MACROMEDIA® DIRECTOR® 6 FOR DUMMIES®

by Lauren Steinhauer

IDG Books Worldwide, Inc.
An International Data Group Company

Foster City, CA ♦ Chicago, IL ♦ Indianapolis, IN ♦ Southlake, TX

Macromedia® Director® 6 For Dummies®

Published by
IDG Books Worldwide, Inc.
An International Data Group Company
919 E. Hillsdale Blvd.
Suite 400
Foster City, CA 94404
www.idgbooks.com (IDG Books Worldwide Web site)
www.dummies.com (Dummies Press Web site)

Library of Congress Catalog Card No.: 97-73301

ISBN: 0-7645-0224-7

Printed in the United States of America

10 9 8 7 6 5 4 3 2 1

1B/QY/QZ/ZX/IN

Distributed in the United States by IDG Books Worldwide, Inc.

Distributed by Macmillan Canada for Canada; by Transworld Publishers Limited in the United Kingdom; by IDG Norge Books for Norway; by IDG Sweden Books for Sweden; by Woodslane Pty. Ltd. for Australia; by Woodslane Enterprises Ltd. for New Zealand; by Longman Singapore Publishers Ltd. for Singapore, Malaysia, Thailand, and Indonesia; by Simron Pty. Ltd. for South Africa; by Toppan Company Ltd. for Japan; by Distribuidora Cuspide for Argentina; by Livraria Cultura for Brazil; by Ediciencia S.A. for Ecuador; by Addison-Wesley Publishing Company for Korea; by Ediciones ZETA S.C.R. Ltda. for Peru; by WS Computer Publishing Corporation, Inc., for the Philippines; by Unalis Corporation for Taiwan; by Contemporanea de Ediciones for Venezuela; by Computer Book & Magazine Store for Puerto Rico; by Express Computer Distributors for the Caribbean and West Indies. Authorized Sales Agent: Anthony Rudkin Associates for the Middle East and North Africa.

For general information on IDG Books Worldwide's books in the U.S., please call our Consumer Customer Service department at 800-762-2974. For reseller information, including discounts and premium sales, please call our Reseller Customer Service department at 800-434-3422.

For information on where to purchase IDG Books Worldwide's books outside the U.S., please contact our International Sales department at 415-655-3200 or fax 415-655-3295.

For information on foreign language translations, please contact our Foreign & Subsidiary Rights department at 415-655-3021 or fax 415-655-3281.

For sales inquiries and special prices for bulk quantities, please contact our Sales department at 415-655-3200 or write to the address above.

For information on using IDG Books Worldwide's books in the classroom or for ordering examination copies, please contact our Educational Sales department at 800-434-2086 or fax 817-251-8174.

For press review copies, author interviews, or other publicity information, please contact our Public Relations department at 415-655-3000 or fax 415-655-3299.

For authorization to photocopy items for corporate, personal, or educational use, please contact Copyright Clearance Center, 222 Rosewood Drive, Danvers, MA 01923, or fax 508-750-4470.

 is a trademark under exclusive license to IDG Books Worldwide, Inc., from International Data Group, Inc.

About the Author

After moving from special effects at Universal Studios, marketing campaigns for major Hollywood movie studios, and graphic design for numerous agencies, studios, and clients in Los Angeles, Lauren Steinhauer began his computer career in San Francisco with the Lisa, Apple's precursor to the original Macintosh 128K.

Since the release of VideoWorks in 1985, the original version of Director, Lauren has provided multimedia creative services to clients such as Apple Computer, Claris Corporation, Pacific Bell, SPRINT, and Novell. With the publication of *Macromedia Director 6 For Dummies*, Lauren has authored four books for IDG in addition to numerous other books and workbooks. Lauren is also working to complete a Sherlock Holmes pastiche in his (ha-ha) spare time with his eye on a theatrical release to follow, starring. . . .

He has led countless one- and two-day workshops featuring major multimedia applications including Director; he has been a faculty member of San Francisco State University's Multimedia Studies Department nearly from its inception where he has conducted basic and advanced multimedia courses. Lauren is also a faculty member of Center for Electronic Art, a prestigious multimedia training facility in San Francisco where he conducts Director and Lingo courses and multimedia intensive workshops.

Lauren offers multimedia and Web-related creative services and training through his own San Francisco-based business, Steinhauer & Associates.

ABOUT IDG BOOKS WORLDWIDE

Welcome to the world of IDG Books Worldwide.

IDG Books Worldwide, Inc., is a subsidiary of International Data Group, the world's largest publisher of computer-related information and the leading global provider of information services on information technology. IDG was founded more than 25 years ago and now employs more than 8,500 people worldwide. IDG publishes more than 275 computer publications in over 75 countries (see listing below). More than 60 million people read one or more IDG publications each month.

Launched in 1990, IDG Books Worldwide is today the #1 publisher of best-selling computer books in the United States. We are proud to have received eight awards from the Computer Press Association in recognition of editorial excellence and three from *Computer Currents'* First Annual Readers' Choice Awards. Our best-selling *...For Dummies®* series has more than 30 million copies in print with translations in 30 languages. IDG Books Worldwide, through a joint venture with IDG's Hi-Tech Beijing, became the first U.S. publisher to publish a computer book in the People's Republic of China. In record time, IDG Books Worldwide has become the first choice for millions of readers around the world who want to learn how to better manage their businesses.

Our mission is simple: Every one of our books is designed to bring extra value and skill-building instructions to the reader. Our books are written by experts who understand and care about our readers. The knowledge base of our editorial staff comes from years of experience in publishing, education, and journalism — experience we use to produce books for the '90s. In short, we care about books, so we attract the best people. We devote special attention to details such as audience, interior design, use of icons, and illustrations. And because we use an efficient process of authoring, editing, and desktop publishing our books electronically, we can spend more time ensuring superior content and spend less time on the technicalities of making books.

You can count on our commitment to deliver high-quality books at competitive prices on topics you want to read about. At IDG Books Worldwide, we continue in the IDG tradition of delivering quality for more than 25 years. You'll find no better book on a subject than one from IDG Books Worldwide.

IDG
BOOKS
WORLDWIDE

John Kilcullen
CEO
IDG Books Worldwide, Inc.

Steven Berkowitz
President and Publisher
IDG Books Worldwide, Inc.

*Eighth Annual
Computer Press
Awards ≥1992*

*Ninth Annual
Computer Press
Awards ≥1993*

*Tenth Annual
Computer Press
Awards ≥1994*

*Eleventh Annual
Computer Press
Awards ≥1995*

IDG Books Worldwide, Inc., is a subsidiary of International Data Group, the world's largest publisher of computer-related information and the leading global provider of information services on information technology. International Data Group publishes over 275 computer publications in over 75 countries. Sixty million people read one or more International Data Group publications each month. International Data Group's publications include: **ARGENTINA:** Buyer's Guide, Computerworld Argentina, PC World Argentina; **AUSTRALIA:** Australian Macworld, Australian PC World, Australian Reseller News, Computerworld, IT Casebook, Network World, Publish, Webmaster; **AUSTRIA:** Computerwelt Österreich, Networks Austria, PC Tip Austria; **BANGLADESH:** PC World Bangladesh; **BELARUS:** PC World Belarus; **BELGIUM:** Data News; **BRAZIL:** Annuário de Informática, Computerworld, Connections, Macworld, PC Player, PC World, Publish, Reseller News, Supergamepower; **BULGARIA:** Computerworld Bulgaria, Network World Bulgaria, PC & MacWorld Bulgaria; **CANADA:** CIO Canada, Client/Server World, ComputerWorld Canada, InfoWorld Canada, NetworkWorld Canada, WebWorld; **CHILE:** Computerworld Chile, PC World Chile; **COLOMBIA:** Computerworld Colombia, PC World Colombia; **COSTA RICA:** PC World Centro America; **THE CZECH AND SLOVAK REPUBLICS:** Computerworld Czechoslovakia, Macworld Czech Republic, PC World Czechoslovakia; **DENMARK:** Communications World Danmark, Computerworld Danmark, Macworld Danmark, PC World Danmark, Techworld Denmark; **DOMINICAN REPUBLIC:** PC World Republica Dominicana; **ECUADOR:** PC World Ecuador; **EGYPT:** Computerworld Middle East, PC World Middle East; **EL SALVADOR:** PC World Centro America; **FINLAND:** MikroPC, Tietoverkko, Tietoviikko; **FRANCE:** Distributique, Hebdo, Info PC, Le Monde Informatique, Macworld, Reseaux & Telecoms, WebMaster France; **GERMANY:** Computer Partner, Computerwoche, Computerwoche Extra, Computerwoche FOCUS, Global Online, Macwelt, PC Welt; **GREECE:** Amiga Computing, GamePro Greece, Multimedia World; **GUATEMALA:** PC World Centro America; **HONDURAS:** PC World Centro America; **HONG KONG:** Computerworld Hong Kong, PC World Hong Kong, Publish in Asia; **HUNGARY:** ABCD CD-ROM, Computerworld Szamitastechnika, Internetto online Magazine, PC World Hungary, PC-X Magazin Hungary; **ICELAND:** Tolvuheimur PC World Island; **INDIA:** Information Communications World, Information Systems Computerworld, PC World India, Publish in Asia; **INDONESIA:** InfoKomputer PC World, Komputek Computerworld, Publish in Asia; **IRELAND:** ComputerScope, PC Live!; **ISRAEL:** Macworld Israel, People & Computers/Computerworld; **ITALY:** Computerworld Italia, Macworld Italia, Networking Italia, PC World Italia; **JAPAN:** DTP World, Macworld Japan, Nikkei Personal Computing, OS/2 World Japan, SunWorld Japan, Windows NT World, Windows World Japan; **KENYA:** PC World East African; **KOREA:** Hi-Tech Information, Macworld Korea, PC World Korea; **MACEDONIA:** PC World Macedonia; **MALAYSIA:** Computerworld Malaysia, PC World Malaysia, Publish in Asia; **MALTA:** PC World Malta; **MEXICO:** Computerworld Mexico, PC World Mexico; **MYANMAR:** PC World Myanmar; **NETHERLANDS:** Computer! Totaal, LAN Internetworking Magazine, LAN World Buyers Guide, Macworld Netherlands, Net, WebWereld; **NEW ZEALAND:** Absolute Beginners Guide and Plain & Simple Series, Computer Buyer, Computer Industry Directory, Computerworld New Zealand, MTB, Network World, PC World New Zealand; **NICARAGUA:** PC World Centro America; **NORWAY:** Computerworld Norge, CW Rapport, Datamagasinet, Financial Rapport, Kursguide Norge, Macworld Norge, Multimediaworld Norge, PC World Ekspress Norge, PC World Nettverk, PC World Norge, PC World ProduktGuide Norge; **PAKISTAN:** Computerworld Pakistan; **PANAMA:** PC World Panama; **PEOPLE'S REPUBLIC OF CHINA:** China Computer Users, China Computerworld, China InfoWorld, China Telecom World Weekly, Computer & Communication, Electronic Design China, Electronics Today, Electronics Weekly, Game Software, PC World China, Popular Computer Week, Software Weekly, Software World, Telecom World; **PERU:** Computerworld Peru, PC World Profesional Peru, PC World SoHo Peru; **PHILIPPINES:** Click!, Computerworld Philippines, PC World Philippines, Publish in Asia; **POLAND:** Computerworld Poland, Computerworld Special Report Poland, Cyber, Macworld Poland, Networld Poland, PC World Komputer; **PORTUGAL:** Cerebro/PC World, Computerworld/Correio Informático, Dealer World Portugal, Mac*In/PC*In Portugal, Multimedia World; **PUERTO RICO:** PC World Puerto Rico; **ROMANIA:** Computerworld Romania, PC World Romania, Telecom Romania; **RUSSIA:** Computerworld Russia, Mir PK, Publish, Seti; **SINGAPORE:** Computerworld Singapore, PC World Singapore, Publish in Asia; **SLOVENIA:** Monitor; **SOUTH AFRICA:** Computing SA, Network World SA, Software World SA; **SPAIN:** Communicaciones World España, Computerworld España, Dealer World España, Macworld España, PC World España; **SRI LANKA:** Infolink PC World; **SWEDEN:** CAP&Design, Computer Sweden, Corporate Computing Sweden, Internetworld Sweden, it.branschen, Macworld Sweden, MaxiData Sweden, MikroDatorn, Nätverk & Kommunikation, PC World Sweden, PCAktiv, Windows World Sweden; **SWITZERLAND:** Computerworld Schweiz, Macworld Schweiz, PCtip; **TAIWAN:** Computerworld Taiwan, Macworld Taiwan, NEW ViSiON/Publish, PC World Taiwan, Windows World Taiwan; **THAILAND:** Publish in Asia, Thai Computerworld; **TURKEY:** Computerworld Turkiye, Macworld Turkiye, Network World Turkiye, PC World Turkiye; **UKRAINE:** Computerworld Kiev, Multimedia World Ukraine, PC World Ukraine; **UNITED KINGDOM:** Acorn User UK, Amiga Action UK, Amiga Computing UK, Apple Talk UK, Computing, Macworld, Parents and Computers UK, PC Advisor, PC Home, PSX Pro, The WEB; **UNITED STATES:** Cable in the Classroom, CIO Magazine, Computerworld, DOS World, Federal Computer Week, GamePro Magazine, InfoWorld, I-Way, Macworld, Network World, PC Games, PC World, Publish, Video Event, THE WEB Magazine, and WebMaster; online webzines: JavaWorld, NetscapeWorld, and SunWorld Online; **URUGUAY:** InfoWorld Uruguay; **VENEZUELA:** Computerworld Venezuela, PC World Venezuela; and **VIETNAM:** PC World Vietnam.

3/24/97

Dedication

To the very special people in my life, my son Dorian, my mother, my brothers, my psychiatrist, my newfound beloved friends Al and Alice, and especially to the sweetest soul I have ever met, Rudi Soriano, without whose support I could not have written this book.

Author's Acknowledgments

Many thanks to Mike Kelly, Acquisitions Editor for IDG, for his support, to Kim Darosett for her many thoughtful and intelligent edits, and especially to Rev Mengle who took such loving care in preparing this book for publication. Many thanks, too, to Jay Lee, Technical Editor, who suggested so many insightful improvements to the manuscript, and to the great IDG production staff for their wonderful work.

Publisher's Acknowledgments

We're proud of this book; please send us your comments about it by using the IDG Books Worldwide Reader Response Card at the back of the book or by e-mailing us at feedback/dummies@idgbooks.com. Some of the people who helped bring this book to market include the following:

Acquisitions, Development, and Editorial

Project Editors: Rev Mengle, Pamela Mourouzis

Acquisitions Editor: Michael Kelly

Media Development: Joyce Pepple

Associate Permissions Editor: Heather H. Dismore

Copy Editors: Kim Darosett, Suzanne Thomas

Technical Editor: Jay Lee

Editorial Manager: Colleen Rainsberger

Editorial Assistant: Darren Meiss

Production

Project Coordinator: E. Shawn Aylsworth

Layout and Graphics: Cameron Booker, Lou Boudreau, Linda M. Boyer, Angela F. Hunckler, Brent Savage

Proofreaders: Kathleen Prata, Christine Berman, Kelli Botta, Rachel Garvey

Indexer: Liz Cunningham

Special Help

Joell Smith, Associate Technical Editor; Access Technology, CD Interface Design; Donna Love, Editorial Assistant; Matthew McClure, Editoral Assistant; Stephanie Koutek, Proof Editor

General and Administrative

IDG Books Worldwide, Inc.: John Kilcullen, CEO; Steven Berkowitz, President and Publisher

Dummies, Inc.: Brenda McLaughlin, Senior Vice President and Group Publisher

Dummies Technology Press and Dummies Editorial: Diane Graves Steele, Vice President and Associate Publisher; Kristin A. Cocks, Editorial Director; Mary Bednarek, Acquisitions and Product Development Director

Dummies Trade Press: Kathleen A. Welton, Vice President and Publisher

IDG Books Production for Dummies Press: Beth Jenkins, Production Director; Cindy L. Phipps, Manager of Project Coordination, Production Proofreading, and Indexing; Kathie S. Schutte, Supervisor of Page Layout; Shelley Lea, Supervisor of Graphics and Design; Debbie J. Gates, Production Systems Specialist; Robert Springer, Supervisor of Proofreading; Debbie Stailey, Special Projects Coordinator; Tony Augsburger, Supervisor of Reprints and Bluelines; Leslie Popplewell, Media Archive Coordinator

Dummies Packaging and Book Design: Patti Sandez, Packaging Specialist; Lance Kayser, Packaging Assistant; Kavish + Kavish, Cover Design

♦

The publisher would like to give special thanks to Patrick J. McGovern, without whom this book would not have been possible.

♦

Contents at a Glance

Cartoons at a Glance

By Rich Tennant

page 9

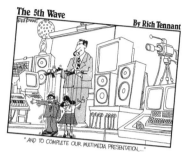

page 213

page 329

page 65

page 293

Fax: 508-546-7747 • E-mail: the5wave@tiac.net

Table of Contents

· ·

Introduction

I know, like everyone else, you want to be in the movies. But because Hollywood hasn't been ringing your phone off the hook the last couple of days — or years, for that matter — what could be better than multimedia with Director 6, the premiere program for creating Hollywood-like movies on your very own PC or Mac? But wait — with just the mention of the word Director, and like a .45 caliber Magnum at your temple in a dark alley on Friday the 13th, your palms begin to sweat, your heart rate triples, and you get acne for the first time in 31 years. Director? Me?

You've heard all the stories. Director's hard, like a shot of cheap bourbon at 2 a.m. after a tough case. It's impossible, like the woman who won't forgive you for turning her in to the cops — your mother yet. It's rough, like five-day-old stubble. (No, I'm not still talking about your mother.) Yes, we've all heard these absurd horror stories.

They're all true.

But thank goodness you have this book. At least it's in your hands. Whether you pay for it is between you, your conscience, and that brawny security guard breathing down your neck. Director has a high learning curve; it doesn't hurt to be a rocket scientist with neurosurgery as a hobby. But ordinary people like you and that brawny security guard can understand how to use Director 6 and make smart-looking, successful multimedia productions with a Mac or PC. Best of all, Director 6 includes a portal to Cyberspace called Shockwave so that you can even create movies for the World Wide Web.

What This Book Offers Mac or PC Users Like You

This book is for Mac or PC users. Actually, it's for PC or Mac users. Truth be told, it's really for Mac *and* PC users. Anyway, after Director is up and running, it's essentially the same program on either type of computer; where important differences exist, I point them out. If you plan on developing Director movies for both Macs and PCs, you'll need to buy separate copies of Director 6 for Macintosh and Director 6 for Windows. Don't look at me for that interest-free loan.

That aside, I've done everything possible to make this book on Director 6 friendly and inviting. Don't be surprised if you start dating it after a couple of reads.

I'm not going to make all those assumptions that other books make — that you were born knowing a *bit* from a *byte* or what a *Lingo script* is all about. Instead, I break down seemingly impossible tasks — such as changing the time on your VCR — into easy, doable steps, making essential features of Director crystal clear. Director 6 has 19 basic windows, give or take, but this book concentrates heavily on the most important ones, including

- The Stage window
- The Cast window
- The Score window
- The Paint window

This book gives you plenty of pictures for reference (get out your crayons) and lots of Director tips and tricks. The last chapter virtually brims with stuff that helps make life more carefree as you read about Director. The last chapter may even clear up your dry, itchy scalp and make your kids behave in public.

Who You Are

This writer's making some basic assumptions about someone who won't ante up more than $24.99 for a book, er, I mean, about someone who buys a book from the *...For Dummies* series. I'm assuming one or more of the following about you:

- You're new to computing.
- You're new to animation.
- You're new to multimedia.
- You're new, period.
- You're intimidated by technical jargon.
- You're not interested in technical jargon.
- You don't know what "technical jargon" means.
- You're running a Mac on some version of System 7.
- You're running a PC under Windows 3.1, 95, or NT.
- You're a fan of *The X-Files*.
- You've had flashbacks of alien abductions lately.

Icons Used in This Book

Some of the aids included for you in this book are marked with distinctive icons. In fact, if you cut them out really carefully and paste them neatly on acid-free card stock, they make really nifty holiday gifts.

This icon points out optional reading for you budding propeller-heads to ease you into a few technical areas and to entice you into trying advanced Macromedia Director techniques.

The Warning icon is meant to alert you to potentially risky or foolhardy software detours and acrobatics. As long as you have good backups — you do make copies of your software, don't you? — the worst thing that may happen is having to reinstall Director or your operating system. And doting father figure that I am, I'll occasionally remind you to save your work and to be sure to eat plenty of leafy, green vegetables.

Your computer is very hale and hardy, which is not to say that you should regularly drop it from a 12-story building. Physically, you can break your computer in only a couple of ways and, even then, only with determination and pluck (you'll find pluck in the notions department of your local drugstore).

Software-wise, you may try something during the course of exploring Director that makes your computer freeze up, display an error message, or behave in some other unusual way, but chances are that it's just a software problem and temporary. Simply restarting your computer clears up at least half of these problems.

Dumb things to do to your computer

Dumb Thing to Do #1

Plugging in or unplugging computer cables while the machine's on. You can easily zap a component on something called the *system board* in your computer. One moment of hedonistic impatience may cost you $1,500 or so to get a new system board.

Dumb Thing to Do #2 (drum roll, please)

The ever popular moving-your-computer-while-it's-running trick, a great way to learn what hard drive crashes and acid reflux are all about. Inside your computer, your hard drive's spinning at about 5,500 revolutions per minute or faster. Moving a running computer places the delicate read-write heads inside your hard drive at great risk of crashing into your data, about the equivalent of your car crashing into a brick wall at 80 miles per hour.

Throughout the book, you find many suggestions to make working with Director more productive and creative — or to just generally make life easier, such as storing avocados in a brown paper bag to make them ripen.

By the way, this book is produced with remarkable state-of-the-art scratch-and-hear technology. When you come to one of these icons, scratch the icon so that you can read while listening to Ed Ames sing, "Try to remember . . . ." Hah, caught you scratching.

This icon indicates that I've got something to say about one of the other elements in Macromedia's Studio suite of related programs.

All you old-timers out there who have used previous editions of Director will appreciate this icon, which points out new-fangled features.

The CD in the back of this book is designed to fit specifically in *your* computer. Try it out and see. Fits, doesn't it? And you'll see this icon whenever I talk about one of the programs on the CD.

Conventions Used in This Book

This book tries to be more helpful than those other books about Director. On the off chance that you need some information from another computer book, you're sure to run into descriptions that seem puzzling to you because "they" won't bother explaining what "they" mean. However, because I love each and every one of you dearly, *I* explain all.

You're welcome.

Okay, everyone, slip on your enclosed decoder rings. The conventions used in this book include the following:

✔ **Menu Name⇨Command Name:** For example, "Choose Edit⇨Paste" means "Press the mouse on the Edit menu, drag the mouse pointer down, and choose the Paste command." Sometimes I say, "Go to the Paste command from the Edit menu" or "Choose Paste from the Edit menu." You run into the generic form frequently when you read more technical books.

✔ **Mac Modifier Key/PC Modifier Key+Character Key:** The Command (⌘) key, Shift key, Option key, and occasionally the Control key are Mac modifier keys. For Windows users, the Control (Ctrl) key usually replaces the Mac's Command key and the Alt key replaces the Option key. By pressing one or more of these modifier keys in combination with a character key, you can use keyboard shortcuts for various menu commands or to apply a specific technique to a selection. For example, "Pressing ⌘/Ctrl+1 alternately hides and shows the menu bar," means, "For a Mac, while pressing the Command key, tap the 1 key; for PCs, while pressing the Control key, tap the 1 key."

✔ In this book, the Mac's Command key is represented by the special character, ⌘ (Apple's "daisy" icon). By the way, newer Mac keyboards emboss both the daisy icon and the Apple icon on the Command key.

✔ Many computer techniques include holding down a modifier key while doing something else such as dragging the mouse. In this book, you'll see sentences such as, "To move a sprite horizontally on the Stage, Shift+drag the sprite." Translation: "While holding down the Shift key, drag the sprite." Or you may see, "To copy a cast member in the Cast window, Option/Alt+drag the cast member to an empty slot in the window." Translation: "While holding down the Option (Macaholics only)/Alt (PC users only), drag the cast member to an empty slot in the window."

✔ **Bold text:** You'll find text that you are to type at some point in a task in bold characters within a paragraph (or non-bold in otherwise bold steps). For example, I may say "At the C prompt, type **WIN** and press Return to go to the Windows Desktop," meaning that you're to enter the characters W, I, and N in the appropriate field and continue the instructions. Be sure to enter the characters exactly as printed, including uppercase and lowercase letters and spaces. Sometimes stuff you enter is case-sensitive, sometimes not. It's usually safest to type exactly what's printed. (If you see "Simon says," ignore the rest of the sentence; I'm just having one of my silly attacks.)

TIP

Lauren's indubitable rules of keystrokes

When using modifier keys for keyboard shortcuts, be sure to follow "Lauren's Indubitable Rules of Keystrokes," which states:

1. For Macs, press the Command key (⌘) first; for PCs, press the Control key (Ctrl) first.

2. Press other modifier keys next.

3. Press the character key last.

4. After pressing the complete sequence, release all the keys unless specifically instructed not to.

Does This Book Cover Everything?

Now that we've come to be so close, such tight, deep personal friends, you have the gall to ask me, "Does this book have everything anyone ever wanted to know about Director?"

No.

What won't you find in this book? Laughs for one, as you've already discovered. You won't find an explanation for every command of every window, either. You won't find detailed pontificating on most Lingo commands. (*Lingo* is Director's name for its built-in computer language.) You won't find many advanced techniques covered, although I touch on a few in passing as teasers for you prospective propeller-heads out there.

But this book does get you started in a very big way. What this book doesn't cover is more than made up for with clear, concise information about Director 6 essentials for the budding computer user and multimedia and Web designer wannabe. Plus, this book has nice, wide margins to doodle on.

How This Book Is Organized

This book contains four major parts or sections, each section containing several chapters, each chapter made up of billions upon billions of molecules. Makes you think, huh?

You do not need to read this book from cover to cover. I've read it cover to cover for you. This book should summon up images of an overstuffed wingback chair, a crackling fireplace, and a Rockwellesque, white-haired grandpa tenderly hugging his grandchild as they peruse a fine, weathered, leather-bound classic together.

Okay, reality sets in. What you've got in your hot little hand is a floppy, softcover edition likely to burst into spontaneous combustion at any second; use your God-given imagination, won't you? What I'm trying to convey is that each topic and exercise is relatively self-contained. By using the Table of Contents or the Index, you can go to any topic of interest and find valuable information on the subject in question and plenty of fine, fire-kindling material to boot.

Part I: What's New, Pussycat?

In Part I, I introduce Director 6, show you how to start the program, and then discuss exciting new features of Director 6 — a major upgrade from Macromedia.

I ask you to think big. Bigger. That's it. Now you're ready to tackle cosmic questions like, "What is the meaning of life?," "Is there absolute good and evil?," and "How do I install this darn software, anyway?" Part I covers all that existential stuff with illustrations and references numerous enough to cut out and use as designer wallpaper. Along the way, you make incredible discoveries, including the fact that *multimedia* really means something. And that the blank screen you first come to in Director has a name and actually has a purpose.

Part II: The Big Picture

With Part II, the book rapidly deteriorates from mediocre to downright useless, unimportant stuff such as how to use Director's Cast, Score, Paint, and Text windows. Just reading about the Cast window makes you want to go out and buy a casting couch. After discovering the secrets of the Score window, you may be swept up in an overpowering urge to pull on riding britches and shiny black boots and watch creaky, old Erich Von Stroheim movies all night. And I deliberately toned down the Paint window stuff so that you're not inclined to decide that you were born with one ear too many. Finally, if the Text window info doesn't bring out the Hemingway in you, I don't know what will.

Part III: More Interaction, Please!

Here's the section where you ease into Director's talents for lifting a presentation beyond a glorified sideshow by taking advantage of your computer's unique powers. Read about how to add special effects to your movies with push-button ease; how to prep your Director movies for the World Wide Web; how to use Director 6's new drag-and-drop behaviors; and how to use Director's computer language, Lingo, to open up a whole new world of interactivity and excess stomach acid.

"More Interaction, Please!" delves gently into numerous ways of adding interactivity with Director 6 and how Director 6 interacts with other programs such as XRes and SoundEdit 16 from Macromedia's suite of programs. Easy-to-follow steps, illustrations, screen shots, and examples provide self-contained blocks of information on each Director topic covered, allowing you, gentle reader, to successfully create cross-platform movies that work in the real world as presentations, CD-ROMs, and Web-based multimedia.

Part IV: The Part of Tens

I don't know why, but whenever I think of the name of Part IV, I can't help picturing Charlton Heston saying it as a line from one of his epics. Can't you just see him exclaiming, "The Part of Tens," with his mouth and chin making those distinctively "Hestonian" gestures? Anyway, Part IV includes ten frequently asked questions such as "What Can I Do to Make My Movies Play Faster?," "Can I Play My Director Movie on a Macintosh and a PC?," and "Should I Worry About My Cat's Intestinal Tract?"

Seriously, Part IV also reviews the ten most important ways to add animation to your Director movies and the ten most common questions and answers.

Part V: Appendix

You budding propeller-heads probably have already figured out that a CD is included inside the back cover of this book. Listen very carefully: Even if that burly security guard has his back turned, do not take the CD out until after you take the book home! Got it? Good.

When you get home (or work, if you play on your computer there), you'll find the CD has lots of great software — including a demo version of Director 6! Appendix A tells you all about the software on the CD, and about the CD's bonus chapters, which include my definitive Director 6 resource list (you're welcome), lists of the top Lingo words and Director 6 behaviors, a chapter on debugging Lingo for you hard-core propeller-heads, and a chapter on using the Director 6 Animation Wizard.

What's Next?

Aside from paying for the book if you haven't already, the next step is to turn the page and dive right into the task of tackling Director 6. Don't forget that burly security guard.

Attention all readers

The pictures of menus, menu bars, and windows were taken from a Mac running on System 7.5.5, the latest version to date of what is now known as the Mac OS (Macintosh Operating System). If you're running Windows or an earlier release of System 7.0 on a Mac, your screen may differ slightly from the illustrations. If you're running the Mac's previous System, System 6.0, your screen will differ a little more dramatically, but after you're in Director, much of what you see will be very similar, if not the same. If you're running an even earlier System, shame on you!

Part I

What's New, Pussycat?

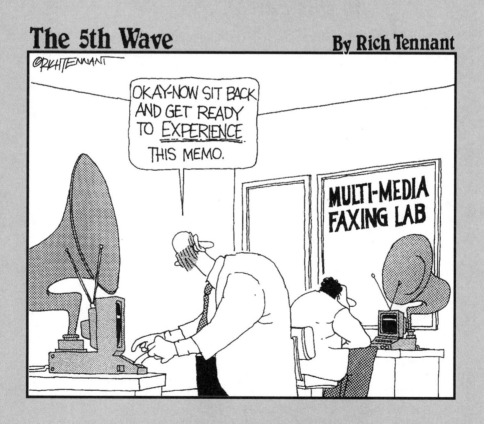

In this part . . .

If you've ever dreamed of creating multimedia of your very own and broadcasting interactive animations on the World Wide Web, now is the time to dive in with Macromedia Director 6, by far the easiest and most powerful version of the program to work with since its humble beginnings back in 1985.

Even if you just began your computer career, this part preps you for your adventure with introductory chapters, where you can find out what multimedia is all about, why Director is the program of choice for so many multimedia and Web site developers, why you should be nutty enough to join their growing ranks, and — if you're an experienced Director user — what new features you can find in Director 6.

Chapter 1

Stars of Director — Graphics, Sound, Animation, and Your CPU

In This Chapter

▶ What do you use Director for?

▶ What exactly is multimedia?

Some of you in ReaderLand may desperately want to learn Macromedia Director 6 without having the slightest notion why. Okay, I'm going to give you some great ammo to fight back with when your spouse finds out that you just plunked down nearly a grand for a piece of shiny iridescent plastic that you defensively insist is called a CD-ROM.

Following in Walt's Mouseprints

First, you can tell your friends and relatives that you're an animator, just like Walt what's-his-name, because Director is an *animation program* first and foremost. In other words, Director gives you the tools to make presentations that don't just sit there, but actually get up and move around. From its humble beginnings in a log cabin — introduced in 1985 as VideoWorks — Director was built to create a unique type of presentation: eye candy that changes over time.

As you explore the latest successor of VideoWorks, you see that Director 6 offers special windows to help build this kind of presentation with relative ease, if not abandon. For example, you run into the Score window, aptly named because it's very much like a musical score, with distinctive shorthand for recording changes in the presentation from frame to frame. In Director's Score window, you can follow the flow of visual information in your presentation, as well as rearrange and modify this information. In another special window, the Stage, you can play back your masterpiece. And when the throng of admirers comes up and asks, "Where do you go from here?" you can proudly exclaim, "I'm going to Disneyland!"

Just a Lincoln Off the Old Log

How'd you like to have your kids smile up at you and boast to their friends, "My dad (or mom) is just like Lincoln"? Aside from the distinctive facial features, maybe they recognize in you a yearning to take advantage of Director's *interactive* features to give The People their freedom — freedom to navigate through tons of information by choosing what they want to find out about and having darn good fun at the same time.

To create an interactive movie with Director, you can integrate graphics, music, narration, sound effects, and digital video into your masterpiece; you can also add buttons for deciding what happens next.

Normally, this type of interactive production is reserved for hard-core programmers — you know, those people who all look vaguely like Bill Gates. But with new drag-and-drop behaviors (which you can learn more about in Chapter 15), Director 6 allows those of you interested in this sort of thing to realize your ideas and present them without learning Lingo programming.

Most exciting of all, Director 6 is raring to run on the World Wide Web. With Shockwave built into Director, you're ready to poster the Web with your own high-quality animations. You can also use Director 6's Shockwave for Audio to compress high-quality sound for the Web, CD-ROMs, and other applications.

By the Way, What the Heck Is Multimedia?

Even if you already know that you want to create animations with Director, I'll still bet that you probably have a pretty murky concept of what Director's other forte, multimedia, is all about. And "I know it when I see it" just doesn't cut it with those Fortune 500 clients you may want to work for. Trust me.

I admit, defining multimedia is a real challenge; I haven't seen the same definition for multimedia in any two books. Multimedia is one of those slippery things to define, like art, truth, and Aunt Edna's holiday fruitcake. But I'll try to decide on a working definition. Oh, one more bit of fatherly advice: Stay away from Aunt Edna's holiday fruitcake.

Working definition of multimedia: *Multimedia* is the presentation of information by combining images, sounds, and movement with the power of the computer.

Now, on to exploring my definition one chunk at a time.

Multimedia is image

Multimedia has something to do with images. Imagining multimedia without graphics, movies, artwork, or photographs is hard. Actually, images represent the strongest component of multimedia.

As it turns out, we're visually oriented creatures receiving about 80 percent of the information around us through our sense of sight; compare the richness of our visual life with our sense of smell, taste, or even touch. The other senses are all exquisite, but slip on a blindfold, and you're lost. You've probably seen those figures about how many advertising messages bombard us each day and how much TV we watch (or endure). Commanding visuals are certainly a dominant constituent of multimedia.

Multimedia is sound

But what would multimedia be without sound? Did you know that "silent" movies were never silent? A pianist or organist accompanied screenings, and sometimes a sound-effects man was there in the dark, too, adding thunder, clattering horse hooves, and, of course, gunshots to the melodrama.

Have you ever turned off the audio portion of your TV and watched a movie or commercial without sound? Think of some of your favorite movie scenes and then imagine them without sound. Picture the climactic scene in Spielberg's *Close Encounters of the Third Kind* when the great mothership appears over Devil's Tower, hovering jewel-like above gaping scientists. Imagine the stargate sequence in Kubrick's *2001: A Space Odyssey* without audio. Very different experiences — and not for the better.

So sound, including sound effects, music, and narration, is also a major player in the multimedia game.

Multimedia is movement

In this age of MTV, with its overpowering imagery and movement, color and movement, and creative abandon . . . and movement, movement is an integral extension of the force of imagery that plays such an important part in defining multimedia.

And movement.

In an attempt to stretch the definition of movement, pioneers of multimedia — ahem, myself included — tried incorporating video into productions with clumsy work-arounds, multiple monitors, separate VCRs, laser disc players, controllers, and wires, wires, and more wires. Then a few years ago, Apple Computer turned the world upside down with something called QuickTime, followed quickly by Microsoft's Video for Windows for you PC users, allowing multimedia types to add video directly within Director with all the Hollywood claptrap — dissolves, fade-ins, fade-outs, really wild special effects, and, oh yes, some content.

QuickTime, QuickTime for Windows, and Video for Windows are additions to the system, extensions in the Mac world and TSRs (Terminate and Stay Resident) programs for PCs. These system extensions allow your operating system to handle the kind of information that changes over time, in the form of a special digital video file type. In addition to Apple's QuickTime for Windows, you PC types can create Audio Video Interleaved (AVI) movie files for your digital video needs, and a number of translators can convert Mac QuickTime mooVs and PC AVI movies into one another.

But here's a point. TV offers photos, graphics, movies, movement, and sounds of every description — and more than a few others beyond description. If you've ever caught *The Geraldo Rivera Show*, you know what I mean. So why isn't TV considered multimedia? Or movies, for that matter?

One other element completes my working definition of multimedia.

Multimedia is your computer

In Lewis Carroll's *Alice in Wonderland*, the White Rabbit wonders how to begin telling a story to the King and Queen of Hearts. Carroll has the King smugly suggest, "Begin at the beginning . . . and go on till you come to the end: then stop."

Historically, most information has been linear, meaning that you start on page one, march in step through subsequent pages, and on the last page, as the King of Hearts suggests, you stop. If you graphed the content, you'd wind up with a straight line — that's traditional, linear information and storytelling.

The power of your computer is the digital glue binding the other elements of multimedia together and adding the final touches: *interactivity* and *hypertext*.

Multimedia has something to do with using the computer to give the user, the person before the computer, the freedom to explore information in a "nonlinear" way.

What do you get when you graph interactive multimedia? A graph that looks more like a tree with hundreds or thousands of branches. In fact, many multimedia products feature such a map to help the user navigate through the product.

Interactive multimedia

Defining interactivity and hypertext is as slippery as defining multimedia. Thanks a lot.

When you use computing power to give the user the ability to decide where to start and which direction to go, you add *interactivity* to multimedia.

As you build your presentation in Director, you add interactivity by presenting the user with options in the form of buttons, sliders, and other controls that look like familiar objects in the real world. Here's where knowing at least a little Lingo scripting is important. Making a mental note to check out Chapter 14 isn't a bad idea.

Hypertext

When you use the power of the computer to add links to text that the user can explore, you create *hypertext* — allowing the user to delve into deeper and deeper layers of information at will. Normally, the user is unaware of how these links work; that is, these links are *transparent* to the user. Ironically, you often go about creating these links with transparent buttons that take the user to deeper levels of information. If you've ever gone surfing on the Web and clicked on underlined text, you've used hypertext links.

Interesting but moldy history of ye olde attempts at interactivity and hypertext

Early insightful experiments in interactivity and hypertext cry out to be cited here. Many illuminated manuscripts, those beautifully gilded pages of hand-drawn text and wondrous illustrations from bygone days, feature hypertext in their structure. As you carefully inspect these venerable, delicate documents — put those white gloves on and, please, no sneezing — note the large central block of text, the smaller text to the left, and yet another smaller block of text to its left. This is hypertext, 12th-century style. In other words, this kind of layout allows the reader to break away from the main text and delve into deeper levels of content on an intellectual whim. Power is transferred to the reader — that's nearly interactive multimedia; just add a gerbil-powered computer, and you're off and running.

I've got to include the magical *Tristram Shandy*, a novel by Laurence Sterne published in 1760, in this stop-over into antiquity. If you've never read it, do yourself a favor: Beg, borrow, or steal a copy. *Tristram Shandy* is not your ordinary book; describing it makes defining multimedia look like a picnic without ants. There are suddenly blank pages, there are pages with one word on them, and there are weird pages. In this inverted Tom Jonesian world, the author tells his story not only with text but with the words themselves — the very pages of the book and how they are or are not laid out. *Tristram Shandy* is certainly an impressive experiment in multimedia, hypertext, and interactivity — the whole she-bang, worthy of reading and studying.

Chapter 2

Launching Director: An Application by Any Other Name . . . .

● ●

In This Chapter

▶ Reviewing the GUI, Director's executive producer

▶ Looking around Director

▶ Exploring Director's About box

▶ Purging Director's memory

▶ Using Director's File menu

▶ Touring Director's other menus

● ●

*W*hy have Apple founders Steve Jobs and Steve Wozniak and Bill Gates of Microsoft fame been so successful in the high-tech world, amassing personal estates well in excess of $1,000 each? Most computer pundits agree: Chili's a whole lot tastier with a big topping of real, shredded cheddar cheese and chopped onions. Also, they agree: These high-tech pioneers owe much of their success to the innovative Graphical User Interface (GUI) of the Mac OS, integral to the Mac since the introduction of the Mac 128K in 1984 and to Windows introduced by Microsoft several years later.

The GUI (pronounced goo-ee, honest) is a set of mostly visual cues used to "communicate" with your computer, in contrast to a CLI, or command line interface, which is like DOS for PCs in the bad old days, where the user faces a text-based screen, reads lines of data generated by a computer program, and types commands to go to the next step between primal screams of frustration and anger.

The graphical user interface of the Mac OS and Windows includes the following:

- ✔ The desktop, which is home base. On the desktop, you find application and file icons and a menu bar. These graphic elements come from your computer's chips or from the hard drive.

- ✔ The menus and windows of programs you open and the visual similarity of one program to another.

- ✔ The general "look and feel" of the interface, its friendliness and patience with users — all built-in, of course — like HAL until he went kookoo for Koko Puffs.

Opening Director 6

Director 6.0

Okay, you're at the desktop. If you're like normal people — although I doubt it because you paid good money for this book — you've already made an Applications folder (Macs) or program group (PC) the night you wore out your pick-up sticks. The Applications folder/group is probably where you installed Director. At any rate, find Director's custom icon, handcrafted by Italian artisans for untold generations, as shown in the margin.

Select Director by moving your mouse pointer over Director's icon and clicking once. On a Mac, Director's icon changes its appearance (reverses it if you have a black-and-white screen or darkens it on grayscale and color monitors); that's the Mac's endearing way of showing you that the icon's selected. On your PC, the icon's title reverses.

Now you can go to the File menu and choose the Open command to start Director. But for the truly rugged, high-spirited, and adventurous out there (the kind of computer user who grew up playing with G.I. Joe and eating splinters for breakfast), rev up your engines. Point to Director's icon with the mouse and double-click to issue the Open command. And you thought skydiving without a parachute was macho.

With either method, Director launches, and the first window comes into view. Multimedia types call this window the "splash screen." Just knowing this terminology and saying, "splash screen," often and in a loud, boisterous voice puts you leagues ahead of old-fashioned multimedia wannabes who actually think hard work and studying will someday pay off.

Finally, with hearts pounding and arms akimbo (I always wanted to use that phrase), you arrive at Director to find . . . a blank screen?

This blank screen is going to change my life? This blank screen is the beginning of a new career for me? This is why I paid good money for this book — a blank screen?

All these reactions are typical; if I've heard them once, I've heard them once. Trust me; there's more to Director than a blank screen. By the way, this blank screen just happens to be Director's most important window, the Stage, where all the action takes place. See Chapter 3 for more on the Stage.

Stepping Up to the Bar (Graph)

You can learn some important information about Director by choosing Windows⇨Inspectors⇨Memory. The bar graph in the Memory Inspector palette, shown in Figure 2-1, gives you a quick overview of how well Director is managing memory for you as you work on a movie.

Figure 2-1:
The Memory Inspector palette displays Director's use of memory in a bar chart and allows you to purge unneeded memory.

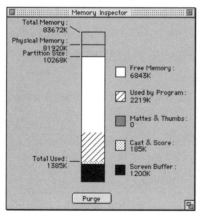

The elements in the bar graph area include the following:

✔ **Total Memory:** Indicates the sum of real memory or so-called RAM SIMMs (DIMMs if you own a Power Mac) installed in your computer and any virtual memory you may be using. *Virtual memory* is a high-tech trick that makes your computer think part of your unused hard drive is extra memory. You PC types use virtual memory when you run in 386 enhanced mode, which pretty much takes care of itself, thank you very much.

✔ **Physical Memory:** Reflects the amount of real memory in the form of RAM chips installed in your computer. This element of the Memory Inspector is visible only when virtual memory is turned on to differentiate physical from total memory that includes virtual memory. See the preceding bullet for more on RAM and virtual memory.

✔ **Partition Size:** Represents the amount of memory reserved for Director's exclusive use. This figure echoes the value set in the Preferred size field of the Mac's Get Info box. Windows has no exact equivalent for manipulating an application's memory except by increasing the amount of RAM or eliminating TSRs (Terminate and Stay Resident), fonts, and other System-related files.

Upon opening, Director reserves a specific amount of memory for its exclusive use, piggy that it is. As long as Director runs — even in the background — the reserved memory remains unavailable to any other program, the system, or any other component of your computer. You PC types know it as extended memory, which pretty much takes care of itself. For Mac users, the reserved memory is called the program's application partition. Out of the box, the initial or default value of the partition is set to the suggested value, but you can change the value to increase the application's performance. (See the section, "For Mac users only: changing Director's application partition," later in this chapter.) More memory = better performance — kind of like presidents.

✔ **Total Used:** Represents the amount of memory being used by the current Director movie.

On the right side of the Memory Inspector, you find the following information with corresponding shaded areas in the bar graph:

✔ **Free Memory:** The white section of the bar. Indicates the current amount of unused memory. This value is the same value as in the Largest Unused Block, which you can find in the About This Macintosh box under the Apple menu at the Finder.

✔ **Used by Program:** Represented on the bar with the light gray section. Indicates how much of Director's program code is currently copied to Director's reserved memory.

✔ **Mattes & Thumbs:** Displays the amount of Director's reserved memory as you create an animation sequence. This value appears in the bar as a medium gray section. *Matte* refers to a special ink type you can use with graphics in Director. *Thumbs* refers to the collection of miniature images you see in the Cast window as you develop an animation. Each matte and thumb, or thumbnail image, takes up a small amount of Director's reserve of memory.

✔ **Cast & Score:** This value is 0 for a blank Director file but grows as you develop your animation sequence. The value is represented in the bar as a dark gray section. *Cast* refers to the actual set of graphics and text represented in the Cast window by thumbnail images. *Score* refers to one of Director's main windows, the Score window, which increasingly takes up Director's reserved memory as you build your animation.

✔ **Screen Buffer:** Represented on the bar as a black section; refers to the amount of Director's reserved memory used to display graphics on the Stage. Screen Buffer size is directly related to the height and width of the Stage window, which you can set and modify in Director at any time from the Modify menu.

Beneath the bar area is the Purge button. The Purge button . . . well, that's what the next section's for.

Purging Director's memory

The Memory Inspector palette gives you critical information about Director's management of memory. Even more unique is the Purge button at the bottom of the palette. When you click Purge, Director tosses out of memory any unneeded data and cast members with Purge Priorities (which you can set) other than 0. One thing every animation or multimedia program cries out for when it comes to memory is, "More, more, more!" Clicking Purge is one of Director's simplest, built-in ways of freeing up memory.

To purge Director's memory, try the following steps. (What you see on your screen will come closer to matching these steps if you quit Director first and return to the desktop, so if you're currently running Director, choose Quit from the File menu.)

1. **Double-click Director's application icon to open Director.**

   You arrive at Director's Stage window.

2. **Choose Window⇨Inspectors⇨Memory.**

   Note the striped light gray section in the bar chart in Figure 2-1 and the number below Used by Program. In my example, the value is 2219K. By the way, I've made this section in Figure 2-1 and 2-2 lighter than it really appears on-screen to increase the contrast.

3. **Click the Purge button.**

   Note the change in the Used by Program value and the height of the light gray section of the bar. Figure 2-2 shows a drop in value from 2219K to 1719K, freeing up about 500K of memory just in this area of memory. Notice that Cast & Score memory use dropped, too.

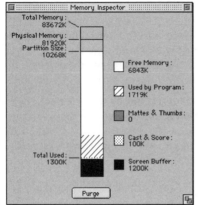

Figure 2-2:
Congrat-
ulations —
you freed
up some
memory.

K stands for kilobytes; each kilobyte equals 1,024 bytes of memory. Don't ask why. The number in Figure 2-1 tells you that 2219K of Director's programming code was loaded into memory when you opened the application, only a portion of Director's total code.

After you click Purge, various built-in routines clean up Director's application partition, which is the amount of memory reserved for the program's exclusive use, and free up memory.

For Mac users only: changing Director's application partition

The amount of memory reserved for a program is often insufficient to run the program at maximum efficiency. With a Macintosh, you can increase the amount of memory yourself with the Info box. Follow these steps:

1. Close Director by choosing Quit from the File menu.

If this step doesn't take you to the Finder, choose Finder from the Application menu. To modify any program's application partition, you *must* first quit the program. If you ever come to a program's Info box and the values in the Memory Requirements panel are grayed out, you forgot to quit.

2. Choose About This Macintosh from the Apple menu.

Note the number to the right of Largest Unused Block. This number represents the memory you have left to play with measured in kilobytes. If the number is 6,000K (kilobytes) or less, run to the store and buy more memory. You shouldn't even try to run Director; really, you don't have enough memory. If the number is at least 9,000K, click the Close box in the upper-left corner of the About window and go to the next step.

3. **At the desktop, find Director's icon in the Director folder and select it with one click of the mouse.**

4. **Choose Get Info from the File menu.**

   The Director 6.0 Info window appears, as shown in Figure 2-3.

Figure 2-3:
Director 6's
Info
window,
where you
can give the
program
more RAM.

Look at the Memory Requirements panel at the bottom of the Info box. The Suggested size is the developer's recommended application partition size and cannot be altered. Notice the value is not in an entry field. Director's suggested size is 10,240K.

The value entered in the Minimum size field is the smallest amount of memory Director may reserve for itself on opening. The minimum size is in an entry field, so you can replace the default value to a smaller number at your own risk. Usually, that's a very bad idea. In my example, the minimum size is set at 6,000K. The idea behind the minimum size is to determine the range of memory that you allow Director to work in. In other words, if you decided you wanted Director to reserve between 6,000K and 10,240K of memory when opened, you would enter 6,000 in Minimum size and leave Preferred size at the default value, 10240. On the other hand, if you wanted to force Director to always open at the preferred size, you'd enter 10240 in the Minimum size field, too.

The value in the Preferred size field is exactly what it says, what the developer would like to see you set Director's application partition to provided you have enough memory. But the trick is to enter an even higher value than the default preferred size for increased performance, especially for high-powered programs such as Director 6.

At this point, I'm going to make some assumptions. One, if you've come this far you have 9000K of available memory (as in Step 2). In this case, you would need to lower the preferred size in Director's Info box to the amount of free memory revealed in the About This Macintosh box in Step 2.

Actually, for the following example, I'm going to be generous and pretend that you have 16MB (megabytes) of extra memory. No, no need to thank me. I'm also going to assume the preferred size value is currently set to 10,240K, which isn't too shabby, but you can do better.

5. **Double-click the field labeled Preferred size to select the current value.**

6. **In the Preferred size field, enter a higher value than the default preferred size.**

   Don't include a comma or K character. In this example, I want you to enter 10240.

7. **Click the Close box in the upper-left corner of the Director 6 Info window.**

You just upped Director's application partition, which is fine for the sake of this example, but . . . remember Real Life? When you're not watching TV? In Real Life, you'd want to set Director's application partition much higher if you have the memory and the money. For a typical animation production, you want to set the Preferred size field to 20,000K (or higher). That's nearly 20MB. Yikes! PowerMacs generally need even more memory. If you don't have at least 32MB of RAM, get it. You'll thank me later.

The Toolbar

Choose Toolbar from the Window menu to view a line of buttons that goes clear across the screen, looking incredibly like the facsimile shown in Figure 2-4. If you're comfortable with the toolbar in Microsoft Word 6.0, you'll like this new feature. The Director 6.0 toolbar offers lots of basic commands at the click of your mouse.

Figure 2-4:
The
Director 6.0
toolbar.

Table 2-1 summarizes the function of each mysterious button.

Table 2-1	Toolbar Buttons	
Button	*Button Name*	*What It Does*
	New Movie	Creates a new movie. If you haven't saved the current movie, Director prompts you to save it. Director can show only one movie at a time.
	New Cast	Creates a new Cast window. You may choose to make it an internal or external cast. See Chapter 5 for more info on internal and external Cast windows.
	Open	Displays the Open File dialog box, where you can choose a different movie to work with.
	Save	Updates the current movie to disk or to your internal hard drive.
	Print	Displays the Print dialog box with many options, including an Options button with additional buttons.
	Import	Displays the Import File dialog box, where you recruit cast members for your movie. For more on importing files, see Chapter 5.
	Undo	If you make a mistake and you know it, immediately stop. Do not pass Go. Click this button once to step back one giant step to degoof your movie.
	Cut	Removes the selection from the movie and places it in the Clipboard, same as the Cut command in the Edit menu.
	Copy	Puts a copy of the selection into the Clipboard, your Mac and PC's little liaison between files and applications.
	Paste	Inserts the current contents of the Clipboard into the current window or insertion point, if appropriate. This option is grayed out or disabled if it's not an appropriate command at the time.
	Find Cast Member	Displays the Find Cast Member dialog box, where you can search by Name, Type, Palette, or Usage.

(continued)

Table 2-1 *(continued)*

Button	Button Name	What It Does
	Exchange Cast Members	Exchanges the selected sprite in the Score window with the selected cast member in the Cast window.
	Extend Sprite	Stretches the end of each selected sprite in the Score to the current frame in a movie.
	Align	Displays the Align floating palette to line up selected sprites on the Stage in one of nine different ways.
	Rewind	Rewinds the current movie to Frame 1, usually what you want to have happen just before you play back your production.
	Stop	Halts playback of the current movie.
	Play	Begins playback of the current movie from the current frame, not necessarily from the beginning of the movie.
	Cast window	Displays the Cast window, where all good actors hope to arrive. The equivalent of choosing Window⇨Cast or pressing ⌘/Ctrl+3.
	Score window	Displays the Score window, where you design and choreograph your movie. The equivalent of choosing Window⇨Score or pressing ⌘/Ctrl+4.
	Paint window	Displays the Paint window, where you create new Bitmap Cast Members or edit imported bitmaps. The equivalent of choosing Window⇨Paint or pressing ⌘/Ctrl+5.
	Text window	Displays the Text window, where you enter rich text. The equivalent of choosing Window⇨Text or pressing ⌘/Ctrl+6.
	Behavior Inspector	Displays the Behavior Inspector (discussed in Chapter 15) where you can modify a behavior or create a new behavior.

Button	Button Name	What It Does
	Script window	Displays the Script window, where you can play mad doctor conducting cruel and inhuman experiments with Lingo, Director's built-in scripting language. The equivalent of choosing Window⇨Script or pressing ⌘/Ctrl+0 (zero).
	Help pointer	Turns the mouse cursor into America's newest super hero, Help pointer! Choose any menu command or click virtually any location of interest in a window with Help pointer, and you're taken to that very section in Director's built-in, context-sensitive help system.

Director's File Menu

Are you ready to dive into Director's menu bar? Personally, I'd rather go for a pastrami sandwich. To take a look at Director's File menu, press the mouse on File. The File menu drops down, as shown in Figure 2-5, which is why Director cleverly calls it a drop-down or pull-down menu.

Table 2-2 shows you what to expect from each File menu command.

Table 2-2	File Menu Commands
Command	What It Does
New⇨Movie	Asks you to save any changes to the current movie, closes the current file, and creates a new movie.
New⇨Cast	Creates a new internal or external Cast window. See Chapter 5 for more on internal and external casts.
Open	Takes you to the Open dialog box to find an existing Director movie.
Close	Closes any window other than the Stage window, which is always visible for the current movie.
Save	Updates a movie and linked casts that you've already named and saved to the hard drive.

(continued)

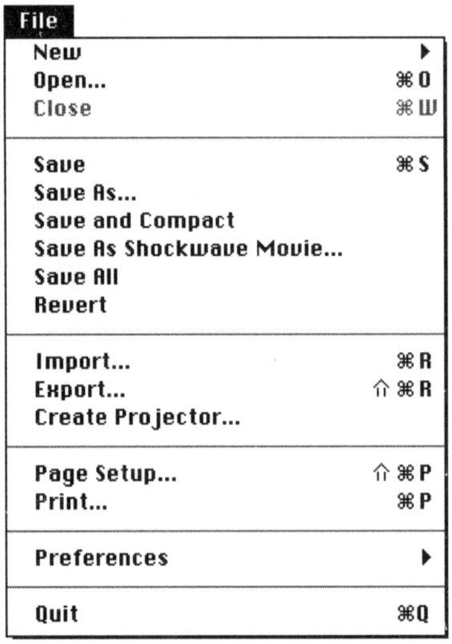

```
┌─────────────────────────────────────┐
│ File                                 │
├─────────────────────────────────────┤
│ New                              ▶   │
│ Open...                        ⌘ O   │
│ Close                          ⌘ W   │
│                                      │
│ Save                           ⌘ S   │
│ Save As...                           │
│ Save and Compact                     │
│ Save As Shockwave Movie...           │
│ Save All                             │
│ Revert                               │
│                                      │
│ Import...                      ⌘ R   │
│ Export...                    ⇧ ⌘ R   │
│ Create Projector...                  │
│                                      │
│ Page Setup...                ⇧ ⌘ P   │
│ Print...                       ⌘ P   │
│                                      │
│ Preferences                      ▶   │
│                                      │
│ Quit                           ⌘ Q   │
└─────────────────────────────────────┘
```

Figure 2-5:
Director's
File menu.

Table 2-2 *(continued)*

Command	*What It Does*
Save As	Opens the Save As dialog box to save the current movie as a new movie to the hard drive.
Save and Compact	Similar to the Save command, but compresses the movie and removes unneeded data for better performance.
Save as Shockwave Movie	Saves the movie in compressed form as a Shockwave movie for publishing Director movies on the Web.
Save All	Updates the movie and all casts, internal and external and linked or unlinked. For more on linked and unlinked casts, see Chapter 5.
Revert	Returns the current movie to its last saved version on the hard drive.
Import	Allows you to add several graphics file types and sound file types as cast members in your Director movie.
Export	Turns a Director file into different external file types.
Create Projector	Creates a stand-alone version of selected movies for distribution.

Command	*What It Does*
Page Setup	Sets up a current movie to print with Page Size, Scaling, and Orientation settings.
Print	Allows you to print all or a portion of the current movie, including the contents of selected windows.
Preferences⇔General	Allows you to set Stage Size, User Interface options, and Text Units (inches, centimeters, or pixels) and allows you to determine whether to temporarily borrow from unused system memory.
Preferences⇔Network	Opens the Network Preferences dialog box where you can customize communications between Director and the World Wide Web.
Preferences⇔Score	Allows you to set options like colored cells and drag and drop and to set information in the extended display mode of viewing cast members in the Score.
Preferences⇔Sprite	Allows you to determine how sprites are displayed in the Score window and on the Stage.
Preferences⇔Cast	Allows you to set the maximum number of cast members visible in the Cast window, the width of each row, the thumbnail size, the format of cast member labels, the types of media icons visible, and whether to show cast member script icons.
Preferences⇔Paint	Allows you to set the way brushes behave in the Paint window, whether color cycling repeats by jumping back from end to starting point or by reversing the sequence of a color cycle, custom line widths, the percentage of Director's blending feature, how fast Lighten/Darken effects work, and the way Director handles changes in color palettes or interpolation. For more on color cycling, check out Chapter 11.
Preferences⇔Editors	Opens the External Editors Preferences dialog box where you can link an external application (what Director refers to as an editor) with a bitmap, video, or sound cast member.
Quit	Closes Director and takes you to another open program or to the desktop.

What's an active window?

In the world of graphic user interfaces, only one window is available at any one time (with one exception coming up). The most recent window you've selected is the currently active window; all other open windows are inactive. Looking at title bars is the key to knowing which window is active. On the Mac, the active window displays its name in reversed text in the title bar at the top of the window, and gray, horizontal stripes adorn the width of the title bar; in Windows, the title bar of the active window displays the brightest color of the open windows. In either case, all other open windows become inactive.

Ah, the exception — I'm glad you reminded me. A special type of window called a *floating palette* appears active at all times and appears to, well, float in front of the regular active window. Director 6's Control Panel and Memory Inspector are good examples of floating palettes.

Well-designed Mac and Windows programs are supposed to share the same look and feel, but even the best of them have individual quirks. The following list is a collection of some of Director's idiosyncrasies reflected in the File menu:

- ✔ Director allows only one open movie at a time. When you choose the New Movie command, Director asks you whether you want to save changes to the current movie, closes the current movie, and then presents you with the new, blank Director file. In most other programs, you can open as many files as your available memory can handle.

- ✔ You can't close the current movie's Stage window. If the only window visible is the Stage window, choosing Close Window from the File menu does nothing, kind of like politicians. Your only options are to switch to another file with the Open command or quit.

- ✔ Director has always been infamous for making heavy demands on your computer's limited memory. Use the Save and Compact command when you've nearly completed your animation to bring down the size of the file and to help it copy into memory faster. And remember that the Purge button in the Memory Inspector frees up the maximum amount of memory.

By the way, many of the File commands take you to a window or dialog box featuring a Help button, one more way to access Director's online help, only one step better. For example, if you choose File➪Import and then click the Help button from the Import dialog box, lo and behold, you come to the Help window for the Import command. No looking up topics or keywords!

Touring Director's Other Menus

Director's other menus are no slouches, either, including

- ✔ Edit
- ✔ View
- ✔ Insert
- ✔ Modify
- ✔ Control
- ✔ Xtras
- ✔ Window
- ✔ Help

Some menus that appeared in earlier versions of Director are gone. For example, Lingo, Director's built-in scripting language, doesn't get a menu on the menu bar anymore. Instead, you find two pop-up menus in Script Cast Member dialog boxes, an alphabetical list of Lingo properties and commands and the same list organized by category. To see the pop-up menus, try the following steps:

1. **Choose Window⇨Cast or press ⌘/Ctrl+3.**

   The Cast window appears with a row of buttons at the top.

2. **Select any cast member with one click of the mouse.**

3. **Click the Cast Member Script button, the third button from the right.**

   The Cast Member Script dialog box appears with its own set of buttons.

4. **Locate the Alphabetical Lingo button with a large L in the center and press it to view the alphabetized pop-up menu.**

   You see an impressive list of Lingo stuff (see Figure 2-6) beginning with operators, and then you see Lingo commands in alphabetical order and with submenus.

5. **Locate the Categorized Lingo button just to the right and press it to view the categorized pop-up menu.**

   Believe it or not, you'll be able to make heads or tails of this mess before long.

For you old-timers, the Palette menu is gone, too. No Paint menu. No Script menu. Actually, you'll find that the menus are much better organized than in previous versions of Director. The menu bar no longer keeps changing what window happens to be active. I get into all the details in upcoming chapters.

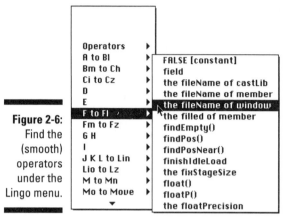

Figure 2-6:
Find the (smooth) operators under the Lingo menu.

Hey, they cheated me out of revert! It's grayed out!

Whoa, pardner. I want to review a basic part of the graphic interface. You've got a new Director file, right? You haven't added a blessed dot to it, right again? So you haven't saved anything to the hard drive — "to disk," as multimedia types like to say.

Now, Revert takes you to the last saved version of your file. If you don't have a last saved version, you've got no Revert. (You've got no bananas, either, but that's another story.) Director is smart enough to know all this even if the rest of us don't, which is why the Revert command may be grayed out. The technical name for this condition is *disabled.* And, yes, last time I looked, that term in this particular situation is still politically correct. Commands that are available to you (not grayed out) are said to be *enabled.* Enabled, disabled. Add these words to your growing vocabulary, and your future's set in stone. Just remember, Hoffa's future was set in stone, too. Or was it his feet?

Chapter 3

Lights, Camera, Action!

● ●

In This Chapter

▶Introducing the Stage

▶Traversing the Stage

▶Sizing up the Stage

▶Channel surfing with the Control Panel

▶These buttons aren't on my remote control!

● ●

*I*f you haven't had the pleasure (hah) of working in the movie industry, have you ever been to Hollywood and wound up at a free taping of a TV show? Wires, cameras, mikes, more wires, more cameras. And where are they pointing? Sure, at the actors or game show host or talk show host; but, more to the point (no pun intended), the cameras point at the stage. Without the stage, there'd be no show.

I know, you've all seen those grainy, old Mickey Rooney films where a convenient barn is always nearby, ready to serve as a stage. But no, the world's grown too sophisticated now, and you probably couldn't get fire insurance for the barn, anyway.

All the World's a Stage: Director's Opening Window

When you open Director 6, the introductory window or splash screen momentarily greets you, and then you finally come to the Stage. Just as a stage is vital for TV shows and sound stages, Director's Stage window is *the* window, where all the action occurs and where your special type of information, moving and changing over time, plays before your eyes.

Wait a minute! The darn Stage is blank as a polar bear in a snowstorm!

I see that you noticed the Stage doesn't offer much to catch your attention. If you think it's bad now, try this:

1. **Find the ⌘/Ctrl key.**

   The ⌘ key for the Mac or Ctrl key for PCs, one of the so-called modifier keys on your keyboard, usually rest just to the left of the spacebar.

2. **Press and hold down the ⌘/Ctrl key.**

   Continue holding down the ⌘/Ctrl key. You're about to perform a keyboard shortcut for selecting the Stage. I know, you're already at the Stage, but watch . . . .

3. **Press 1.**

   (That's the number 1.) Ah, the menu bar disappears. Now *that's* blank!

Stage window forever

Pressing ⌘/Ctrl+1, which is a shortcut way of saying Steps 1 through 3 in the preceding section, is what multimedia types call a *toggle* command. Choosing Stage from the Window menu or pressing ⌘/Ctrl+1 alternately hides and shows the menu bar. After all, a menu bar at the top of your animation would be pretty distracting, not to mention unhygienic.

Notice that the Stage window never disappears; it's the one Director window you can't choose to hide.

The incredible, invisible menu bar

On a slow weekend, you can have a great time with Director's menu bar. Press ⌘/Ctrl+1 so that the menu bar disappears. Or should I say seems to disappear, because it's really still there! Try moving the mouse pointer up to where you think the Window menu belongs, and sure enough, the pull-down menu pops into view. All the menus are operational but invisible when you hide the menu bar.

Give yourself ten points for every window you find and then treat yourself to dinner at your favorite restaurant. Not on me, though.

Hyperactive windows

If the menu bar is visible, press ⌘/Ctrl+1, find the Window menu, and peek at the Window menu commands. Notice the diamond to the left of the Stage window command, which is Director's coy way of telling you that the Stage is the currently active window. Figure 3-1 shows the title bar of an active window.

Figure 3-1:
The title bar
of an active
Color
Palettes
window.

You can read more about active window stuff in the sidebar, "What's an active window?" in Chapter 2.

Not counting the Stage window, which always lacks a title bar, inactive windows lose the horizontal stripes in their title bars, and the window name becomes grayed out or disabled. The Close box in the upper-left corner and the Zoom box in the upper-right corner disappear as well. (See Figure 3-2.)

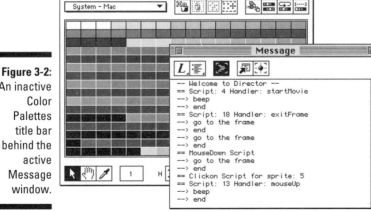

Figure 3-2:
An inactive
Color
Palettes
title bar
behind the
active
Message
window.

Checks and balances

For a fun time, try the following procedure, but be sure that the menu bar is hidden. If the menu bar isn't hidden, press ⌘/Ctrl+1. Display the Control Panel by choosing Window⇨Control Panel or by pressing ⌘/Ctrl+2. Press the Window menu and note the check mark by the Control Panel command. The Stage gets a diamond, and the Control Panel gets a check. What gives?

Director 6 now makes use of a special type of window called a *floating palette*. The Control Panel is an example of such a palette with a skinny title bar at the top, a Close box in the upper-left corner, and the capability to float in front of other windows including the active window. Another peculiar fact about floating palettes in Director: The Close command in the File menu doesn't work with palettes. Try it if you don't believe me, zheech.

Modifying the Stage

Options for modifying the Stage window reside in the Movie Properties dialog box. Choose Modify⇨Movie⇨Properties, and the Movie Properties dialog box appears, as shown in Figure 3-3.

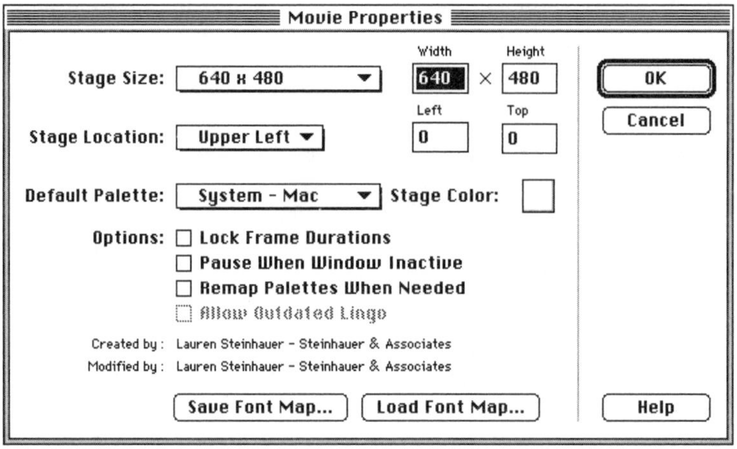

Figure 3-3: The Movie Properties dialog box, where you can modify the Stage window.

Sizing up the Stage

You find a number of size options in the Stage Size pop-up menu, including the following:

- **512 x 342:** The classic Macintosh size for the compact Mac models including the Mac Plus, Mac SE30, and Mac Classic.

- **640 x 480:** The standard size for 13- and 14-inch monitors.

- **832 x 624:** A common size for 16-inch multiple resolution monitors.

- **1024 x 768:** A common size for 19-inch multiple resolution monitors.

- **QuickTime 160 x 120:** The famous "postage stamp" size for QuickTime mooVs; often used when computer resources are known to be limited.

- **QuickTime 320 x 240:** A quarter-screen size often used for CD-ROM publishing because it's large enough to actually see something and small enough to run on all but the slowest computers.

- **Main monitor:** The Stage adopts the dimensions of the main monitor that you designate in the Monitors control panel.

- **Multiple monitors:** The Stage can be spread across several monitors to create a "virtual screen." See the "Double your pleasure, double your fun" sidebar later in this chapter.

- **Custom:** Becomes the selected option when you enter a custom width and height in the boxes to the right of the Stage Size pop-up menu.

That X-Y coordinate thing

Back in the moldy, old 17th century, a Frenchman by the name of Renatus Cartesius was working on a number of grand projects, including changing his name. Better known as René Descartes, he's credited for establishing the foundation of analytic geometry and for the famous saying, "Never put Descartes before the horse." Or was it, "I think, therefore I am?"

Anyway, people are interested in Descartes for his creation of a coordinate system used for pinpointing any location on a surface. You set horizontal locations along the x axis and vertical locations along the y axis. You can designate any point on a surface by giving its location along the x and y axes. Starting from an origin at 0,0 (0 for x and 0 for y), locations move in a positive direction down and to the right and negative directions up and to the left. If this x and y stuff confuses you, you can check out Figure 3-4 to get a better idea.

In the world of Director and most other computer programs, the upper-left corner of the screen monitor is called the *origin.* Window locations are measured by using the horizontal and vertical *offset,* or distance from the origin. With that concept in mind, look at the Movie Properties dialog box options for Stage Location relative to the monitor screen, including

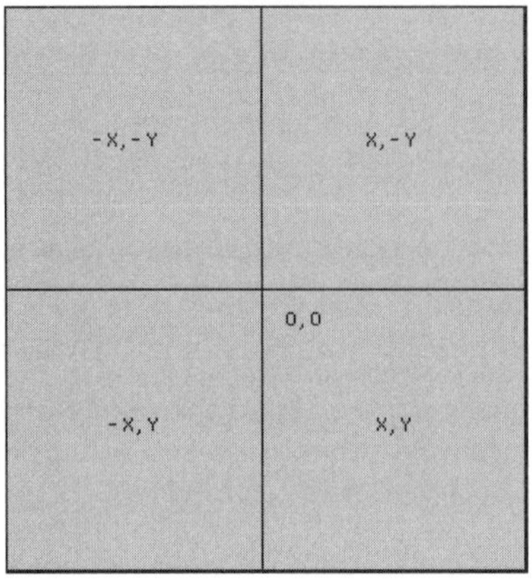

-X, -Y	X, -Y
0,0	
-X, Y	X, Y

Figure 3-4:
The
Cartesian
plane with
its x and y
axes and
origin.

✔ **Centered:** Centers the Stage window in the center of the monitor screen.

✔ **Upper Left:** Places the upper-left corner of the Stage window at the origin of the monitor screen.

✔ **Other:** Enter left and top offsets for the upper-left corner of the Stage window relative to the monitor screen's origin.

You can also set the default palette of a movie in the Movie Properties dialog box from the Default Palette pop-up menu. Beware: Setting the palette to anything other than the standard System palette can have a dramatic and often unpleasant effect on all cast members seen on the Stage. For more information on Director's palettes, see Chapter 8.

Double your pleasure, double your fun

Running two monitors is great for developing Director movies and multimedia. The idea is to drag all those gorgeous windows to the extra monitor and keep a nice, uncluttered view of the Stage on your main monitor. Two monitors make life nice, easy, and expensive.

You can also use multiple monitors as part of the presentation itself. The monitors become one giant "virtual" screen, with each monitor serving as a port into this magical world.

Some Power Macintosh models have built-in multiple monitor capabilities. Otherwise, you need an extra video card to run each additional monitor for multimedia extravaganzas.

By the way, when you're running two or more monitors, let Director know by choosing Modify⇨Movie⇨Properties and choosing Multiple Monitors from the Stage Size pop-up menu in the Movie Properties dialog box.

Pop-up palette

To the right of the Default Palette pop-up menu in the Movie Properties dialog box is the Stage Color selector. Press the selector to select a color from the pop-up palette.

Multimedia types often measure things with the pixel (for Macs) or pel (for PCs), short for picture element. A pixel or pel is the unit that makes up the pictures you see on your monitor. A standard for computer displays is a 13-inch monitor measuring 640 pixels width x 480 pixels height. By the way, the resolution of your screen is usually 72 pixels or pels per inch (ppi).

The Stage's Grid

As another helpful feature of Director 6, the Grid helps you align sprites on the Stage while the Grid's Snap To command, depicted in Figure 3-5, is turned on.

Figure 3-5:
The Snap
To submenu
under the
Grids
command in
Director's
View menu.

The Snap To command makes the Grid magnetic; sprites seem to, well, snap in place, aligning along the Grid's array of squares. The Grid's submenu also includes the Show command, which is another toggle command alternatively showing and hiding the Grid on the Stage. You can choose Settings from the submenu to custom-tailor the Grid to your every whim with the Grid Settings dialog box shown in Figure 3-6.

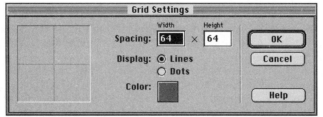

Figure 3-6:
Customize
Director's
Grid with
abandon in
the Grid
Settings
dialog box.

Channel Surfing with the Control Panel

Borrowing metaphors from TV has become very popular in MultimediaLand, especially the VCR metaphor. You see a lot of interfaces that look familiar because their buttons echo controls on your VCR remote. Actually, using familiar interfaces isn't a bad idea when developing animation and multimedia, where communicating quickly and presenting intuitive interfaces are ever-present challenges.

The next Director window to check out under the Window menu is the Control Panel, which sports a familiar VCR interface and duplicates basic commands under the Control menu. These commands include the familiar (Play, Stop, and Rewind) and the not so familiar (Loop Playback). Figure 3-7 shows the Control menu in all its glory.

Control

Play	⌐ ⌘ P
✓ Stop	⌐ ⌘ .
Rewind	⌐ ⌘ R
Step Forward	⌐ ⌘ --→
Step Backward	⌐ ⌘ ←--
✓ Loop Playback	⌐ ⌘ L
Selected Frames Only	
Volume	▶
Disable Scripts	
Toggle Breakpoint	⇧ ⌐ ⌘ K
Watch Expression	⇧ ⌐ ⌘ W
Remove All Breakpoints	
Ignore Breakpoints	⇧ ⌐ ⌘ I
Step Script	⇧ ⌐ ⌘ ↓
Step Into Script	⇧ ⌐ ⌘ --→
Run Script	⇧ ⌐ ⌘ ↑
Recompile All Scripts	⇧ ⌐ ⌘ C

Figure 3-7:
The Control
menu for all
you control
freaks.

The Control Panel also allows you to

✔ Zoom forward and backward through the frames of your movie.

✔ Set the pace or tempo of your movie.

✔ Select the way you time your movie.

✔ Set displayed time values to real times for the specific computer model running the movie.

These Buttons Aren't on My Remote Control!

The Control Panel is chock full of buttons and icons and more buttons (see Figure 3-8). The buttons are pretty intuitive, as multimedia types like to say. In other words, you should have an easy time guessing their functions because most of the buttons resemble controls on your VCR remote.

After you click a button, it looks *depressed* — no, silly goose, not sad, depressed as in pressed in — if you're running in grayscale or color. If your monitor is set to black and white, the selected button turns into a negative image.

Figure 3-8:
Director's
Control
Panel:
Nirvana for
remote
control
junkies
everywhere.

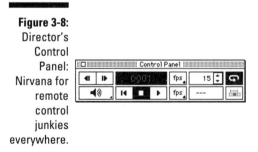

Notice the little black corner in the lower right of some Control Panel buttons, indicating a hidden pop-up menu of options you can display by pressing the mouse.

Look over the buttons in the top row of the Control Panel from left to right:

- ✔ **Step Backward:** Moves you back one frame of your movie with each click.

- ✔ **Step Forward:** Moves you to the next frame of your movie with each click.

- ✔ **Frame Counter:** Displays the current frame of your movie. Period.

- ✔ **Tempo Mode:** Toggles the Tempo panel between frames per second (fps) and seconds per frame (spf) with a pop-up menu.

- ✔ **Tempo:** Displays the current tempo. You can increase or decrease the movie's tempo by clicking the up/down arrow controls.

- ✔ **Loop Playback:** Sets your movie to play itself over and over, forever — you'd better like your movie a lot. Actually, you have many outs, like clicking the Stop button in the Control Panel or pressing ⌘/ Ctrl+Option/Alt+period. If you want your movie to play once, click Loop again; the button becomes a straight-line icon.

As if that weren't enough excitement, turn your attention to the Control Panel's bottom row of buttons, described from left to right:

- ✔ **Sound:** Mute your movie's sound level or choose levels 1 to 7 with the button's pop-up menu.

- ✔ **Rewind:** Faster than your VCR or a speeding bullet, clicking Rewind instantly zips you to Frame 1 of your movie.

- ✔ **Stop:** One click stops your movie dead in its tracks (no pun intended).

- ✔ **Play:** Start your movie like a pro; one click of the mouse does the job.

- ✔ **Actual Tempo Mode:** The pop-up menu allows you to see how fast your movie is playing in real or "actual" time and to set how the actual time is displayed: Frames Per Second (fps), Seconds Per Frame (spf), Running Total, or Estimated Total. Running Total gives you the total actual time a movie plays. The Estimated Total setting is considered more accurate for sequences that play longer than a few seconds.

- ✔ **Actual Tempo:** Displays the actual tempo as set in the Actual Tempo Mode pop-up menu.

- ✔ **Selected Frames Only:** Click to play only the range of frames selected in the Score window.

Chapter 4

Major Improvements

In This Chapter

▶ Exploring Director 6's improved Help system

▶ Cozying up to new types of files

▶ Schmoozing with media editors

▶ Discovering Xtras embedding

▶ Sprinting ahead with sprite improvements

*D*irector 6 has come a long way from its roots as a black-and-white only animation program called VideoWorks. Each new version of Director has become more powerful with additions such as a built-in 24-bit painting program, a built-in programming language called Lingo that adds interactivity to Director movies, Shockwave technology that turns movies into multimedia for the World Wide Web, built-in child care for working mothers, and many other improvements.

Now enjoy reading about some of Director 6's new wonders — from an improved Help system supporting lots of new file types to extras for Xtras, Director's name for its plug-ins.

Calling S.O.S. with D.O.L.H. (Director's Online Help)

Let's face it. Director is a complex program (not complicated, mind you, but complex) with 19 plus windows, a myriad set of commands, and options in a multitude of dialog boxes. So it's a real relief to find that Macromedia took a good Help system and made it even better in Director 6 with a streamlined interface, a searchable index, a handful of Director-based tutorials, and a built-in vending machine that dispenses M&Ms at random intervals.

Actually, Director's help isn't really Director's help. That is, it's Director's help, but it doesn't belong to Director. In other words, h-m-m-m, Director's Help system is really a separate application called QuickHelp.

One of Director's marvels, QuickHelp is what multimedia types call online help, meaning that it's available on your computer while you're running Director. You don't have to look up anything in those old-fashioned books. Saying "online help" loudly often assures you a place in multimedia history. Or maybe psychiatric history. Figure 4-1 shows QuickHelp's main menu. From this menu, you can search through Help's numerous topics.

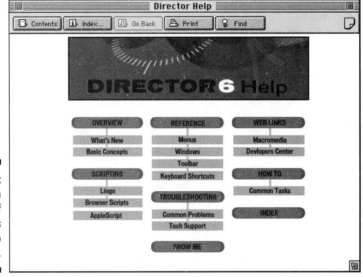

Figure 4-1:
The main menu of Director's Help window.

To access Director's online help, choose Guide (Balloon Help)⇨Director Help, as shown in Figure 4-2. Notice all the other Director options under the Guide menu from specific topics covered in online help to registering and participating in a survey.

Using Context-Sensitive Help

Director's online help has more going for it than good looks. It features *context-sensitive help,* meaning that Director can go straight to your topic of interest instead of always landing on Director Help's main menu. How can you access online help? I'm glad you asked.

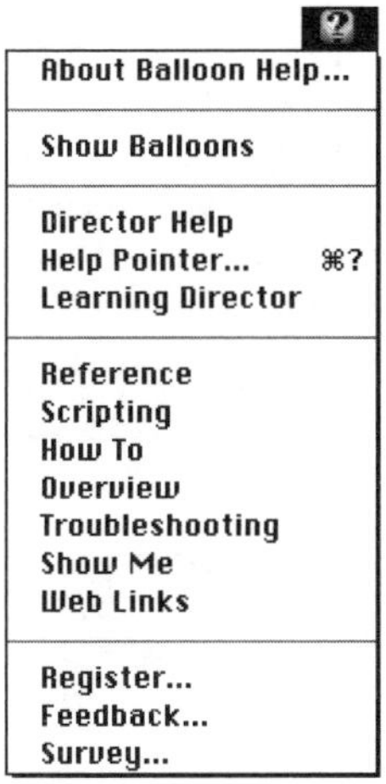

| About Balloon Help... |
| Show Balloons |
| Director Help |
| Help Pointer... ⌘? |
| Learning Director |
| Reference |
| Scripting |
| How To |
| Overview |
| Troubleshooting |
| Show Me |
| Web Links |
| Register... |
| Feedback... |
| Survey... |

Figure 4-2: You find a number of online help topics under the Guide menu.

The Help pointer

 Director provides a number of ways for you to access online help. One way is to transform that ordinary drab mouse pointer into the cool Help pointer, a cursor that looks like a question mark preceded by a small asterisk, as shown in the margin. You can access the Help pointer a number of ways. Choose Window⇨Toolbar to display Director's Toolbar feature just under the menu bar and then click the Help pointer icon on the far right of the Toolbar. You can also press ⌘/Ctrl+? or choose Guide (Balloon Help)⇨ Help Pointer on a Mac or Help⇨Help Pointer on a PC.

Now for the fun, context-sensitive part. Click any window or choose any menu command with the Help pointer, and Director (usually) takes you right to that topic in the Help window, as shown in Figure 4-3. In my example, I clicked the Stage with the Help pointer, and Director took me to the help section about the Stage window.

Dialog box buttons

Another way to access context-sensitive help is from dialog boxes. Virtually every one of Director's dialog boxes includes a Help button in the lower-right corner. Click Help to go to the appropriate info in the Help window that relates to the dialog box function(s). Often, you'll see a screen shot of the dialog box with notes on each of its options along with additional links to related topics.

An intriguing conundrum

To access the Help pointer, should you press the ⌘/Ctrl+? keys or the ⌘/Ctrl+Shift+? keys? Don't you type a question mark by pressing the Shift key first?

Know what? In Real Life, it doesn't matter. I just mentioned it to pad this section; it was looking a little lean.

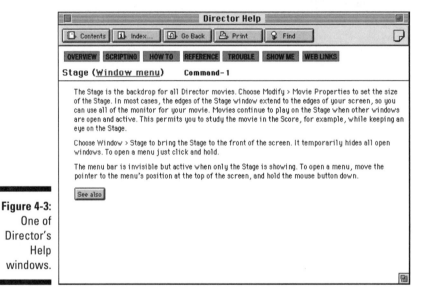

Figure 4-3:
One of
Director's
Help
windows.

Exploring QuickHelp's Interface

When you arrive at Director's Help system, QuickHelp provides a rich interface for you to move around in. All the Help windows other than the main menu sport two rows of buttons to play with. QuickHelp features a custom menu bar to explore. You can even kill a whole weekend delving into the intricacies of QuickHelp's Topics window.

QuickHelp buttons

The interface features two rows of buttons filled with wondrous functions. Table 4-1 summarizes the functions of the items in the first row of buttons at the top of Director 6's Help window, a full collection of tools for maneuvering through Help's contents. To use all the features discussed, you need access to the Web with an ISP (Internet Service Provider) and a good browser such as Netscape Navigator or Internet Explorer. AT&T WorldNet Service software is included on the CD.

Table 4-1	Help Window Buttons, Row 1
Item	*What It Does*
Contents	Takes you to the Director Help Contents window, a main menu featuring eight topics and several subtopics. Clicking one of the topics or subtopics takes you to a list that you can explore with a click of the mouse.
Index...	Takes you to the Topics window with two tabs, Index and Find. *Index* features a key word search and a scrolling index of topics. *Find* offers an extended search interface similar to the Find command available on the Macintosh desktop.
Go Back	Jumps you back to previous screens in reverse order.
Find	Displays the Find interface in the Topics window where you can set up an extended search.

Table 4-2 summarizes the function of the buttons in the second row of the Director 6 Help window, an echo of the graphical Main Menu that you come to by clicking the Contents button.

Table 4-2	Help Window Buttons, Row 2
Button	*What It Does*
OVERVIEW	Takes you to a screen with two options: What's New, a discussion of Director 6's new features; and Basic Concepts, a discussion including subjects such as Working with Cast Members, Working with Sprites, and Creating Interactivity.
SCRIPTING	Takes you to a screen with three options: Lingo, with a set of linked screens about Director's built-in programming language; Browser scripts, a discussion of how Director Shockwave movies can interact with Web browsers such as Netscape Navigator and Microsoft Internet Explorer; and AppleScript, a discussion of how Director can be controlled by AppleScript, a scripting language from Apple Computer that allows applications to "talk" to each other.
HOW TO	Takes you to a set of options about how to do common tasks in Director 6 such as Creating Interactivity, Editing Media, and Completing Movies. Click a category to explore related topics.

(continued)

Table 4-2 *(continued)*

Button	What It Does
REFERENCE	Takes you to a window of categories organized by Menus, Windows, Toolbars, and Keyboard Shortcuts. Click a listing to explore related topics.
TROUBLE	Takes you to a window brimming with Director information about common problems and provides a hot link to Macromedia's technical support.
SHOW ME	Your key to accessing new interactive tutorial movies, shown in Figure 4-4, that explain a number of critical Director techniques and features such as Cast Members and Sprites, Color Palettes, and Film Loops as well as new features including Behaviors and Streaming Shockwave.
WEB LINKS	Takes you to a window listing Macromedia's Web site where you can find: topics, such as How do I . . . ?, where experts answer your toughest Director questions online; Updates & Downloads, where you can download product updates, new Xtras (Director's plug-ins), and other goodies; and Interact, where you may leave messages for Macromedia's staff (keep it clean). By the way, if you have access to the World Wide Web, the Macromedia listing is a hot link that takes you straight to the Web site with your favorite browser.

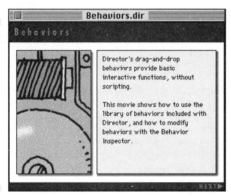

Figure 4-4:
You can
access
tutorials
such as the
Behaviors
tutorial in
Director's
Help
window.

As you explore Director's Help system, you find screen shots of various windows. You can click different features of a window to display a panel of relevant information.

For example, the topic, "Message window toolbar," appears when you type **mes** in the Index window; after you click Display, you come to the Message window toolbar window where you can explore the depicted toolbar buttons. Clicking the first depicted button displays a panel where you discover that the button is called the Alphabetical Lingo pop-up menu, listing all of Director's Lingo commands in alphabetical order. You can close the panel by clicking anywhere outside the panel. Many panels also include a See Also button that displays additional links to related topics.

The Help menu

QuickHelp has its own menu bar. Although most of the commands are self-explanatory, I just want to go over some that are puzzling enough to warrant a brief explanation.

- ✔ **File⇨Print All Topics:** To print out a hard copy of *all* the help material, choose this command. The hard copy's great for leveling tables.

- ✔ **Edit⇨Delete Note:** If you want to trash a note, click the note and choose Edit⇨Delete Note or drag the note out of the Help window. (You'll see the cute hand icon turn into a smelly old trash can.)

- ✔ **Edit⇨Undo Delete Note:** If you foolishly tossed out a gem of a note, you can reclaim it with this command if you act immediately after choosing File⇨Delete Note.

- ✔ **Edit⇨Copy Topic as a Picture:** Choose this command to make what amounts to a screen shot of the current screen. If you want to create your own wallpaper, choose this command in various windows, print them out, color them with crayons, and buy a wallpaper-hanging setup. Great family fun. If you want to copy text within a help window, drag through the text and use the old-fashioned Copy command under Edit.

- ✔ **Bookmarks⇨Set Bookmark:** Choose this command to create a kind of electronic bookmark for the current topic in the Set Bookmark dialog box, as shown in Figure 4-5. A nice feature is that you can select a keyboard shortcut from a pop-up menu to return to the marked topic at any time. Director lists any bookmarks that you create under the Bookmarks menu.

Figure 4-5:
Create a
custom
bookmark
in the Set
Bookmark
dialog box.

✔ **Bookmarks⇨Edit Bookmarks:** This command takes you to the Edit Bookmarks dialog box, listing all bookmarks in a scrolling field. You can change the name of a selected bookmark or its keyboard shortcut or even delete the bookmark if you feel particularly destructive. You can also click the View button to take you to the page corresponding to the selected bookmark in the list.

✔ **Options⇨History Window:** This command takes you to the History scrolling palette that lists the last several windows you visited. To revisit a window, select the listing and click View Topics at the bottom or double-click the listing in the palette.

✔ **View⇨Show Notes:** This is one of those infamous toggle commands. Choose once to show your notes. Choose again to hide them. Top security feature. Good thinking, Macromedia. No one's going to figure this one out.

✔ **View⇨Director Help:** This one's got me stumped. Send in your best guess to me personally, in care of IDG Books Worldwide, Inc.

Help notes

Did you notice the little yellow square in the upper-right corner of the Help window? It represents an electronic stick-on note. Press the square, drag a note into the Help window, and then write yourself a memo! If you don't enter any text, the note disappears when you jump to another page. To delete a note, choose Edit⇨Delete Note or drag the note off the Help window where it turns into a cute trash can cursor until it disappears when you release the mouse.

Topics window

When you click the Index button at the top of the Help window, the Topics window, shown in Figure 4-6, appears in a blinding flash of light. It features an interface with two tabs, Index and Find.

In Index mode, you can enter a keyword at the top, which is great fun because Director tries to anticipate what you're typing, jumping to the topic in the scrolling list below the keyword entry box. If Director guesses right, just stop typing and click the Display button at the bottom-right of the Topics window or press Enter; otherwise, continue entering the keyword that you want to search for and then press Enter.

In Find mode, you can do an extended search using pop-up menus and the More Choice button. Choose the desired modifiers in the two pop-up menus. Each time that you click More Choices, a duplicate set of pop-up menus appears where you may further refine your search.

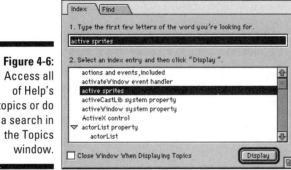

Figure 4-6:
Access all
of Help's
topics or do
a search in
the Topics
window.

Note the Recent Searches pop-up menu in the upper-right corner of the
Topics dialog box that keeps a record of your last several setups for a
search. Choosing a listing recreates the settings in the Topics dialog box.

When you click the Options button, the Find Options dialog box, shown in
Figure 4-7, appears where you can refine your search even more with the
following settings:

✓ **Nearby:** With two or more sets of pop-up menus in the Topics window,
you can narrow down your search by specifying a second search word
(or phrase) that is close to or *nearby* the first search word within a
certain number of words. Use the Up and Down arrow controls to set
how many words apart the two search words can be to be considered a
valid *hit.*

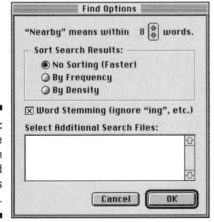

Figure 4-7:
Fine-tune
your search
in the Find
Options
dialog box.

✔ **Sort Search Results:** A successful search produces one or more *hits* that are listed in the scrolling field of the Topics window. Select *No Sorting* for the fastest search producing a list of topics in the order found. *Frequency* sorts the hits by the number of times the search words appear in a particular category whereas *Density* sorts the hits by the number of related topics found.

✔ **Word Stemming:** Selecting Word Stemming allows related categories with "ing" at the end to be considered successful hits.

✔ **Select Additional Search Files:** When and if Macromedia releases additions to the Help system, you can choose to include them in the search from this scrolling field.

Occasionally, Director can't seem to find the Help system when you try to access it. If you have this problem, find Director 6.0 Help inside the Help folder/directory of Director and open it the old-fashioned way (by double-clicking the file).

New, Improved, Taste-Tested Import Formats

One of the major ways to make artwork part of your Director movie is to use the Import command under the File menu. Director has long supported importing paintings or bitmaps. For the Macintosh, that's the PICT format, and for you Windows people the BMP and PNT file formats.

Now, Director 6 supports a new set of file types such as GIF and JPEG. Director supports the new file formats in the sense that it recognizes the new file formats in the Import Files dialog box (discussed in Chapter 5), allowing you to import the files into Director. But on the way, Director *changes* each type of file to a bitmap. For example, Director now allows you to select a native Photoshop file in the Import Files dialog box and then click the Import button; however, when the graphic winds up in Director, it's no longer a Photoshop file but a regular, old-fashioned bitmap.

Director for Macintosh and Director for Windows both support the following new file formats:

✔ **BMP:** For bitmap; this file format is for bitmaps created in Windows painting programs. Like graphics created in Adobe Photoshop or within Director's built-in Paint window, BMP files are a collection of pixels and are similar to mosaics in the way that the image is built up from small dots of color and shading. For more on bitmaps and the Paint window, see Chapters 7 and 8.

✔ **GIF:** For Graphics Interchange Format; this 8-bit file format is from CompuServe, the popular commercial online service and has been a popular format for graphics in World Wide Web pages because of its ability to be compressed to very small file sizes. For more on Director 6 and the Web, see Chapter 18.

✔ **JPEG:** For Joint Photographic Experts Group; this file format is favored by multimedia developers because of its compression capabilities and because JPEG supports 24-bit color, which comes close to photographic quality.

✔ **LRG:** Yet another bitmap file; the native file format is created by Macromedia's xRes application, a painting and compositing program especially for large bitmap graphics.

✔ **Photoshop 3.0:** The bitmap file format for Adobe Systems's popular and very sophisticated painting program.

Director 6 does not currently support the most recent version of Photoshop (version 4). Until there's an update, be sure to save files in Photoshop format using Photoshop 3.0 or save files using Photoshop 4.0 as Photoshop 2.0 format (or as a PICT).

✔ **PNG:** Another bitmap file format created by Windows painting programs.

✔ **TIFF:** For Tagged Image File Format; the best file format for bitmap images, usually chosen for saving scanned photographs.

Director for Macintosh still supports MacPaint, PICS, PICT, and Scrapbook files. Director for Windows still supports PhotoCD, PCX, WMF, PostScript, and the FLC and FLI multiple image formats. For more on importing files into Director 6, see Chapter 5.

Media Editors

Within Director, you can edit only bitmaps created in the Paint window and from painting programs such as Macromedia's own xRes, Adobe Photoshop, and Fractal Design Painter. With Director 6 supporting so many new file formats (see "New, Improved, Taste-Tested Import Formats," the previous section), Macromedia now thoughtfully provides a new feature allowing you to designate one or more applications as *media editors* for individual types of files. A media editor is simply an external application you select to modify specific types of files used in the current Director movie. Double-clicking artwork from a special file type automatically opens the designated media editor where you may make your edits. When you're ready to return to Director, quitting out of the media editor does the trick and automatically updates the artwork in the movie.

To designate a media editor in Director 6:

1. Choose File⇨Preferences⇨Editors.

The Editors Preferences dialog box appears, as shown in Figure 4-8.

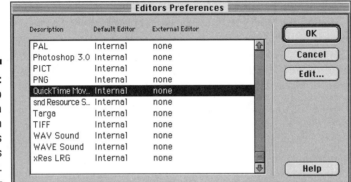

Figure 4-8:
Set up
media
editors in
the Editors
Preferences
dialog box.

2. Select a file type in the Editors Preferences dialog box.

3. Click Edit.

The Select Editor dialog box appears, as shown in Figure 4-9.

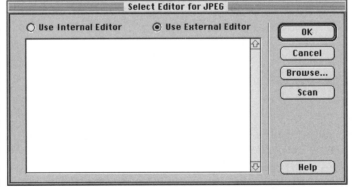

Figure 4-9:
Select Use
External
Editor
and click
Browse to
select a
media
editor.

4. Select Use External Editor and click Browse.

When the Directory window appears, locate the application that you
want to designate as a media editor. You can also click Scan for Director
to search through your drive for the correct applications.

5. **Select the desired application in the Directory and click Open.**

   Director lists the application in the Select Editor dialog box.

6. **In the Select Editor dialog box, click OK.**

   When you return to the Editors Preferences dialog box, your chosen application is now listed as the external editor and the default editor label is listed as External.

7. **Click OK.**

To use a media editor for editing artwork in Director that came from a special file format:

1. **Double-click the special artwork, either in Director's Cast window or on the Stage.**

   For information on the Cast window, see Chapter 5. For info on the Stage, see Chapter 3.

   The MIX Editing in Progress dialog box, shown in Figure 4-10, appears very briefly. Director automatically opens the program you've designated as the media editor where you can edit the artwork.

Figure 4-10:
The MIX
Editing in
Progress
dialog box.

2. **Press Done in the MIX Editing in Progress dialog box.**

   Your edits are saved, and when you return to Director, the artwork is automatically updated.

Xtra, Xtra! Xtras Embedding!

In Director, you can turn a movie into a self-running file called a *projector,* as discussed in Chapter 20. In the bad old days before Director 6 and underarm deodorants, if the projector used one or more of Director's plug-ins called Xtras, you needed to manually install the Xtras onto your system. Yuck, so unhygienic. During the projector-making process, Director 6 can now incorporate these Xtras into the projector as long as you prep the Xtras in the Movie Xtras dialog box.

To prepare Xtras for embedding into a projector:

1. Choose Modify⇨Movie⇨Xtras.

The Movie Xtras dialog box, shown in Figure 4-11, appears in Technicolor, CinemaScope, and THX stereo sound.

Figure 4-11:
Use the Movie Xtras dialog box to list Xtras that are used in a movie.

Director lists Xtras that appear in the Score in the scrolling field of the Movie Xtras dialog box. Xtras may also be used from within Lingo scripts, but they do not show up in the list. When you use Xtras within Lingo scripts, go to Step 2. Otherwise, jump to Step 6.

2. Click the Add button to display a list of the Xtras stored in the Xtras folder, which you can find within the Macromedia folder in your System folder/directory.

3. In the Movie Xtras dialog box, select the Xtra that you used in a Lingo script and want to add to the list.

4. Click OK.

5. If you want to include more Xtras in the list, repeat Steps 2 through 4.

6. Click OK.

Sprite Overhaul

Whether you import artwork — *media* as high-falooting multimedia types like to say — into Director or create bitmaps directly in the Paint window, you actually create your movie by manipulating entities called *sprites* on the Stage and in the Score, two of Director's most essential windows. Director 6 includes several new powerful features for handling and managing sprites. Now if only Director 6 could make paying my taxes easier . . . .

Sprite what?

Here's a concept that's a little hard to get when you first start working with Director. Each time you create a graphic in Director's Paint window or import a graphic by choosing File⇨Import, the graphic winds up in a window called the Cast. In the Cast window, all the graphics (and other types of items) found therein are referred to as cast members. You can drag a cast member on the Stage or to the Score window as described in the appropriate chapters. But when the cast member is on the Stage or in the Score, the same entity is called a sprite, as shown in Figure 4-12.

On the Stage, a sprite looks like its counterpart in the Cast window, so you may be tempted to call the sprite a copy. Don't. The sprite police will come cart you away in the dark of night.

A sprite simply refers to the cast member in the Cast. If you work with a Macintosh, a sprite is very much like an alias that you can create for a file or application from the desktop. An alias isn't a copy; it's like a little map (techies call it a pointer) that directs your computer to the real document or program on the hard drive. Same idea with sprites.

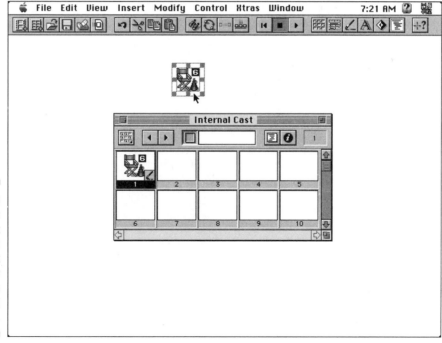

Figure 4-12:
A Bitmap Cast Member in the Cast window and its sprite on the Stage.

Sprite Overlay

Sprite Overlay is a completely new feature for Director 6 that can display a panel of information, shown in Figure 4-13, by each sprite on the Stage. You can use commands under the View menu to decide if a sprite overlay appears and to customize how the display looks. To turn on Sprite Overlay, choose View⇨Sprite Overlay⇨Show Info.

Sprite overlay info

A sprite overlay displays buttons you can click to go to important windows for the sprite. From top to bottom, the buttons include the Cast Member Properties dialog box button, the Sprite Properties dialog box button, and the Behavior Inspector button. In addition, sprite overlays show condensed information from each of the dialog boxes, kind of a *Reader's Digest* of sprite goodies. You can read about sprite preferences in the next section, "Sprite overlay settings"; you can find out more about the Cast Member Properties dialog box in Chapter 5.

Sprite overlay settings

To customize how sprite overlays look on the Stage, choose View⇨ Sprite Overlay⇨Settings. The Overlay Settings dialog box, shown in Figure 4-14, appears in a puff of smoke; but don't worry, this second-hand smoke isn't hazardous to your health.

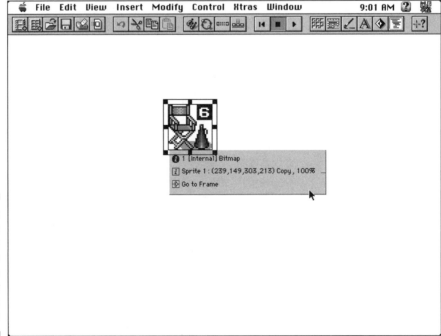

Figure 4-13:
A sprite on the Stage with its sprite overlay showing. Is this legal?

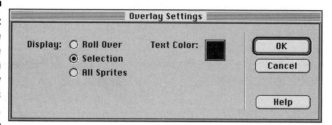

Figure 4-14:
Customize
sprite
overlays in
the Overlay
Settings
dialog box.

On the left side of the Overlay Settings dialog box, the Display options
include:

- ✓ **Roll Over:** Displays the sprite overlay only when the mouse pointer
  moves over a sprite on the Stage.

  The term *Roll Over* comes from a Lingo scripting technique that allows
  an action to occur when the mouse pointer moves or "rolls over" a
  specific sprite.

- ✓ **Selection:** Displays sprite overlays only for selected sprites on the
  Stage. You can Shift+select two or more sprites on the Stage to display
  their sprite overlay information.

- ✓ **All Sprites:** Displays overlays for all sprites on the Stage. More annoying than fingernails on a blackboard, but I'll let you decide.

In the Overlay Settings dialog box, the little black square next to Text Color
is actually a pop-up menu of colors that you can use to set — of all things —
the text color of info in your sprite overlays. In my mind, there's nothing like
black text for readability. Hey! Little things mean a lot.

Sprite overlays are semitransparent. If the background underneath an
overlay is very "busy" (contains a lot of detail) and/or if you've set a relatively light color for overlay text, the information in the overlay may be
unreadable.

Show Paths

You may have noticed another overlay-related command, Show Paths,
located under the View submenu. When you turn on Show Paths, Director
shows the movement trail or path of an animated sprite on the Stage, as
shown in Figure 4-15. I discuss how to use Show Paths in Chapter 6, where I
discuss using a technique called tweening.

Assorted new sprite stuff

Here's a roundup of all sorts of weird, wacky, wonderful things that you can
now do with sprites in the privacy of your own home. Just be sure to put the
kids to sleep first.

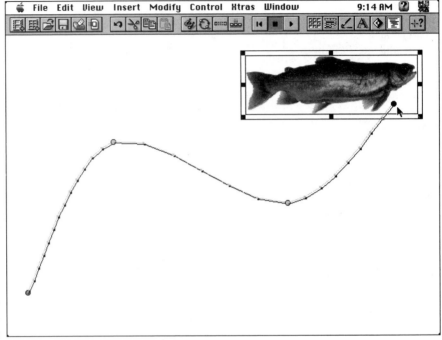

Figure 4-15:
When you turn on Show Paths in the View menu, you can see the trail of a moving sprite on the Stage.

✔ **Changing the duration of a sprite.** A really great feature of this new kind of sprite is how easily you can change the duration of a sprite. To change the number of frames of a sprite, simply stretch the sprite. Drag either end of the sprite until its sprite bar covers the number of frames that you want.

One feature that Director 6 does *not* yet include is morphing, an over-used and abused special effect that every other movie and commercial throws your way. The implication for sprites is that in Director, when you stretch a sprite, you do not create a morphing effect (where one image transforms into another image); instead, your actual result depends on the specific sprite that you stretch. Stretching a sprite containing keyframes creates additional in-between frames and has the effect of smoothing out motion; stretching a sprite without keyframes simply increases the number of frames in its sprite bar. For more on keyframes, see Chapter 6.

✔ **Moving a sprite bar in the Score window.** Now that the new default setting for a sprite in the Score window includes a sprite span of 28 frames, the first and last sprites in the sprite bar are special types of sprites referred to as keyframes. These special sprites are a part of a technique for creating animation called tweening, which defines the most important frames in an animation sequence and lets Director create the missing, intermediate frames. Trying to move the whole sprite bar to another channel by dragging either of the keyframes doesn't accomplish much (except that you may inadvertently change the width of the sprite bar).

To move a sprite's entire sprite bar to another location in the Score window, you need to drag any part of the sprite bar *other* than a keyframe. As you drag the sprite, you find that the mouse pointer turns into the Hand cursor and that you can change the entire sprite's location in the Score.

✔ **Moving a sprite on the stage.** The result of moving a sprite on the Stage is dramatically affected by whether the sprite is a so-called keyframe. Moving a nonkeyframe sprite on the Stage moves its entire sprite bar in the Score window. Moving a keyframe sprite on the Stage makes Director automatically recreate the intermediate frames of the entire keyframe animation sequence.

✔ **Placing two or more cast members into one sprite bar.** Another result of Director 6's new type of sprite is that a sprite's sprite bar can incorporate two or more different cast members from the Cast window. How is this possible? Well, it can happen when you use the Cast to Time command, a technique for placing a sequence of cast members into Director's Score window. After you select cast members in the Cast window and choose Modify⇨Cast to Time, the selected cast members become one sprite in the Score window, one cast member per frame of the sprite's sprite bar.

Sprite Labels

You can turn on Sprite Labels, one of Director 6's new features, to list a sprite's cast member in the sprite's sprite bar by choosing View⇨Sprite Labels and choosing an option in the submenu, as shown in Figure 4-16.

Figure 4-16: Customize the way a sprite bar looks in the Score window with the Sprite Labels submenu.

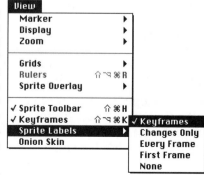

The Sprite Labels submenu includes the following options:

✓ **Keyframes:** Displays the sprite's cast member number next to each keyframe.

✓ **Changes Only:** Displays a keyframe's cast member number only if the keyframe is different from the previous keyframe.

✓ **Every Frame:** Numbers every frame of a sprite with its cast member number.

✓ **First Frame:** Numbers only the first frame of a sprite with its cast member number.

✓ **None:** Come on, you can figure this one out, right?

Sprite preferences

Now that sprites are so hoity-toity that they have their very own Sprite Preferences dialog box, shown in Figure 4-17, you can customize some characteristics of sprites on the Stage and within the Score window.

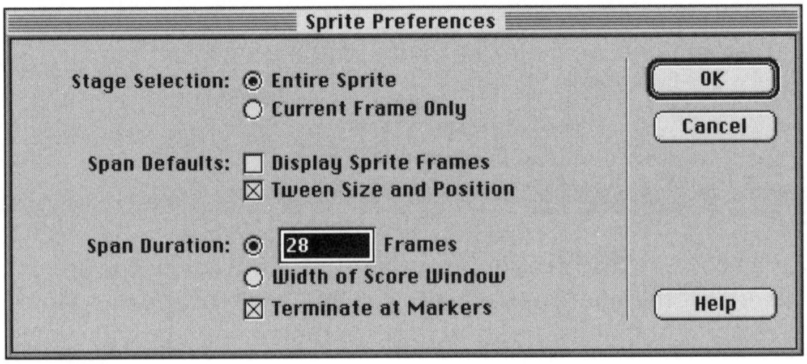

Figure 4-17:
Modify
sprite
character-
istics in the
Sprite
Preferences
dialog box.

The Sprite Preferences dialog box includes the following options:

✓ **Stage Selection Radio Buttons:** Changes how a selected sprite on the Stage is displayed in the Score window. Choose Entire Sprite for Stage Selection to select the entire sprite bar in the Score. Choose Current Frame Only to select the sprite in only the current frame.

✓ **Span Defaults Check Boxes:** These options affect the look and behavior of *new* sprites; changing settings does not affect sprites that are already in the Score window. Choosing Display Sprite Frames is the same as manually choosing Edit➪Edit Sprite Frames for a new sprite.

Note: When you turn on Edit Sprite Frames in the View menu and click a sprite on the Stage, you select the sprite in only the current frame of the Score. By modifying the sprite, you automatically turn it into a new keyframe. See Chapter 6 for more info on keyframes and tweening.

Tween Size and Position is Director's default setting. It tells Director to alter a sprite's size and location from keyframe to keyframe, automatically creating an animation with a technique called tweening.

A sprite in Director 6, represented by the bar or "sprite span" in the Score, may represent one or more cast members.

✔ **Span Duration Radio Buttons:** You can change the default setting of 28 frames for a sprite's span in the Score window by typing a different value in the Frames entry box. Selecting the Width of Score Window radio button sets the sprite bar to the current width of the Score window.

Note: After you choose the Width of Score Window, a sprite's span keeps the original width of the Score window, even if you later resize the Score.

✔ **Terminate at Markers Check Box:** Markers are little signposts that you can add in the Score window at specific frames. Select this radio button to make a new sprite's sprite bar stop one frame away from the first marker to the right in the Score. For example, if you have a marker in Frame 10 and you drag a sprite into Frame 5, the sprite's sprite bar stretches from Frame 5 to 9.

Sprite Inspector

Director 6 adds the Sprite Inspector, shown in Figure 4-18, to the Inspectors submenu of the Window menu to join the Text and Memory Inspector floating palettes. The Sprite Inspector collects useful info and settings for a sprite that you select on the Stage or in the Score window and allows you to change the sprite from the palette.

After you select one sprite, the full range of settings in the Sprite Inspector is available. You can also select several sprites and alter them with a more limited group of settings.

The info and settings that you can find in the Sprite Inspector are exactly the same as the display of the Sprite toolbar (described in full in Chapter 6) at the top of the Score window, except that the Sprite Inspector's layout is vertical, not horizontal.

Figure 4-18:
As a new
floating
palette, the
Sprite
Inspector
displays
lots of info
on a sprite
selected on
the Stage or
in the
Score.

Part II
The Big Picture

In this part . . .

One reason why Director is such a wonderful program to work with is its richness of windows and options therein. In this part, I focus on the major players in the Window Department, where you get to become close, personal friends with Mr. Cast, Mr. Score, Ms. Paint, and that ever popular gad-about, the Text window.

Chapter 5

Casting Coach or Couch?
The Cast Window

- -

In This Chapter

▶ Casting your movie with the Cast window

▶ Adding cast members to your movie

▶ A brief tour of the Cast menu

- -

Director 6's Cast window is how Director types make a casting call in the world of digital moviemaking. All the files on your hard drive get all excited, slap down their copy of *Variety,* and come running to queue up with hearts aflutter, hoping against hope to find themselves among the chosen, on their way to stardom, wealth, and interviews with Robin Leach.

Calling All Cast Members

Now that you know how exciting the Cast window is, take a look at it by choosing Window⇨Cast or pressing ⌘/Ctrl+3.

Your Cast window appears like a blinding bank of klieg lights streaming into the crisp, Hollywood night sky! Pretty exciting, huh?

Can I believe my ears? Did I hear someone say, "Not exactly"? Hmm, maybe you're not the right file type. Director's pretty picky about the type of file it accepts in the Cast window, you know.

Defining the Cast

First, I'll define the Cast.

Anyone working in the food industry in L.A. No, cut. Over and out. A cast member is any media or script that is used within your movie. The type of cast members that Director handles varies with the package you use, Macintosh or Windows.

The native graphics type of file for Director is the *bitmap,* the kind of graphic made up of pixels of color and/or brightness levels. Bitmaps are cousins to mosaics and halftone images in magazines in the way they create the illusion of an image with small dots of information. Director also handles sound, digital video, and other type of cast members. As listed in the Import Files dialog box, Macintosh cast members include

- **Picture:** PICT images containing drawings and/or bitmaps.

- **MacPaint:** Simple 1-bit black and white bitmaps.

- **Sound:** System 7 sounds, AIFF (Audio Interchange File Format) sound files, and AIFC (compressed AIFF) sound files.

- **Scrapbook:** Bitmap graphics in the current Scrapbook.

- **PICS:** A special file format containing a set of PICTs.

- **Director Movie:** Any other Director movie, imported as a film loop along with individual cast members.

- **Director Cast:** Cast members of an external Cast window.

- **QuickTime:** Digital videos often compressed with various Apple compression schemes (codecs), always imported as linked files.

- **Text:** Imported text documents and text directly entered in Text and Field windows within Director 6.

Additional types of Macintosh cast members not directly listed in the Import Files dialog box include

- **Palettes:** Sets of colors optionally imported along with an external bitmap or created directly in Director's Color Palettes window.

- **Film loops:** A sequence of frames from the Score window copied into one cell of the Cast window as a single cast member.

- **Scripts:** Imported along with Director movies or created within Director's Script window.

As listed in the Import Files dialog box, Windows cast members include

- **Bitmap files:** Paintings from programs like Corel PHOTO-PAINT or created directly in Director's Paint window.

- **JPEG files:** An acronym for Joint Photographic Experts Group, compressed files that can contain 24-bit bitmaps.

- **CompuServe GIF files**: An acronym for Graphics Interchange Format, compressed bitmaps with up to 256 colors.

- **TIFF files:** An acronym for Tagged Image File Format, high-quality bitmaps often used to save scanned photographs.

- **EPS files:** An acronym for Encapsulated PostScript, high-quality drawings or vector-based graphics created with drawing programs such as CorelDRAW and Adobe Illustrator.

- **PhotoCD files:** Graphics from Kodak's proprietary scanning service producing a CD-ROM from photographic film formats.

- **PC Paintbrush files:** Graphics created with the Paintbrush application, extension type PCX.

- **Windows metafiles:** Developed by Microsoft, a graphic container for bitmap and/or vector-based images that can handle up to 24-bit color depth.

- **Palettes:** Collections of colors that can be imported or directly created in Director's Color Palettes window.

- **Sounds:** WAV (Wave Audio) sound files, AIFF sound files, and AIFC sound files.

- **Director movies:** Any other Director movie, imported as a film loop and individual cast members.

- **Cast files:** Cast members of an external Cast window.

- **Video clips:** Linked Digital Video Cast Members from QuickTime and AVI (Audio Video Interleave) files.

- **FLC and FLI files:** Proprietary multiple image animation file types created in Autodesk Animator Pro and Autodesk Animator.

- **Macintosh PICTs:** The Macintosh metafile format, containing bitmap and/or vector-based graphics.

- **MacPaint files:** Simple 1-bit black and white bitmaps.

- **Text files:** Imported text documents and text directly entered in Text and Field windows within Director 6.

Additional types of Windows cast members not directly listed in the Import Files dialog box include

- **Film loops:** A sequence of frames from the Score window copied into one cell of the Cast window as a single cast member.

- **Scripts:** Imported along with Director 6 movies or created within Director's Script window.

"Invisible" support for new file formats

Director 6 for Macintosh now supports BMP, GIF, JPEG, LRG (xRes), Photoshop 3.0, PNG, and TIF graphic file formats. I call Director 6's new support of these file formats "invisible" because you don't see the formats listed in the Import Files dialog box's Show pop-up menu. But you do see files of these file formats listed in the Directory area of the dialog box; Director kind of lumps them all together as bitmap-type graphics (which they are, by gosh). Here's a brief description of the newly supported file formats:

- **BMP:** The PC world's most basic bitmap-type file format.

- **GIF:** For Graphics Interchange Format, the World Wide Web's most prevalent file format featuring compression and support for up to 256 colors.

- **JPEG:** For Joint Photographic Experts Group, a sophisticated (always wears top hat and tails) file format featuring compression and either 24-bit color or 256 grayscale graphics.

- **LRG:** The native file format of Macromedia's own xRes, a solid painting and compositing program that comes bundled with Director 6 Studio.

- **Photoshop 3.0:** The native file format for files created with Adobe's renowned painting program.

- **PNG:** Another bitmap-type file format prolific in the PC world.

- **TIFF:** For Tagged Image File Format, the file format of choice for scanned images in both the Mac and Windows worlds.

Interesting enough, Director 6 for Windows isn't so sneaky about now supporting BMP, GIF, JPEG, PNG, and TIF graphic formats; the program not only supports the new file formats but lists them in the Import Files dialog box's Show pop-up menu. Director 6 for Windows also now supports Macintosh PICTs and MacPaint files and lists them as well in the Show pop-up list.

For some unexplainable cosmic reason, Director 6 for Windows becomes sneaky about supporting LRG (xRes) and Photoshop 3.0 file formats, supporting these new file formats but not listing them in the Show pop-up menu.

Although Director 6 now supports new file formats such as JPEG and GIF compressed file types, don't think you can create movies with compressed cast members showing up in your Cast window and on the Stage. Director supports the new file types only in the sense that files of the newly supported types are now visible and selectable in the Directory area of the Import File dialog box. When you actually import the new file types, Director changes them into standard, old uncompressed bitmaps. Too bad, huh?

Of drawings, paintings, PICTs, and PICS

Many years ago, Charlton Heston parted the world of computer graphics into the two realms of drawings and paintings. Drawings come from drawing programs such as ClarisDraw for the Mac and CorelDRAW for the PC. You hear computer nerds refer to this type of file as an object-oriented or vector-based graphic, too. Drawings describe shapes with hidden computer code, are easily enlarged or reduced, and print smoothly at virtually any size on most printers.

Paintings come from Mommy and Daddy paintings, that is, paintings come from applications such as Macromedia's xRes, bundled with the Director 6 Studio package, as well as Adobe Photoshop and Fractal Design Painter for the Mac and PC. Director 6's Paint window offers a built-in 24-bit painting program, too. Paintings are built up from units of color called pixels or pels (picture elements), very similar to mosaics made up of individual tiles or magazine photos made up of halftone dots. Also referred to as bitmapped graphics, paintings can display very subtle, photographic-like shading and detail but do not reduce or enlarge well. With low-resolution printers, they print out with distracting ragged edges referred to as the infamous *jaggies*.

In the world of Mac, a PICT is an all-purpose file type that may contain a vector-based or bitmapped graphic. A PICS file contains a set of individual PICTs — each PICT stored as a "resource" in the file. Mac files have unique structures called data and resource forks. When you type a memo, typically the text of the memo goes in the data fork. When you create a PICS file, each PICT you include in the PICS file becomes a resource in the Mac file's resource fork. When you import a PICS file into Director 6, each PICT resource within the PICS file becomes an individual cast member in the Cast window. You can also export a Director movie as a PICS file, turning each frame of your movie into a PICT resource in the PICS's resource fork.

Such power is truly frightening.

Adding cast members to the Cast window

You can't wait to add a cast member to the Cast. I know the feeling, far stronger than a Big Mac attack. Adding a cast member is what the Import command has been waiting so patiently to do for you.

Import is a pretty common command in most programs and does pretty much the same thing in each program: adding the contents of a file on disk to the program's currently open document. Some programs such as PageMaker call the Import command the Place command. Same thing.

To add a cast member, just follow the Yellow Brick Road, er, these steps:

1. Choose File⇨Import or press ⌘/Ctrl+R.

The Import Files dialog box appears where you can set import options. Notice that All Files is the first option in the Show pop-up menu shown in Figure 5-1. With All Files chosen, you see a list of all importable files on your hard drive. Choosing any other option for Show lists only that file type. PICT is the workhorse file type for the Macintosh. With the Mac, most of the cast members you add to Director 6 are PICTs. For PC users, the most ubiquitous file format is the bmp (bitmap) file type.

Figure 5-1:
Options in
the Mac
Import Files
dialog box's
Show pop-
up menu.

Show: ✓All Files
PICT
Bitmap Image
Palette
Sound
Director Movie
Director Cast
QuickTime
Scrapbook
PICS
Text

Notice the pop-up list at the bottom of the Import Files dialog box. You can find more on the dialog box's options in "Linking your imported file" in this chapter. The Import as PICT option imports a vector-based PICT into Director 6 as a PICT Cast Member. Ordinarily, Director 6 transforms imported PICTs into bitmapped graphics with a process called rasterization. For more on vector-based files, check out the sidebar, "Of drawings, paintings, PICTs, and PICS."

2. **Find the desired file in the Directory.**

3. **Click the file(s) in the list that you want to import.**

   You can also choose Add All to import all the files.

4. **Click the Import button.**

   If you import a bitmapped graphic, Director 6 presents the Image Options dialog box, where you can change the file's color depth and palette. Click OK, and Director takes you to the Cast window, where you find the imported file as a new Bitmap Cast Member in the Cast.

Avoid scrolling through long lists in the Directory and come close to a file by pressing the first letter of its filename on the keyboard. For example, if you're looking for a document named PHOTO.BMP in the Directory, type P to select the first file in the Directory beginning with the letter *P*.

You can get even closer to your file, if not right on, by quickly typing **ph** or **pho**. The trick is to type two or more characters quickly enough so that your computer recognizes the key sequence as part of a word.

By the way, this technique works with other scrolling lists, including windows on the desktop and Director's Help windows.

Director 6 has a few more ways to add cast members to the Cast window, including

✔ Painting a new cast member in Director 6 with the Paint window tools. You can find more about Paint window tools in Chapter 8.

✔ Entering text in the Text or Field window. Run, do not walk, to Chapter 9 for more info on Text and Field windows.

✔ Adding a behavior from the Behaviors Library Cast window to a sprite on the Stage. See Chapter 15 for all the dirt on behaviors.

✔ Creating a Lingo script. For more on Lingo scripting, jump to Chapter 14.

✔ Making a custom palette in the Color Palettes window. (See Chapter 11.)

Think of each cast member in the Cast window as a special collection of formatting decisions or "style sheets" that you can apply to any number of frames in your movie. For example, suppose you build a movie with an imported bitmap across several frames and then decide to change one of the colors of the Bitmap Cast Member from puce to aquamarine. Changing the color of the cast member after it's in Director's Paint window ripples through all instances of the Bitmap Cast Member in your movie. Pretty clever, huh?

Internal and external Cast windows

One of Director 6's most important features is support for multiple casts for your movies. You can work with two types of casts, internal and external casts. For Director old-timers, the closest Director came to an external cast was the one SHARED.DIR file allowed for each movie, where cast members and Lingo scripts could be shared among several Director movies.

Use internal and external casts to organize your cast members in some meaningful way (all Palette Cast Members in one cast, all Script Cast Members in another, for example) and reduce the number of cells needed in any one Cast window.

Internal casts

Director 6 starts you off with one internal cast that's saved within the movie itself. Each additional cast you create is added to the movie with advantages and disadvantages. The greatest advantage of internal casts is never needing to go searching for them; they're intrinsic to the file. You can also organize your cast members by using different internal casts; for example, you can put all Text Cast Members in a Text Cast Member internal cast, all Bitmap Cast Members in another Bitmap Cast Member internal cast, and so on. But you can't share internal cast members with other movies. Each new internal cast bloats the Director movie's size and may put performance at risk on slower machines.

External casts

External casts are saved external to any one Director movie and can be shared among movies common to a production. An external cast is not necessarily linked to the movie currently open in Director; you need to choose to link the external movie. Why would you want to do such a ridiculously civil thing?

A linked external cast opens automatically with its designated movie. Even if you move the cast file inadvertently, Director 6 prompts you to locate the cast on your hard drive. Sounds great, although the prompt could be very distracting during a presentation. Back on the plus side, Director updates linked casts whenever you choose Save from the File menu. You need to save unlinked casts individually.

Choose Modify⇨Movie⇨Casts to link or unlink selected casts from within the Movie Casts dialog box, as shown in Figure 5-2.

Figure 5-2:
The Movie Casts dialog box, where you can link an external cast to the current movie.

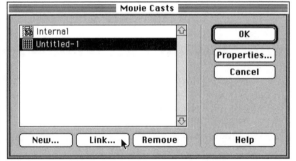

Linking your imported file

Choose File⇨Import to display the Import Files dialog box. Locate the Link to External file command in the Media pop-up menu at the bottom of the dialog box. (See Figure 5-3.)

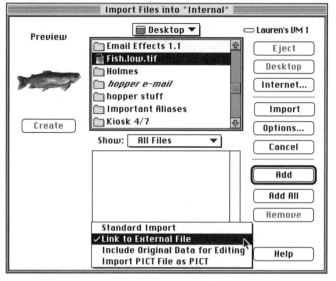

Figure 5-3:
Choose Link
to External
File from
the Media
pop-up list
to import a
linked cast
member
into
Director.

If you choose Standard Import instead, the imported file becomes part of your movie, increasing the movie's file size. Benefits? No need to keep track of the imported file; it's part of your movie. On the other hand — no, the other hand — choosing Link to External File gives you a bouquet of advantages, including the following:

✔ Creating a relationship with the imported file so that you can view the file without physically adding it to your movie, keeping the movie file size down.

✔ Automatically updating a linked file after you make changes to the file in its parent application. For example, if you import a Photoshop file to Director 6 as a linked file and then later open, modify, and save the file in Photoshop, Director automatically updates the linked cast member the next time you open the movie.

✔ Sharing an external, linked file among several movies without increasing the size of each movie.

✔ Launching the original application, referred to as the External Editor, from within Director 6 to edit the selected linked cast member. After setting up an application as an External Editor in the Editors dialog box, shown in Figure 5-4, you can simply double-click the linked cast member in the Cast window to launch the file's parent program. For inquiring minds, see "External Editor stuff," later in this chapter to see how to set up external editors.

After importing linked files, do a good job of tracking them. If a file's location changes after you import it as a linked cast member, the next time you open the movie, Director 6 asks where the heck the file is, spoiling your presentation with catcalls and boos from the disappointed and unruly audience.

The safest way to ensure that Director 6 never loses track of linked files is to create a project folder for each presentation and to keep all linked files and movies in that one folder. If you're working on a Mac and you must move a file out of the project folder, take advantage of System 7's Alias command. At the desktop, select the file, choose File➪Make Alias, and move the alias to a new location. You Windows 95 people can create a so-called shortcut to accomplish the same objective. Simply select the file from within Windows Explorer or the My Computer window and choose File➪Create Shortcut. Then drag the shortcut to the new location.

Whenever you import digital video like a QuickTime movie or AVI (Audio Video Interleave) movie, Director 6 automatically links it to the current movie.

Moving cast members around in the Cast window

You may want to move a cast member from one slot to another in the Cast window. Director 6 helps you out with special cursors to keep you on track and prevent you from making embarrassing mistakes that may turn you into a social misfit. Come along with me on a little tour of this fascinating experience of moving cast members:

1. **Choose Window➪Cast or press ⌘/Ctrl+3 to display the Cast window.**

2. **Move the mouse pointer over the cast member that you want to move.**

   Notice that the mouse pointer or cursor changes to the Hand cursor, illustrated in Figure 5-5.

Figure 5-5:
The mouse
pointer
changes to
the Hand
cursor
when
moved over
a cast
member.

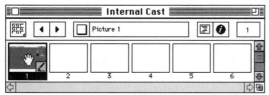

3. **At this point, press the mouse and begin dragging the cast member in the direction of an empty cell in the Cast window.**

   A couple of things happen at this point. The Hand cursor turns into the menacing Fist cursor, and the cast member follows the mouse in ghostly outline form, both visible in Figure 5-6.

Figure 5-6:
An outline
form
follows the
mouse
when
moving a
cast
member.

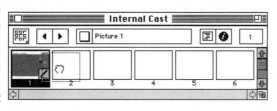

4. **When the cast member outline and Fist cursor loom over an empty cell in the Cast window, release the mouse button.**

   You moved your cast member from one cell to another.

When you drag a cast member from the Cast window and you try to release the mouse button at an inappropriate time, Director tattoos the Fist cursor with the international "no way" sign (you know, the circle with the slash through it).

Editing cast members 101

Considering how many types of graphics you can import, you may be wondering which cast members you can edit directly in Director. Here's the list; it's real long, so I hope you don't get eyestrain:

- ✔ Bitmaps

Bitmaps only need apply

Director's built-in editor, the Paint window, can handle only the file type called a bitmap, which comes from paint programs such as Macromedia xRes, bundled with the Director 6 Studio package (a demo version is included on this book's CD); Photoshop, or Corel PHOTO-PAINT. A bitmap is s just a collection of colored pixels that you can turn on and off or change color with the Paint window's various tools. For more on the Paint window, jump to Chapter 8.

Ah, you're wondering why QuickTime isn't in my nifty list. You've heard that QuickTime movies are nothing more than a collection of bitmapped images. Almost won the turkey but not close enough. QuickTime frames may start out as bitmaps, but after you incorporate them into a QuickTime movie, they transform into a special QuickTime format that Director's built-in Paint tools can't modify.

By the way, Director 6 includes PICTs in the Import dialog box, but, when you click Import, Director changes imported PICTs into bitmapped graphics that you can edit in the Paint window. For more on PICTs and bitmaps, see the sidebar "Of drawings, paintings, PICTs, and PICS" earlier in this chapter.

If you're determined to add a real PICT to your movie, you have two choices:

 ✔ Before importing the PICT, be sure to choose Link to External File from the Media pop-up menu at the bottom of the Import Files dialog box.

 ✔ With a PICT already in the Clipboard, click an empty cell in the Cast window and be sure to choose Edit➪Paste Special➪Paste as PICT. If you use the standard Paste command to copy a PICT from the Clipboard to the Cast window, you wind up with a bitmap (another way to add a bitmap to the Cast window but not necessarily what you may want to accomplish).

Either way, you wind up with a real PICT in your movie, but you can't edit the image in Director's Paint window. Unless. . . .

That's where the External Editor comes in — one of Director 6's nifty new features.

External Editor stuff

When you can't edit a linked cast member within Director 6 because the cast member is not a bitmapped graphic, or if you prefer to use another program to edit the linked cast member, set up an external editor. To create an external editor, follow these steps:

1. Choose File➪Preferences➪Editors.

You see a scrolling list in the Editors Preferences dialog box with a list of file types that Director supports in the first column.

2. **Select the type of file to edit in an external editor.**

3. **Click Edit.**

4. **Click Use External Editor.**

5. **Click Browse or Scan to locate and select the desired application on your hard drive.**

6. **Click OK through various dialog boxes to return to Director's Stage.**

Simple, isn't it? You could do this editing stuff in your sleep, right? Now, wake up.

Why would you want to import a real PICT into Director? Because you can enlarge or reduce PICTs more successfully than bitmapped graphics, and they print smoothly from most printers. Disadvantages? PICTs animate more slowly than bitmaps in Director, and you won't be able to apply Director's special ink effects to a PICT. For more info on ink effects, jump to Chapter 6.

Exploring the Cast Windows

If you walked through the steps in the previous sections and imported a cast member into the Cast window, are you happy now? Good, now that that's out of your system, you can go back to exploring the Cast window itself. Notice the custom features of the Cast window.

Custom features

At the top of the Cast window is a row of buttons and text areas. From left to right, they include

- ✔ **Choose Cast:** Press to choose a Cast window from the pop-up menu or to create a new Cast window.

- ✔ **Previous Cast Member:** Each click selects the previous cast member. When you get to the first cast member, the next click loops you back to the last cast member and away you go in reverse gear, again.

- ✔ **Next Cast Member:** Each click selects the following cast member. When you get to the last cast member, the next click loops you back to the first cast member, where you continue the forward cycle.

- ✔ **Drag Cast Member:** Press and drag to drag the currently selected cast member(s) to the Score window or on the Stage. You can also press the cast member thumbnail directly and drag it to the Score window or on the Stage.

The nice feature of the Drag Cast Member button is that you can place a selected cast member or group of selected cast members even if they are not currently visible in the Cast window. For example, say you have your Cast window set to show six thumbnails at a time; the Cast window currently displays cast members 1 to 6, but you've selected cast members 35 to 42 farther down in the unseen set of cells. Use the Drag Cast Member button to place the selection on the Stage or in the Score window.

✔ **Cast Member Name:** Displays the name of the currently selected cast member. An imported cast member adopts its original filename, but you can change its name in this field at any time.

✔ **Cast Member Script:** Takes you to the Script window for the currently selected cast member. In the Script window, you can play with Lingo, Director's easy-to-use, built-in language. Every cast member can have a script associated with it. For more info on Lingo and scriptwriting, see Chapter 14.

✔ **Cast Member Properties:** Takes you to the Cast Member Properties window for the currently selected cast member, where you can change the name, palette, and purge priority of the cast member. For more info on palettes, see Chapter 11. For more info on purge priorities, see Chapter 9.

✔ **Cast Member Number:** Displays the selected cast member's cell number. As you import and create cast members, Director 6 places them sequentially in the Cast window, but you can always drag one or more cast members to other locations in the Cast window.

Cast Member Properties button

You can call up the Cast Member Properties window a number of ways — so many choices, so little time:

✔ Click the Cast Member Properties button in the Cast window.

✔ Choose Modify⇨Cast Member⇨Properties.

✔ Press ⌘/Ctrl+I.

✔ Super secret way: After signing 15 copies of the enclosed nondisclosure form, feel free to read the sidebar, "Super secret menu."

Super secret menu

One of Director 6's great features is its hidden context-sensitive menus, which work on most of Director's windows. For example, to view hidden menus in the Cast window, you Mac types press the Control key. PC types, use the right mouse button instead. Everybody, press the mouse on one of the cells of the Cast window. If the cell contains a cast member, the secret menu contains a mix of menu commands from the Edit, Modify, and other menus in Director's menu bar. Even a blank cell gives you Paste Text, Import, and Cast Properties commands.

Because the Cast Member Properties button is so essential, the following steps show you how to take advantage of its options:

1. **Make sure that a Bitmap Cast Member is selected in the Cast window.**

2. **Click the Bitmap Cast Member Properties button.**

   Director takes you to the Bitmap Cast Member Properties dialog box, similar to Figure 5-7.

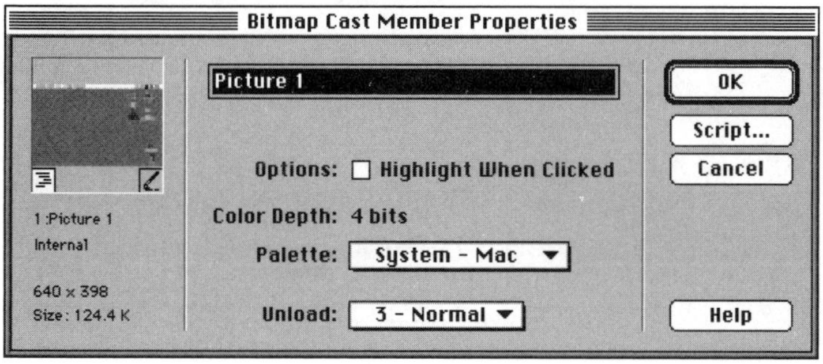

Figure 5-7:
A Bitmap Cast Member Properties dialog box bursting with information and options.

Bitmap Cast Member Properties
Picture 1 — OK
Script...
Options: ☐ Highlight When Clicked — Cancel
1 :Picture 1 / Internal — Color Depth: 4 bits
Palette: System - Mac ▼
640 x 398 / Size : 124.4 K — Unload: 3 - Normal ▼ — Help

In the left panel of the dialog box is a thumbnail preview of the cast member. Underneath the preview is the Cast Member Number, the current Name, whether the cast member is an internal or external cast member, its dimensions, and its size.

In the center panel is the Name field. Notice that Director has even highlighted the name for you so that you can change it on a whim — such decadence. If you check the Highlight When Clicked check box, Director highlights the cast member like a button when you add a script or behavior to the cast member and press the cast member during playback; add a behavior to the cast member and you have a fully functioning button. You can get up to speed with behaviors by jumping to Chapter 15.

Below the Options check box, the color depth is displayed. Next, the Palette pop-up menu allows you to change the set of colors for the Bitmap Cast Member. Underneath is the Unload pop-up menu, which you can use to alter how Director manages computer memory. In the right panel are OK, Script, Cancel, and Help buttons.

3. If you're so inclined, type a new name for your cast member.

The text that Director preselected for you is replaced with the name you enter.

When you name a cast member, be sure to enter a meaningful title. Naming a cast member "#1," for example, isn't going to be very significant to you a week or month later. Or to a colleague today.

4. Press the Palette pop-up menu to view a list of Director's built-in palettes and custom-made palettes.

A list of Director's built-in palettes and custom-made palettes appears, as shown in Figure 5-8.

Figure 5-8:
A sparkling array of colors is available in the Palette pop-up menu.

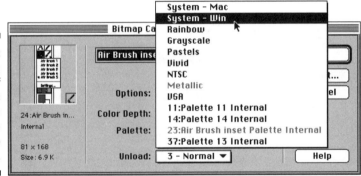

5. Select the desired palette from the Palette pop-up menu.

When you select a new palette, be prepared for a potentially startling color shift on your screen. As soon as you switch palettes, colors on-screen are *remapped* to the new set of colors. For example, if you switch from the regular Mac System palette or the Windows palette to the NTSC palette, you see a big difference in colors. For a full description of palettes included with Director 6, including the NTSC palette, check out Chapter 11.

6. Press the Unload pop-up menu.

This pop-up menu allows you to modify the way Director purges RAM (Random Access Memory).

Did someone say something about purge? I know, this command's a little scary. You've heard of purges in other parts of the world. That's bad enough, but tell me it's not happening in the good old U.S. of A.

Wait, this is a different kind of purge.

Purging in Director 6 is a way of managing memory. When memory runs low, Director starts trashing or purging stuff from memory, including cast members. The Unload pop-up menu lets you decide what gets tossed and when by selecting a cast member from the Cast window, opening the Cast Member Properties box, and setting a purge priority based on the following criteria:

✓ **Priority 0:** Gives a very important cast member that is going to be used frequently in the movie Priority 0, meaning, "Never purge Mr. Big Shot from memory. Too important."

✓ **Priority 1:** A little lower on the totem pole than Priority 0; giving a cast member Priority 1 means, "Save this puppy for last."

✓ **Priority 2:** The normal setting, meaning, "Expendable but nice to hang around with. Keep it if you can."

✓ **Priority 3:** The lowest priority; mow 'em down along with gaffers, technicians, accountants, and assistant directors.

Director's hard cell

The Cast window is mainly a set of 32,000 rectangular cells. If you have a screen large enough to display them all, congratulations. (By the way, I know where you can get a great deal on industrial-size sun blocker; give me a call.)

Each occupied cell in the Cast window represents one cast member with a thumbnail preview and gives you the following information:

✓ The type of cast member

✓ The position of the cell in the window by number

✓ An optional name for the cell

You can learn a lot about a cast member by noting its thumbnail's so-called Media Type icon, listed directly ahead in Table 5-1, that signals the type of file the cast member is derived from.

Table 5-1	**Media Type Icons**
Icon	*What It Represents*
	Bitmap. A painting, may have been imported from a PICT, PICS, MacPaint, Scrapbook file, ClarisDraw file, CorelDRAW file, or bmp file or created in Director 6 with Paint window tools. May be edited in Director's Paint window.
	Button. Created with one of three Button tools in the Tools window.
	Digital Video. Typically an imported QuickTime mooV or AVI movie; plays in its own Digital Video window on the Stage. Digital Video Cast Members are always linked to the original external files on disk.
	Field. Text-based cast member created with the Field tool in the Tool window or by choosing Insert⇨Control⇨Field. Can be set as editable text during playback, but fields in motion tend to slow down animation sequences.
	Film Loop. A sequence of Director frames organized into a single cast member in the Cast window. An imported, unlinked Director movie becomes a film loop, too; each of its cast members is added to the current movie's internal cast. Film loops are often used for animations that, well, loop — for example, a bird with constantly flapping wings.
	Linked Movie. A Director movie that has been imported as a linked cast member. The linked movie's cast members are not added to the internal cast.
	Linked PICT. A PICT imported with the As PICT and Linked check boxes selected in the Import Files dialog box.
	Linked Sound. Imported sound file with the Linked check box selected in the Import Files dialog box.
	Palette. A collection of colors imported with an external graphic file or chosen from the Color Palettes window. Director 6 comes with a set of palettes, but you can also create your own custom palette in the Color Palettes window.
	PICT. A PICT imported with the As PICT check box selected in the Import Files dialog box. You can also copy a PICT to the Cast window from the Clipboard by choosing Edit⇨Paste Special⇨As PICT.
	Script. Each Lingo script you write in the Script window becomes a Script Cast Member in the Cast window or may be added when you import a linked Director movie.

Icon	What It Represents
⊞	Shape. A shape created with one of the Shape tools in the Tools window; similar to object-oriented drawings created with programs like ClarisDraw and CorelDRAW. Shapes use less memory than bitmaps but animate more slowly on the Stage and aren't recommended for movies running on slower computers.
🔊	Sound. An imported sound file from among many file types including snd resources, Windows WAV sound files, and Macintosh AIFF (Audio Interchange File Format) sound files. AIFF sounds may be linked to the original file on disk. An AIFF sound also plays from disk, reducing the load on memory, and can be used for both Mac and Windows Director movies. For more on sounds, see Chapter 16.
Ⓐ	Text. A Text Cast Member created when you enter text in the Text window. Director 6 includes expanded text support for Text Cast Members, including tabs, indents, paragraph formatting, and anti-aliasing. However, Text Cast Members are not editable on playback.
◧	Transition. Each transition effect you select in the Score becomes a cast member. For more on transitions, see Chapter 6.
☐	Xtra. An Xtra Cast Member indicates a special transition, effect, or other feature added to the movie by way of an Xtra, Macromedia's name for its plug-in like additions to Director's feature set.

In addition, a cast member containing a script may display a special Cast Member Script icon in the lower-left corner of its thumbnail. To turn on this feature, choose File⇨Preferences⇨Cast. In the Cast Preferences dialog box, highlight the Show Cast Member Script Icons check box and click OK.

Selecting multiple cast members

Director's a little strange when it comes to making multiple selections in the Cast window. Shift+selecting works for most applications but not for Director. No, that's not good enough for Mr. Fancy Pants Director. When you need a noncontiguous selection of cells, ⌘/Ctrl+click the desired cells, which is useful for selecting cast members throughout the Cast window to drag to the Stage or to change their palettes. However, to make a contiguous selection of cells in the Cast window, that is, without jumps, stay with the old Shift+click trick. Click the first cell to highlight it. Move to the last cell to be included in the selection and Shift+click the last cell. You wind up with a contiguous range of selected cells.

Chapter 6

As Time Goes By: Opening Director's Score Window

• •

In This Chapter

▶ Exploring the Score window

▶ Using icons in the Score window

▶ Adding cast members to the Score window

▶ Finding the hidden cells

▶ Coloring in the Score window — stay inside the lines!

▶ Manipulating cells

▶ Manipulating sprites

• •

*F*rom its start as VideoWorks in 1985, Director was designed to handle information that changes over time, information that cries out for a Score-type window. You design your Director movie in the Score window, deciding which cast members appear and vanish on the Stage at your every whim (with client approval, of course). Of all Director's windows, the Score window allows you to play director to the hilt.

The Score Window: And You Thought NeuroLinguistics 101 Was Complicated

Choosing Score from the Window menu calls up the Score window. I've got to admit, the Score's a mighty intimidating window. Everything has its place for a purpose, though, and soon you can read the Score window like the back of your hand. You can read the back of your hand, can't you? That's a must quality for multimedia types. Good.

Miss your old Score window?

If you're familiar with Director 5, you may notice that the Score window has been given a facelift, tummy tuck, manicure, and pedicure (with a perm thrown in for good measure) for Director 6. If this seems too much for a longtime Director 5 user to face, take heart. Macromedia graciously includes an option to make Director 6's Score look more like the old version while you wean yourself away from Director 5. Choose File➪Preferences➪Score and then select Director 5 Style Score Display to make the Score's interface look more like Director 5's cozy, comfortable, old Score.

The Score window is where you really create your movie. In our culture, lots of stuff moves from left to right: type, days in the calendar, pages of a book, even images. Ever notice how figures in a film moving left to right seem effortless? Film the same scene moving right to left, and it's uphill all the way. Add a little dramatic music, some popcorn, and you've got great dramatic footage. So think of the Score as a graph of time moving left to right in your animation — earlier stuff to the left, later stuff to the right.

That's MISTER cell to you, Bud

The small, white rectangles in the Score window are called cells. These cells are better delineated in Director 6 than in previous versions. Cells hold sprites that come from the Cast window and serve as building blocks for the visual timeline that you develop in the Score window. You can change the view of these cells in the Score window. For example, if motion info is most important to you at a particular time in your movie's development, you can switch to Motion view from the Display pop-up menu.

To move one frame to the right in the Score window, press ⌘/Ctrl+Option/Alt+→. Alternatively, just press 3 on the numeric keypad. To move left one frame, press ⌘/Ctrl+Option/Alt+← or press 1 on the keypad.

Sprite toolbar

I guess you noticed plenty of new icon thingies to explain. The top row is called the sprite toolbar, which you can show or hide (to buy some extra real estate) by choosing View➪Sprite Toolbar. Start from the top left of the Score window, shown in Figure 6-1, and note the following:

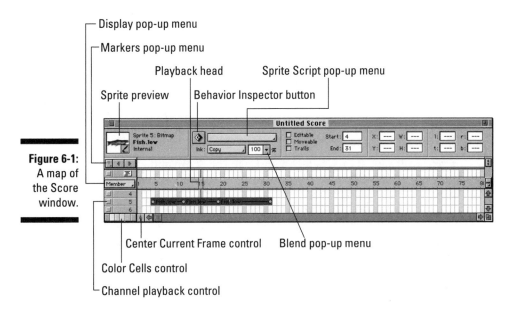

Display pop-up menu

Markers pop-up menu

Playback head   Sprite Script pop-up menu

Sprite preview   Behavior Inspector button

Figure 6-1:
A map of
the Score
window.

Center Current Frame control   Blend pop-up menu

Color Cells control

Channel playback control

✔ **Sprite Preview:** A small preview area for the currently selected sprite in the Score window. A thumbnail appears for a bitmap sprite. Director displays the sprite's distinctive icon in the lower-right corner of the preview area. If the sprite is a script, the Cast Member Number and external or internal label appears. Double-clicking the preview area takes you to the Paint or Script window for the sprite, where you can make modifications. To the right of the preview is the sprite's channel number, the type of sprite, its Cast Member Number, and which cast it comes from.

✔ **Behavior Inspector button:** Displays the Behavior Inspector listing any behaviors added to the currently highlighted sprite. (See Chapter 15 for more about Behaviors.)

✔ **Sprite Script pop-up menu:** A long, white, shadowed box (usually indicates a pop-up menu) that displays any scripts the currently selected sprite contains. You can also clear a script or start a new script with the Clear Script and New Script commands at the bottom of the pop-up menu.

✔ **Ink pop-up menu:** Under the Sprite Script pop-up menu is the Ink pop-up menu listing an impressive set of ink effects worthy of George Lucas. The idea is to select one or more bitmap sprites and apply an ink effect to them with impressive results, while keeping the following caveat in mind: Ink effects can seriously degrade the performance of your movie, especially on a low-powered computer.

✔ **Blend pop-up menu:** To the right of the Ink pop-up menu; displays percentages of blend effect for a sprite set to Blend ink in the Ink pop-up list.

✔ **Editable check box:** For Field Cast Members only; select a field sprite in the Score and check this box to allow users to type in a field during playback.

✔ **Moveable check box:** Select a sprite in the Score and check this box to allow users to drag the sprite on the Stage during playback.

✔ **Trails check box:** Select a sprite in the Score and check this box to create the effect of using the sprite's shape as a paint brush that leaves a "trail" of itself behind when it moves during playback. Take a gander at the sidebar, "Use Trails for easy and unusual special effects," later in this chapter for more on trails.

✔ **Start Frame entry box:** Displays the number of the selected sprite's first frame in the Score. You can also change the value by typing in a new number and pressing Return.

✔ **End Frame entry box:** Displays the number of the selected sprite's last frame in the Score. You can also change the value by typing in a new number and pressing Return.

✔ **Registration Point Horizontal entry box:** Displays the X coordinate value of the selected sprite's registration point in pixels. By default, the point is at the center of the sprite, but you can change the value by typing in a new number and pressing Return. You can also change the value in the Paint window by clicking the Registration Point tool in a different point horizontally.

✔ **Registration Point Vertical entry box:** Displays the Y coordinate value of the selected sprite's registration point in pixels. By default, the point is at the center of the sprite, but you can change the value by typing in a new number and pressing Return. You can also change the value in the Paint window by clicking the Registration Point tool in a different point vertically.

✔ **Width entry box:** Displays the current width in pixels of the selected sprite, but you can change the value by typing in a new number and pressing Return.

✔ **Height entry box:** Displays the current height in pixels of the selected sprite, but you can change the value by typing in a new number and pressing Return.

✔ **Left, Right, Top, Bottom entry box:** Displays the current values for the selected sprite. You can change the values by typing in a new number and pressing Return.

These values are mirrored in a new inspector palette for Director 6, the Sprite Inspector, discussed in Chapter 4.

Enhanced controls

On the right side of the Score window, above a standard vertical scroll bar, are two additional, enhanced controls.

- **Hide/Show Effects Channels button:** Shows or hides the effects channels above sprite Channels 1 to 120, including the Tempo, Palette, Transition, and two Sound channels. The Script channel above Channel 1, however, remains visible.

- **Zoom pop-up menu:** New for Director 6, Zoom provides a number of ways to customize the width of Score window cells, including Narrower and Wider menu commands and percentages from 12 to 600 percent.

  Although narrow cells show more of the Score, text that appears in Director 6's new sprite bars also becomes condensed and difficult to read.

Under the sprite preview in the upper-left corner of the Score is yet another set of controls. They include:

- **Markers pop-up menu:** Displays the list of markers that you create when developing a Director movie to aid in navigating from one section to the next. You can find out how markers work in Chapter 13.

- **Previous and Next Marker controls:** Moves the playback head to the respective marker in the Score.

- **Display pop-up menu:** Use to customize the view in the Score window, similar to changing the view of a window at the desktop with the View menu. For example, when you choose Extended from the pop-up menu, you get larger cells with additional information. You can even customize what info appears in Extended view by choosing File➪Preferences➪ Score and clicking the items you want to include in Extended view.

  In Figure 6-2, for example, the first line of the Extended view displays the cast member's name, FLOUNDER.BMP. Underneath, all behaviors associated with the sprite are listed. Next, Director displays the Ink type currently chosen for the bitmap. In the Location line, the X and Y coordinates are listed. The Motion line indicates the change of location from the previous keyframe. This information is repeated for each additional keyframe in the sprite's sprite bar.

- **Channel Playback control:** On the left of each of the Score's 120 channels and each of the Effects channels, click to alternately turn on or off a specific channel.

- **Color Cells control:** At the bottom of the Score window; color-codes one or more selected cells. You can use this feature to flag a special range of cells for development or simply to help organize the Score.

- **Center Current Frame control:** Click to display the current frame in the center of the Score window.

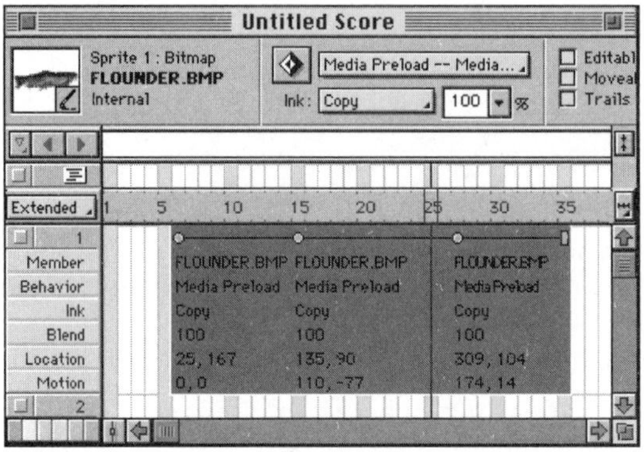

Figure 6-2:
Score
window
cells in
Extended
views.

Channel numbers and frames

A row of cells in the Score constitutes a channel. Director 6 provides you with 120 channels to play with while developing your movie. Think of channels as plastic overlays used in traditional animation. Going along with this analogy, Channel 1 is similar to static background art, such as the canyon where Wile E. Coyote chases Road Runner; Channel 2 is the second rearmost acetate layer with Road Runner running away from you toward the background; Channel 3 is the next layer with Wile E. Coyote tearing after Road Runner; Channel 4 is a great yellow cloud of dust that Road Runner and Wile E. Coyote kick up as they race down the canyon. And look, you still have 116 channels left to play with.

A column of cells represents one frame of your movie. Whatever occurs in that one frame is recorded in one or more of the 120 channels available in each frame. Basically, you have an undetermined number of frames for your movie limited only by your hard drive storage and installed memory.

Use Trails for easy and unusual special effects

Okay, you Roy Rogers fans, happy *Trails* is a special effect you can apply to a selected sprite in the Score so it leaves a copy of itself wherever it moves on the Stage. Basically, the sprite becomes a brush that paints its own image along its path of movement to build unusual shapes and patterns on the Stage. In addition, when you turn off Trails in a subsequent frame, the same sprite begins to erase its own trail wherever it passes over the trail on the Stage.

You nostalgia buffs can build your own psychedelic "flower power" happenings on Director's Stage. (Don't forget beads, flowers in hair, and tie-dyed bell bottoms.)

One of the new Director 6 Score window features are data tips that appear in channels as you move the mouse. Data tips work like the tooltips feature that displays little yellow labels next to key interface items, such as buttons and pop-up menus, except that data tips display info about sprites in the Score. To turn off data tips, choose File⇨Preferences⇨Score and uncheck Show Data Tips in the Options panel of the Score Window Preferences dialog box.

The playback head

To the right of the Display pop-up menu is the channel where Director displays frame numbers in five frame increments. The Score's playback head rides horizontally in this channel and indicates the current frame. Normally, the playback head moves from left to right in this channel during movie playback. During development, you can drag the playback head left or right like the fast shuttle control on your VCR remote. A nice improvement over previous versions of Director, a thin vertical line follows the playback head's location from the Tempo channel to the bottom of the Score window.

If you're familiar with Director 5, you may notice the playback head in Director 6 looks different. Whereas Director 5's playback head was a black rectangle that rode above frame numbers in its own channel, the new playback head looks transparent — like a lucite tab — moving within the row of frame numbers.

Hidden, top-secret channels

Pith helmets on now, everyone. Above the row of frame numbers in the Score window is the Script channel. You can display an additional set of special channels, shown in Figure 6-3, by clicking the Hide/Show Effects Channels control described earlier in this chapter in "Enhanced controls".

Figure 6-3:
Hidden
channels in
the Score
window.

Table 6-1 reviews the special score channels, one by one.

Table 6-1		Special Score Channels
Icon	*Channel*	*Description*
⊕	Tempo	Sets the pace and adds limited interactivity to your movie from the selected frame.
⊞	Palette	Changes the set of colors used in your movie starting from the selected frame.
▶◀	Transition	Sets dissolves, wipes, and other transition effects; by the way, the transition actually begins on the previous frame. By gosh, you can peruse more about transitions in "Transitions, transitions! (To the tune from *Fiddler on the Roof*)" later in this chapter.
◀1	Sound Channel 1	Plays imported sounds including SoundEdit, AIFF, AIFC files, WAV files, and SND resources.
◀2	Sound Channel 2	Plays left and right stereo sound from stereo-capable Macs (Quadra and Power Mac AV models) and PCs with stereo-capable sound cards by adding sound to Sound Channels 1 and 2.
▤	Script	Double-click a frame in this channel to add Lingo commands that Director normally executes when the playback head leaves the frame.

A SoundEdit sound file is the proprietary file type for Macromedia's SoundEdit 16 2.0, a Macintosh application for editing sampled sounds that comes bundled with the Director 6 Studio package. An AIFF (Audio Interchange File Format) file is a cross-platform capable sound file type that has been promoted as an industry standard. AIFC files are similar to AIFF files but compressed. And SND files are bits of code that become part of the movie file itself when imported into a Macintosh Director movie. WAV files are a common PC sound file type.

If you intend to import and play back sound from both Sound channels, make sure that you Mac types have Sound Manager 3.0 or later installed in your System folder or that your PC sound card supports stereo sound and that you have the latest sound driver installed; update drivers with Windows 95's Drivers control panel.

Getting into the habit of entering a Tempo setting in the first frame of the Tempo channel for each movie is not a bad idea. Otherwise, Director plays your movie at 15 fps (frames per second), the default tempo setting that may not necessarily match your needs. Oh, and be sure to floss after each and every meal.

Transitions, transitions! (To the tune from Fiddler on the Roof)

Director's transitions are a set of special effects that occur when the play-back head moves from one frame to the next. Built-in transitions help you quickly build professional-looking multimedia. You can heighten the drama of a bullet chart by setting a new line of text to dissolve into place on the Stage. Or you can create quick animation effects by wiping from one frame to another. You can use this trick to create an animation sequence with only two sprites and one wipe transition.

Imagine a sprite in Frame 1 that looks like a deck of cards neatly squared on the table. The second sprite in Frame 2 depicts the deck fanned out across the Stage. You double-click Frame 2 in the Transition channel and choose Wipe Right from the pop-up menu of transitions. When you rewind your movie in the Control Panel window and click the Play button, the Wipe transition creates a slick illusion that the deck of cards has magically fanned itself.

In case you didn't notice, the Transition pop-up menu gives you over 50 transitions to choose from. In other words, if you think I'm going to cover each one of them in this book, I've got a great piece of property I'd love to show you in a quaint little village called Chernobyl. Anyway, after you choose a transition, Director allows you to modify most of the transitions with one or more of the following options:

- ✔ **Duration:** Available for most transitions; you can set a duration in 500th of a second units.

- ✔ **Smoothness:** Affects the number of pixels that change in the image from one unit of time to the next. Generally, the lower the smoothness setting, the coarser the effect of the transition.

- ✔ **Stage Area/Changing Area:** With some transitions, you can apply the effect only to the part of the Stage that changes. For example, choosing Changing Area displays a new sprite dissolving into view on the Stage, but the background doesn't show any transition effect.

Never set a transition in the first frame of a movie. Transitions are designed to start on the previous frame. When you set a transition in the first frame, no previous frame exists to begin the transition.

Adding a Cast Member to the Score

Have you noticed one thing the Score shares with other windows? Aside from the gizmos, numbers, and icon thingies, the Score's pretty bare when you first open it. You see, the folks at Macromedia made a deal with you when you bought Director. Macromedia makes the software; you make the movie. You're responsible for putting content into the Score, which is pretty frightening considering those old SAT scores. But you've come a long way, and something that may brighten up that old Score window, aside from a couple of throw rugs and a little paint, is to add a cast member. Build your movie by adding cast members from the Cast window to the Score like so:

1. **Open the Stage window by choosing Window⇨Stage or by pressing ⌘/Ctrl+4.**

2. **Open the Cast window by choosing Window⇨Cast or by pressing ⌘/Ctrl+3.**

3. **Press the mouse over the cast member of choice in the Cast window.**

   Notice that when you first move the mouse pointer over the cast member, the mouse pointer transforms from a drab, ordinary arrow into the Hand cursor, as shown in the margin. When you press the mouse button down, it changes into the infamous and diabolical Fist cursor, as shown in the margin.

4. **Keep the mouse button held down and begin dragging the mouse pointer toward the Score window.**

   Notice the "ghost icon" of the chosen cast member following the Fist cursor. As you drag over areas where you shouldn't release the mouse, the cursor changes into the Fist cursor with the international "No-No" symbol inside, as shown in the margin. Kind of like Robert Mitchum with Love and Hate tattooed on his knuckles in that old black-and-white movie. Now that's macho.

5. **With the mouse button still pressed, drag the cast member over the Score window.**

   The cursor changes to the pointer and a bold outline of what Macromedia calls the *sprite bar* becomes visible. The playback head follows the first frame of the sprite bar as you move left or right. I capture all this fascinating action in Figure 6-4.

6. **Release the mouse button to place the sprite at the desired location in the Score.**

Now a number of events take place at the same time. See if you catch them all; no fair peeking at Figure 6-5, which reflects most of these changes:

✔ Your pants fall down. If not, the program's defective; return it immediately and demand a fresh copy. Pull your pants up first.

✔ Your cast member instantaneously appears, centered on the Stage.

✔ A small preview of your cast member appears in the upper-left corner of the Score window.

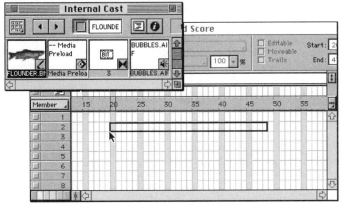

Figure 6-4:
The playback head in the Score window.

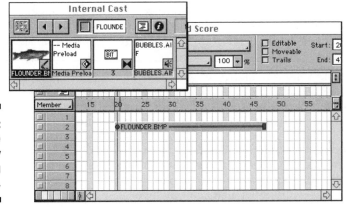

Figure 6-5:
The Score window after adding a sprite.

Take my advice and tattoo the following on your forehead. Call the contents of the Cast window *cast members*. After you drag a cast member into the Score window, refer to the cast member in the Score as a *sprite*. Hey, I didn't make this up; blame Macromedia. It's the honest truth, I swear. So a bitmap in the Cast window is a cast member. The same bitmap in the Score is a sprite. Good. Cut. Print.

All This Ink and Not a Drop on Me — Oops

I know, I whizzed by that Ink pop-up menu pretty quickly in the "Sprite toolbar" section earlier in this chapter. Now you can relax, get a cup of coffee, loosen your belt, take off your shoes — wait, better put your shoes back on — and investigate the mysterious world of ink effects in Director.

The most useful and frequently used inks in the Ink pop-up menu include

- **Copy:** The out-of-box or default ink for sprites; it uses the least amount of memory and is the fastest running ink of all. On the Stage, the sprite is contained in a rectangular *bounding box* that reflects the sprite's maximum width and height. The bounding box is filled with opaque pixels that obscure the background. The default color of the pixels is white. You can change the color by selecting the sprite, choosing Window⇨Tool palette, and changing the background color.

- **Matte:** Makes pixels surrounding a sprite in its bounding box (the imaginary frame defining the width and height of the sprite) transparent so that the sprite displays a cut-out effect against the background.

- **Bkgnd Transparent:** Similar to Matte but turns all background-colored pixels surrounding and within the sprite transparent, allowing you to achieve the infamous "donut" effect. You can use Bkgnd Transparent to make a sprite, such as a large *A,* dance around the Stage. The so-called counter in the center of the *A* appears transparent, allowing sprites and the background to show through. Why the *A* is dancing around is between you and your conscience.

- **Mask:** Similar to Matte but goes a step further. When set up correctly, Mask allows selective background-colored areas in a complex sprite image to remain opaque yet still deliver the "donut" effect. For intimate details on the mask-making process, turn to Chapter 8.

Other inks allow you to create some very unusual effects, especially when two or more sprites overlap, but beware. These inks can tax your computer's hertzpower to the limit and force your movie to its knees (not a pretty sight). Additional ink effects include

- **Transparent:** Intended mainly for black-and-white screens; makes any background-colored pixels in the selected sprite transparent.

- **Reverse:** Intended mainly for black-and-white screens; black or foreground-colored pixels in a selected sprite become white, and white or background-colored pixels become transparent, revealing the background. With color monitors, color-on-color effects are hard to predict, so save time for plenty of experimentation and breaking of fine china against the wall in fits of aesthetic frustration.

- **Ghost:** Intended mainly for black-and-white screens; black pixels in the selected sprite turn pixels of underlying sprites white and transparent.

- **Not Copy, Not Transparent, Not Reverse, Not Ghost:** Not as in "The check is in the mail . . . NOT," first reverses pixels of the selected sprite and then adds the corresponding ink effect to them.

Technical drivel about color values

To really understand how ink effects do their magic, you need to understand how a color image appears on your screen. Each pixel you see on your screen is the result of red, green, and blue light mixing together, which is why monitors are often referred to as RGB displays (or as #@%%^&*!! displays when they're not working).

By the way, these red, green, and blue lights come from three tiny electronic "guns" inside your monitor, one for each color, pointed at the phosphorescent surface of your screen. Your color TV at home works basically the same way.

Each color has its own recipe of red, green, and blue light. Where you see a black pixel, no red, green, or blue beams of light strike that particular area of the monitor. So another way of saying black is: Red = 0 (for 0 percent), Green = 0, and Blue = 0. Where you see a white pixel, maximum (or 100 percent) red, green, and blue light meet and mix at that precise point on your screen. You can designate white as Red = 100, Green = 100, and Blue = 100.

When you mix light together instead of crayons, red and green equal yellow — believe it or not. Here's a simple test to prove I'm right. Rent three standard klieg lights and three filters — red, green, and blue — each about two yards wide. Overlap their mega-volt beacons on the wall of any nearby skyscraper and what do you get in the center? That's right, pure white light. Now turn off the blue klieg light (watch your fingers, those klieg lights get hot). Voilà, a beautiful, diaphanous yellow. And it only cost you a few thousand dollars in equipment and hauling to demonstrate the additive approach to mixing color. Don't worry, it's probably tax-deductible.

So with so-called additive color, you can designate any color with a set of red, green, and blue values. When you select a sprite from the Score and apply the Add ink effect, Director adds the red, green, and blue values of each pixel in the selected sprite to the red, green, and blue values of each underlying pixel. Remember, these values are percentages of color, so you may see a case where adding values gives you a sum over 100 percent. When this situation occurs with the Add ink effect, Director makes the excess percentage the new value. On the other hand, when you choose Add Pin, you tell Director to ignore color values over 100 percent, resulting in a number of new colors with 100 percent red, green, and/or blue.

- ✔ **Blend:** Averages the selected sprite's color with the color of underlying sprites, creating a transparency effect.

- ✔ **Darkest:** Compares pixels of the selected sprite to the current foreground color, and colors only pixels in the selected sprite that are darker than the foreground color.

- ✔ **Lightest:** Compares pixels of the selected sprite to the current foreground color, and colors only pixels in the selected sprite that are lighter than the foreground color.

- **Add:** Adds the color values of each pixel in the selected sprite to the color values of each underlying pixel. The Add ink effect looks like a blend at first glance but doesn't hold true on close inspection. Also, as its name implies, Add often makes a new, lighter color after the addition, but not necessarily. Some color combinations in Add loop past the highest color value in a palette, white, to the lowest color value, black, or to a subsequent color in the palette, resulting in surprising color changes. Check out the sidebar, "The wild, wacky world of foreground color, background color, and pattern," coming soon to your neighborhood, about colors and their associated values to see how all this works, as if anyone cares.

- **Add Pin:** Similar to Add, but doesn't allow the final color to loop past the highest color value. The result is that many color additions with Add Pin wind up white, the highest color value that a pixel can register.

- **Subtract:** Subtracts the color values of each pixel in the selected sprite from the color values of each underlying pixel, resulting in a new color. If the result is a negative value, the color restarts from black to subsequent colors in the palette.

- **Subtract Pin:** Similar to Subtract, but doesn't allow a color value to loop back and continue up the scale of color values. Applying Subtract Pin to a sprite often results in many black pixels, the lowest color values that a pixel can register.

The wild, wacky world of foreground color, background color, and pattern

When you explore ink effects, you need to keep in mind that Director always recognizes a set of three related settings: current foreground color, current background color, and current pattern. Because inks make use of these two colors and the current pattern in creating their effects, being aware of these conditions can help you anticipate an effect. Even if you're running a black-and-white monitor, you have a current foreground color, black, and a current background color, white. Running color, you can switch from black to a color chip with the foreground color selector and switch from white to another color — including black — from the background color selector in the Paint or Tools window.

When you paint with solid black paint, the current pattern is simply solid black. If you're considering a waffle pattern in the Pattern pop-up menu, the pattern itself is black, its negative space white. Running in color mode, the current foreground color replaces black and the current background color replaces white.

Up Close and Personal with the Score Window Preferences Dialog Box

Chances are, you guessed that the Score Window Preferences dialog box, majestically photographed in Figure 6-6, is related to what goes on in the Score window. Glad to see that you're not asleep out there in ReaderLand. Why don't you see what's inside? Options for customizing what you see in the Score include

Figure 6-6:
The Score
Window
Preferences
dialog box,
where you
can set
many
options.

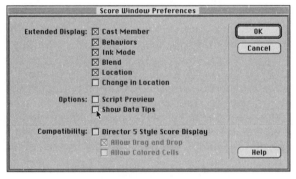

✔ **Extended Display:** Makes Score window cells larger to display information you select from check boxes including Cast Member (name and number), Behaviors, Ink Mode, Blend (percentage of transparency with Blend ink), Location (the sprite's centerpoint relative to the upper-left corner of the Stage), and Change in Location.

✔ **Options:** Offers two selections, Script Preview, which displays the first few lines of a script under the sprite toolbar; and Show Data Tips, which displays the Cast Member Name if available and Cast Member Number when the mouse is positioned over a sprite.

✔ **Compatibility:** Offers one major option, displaying the Score with an interface similar to Director 5. Also includes a subset of options including Allow Drag and Drop, to drag a selection in the Score from one location to another, and Allow Colored Cells, to color-code selected cells by clicking a color in the Allow Colored Cells control at the bottom-left of the Score.

Using Space to Time

One of the monster challenges you face when you use Director is to get cast members from the Cast window to the Score. Space to Time under the Score menu is the instant coffee of Director commands. This command allows you to select a number of cast members from the Cast window and instantly place them as sprites in consecutive frames of the Score. When you choose this command from the Modify menu, the Space to Time dialog box appears. In the Space to Time dialog box, you can set the number of frames separating each sprite as it becomes part of the Score. The default value is 1, but you can enter whatever value you please. The reason you may want to add additional frames between sprites is to take the process one step further and smooth the animation by allowing Director to create the intermediate frames, a technique called tweening. You can read all about tweening in Chapter 20.

Sometimes you want to visually check how a set of selected cast members relate to each other by dragging them on the Stage as sprites. What happens when you drag cast members on the Stage? Excellent; have a lump of sugar. Director places them in separate channels under the same frame in the Score. After you check each sprite's position and possibly modify the location of some of the sprites, you can select the sprites from the Score by dragging out a selection marquee or by pressing Shift and clicking the sprites; then choose Space to Time from the Score menu to rearrange the sprites' cells from consecutive channels in the same frame to consecutive frames. This action places the sprites in the Space-Time Continuum that Einstein proposed, and the end of the world occurs in a blinding flash of searing heat. Or maybe it just places the sprites in adjacent frames of your movie. Are you brave enough to take the chance?

Sprite Makeover

Sprites, those images that you place on the Stage and coax into leaping through rings of fire (and other daring feats), refer to cast members in the Score the same way an exit sign refers to a special doorway. If I were talking about Director 5, I could condense all you'd need to know about sprites in the previous, brilliantly terse sentence. With Director 6's entrée, I need Chapter 4 and this chapter to cover new and important info about sprites. The most dramatic differences in Director 6 relate to how sprites are displayed and new ways of working with special animation frames called keyframes.

Sprites as objects in the Score window

Ironically, now that the powers that be at Macromedia have made sprites easier to use, they're also more complex. They're so simple, so complex, that they're now called *objects* as in OOP (Object Oriented Programming). To tell you the truth, sprites, buttons, and other Director items have long been objects. "Say what?"

Maybe the simplest approach to understanding the concept of an object is to talk about things that aren't objects. A traditional way of creating computer stuff is to separate function from information. A good example of this approach is just about any application that you're familiar with. The program or application is the *function;* the documents that you create with the software are the *info.* Objects are a blend of function and info ("data" for the coneheads among you).

In Director 6, a sprite is now a combination of function and data. Each sprite knows it's a sprite and knows its own characteristics.

The most visible difference between sprites in Director 5 and Director 6 is apparent in the Score window. In Director 5, each sprite in the Score occupied only one frame. With Director 6, the default setup is for each sprite to occupy 28 frames in the Score, referred to as its *sprite span*. Visually, a sprite's span is the sprite's sprite bar in the Score. You can change the sprite span in the new Sprite Preferences dialog box, discussed in Chapter 4.

Director does *not* modify the sprite span of sprites already in the Score, regardless of what option(s) you choose for Span Duration.

When sprites become keyframes in Director 6

The folks at Macromedia have made major changes to the way that you handle those special frames in the Score window called keyframes. Did I hear you ask, "What per chance are keyframes?" I'm glad you asked. A keyframe marks a significant frame in an animation sequence, such as the beginning and ending of a sequence or the high point of a bouncing ball animation. A keyframe is a milestone frame that you use in both traditional and computer-generated animation.

In traditional animation, the idea is: A master animator creates the milestone frames or keyframes that are then passed on to the rest of the animators who generate the intermediate frames. This discussion brings me to two other important concepts in this whole crazy process: the intermediate frames that are referred to as in-between frames and the process itself that is called in-betweening or tweening, for short.

In Director 6, you can create keyframes and leave creating the intermediate frames to Director with its new automatic in-betweening (or tweening, for short) feature. Each sprite begins with a default sprite span of 28 frames in the Score window. The first frame in its sprite bar is a token keyframe marked with a hollow white ball. But a sprite with only one keyframe is like an auto without an engine: It can't go very far. You need to create a minimum of two keyframes to tween an animation.

A word about the sprite tweening command

Objects in the Real World don't usually start and stop in equal units of space from moment to moment. For example, imagine a bouncing ball. The ball speeds up or accelerates as it approaches the floor, bounces off the ground with stored up energy, and begins to slow down or decelerate as it reaches its highest point in the air because of the effects of gravity.

By calling on the Sprite Tweening command (what was referred to in previous versions as In Between Special), you can add an Ease In and Ease Out value to make an animation more realistic. You can also set up complex, nonlinear movements for sprites. Take a peek at the section on using the Sprite Tweening command in Chapter 20.

Following are some of the new techniques that you can use with keyframes and tweening:

Using automatic tweening

When you create a new keyframe (for more information see "Creating new keyframes" later in this chapter) or when you modify a keyframe in the Score or on the Stage, Director 6 automatically updates the in-between frames. If the keyframe thing is a little shaky to you, try rereading the intro to "When sprites become keyframes in Director 6" earlier in this chapter. For more fun, try reading it upside-down (especially effective on slow weekends).

Selecting keyframes

In a sprite's sprite bar, you can individually select and modify each keyframe (marked with a white ball) by using controls in the Score, such as the new sprite toolbar at the top of the Score (see the section "Sprite toolbar" earlier in this chapter). You can also change the keyframe on the Stage by moving the keyframe or resizing it.

Selecting non-keyframes

When you click a non-keyframe part of a sprite's sprite bar in the Score, you select the entire sprite. Then you can move the sprite as a whole from one channel to another or to another set of frames in the Score.

Using the new Edit Sprite Frames command

You may want to select an individual cell in a sprite's sprite bar. In this case, try the following:

Figure 6-7:
When you
choose
Edit⇨Edit
Sprite
Frames, you
select the
individual
cells of a
sprite's
sprite bar.

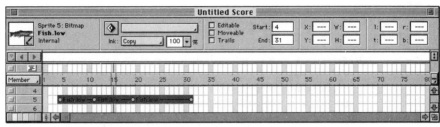

1. **Click the sprite in a non-keyframe part of its sprite bar in the Score.**

2. **Choose Edit⇨Edit Sprite Frames.**

   In the Score, the sprite's sprite bar suddenly looks very different, clearly delineating individual frames of the sprite with selected cells, as shown in Figure 6-7.

3. **Click an individual cell in the sprite's sprite bar.**

   At this point, you can drag the cell independently from the rest of the sprite's sprite bar. For example, you can drag the cell to a different channel in the Score, basically breaking the original sprite in two. You can also Shift+click a range of sprite cells or ⌘/Ctrl+click a set of non-contiguous cells in a sprite's sprite bar.

Instead of choosing Edit⇨Edit Sprite Frames, you can Option/Alt+double-click the sprite in the Score window.

Using the new Edit Entire Sprite command

If you've already chosen Edit⇨Edit Sprite Frames (see the previous section, "Using the new Edit Sprite Frames command") and you've changed your sprite's sprite bar to a set of separate cells, you can return the sprite to its regular setting by choosing Edit⇨Edit Entire Sprite. In its regular setting, clicking a non-keyframe area of a sprite selects the entire sprite's sprite bar when you can move the sprite as a whole in the Score window or on the Stage.

Instead of choosing Edit⇨Edit Entire Sprite, you can Option/Alt+double-click the sprite in the Score window.

Creating new keyframes

Each sprite begins with one keyframe at the beginning of its sprite span, marked with a hollow, white ball. To create a new keyframe:

1. **Click somewhere in the sprite's non-keyframe area of the sprite bar to move to a specific frame.**

   When you click a non-keyframe part of the sprite, you select the entire sprite in the Score window. That's okay, Director knows that you're in a specific frame of the sprite.

2. **Choose Insert⇨Keyframe.**

   A new keyframe appears in the sprite's sprite bar in the current frame. Visually, the sprite still looks the same on the Stage because you haven't modified the sprite yet.

3. **While the keyframe is selected in the Score window, modify the sprite by using one or more of the controls in the sprite toolbar (for more information, see "Sprite toolbar" earlier in this chapter).**

   You can also change the sprite directly on the Stage. For example, you can move the sprite to a new location or resize it. Director 6 automatically creates the intermediate or in-between frames.

Another way to create a new keyframe is the famous Combo method:

1. **Click the sprite in a non-keyframe area of its sprite bar.**

2. **Choose Edit⇨Edit Sprite Frames.**

3. **Click one of the non-keyframe cells of the sprite's sprite bar.**

   Note that in this case, the only selected part of the sprite's sprite bar is the cell in the current frame.

Instead of choosing Edit⇨Edit Sprite Frames, you can Option/Alt+click on a non-keyframe cell of a sprite's sprite bar, skipping the first three steps in this demo. By using this technique, in a lifetime you can save enough time to read an extra MAD magazine. Yikes!

4. **In the Score, modify the sprite — for example, change its location or resize it.**

   Director 6 turns the sprite in the current frame into a new keyframe (note the change in the sprite's sprite bar in the Score) and automatic tweening kicks in, creating in-between frames from the original keyframe at the beginning of the sprite's sprite bar (or the first keyframe to the left of the new keyframe) to the new keyframe in the current frame.

Chapter 7
Paint Window Tool Time

• •

In This Chapter

▶ Accessing the Paint window

▶ Reviewing some familiar icons

▶ Hammering away at Director's Paint tools

• •

*Y*ou know, Director's pretty generous. For the price of the top animation program in Computerdom, the Macromedia people throw in a pretty slick paint program just because they like you so much. Oh, you think the company may have an ulterior motive? Well, Director is a good program anyway.

With the built-in paint program hiding under the Paint window, you can handle any kind of bitmap from 1-bit, black-and-white graphics to what techies call 24-bit images, meaning graphics with over 16 million colors. How did I get that figure? You don't want to know. (If you'll just burst not knowing, read the sidebar, "Colors, colors everywhere," later in this chapter.)

Director also gives you a number of ways to display and use the Paint window, including:

✔ **Choosing Paint from the Window menu:** When you want to start from scratch, call up the Paint window and begin splashing away on a blank, electronic easel. Not an easy thing to do, even with a degree from the Sorbonne and the big set of crayons you got for Christmas.

✔ **Double-clicking a Bitmap Cast Member:** With one or more cast members eagerly awaiting the role of their lives, you can double-click a Bitmap Cast Member's preview in the Cast window and find the actual-size bitmap in the Paint window ready and willing to be edited. This route is a lot easier than starting from scratch. Where did the cast member come from? Well, there are Daddy Cast Members and . . . no, that's another story. The cast member can be an import from a good collection of clip art; an image you scanned yourself and saved as a bitmap; a screen shot you took with the old ⌘+Shift+3 trick on a Mac or by pressing the Print Screen key, sometimes labeled PrtSc, on your trusty PC (some keyboards insist that you hold down the Shift key, too); a chart generated from raw data in Excel; or a roll of film that you had your friendly photo dealer turn into a PhotoCD for you.

Colors, colors everywhere

Getting over 16 million colors from 24-bit graphics comes from the way computers understand information. In the end, all computers know is number 0 and number 1, a counting system called the binary system, which is why computers make such rotten house guests for the weekend. Boring, boring, boring! Anyway, to your computer, 0 stands for off (as in the light switch is off), and 1 means on.

However, various combinations of 0s and 1s, on and off states, have unique coded meanings to your machine. To a computer, 24-bit means a number in binary that looks to you like a string of 24 1s in a row. Rocket scientists like to call this value "2 to the 24th power." 24-bit, 24 binary 1s in a row, 2 to the 24th power — they all stand for the same value — 16,384,000.

✔ **Double-clicking a bitmap sprite in the Score window:** As long as the sprite is a bitmap, you get the Paint window with the bitmap ready for editing in its own cozy easel. See Chapter 4 for more info about sprites.

✔ **Double-clicking the small thumbnail preview of the currently selected sprite in the Score window:** You wind up with the bitmap staring back at you from the Paint window, anxiously awaiting your latest directorial changes.

Oh, No! Thousands of Icon Thingies!

Okay, hold on. You went to the menu bar and chose Paint from the Window menu, or you pressed ⌘/Ctrl+5, the Paint window keyboard shortcut. Now you see icon thingies everywhere staring back at you wondering who you are, as shown in Figure 7-1.

Now come on, you're exaggerating. The number of icons is far less than a hundred, let alone "thousands." A lot of the icons are standard interface stuff for your Mac or PC. So far, so good. Then there's the mysterious stuff: You have a row of icons just under the title bar of the Paint window. To the left, you see a double column of enticing icons and, below the enticing icons, a number of small panels. Come on, you can handle this.

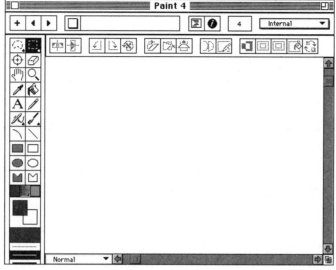

Figure 7-1:
In the Paint window, you can edit an existing bitmap or create a new cast member from scratch.

Paint window's top row of icons

Hello, row of icons in the Paint window. Explore them, if you dare, from left to right:

- ✔ **The New Cast Member icon (+ icon):** Gives you a new electronic easel to paint in with each click; this action also creates a new cast member that occupies the next available cell in the Cast window.

- ✔ **The Previous and Next Cast Member icons:** Allow you to click through the easels of Bitmap Cast Members in the Cast window.

- ✔ **The Drag Cast Member icon:** Lets you drag the contents of the Paint window on the Stage or in the Score window.

- ✔ **The Cast Member Name field:** Shows you the current name of the cast member.

- ✔ **The Cast Member Script icon (the i icon):** Takes you to the Cast Member Script dialog box, where you can tinker with Lingo scripts.

- ✔ **The Cast Member Properties icon:** Takes you to the Cast Member Properties dialog box, where you can modify basic options for the cast member displayed in the current easel.

- ✔ **The Cast Member Number icon:** Shows you the location of the cast member in the Cast window.

- ✔ **The Choose Cast pop-up menu:** Displays a list of Cast windows. Multiple Cast windows, both internal and external, are features introduced with Director 5. For more on internal and external Cast windows, see Chapter 5.

Paint toolbar

Whooh, and that's just the first row. Director 6 sports a wonderland of icons underneath as well. While you're still feeling adventurous, check out this second row — called the Paint toolbar — that allows you to apply various effects to a bitmap with the click of a button. From left to right, the Paint toolbar buttons include

- **Flip Horizontal:** Flips the selection in the Paint window along the horizontal axis. If a portrait of your Aunt Tillie was facing left, it's facing right now, her best side.

- **Flip Vertical:** Flips the selection in the Paint window along the vertical axis. If a portrait of your Aunt Tillie shows her standing by the porch, now she's standing on her head.

- **Rotate Left:** Rotates Aunt Tillie 90 degrees counterclockwise around her center point.

- **Rotate Right:** Rotates Aunt Tillie 90 degrees clockwise around her center point.

- **Rotate Free:** Rotates Aunt Tillie freely around her center point as you drag the mouse pointer hither and thither.

- **Skew:** Places *handles* or tiny rectangles around the current selection in the Paint window that you can use to distort the bitmap along the horizontal or vertical axis.

- **Warp:** Places handles around the current selection in the Paint window that you can use to distort the bitmap in any direction, one handle at a time.

- **Perspective:** Places handles around the current selection in the Paint window that you can drag to shrink or stretch the bitmap horizontally or vertically, giving a three-dimensional effect to the bitmap.

- **Smooth:** Director's way of eliminating the infamous stairstep appearance common to bitmaps because of the way they are built up with square pixels or pels. Smooth softens edges of the selection by adding pixels of intermediate values to subdue the stairstep effect, often referred to as *jaggies*. Another name for smoothing is *anti-aliasing*.

- **Trace Edges:** Paints a border around the shapes that Director finds in the current selection.

- **Invert Colors:** Reverses colors in the current selection, turning black to white, white to black, and creating some wild psychedelic neohippie effects with colored artwork. You may want to find your love beads.

- **Lighten:** Brightens all shades in the current selection by one step in value. Value is the lightness or darkness of an image.

> ✔ **Darken:** Darkens all shades in the current selection by one step in value.
>
> ✔ **Fill:** Pours the current Foreground color and Pattern into the currently selected shape. Keeping up with all these current events?
>
> ✔ **Switch Colors:** Exchanges Foreground color paint in the selection with the current Destination color, another color Director keeps track of for making smooth gradations of color and shading.

Director's Paint Tools

Other mysterious icons of the Paint window represent tools to modify a bitmap in the current easel or create a new cast member from scratch. Remember, these are Paint tools. You build a graphic by turning on units of "electronic paint" or pixels/pels with the Brush or Pencil tool in the Paint window's easel. It's really like a magician's trick. Step up close to the image and watch it break down into separate pixels with no distinguishable shape. Step away and view the image at a normal distance and the image comes together — a distant cousin to mosaic art, what the Impressionists were trying to accomplish with dabs of oil paint and the use of halftones in magazines and newspapers to give the illusion of great tonal depth with microscopic flecks of ink on paper.

Each Paint tool has a so-called *hot spot,* one or more pixels in its cursor from which the "electronic paint" flows like crazy. For example, the Pencil tool's hot spot is right where you'd expect it, at the tip of the pencil point. Knowing where the hot spot is in each tool is important for full control of the image you're building in the Paint window.

The following sections describe Director's Paint tools from left to right, row by row.

Lasso tool

 Use the Lasso tool to create irregularly shaped selections in the Paint window by dragging the Lasso around the desired graphic. The Lasso's hot spot is at the tip of the free end of the rope. Think of using the Lasso as "roping in" an area that you want to include in a selection.

To modify the way the Lasso tool works, press the Lasso tool in the Paint tool palette to display a pop-up menu and choose one of three options, as described in Table 7-1.

Table 7-1	Lasso Pop-Up Menu
Command	*How the Lasso Tool Works*
Shrink	Tightens around the silhouette of a bitmap, eliminating background-colored pixels from the selection
No Shrink	Sets the selection to include all pixels "roped in" with the Lasso
See Thru	Sets background pixels within the selection to Transparent ink

To make a polygonal selection with the Lasso tool, follow these steps:

1. **Option/Alt+click a point outside the target image to establish a starting point for the polygonal selection.**

2. **Click the Lasso tool once for each segment of the polygonal selection.**

3. **For the last segment of the polygonal selection, double-click the Lasso tool to create the last segment and close the polygonal selection shape.**

To create an identical copy or clone of a selection, Option/Alt+drag the selection to a blank area of the Paint window. Each time you release and then re-press the mouse button, you can Option/Alt+drag a new clone to another area of the easel. If you want to constrain movement horizontally or vertically as you clone a selection, add the Shift key to the set of modifier keys.

Selection Rectangle tool

 The Selection Rectangle tool is another basic selection tool for making, of all things, rectangular selections. When you choose the Selection Rectangle tool, the mouse cursor changes to a crosshair (small crossed lines). This tool's hot spot is where the crosshairs intersect. Make a selection by moving above and to the left of what you want to select, pressing the mouse, and dragging the pointer down and to the right until the graphic is enclosed in the selection marquee (sometimes referred to as the marching ants, although my personal belief is that they're termites).

Modify the way the Selection Rectangle tool works by clicking the tool in the Paint tool palette and choosing one of four options from the pop-up menu, as described in Table 7-2.

Table 7-2	Selection Rectangle Pop-Up Menu
Command	*Behavior*
Shrink	Snaps to the height and width of a graphic, eliminating background-colored pixels from the rectangular selection
No Shrink	Includes all pixels enclosed in the selection rectangle
Lasso	Notes the color first pressed and eliminates matching pixels from the selection; also switches to the Lasso tool
See Thru Lasso	Notes the color first pressed, turns all matching pixels in the selection and all background-colored pixels transparent, and then switches to the Lasso tool

The Selection Rectangle tool is also the key to quickly making copies of bitmaps and resizing them, either proportionally or to distort a bitmap horizontally or vertically. Table 7-3 outlines the result of applying modifier keys to the Selection Rectangle tool.

Table 7-3	Using the Selection Rectangle Tool
Action	*Result*
Press Option/Alt	Creates an identical copy, or clone. Each time you stop and drag a selection and re-press the mouse, you can press Option/Alt and then drag a new clone to another area of the easel.
Press Option/Alt+Shift	Creates a clone and constrains movement of the clone and drags a selection horizontally or vertically, depending on the direction of the initial move.
Press ⌘/Ctrl and then drag a corner of a selection	Resizes the selection horizontally and/or vertically. Dragging away from the selection increases the selection's size. Dragging into the selection's center reduces the selection's size.
Press ⌘/Ctrl+Shift and drag a corner of a selection	Proportionally resizes the selection horizontally and vertically. Dragging away from the selection increases the selection's size. Dragging into the selection's center reduces the selection's size.

Some kindly advice for scaling graphics in Director

✔ Reducing a bitmap always works better than enlarging it in Director. Whenever possible, create the largest size bitmap needed for a particular cast member. You can always duplicate the cast member, choose Modify⇨Transform Bitmap, and type a new percentage in the Scale entry field.

✔ If a bitmap is moving, a loss of quality is harder to detect and less critical to the eye.

✔ If you know that changing scale is going to be an important part of a cast member's role, add the cast member to the Cast as a real PICT: From the Clipboard, paste the PICT into the Cast window by choosing Edit⇨Paste Special⇨As PICT. Or import the PICT, being sure to choose Import Pict File as PICT from the pop-up menu at the bottom of the Import Files dialog box. Then resize the PICT as a sprite on the Stage by Shift+dragging a corner handle (for proportional scaling) of the highlighted sprite.

✔ If you've pulled and stretched a sprite, bitmap, or PICT on the Stage beyond recognition and want to magically turn it back to its original form, choose Modify⇨Sprite⇨Properties and click the Restore button in the Sprite Properties dialog box.

 One of Mr. Bitmap's most serious disadvantages is how poorly it resizes up or down. A bitmap resized in Director's Paint window rarely results in an acceptable image for professional work. Notwithstanding Director's fine built-in Paint program, the best approach to resizing a bitmap is to use a sophisticated paint program such as xRes or Photoshop. A program on xRes's level calls on highly refined routines for scaling graphics that even allow for a successful, limited enlargement of a bitmap. Limited is the key word.

Registration Point tool

 In traditional animation, artistes drew their initial sketches on highly translucent paper called onion skin. They learned to hold several pages in one hand and, with inconceivable dexterity, flip back and forth through the pages to test the sequence. In a fit of creative exuberance, the artistes christened this technique *onion-skinning*. Artistes with 12 or more fingers per hand were highly prized, chained to their desks, fed special high-protein diets, and groomed daily with Mr. Ed's horse hair pomade.

Viewing a sequence of bitmaps in the Paint window by pressing the Next Cast Member button is like the traditional onion skinning technique. Each bitmap in the Paint window starts out in life, as it should be, equal under the law and with a registration point centered in the graphic. You can see the registration point of a bitmap by choosing the Registration Point tool and noting where special dotted lines intersect on the easel. Click the Registration Point tool to fine-tune a bitmap's registration point.

To test an animation sequence using the Next Cast Member in the Paint window, follow these steps:

1. **If the Cast window is not already displayed, choose Window⇨Cast or press ⌘/Ctrl+3.**

2. **Press Shift and select a range of contiguous cast members in the Cast window belonging to a particular animation sequence.**

   If necessary, manually rearrange cast members by dragging them into the correct sequence so that they occupy contiguous cells. Director takes good care of all the accounting stuff to keep the Score and Stage windows in sync with the changes you make in the Cast window.

3. **Double-click the first cast member of the animation sequence.**

   Director takes you to the Paint window, where you see the cast member's bitmap.

4. **Simulate onion skinning by pressing the Next Cast Member button and letting subsequent bitmaps pass by.**

5. **If necessary, adjust one (or more) bitmap's registration point by clicking in the desired location with the Registration Point tool.**

By default, each bitmap's registration point rests in its center. To recenter a bitmap's registration point in the Paint window, double-click the Registration Point tool.

Eraser tool

 Use the Eraser tool to remove pixels from a bitmap in broad strokes.

Director doesn't allow you to change the shape of the Eraser. For critical, pixel-by-pixel erasing, follow these steps:

1. **Select the Pencil tool.**

2. **Set the background color to the color behind the graphic.**

   For more information about the Background color chip, see "Additional Paint window areas" at the end of this chapter.

3. **Press Option/Alt to paint with the background color and "erase" unwanted pixels by clicking them with the Pencil tool.**

To instantly erase the entire Paint window, double-click the Eraser.

Some programs are thoughtful enough to warn you when you're about to do something drastic, such as erasing the entire contents of a file or window. They bring up an alert box asking, "Are you sure you want to erase the entire window?" giving you an out by allowing you to click a Cancel button. Not Director. So think twice before using the double-click Eraser trick. Be certain that you want to erase everything in the window. If you do erase the entire easel by mistake, stop. Do not pass Go. Do not collect $200. Immediately choose Edit➪Undo Bitmap or press ⌘/Ctrl+Z to restore the graphic.

Hand tool

 Pressing the Hand tool button within the easel of the Paint window allows you to shift the view on-screen so that you can view hidden sections of full-size bitmaps such as screen shots or oversized bitmaps.

A common fear of novice Director types is that moving a bitmap in the Paint window may mess up the position of artwork on the Stage. Director is smart enough to know better. Give Director some credit, will you? Sheesh!

Press the spacebar to temporarily change the currently selected tool in the Paint window to the Hand tool. This trick now works with the Text tool in Director 6 as long as you haven't established an insertion point in the Paint window. When you have, try pressing the spacebar and clicking at the same time. If it works, you've got only one problem; you lose the insertion point and any text you've typed becomes a bitmap. It's a jungle out there.

 If you've been scrolling up and down a large bitmap in the Paint window and become lost, click the Next Cast Member button in the upper-left corner of the window and then click the Previous Cast Member button. You find that the bitmap reappears in the Paint window like magic.

Zoom tool

 Each click of the Zoom tool doubles the size of the image in the Paint window while a small window in the upper right of the Paint window displays an actual-size view of the region surrounding the mouse pointer. The actual-size view is displayed to keep you from getting lost at larger magnifications.

To zoom out, press the Shift key and note how the little plus sign (+) in the Zoom tool changes to a minus sign (–). By the way, the Zoom tool echoes the Zoom command in the View menu with a pop-up selection of views up to 800 percent.

Eyedropper tool

 Select the Eyedropper tool, then click it on a pixel to read or sample the pixel's color and pattern and to set the current foreground color and pattern to the sample. The Eyedropper tool's hot spot is the very tip of the glass stopper.

 Shift+click the Eyedropper on a pixel to match the current background color and pattern to the pixel. Option/Alt+click the Eyedropper on a pixel to match the end or destination color in the Gradient Destination color chip to the pixel. By the way, a *gradient* is simply a blend of colors.

Paint Bucket tool

 Use the Paint Bucket tool to fill an area with the current foreground color and pattern. This tool's hot spot is at the very tip of the paint spilling from its bucket.

If you choose Gradient from the Ink pop-up menu, the Paint Bucket tool also fills an area with the current gradient, set in the Gradient Destination color chip. The Paint Bucket tool is designed to work with solid areas of color, or as techie types like to say, contiguous blocks of pixels. You see, the Paint Bucket's hot spot is sensitive to the color you initially select; the Paint Bucket is designed to seek out contiguous pixels of matching color.

Double-click the Paint Bucket tool to go to the Gradient Settings dialog box shown in Figure 7-2. The beginning color is defined by the current foreground color and the ending color by the current color chosen as the Destination color chip.

As you can see, Director offers you many options in this dialog box:

✔ Direction of the gradient

✔ Number of cycles in the gradient

✔ Method of producing the gradient

✔ Spread of the gradient, meaning evenly spread or favoring the first or last color

✔ Range, meaning where Director places the beginning and ending colors of the gradient (for example, across the cast member versus the window size)

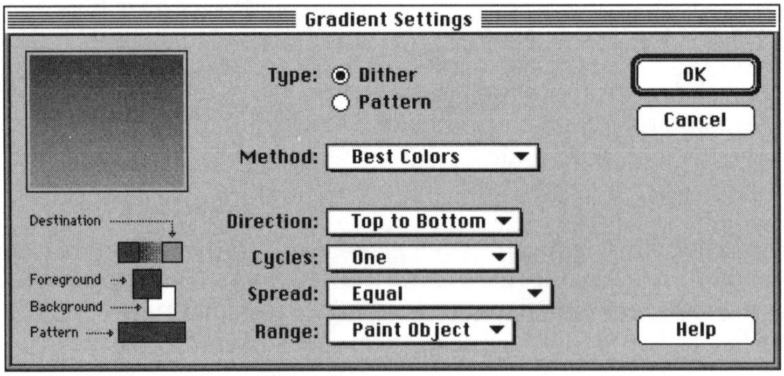

Gradient Settings

Type: ● Dither
○ Pattern

Method: Best Colors ▼

Destination ....→

Direction: Top to Bottom ▼

Cycles: One ▼

Foreground →

Background ......→

Spread: Equal ▼

Pattern ......→

Range: Paint Object ▼

OK

Cancel

Help

Figure 7-2:
The
Gradient
Settings
dialog box.

Text tool

 The Text tool in the Paint window is for creating text that becomes a bitmap as soon as you do just about anything other than type or set text attributes like Font, Size, and Style. Try this out:

1. **Choose Paint from the Window menu.**

2. **Click the New Cast Member (+) button near the upper-left corner of the window.**

3. **Click the Text tool.**

   After you move back to the easel, your mouse pointer looks like the classic I-beam cursor that belongs to word processing programs such as Microsoft Word.

4. **At the I-beam, type some text.**

5. **Type a period and then three spaces.**

   Okay, those of you out there who typed "a period and then three spaces," go stand in the corner for at least three hours. And no supper.

6. **Press the Delete key once.**

Why did I have you add three spaces and then delete a space? The sense of power is intoxicating. Actually, just to give you a better view of the insertion point that looks like an upside-down cross. The short horizontal line at the bottom of the insertion point marks what typographer types call the baseline, where lowercase characters like *x* and *n* rest on the page.

You also see a bold, gray border around the text you type. As long as you retain the gray border and the insertion point, you can modify the text in several ways. For example, you can

✔ Delete characters to the left of the insertion point one character at a time with the Delete key.

✔ Move editable text without losing the border or insertion point by pressing the mouse anywhere within the gray border and dragging the text.

✔ Choose Modify⇨Font or press ⌘/Ctrl+Shift+T to display the Font dialog box, where you can change the font, size, vertical spacing (leading), kerning, and color of the selected text.

✔ Double-click the Color resolution indicator to change the scale, color depth, and/or palette of the text with the Transform Bitmap dialog box. After this operation, you lose the ability to edit the text.

✔ Press the Pattern chip to change the current pattern. You don't see pattern changes until you change the text to a bitmap.

✔ Press the Background color chip to change the current background color; the white space within the bold, gray border that contains the text adopts the new background color. By the way, you don't see background color changes until you change the text to a bitmap.

✔ Press the Foreground color chip to select a new current foreground color; selected text immediately adopts the new foreground color.

✔ Press the Gradient Destination color chip to set up first and last colors for a custom gradient. This action alone does not modify the editable text. To apply a gradient to the editable text, you need to take one more step, selecting Gradient from the Ink pop-up menu. Also, changes are not visible until you turn the text into a bitmap.

✔ Press the Ink pop-up menu to change the current ink effect. Changes are not visible until you turn the text into a bitmap.

Click a blank area of the Paint window to turn text typed with the Text tool into a bitmap, no different from any other bitmap imported or created with one of Director's Paint tools.

The biggest disadvantage of turning text into a bitmap is losing the ability to edit the text. If you want to make edits, you must literally erase and retype bitmapped text; take care to match the previous artwork and blend the text appropriately into its surroundings.

There's an old saying I just made up: Every cloud has a silver lining. You see, a wonderful advantage of bitmapped text is never having to worry if the right typeface is installed in the user's system, a never-ending concern when using editable text. What if the right typeface isn't installed in the computer? What if the user doesn't have the same typeface? What if you have halitosis? And on and on it goes.

Avoid a poor display of text by choosing a TrueType font or installing Adobe Type Manager to your system and restarting your computer before opening Director. For serious type aficionados who want extra-smooth looking type, consider anti-aliased text. For more on anti-aliased text, see Chapter 9.

Pencil tool

 Use the Pencil tool for free-form painting. This tool's hot spot is at the tip of the Pencil point, and it paints with the current foreground color in the Paint window. With the Option/Alt key pressed, the Pencil tool paints with the current background color.

Note: The Pencil doesn't display the current pattern or the current ink effect; its ink effect is always set to Normal, and it always paints with one-pixel-wide paint. (Must be the Republican in the bunch.) See this section's last paragraph for more on ink effects.

Press the Shift key to constrain the Pencil's movement to straight horizontal or vertical lines. Use the Pencil for critical, pixel-by-pixel retouching of a bitmap, too.

Press the ⌘/Ctrl key to temporarily change the Pencil tool or any other tool in the Paint window to Director's Zoom tool.

Air Brush tool

 Use the Air Brush tool to create soft, feathered shapes of color and splatter effects with the current foreground color and pattern.

Note: If you're familiar with xRes or Photoshop, you may be disappointed with Director's Air Brush tool. There's no contest, although Photoshop's Airbrush tool doesn't create the interesting splatter effects that you can achieve with Director's Air Brush, so there. You may just find yourself sneaking away one day from Photoshop to get an effect that you can achieve only in Director.

Double-click the Air Brush tool to display the Air Brush Settings dialog box, shown in Figure 7-3, where you can customize the spray, size of dots, and speed of spraying paint. To modify the Air Brush effect even more, change the current ink effect in the Ink pop-up menu.

Press the Air Brush tool to reveal a pop-up menu of five customizable Air Brush settings.

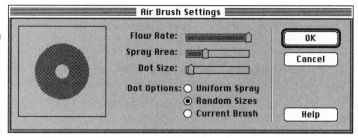

Figure 7-3:
The Air
Brush
Settings
dialog box.

Paintbrush tool

The Paintbrush is perhaps Director's most intuitive Paint tool. It looks and acts just like, well, a brush.

When coupled with ink effects like Smudge or Smear from the Ink pop-up menu, you'd swear you're painting with real oil or acrylic paint. Double-click the Paintbrush tool to display the Brush Settings dialog box shown in Figure 7-4.

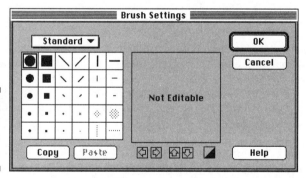

Figure 7-4:
The Brush
Settings
dialog box.

In the Brush Settings dialog box, you can select from 30 installed brush shapes or create custom shapes of your own by pressing Custom in the pop-up menu.

Arc tool

Use the Arc tool to paint curved segments. Select the Art tool and then drag it in any direction to paint an arc, which winds up being a quarter-ellipse on the easel.

Shift+drag to create a perfect quarter-circle with the Arc tool. Option/Alt+drag the Arc tool to paint an arc in the current background color.

Line tool

 Use the Line tool to paint straight lines at any angle in the current foreground color on the Paint window's current easel.

 Using the Line tool, press Shift and then drag the pointer to draw horizontal, vertical, or 45-degree angled lines. Press Option/Alt and then drag the Line tool to draw horizontal, vertical, or 45-degree angled lines in the current background color. Stand on one leg to make this look even more impressive.

Filled Rectangle, Ellipse, and Polygon tools

 Use the Filled Rectangle to paint rectangles, ellipses, and polygon shapes filled with the current foreground color in the current pattern and bordered in the current line width. The border won't display the current pattern.

Hold down the Option/Alt key to paint a filled shape with a border displaying the current pattern, effectively creating a rectangle with no border.

Shift+drag to paint a perfect square or circle. There's no law against tossing in the Option/Alt key to paint a perfect square or circle with a border displaying the current pattern.

Double-click the Filled Rectangle, Ellipse, or Polygon tool to display the Gradient Settings dialog box. For more on the Gradient Settings dialog box, check out the "Paint Bucket tool" section, earlier in this chapter.

Rectangle, Ellipse, and Polygon tools

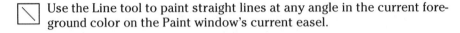 Ah yes, your little friends have a dual personality. Select the regular Rectangle, Ellipse, or Polygon tool to paint a shape with a transparent fill, bordered with the current foreground color in the current line width. To add a little zip to your life, press the Option/Alt key when painting to add the current pattern to the border. And to make life so exciting that you can hardly stand it, add an ink effect from the Ink pop-up menu. Now that's living on the edge. Whooh.

Note: The Polygon tool behaves a little differently than its siblings in the Paint tools palette. Click and drag to establish the first side or segment of the polygon; continue to click and drag to add a side. Double-click the Polygon tool to add the last segment and automatically close the polygon.

Additional Paint window areas

Now, to wake some of you drowsing off in ReaderLand, I'd like you to look at the areas of the Paint window just below the Polygon tools, as shown in Figure 7-1. Top to bottom, these areas include

- **Gradient Destination color chip:** Allows you to select the beginning and ending colors for a *gradient,* or blend of colors, by pressing the left and right sides of the chip and selecting a color from the current palette. Double-click the chip to go to the Color Palettes dialog box, where you can choose a different palette for the bitmap.

- **Foreground color chip:** Allows you to select the current foreground color by pressing the Foreground color chip and choosing a color from the current palette. The number of colors depends on the current color depth setting of your monitor. Double-click the chip to get to the Color Palettes dialog box, where you can select a different palette for the bitmap.

- **Background color chip:** Allows you to select the current background color by pressing the Background color chip and choosing a color from the current palette. The number of colors depends on the current color depth setting of your monitor. Double-click the chip to go to the Color Palettes dialog box, where you can select a different palette for the bitmap.

- **Pattern chip:** Allows you to select the current pattern by pressing the Pattern chip and choosing a pattern. Double-click the Pattern chip to go to the Pattern dialog box, where you can create custom patterns.

- **Line Width indicator:** Allows you to choose the current line width for Director's Paint tools. To set a custom line width, choose File⇨Preferences⇨Paint, from which you can select a line width of up to 64 points with a sliding control in the Paint Window Preferences dialog box. You can also display the dialog box by double-clicking the line 4 `pixels`, in the Line Width indicator.

- **Color Depth indicator:** Displays the color depth of the current bitmap in the Paint window. *Color depth* is techie talk for how many colors a bitmap can display at one time. For example, a 1-bit graphic can show only black and white, while an 8-bit graphic can display up to 256 different colors at one time. Double-click the Color resolution indicator to go to the Transform Bitmap dialog box, where you can, among other options, set the bitmap to a higher or lower color depth.

Note: You can "sample" a pattern or brush shape by clicking the mouse anywhere outside the Patterns or Brush Shapes dialog box. Your sample appears in the large panel on the left of the respective window, where you can click individual pixels to further modify the bitmap into a custom pattern.

Director saves custom tiles in the file where the custom tiles are created. However, Director saves custom patterns to the Director 6 Preferences file in the Preferences folder. If you want to archive custom patterns that you've created, be sure to back up the Director 6 Preferences file before reinstalling the system software or Director; then restore the archived Director 6 Preferences file after installation.

Just to the right of the Line Width indicator is the Ink pop-up menu, which allows you to choose an ink effect for a selection in the Paint window. Many of the ink effects are similar to the inks available in the Score window, but others, such as Smudge and Smear, are specifically used to expand the potential of Director's Paint tools. Double-clicking the Ink pop-up menu several times gives you a terrific headache as the pop-up menu wildly appears and disappears with each click without taking you anywhere else. Great fun on a slow weekend.

Coloring 1-bit cast members

I lied; 1-bit cast members don't have to be black and white. Director gives you a sneaky way to add lots of color to your movie by using just 1-bit graphics. Select a 1-bit sprite on the Stage and give it any color from the palette pop-up panel in the Tool palette, which I cover in Chapter 10. This is a common trick used by developers working under very tight assumptions about user resources, meaning that you're trying to squeeze lots of color into a Director movie that has to fit on a floppy disk. This is also a great trick if you plan to publish on the World Wide Web, where economic graphics are vital for successful design.

Chapter 8

Drawing, er, Painting on Director's Paint Window

· ·

In This Chapter

▶ Setting colors in the Paint window

▶ Exploring mysteries of the Line Width indicator

▶ Handling graphics that are too big for their own good

▶ Making masks, even when it's not Halloween

· ·

*O*kay, if you read Chapter 7, you've perambulated through the mysteries of the Paint window, although I'm not sure that perambulating in public is legal, at least not until the kids are sound asleep. Anyway, there are some people whose ice cream always falls from the cone one minute after they buy it, who wind up with an odd sock at the laundromat, and who always choose Brand X in those taste tests. For those of you out there in ReaderLand whose Paint window comes up with black as the current foreground color and white as the current background color, let me assure you that Director is a 24-bit program; it can handle over 16 million colors at one time, provided that your monitor, computer, and video card can handle 24-bit color.

No, You're Not Limited Just to Black and White

Changing colors is a cinch. The Foreground color chip on the Paint window is actually a pop-up menu. When you press the chip with the mouse, a palette, or collection of colors, appears; select any one of the colors to make it the new foreground color. It's that simple.

Even if you're set for displaying 24-bit color, or over 16 million colors, you can have only one current foreground color at a time. You paint with this color, unless you alter the Paint tool's behavior with modifier keys.

Director's Paint window also provides you with a Background color chip that's located underneath the Foreground color chip. The Background color chip is a pop-up menu, too.

After you decide on your Foreground and Background colors, you have one other important color option to address. You know which one? Wonderful, here's an extra large lump of sugar. That's right — the destination or ending color in the Gradient Destination color chip, your key to creating gradients or color blends in Director. Both the beginning and ending colors in the chip — tantalizingly alluded to in Figure 8-1 — are actually pop-up menus hiding a full palette of available colors.

Figure 8-1:
The Gradient Destination color chip, your key to creating color blends in Director.

How Do I Change the Size of My Lines?

You're painting with the Line tool, and you're getting frustrated because you can't figure out how to change the size of the line. You've cursed at it, which is usually effective with high-technology equipment, but this time, zippo. You've pouted, but with the same result.

You must have forgotten the Line Width indicator in the Paint window, lovingly hand-painted in Figure 8-2.

The Line Width indicator offers you the following:

✔ **Dotted line:** Click this option to paint an invisible line. The invisible line affects only the shape tools — the Rectangle, Ellipse, and Polygonal tools — and when the invisible line is selected, the shape tools produce an object without a border (useful if you're too lazy to press the Option/Alt key).

Figure 8-2:
The Line
Width
indicator is
in the
lower-left
part of the
Paint
window.

✔ **1-pixel, 2-pixel, 3-pixel lines:** Click to choose one of three ready-made line widths for down-to-the-wire, heart-thumping, last-15-seconds-on-the-clock line making.

Choose File⇨Preferences⇨Paint to go to the Paint Window Preferences dialog box, where you can use a sliding control to select a line width of up to 64 points.

When a Graphic's Too Big for Its Own Good

What's a person to do when a graphic's too big to see everything at once in the Paint window? Unfortunately, you can't zoom back smaller than actual size. The following sections give you a clue.

First, view your cast member in the Paint window. Should you choose to accept it, you can accomplish your mission in a number of ways:

✔ Find the cast member in the Cast window and double-click its thumbnail.

✔ Find the cast member in the Score and double-click the sprite.

  ✔ Select the cast member in the Score and double-click the small preview in the upper-left corner of the Score window.

  ✔ Select the cast member in the Score and double-click its sprite on the Stage.

  ✔ Throw chicken bones on the floor, chanting, "Aboo — abow — aboo" (archaic language predating pig Latin).

Using scroll bars

When a full-size bitmap is too large to see at one time in the Paint window, a wonderful invention should come to mind: scroll bars. A vertical scroll bar is on the right side of the Paint window with an up arrow at the top, a down arrow at the bottom, and a weird little box in between that techies call the elevator. Also, a horizontal scroll bar with its own arrows and elevators is located at the bottom of the Paint window.

To see a different portion of the Paint window, you can do any of the following:

  ✔ Click the up or down arrow on the vertical scroll bar.

  ✔ Click the right or left arrow on the horizontal scroll bar.

  ✔ Press and drag the elevator on the vertical or horizontal scroll bar.

Now you know all you ever wanted to know about scroll bars. Aren't you glad you asked?

Using the Hand tool

Another tool that should come to mind when you have a bitmap too large to see at one time is the Hand tool, which lets you drag the bitmap around within the Paint window like a loose sheet of drawing paper. Either choose the Hand tool from the Tool palette or press the spacebar, and any other tool temporarily becomes the Hand tool. One exception: The Text tool won't turn into the Hand tool until you press the spacebar and then press the mouse in the Paint window.

Using the Hand tool changes the location of the bitmap within the Paint window but does not change its position on the Stage or its recorded position in the Score window.

Wow! More Special Effects

When you work in the Paint window, certain commands in the View and Xtras menus become very enticing. I know you're just dying to see what these menus are all about, so dive in; the paint's fine.

Special commands in the View menu

The View menu, shown in Figure 8-3, contains three commands related to the Paint window. These commands include Panel, Rulers, and Onion Skin.

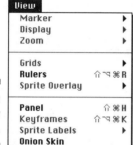

Figure 8-3: The View menu.

Panel

Panel is a *toggle* command, a kind of command that alternates or toggles between turning a command on and off or making a display element visible or invisible, in this case showing or hiding the set of Paint tools on the left side of the Paint window. At times, you may find the Paint tools distracting, so Director is thoughtful enough to include a command that lets you hide the tools whenever you want. Hiding Paint tools with the Panel command is also a way of eking out a little extra real estate on a small monitor. Today, any monitor 14 inches or smaller is considered small.

Rulers

As another toggle command like the Panel command, Rulers allows you to show or hide vertical and horizontal rulers in the Paint window, as shown in Figure 8-4. Notice the dotted line in each ruler; the dotted line marks the current position of the mouse pointer. Strangely enough, the size of the ruler doesn't change when you enlarge the view with the Zoom tool. So for accurate measurements, you need to do a little old-fashioned arithmetic based on the current view of the bitmap.

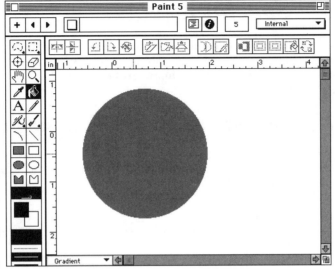

Figure 8-4:
Horizontal
and vertical
rulers that
you can
show or
hide in the
Paint
window.

Monitoring monitor size

The whole topic of working around extra large bitmaps shows why multimedia developer types like monitors larger than the standard 13-inch variety. With a 17-inch monitor or larger, you can place all those tricky windows to the side of the screen and still see the entire Stage, which you probably set to the ever-popular 13-inch size. If you opt to get a larger monitor, find out whether your computer or video card allows you to install extra VRAM, the video RAM that provides a larger screen without losing colors.

Another solution to the large bitmap dilemma is to install a second monitor, not necessarily

color, where you can place all those annoying extra windows and palettes. The prime monitor and any additional monitors can be joined into one virtual screen so that you can literally drag a palette from one screen to the next. Adding another monitor usually means adding another video card to the innards of your computer, although those of you with Power Macs get a bonus — Power Macs are set up for running two monitors without additional add-ons. Check your particular model of Mac or PC to see what you need.

Shhhh — secret features of Paint window rulers

Notice the small box in Figure 8-4, where the vertical and horizontal rulers intersect in the upper-left corner of the Paint window; it includes the letters *in* for inches. You can change the unit of measure on the rulers simply by clicking the small box and choosing the appropriate unit. The other units of measure available to you include

✔ cm = centimeters

✔ Pixel = $^{1}/_{72}$ of an inch (your display's unit of measure)

✔ Pica = $^{1}/_{6}$ of an inch (a typographic unit of measure)

The small box also marks the zero point, or origin, of the rulers, where measurement begins. You can set the zero point to any other location by positioning the mouse pointer in either ruler and pressing and dragging it to some point on the current easel. Resetting the zero point allows you to take measurements from the center of a bitmap or its upper-left corner or any other arbitrary point on the easel.

To return the zero point to its default setting by using the small box, position the pointer in either ruler and press and drag it into the small box.

Onion Skin

Believe it or not, Onion Skin is not the name of a new John Lynch movie; it's a command under the Paint window's View menu that displays the Onion Skin palette, a special kind of window that floats in front of other windows. The term *onion-skinning* comes from traditional animation, when animators hold several pages of translucent paper in one hand and preview an animation sequence by flipping back and forth through the pages.

To begin peeling away Onion Skin's mysteries, call up the Onion Skin palette, depicted in Figure 8-5, by choosing View⇨Onion Skin. By the way, Onion Skin is one of those famous toggle commands; next time you choose Onion Skin, the palette will run off and hide itself.

Onion Skin works by displaying cast members trailing and following the current bitmap as ghost images in the same Paint window easel. You can specify how many cast members are displayed at one time. Normally, these cast members represent the frames of a particular animation sequence; use the Onion Skin palette in order to check whether any bitmaps are out of sync or need refining or for tracing purposes.

I bet you're wondering just what those Onion Skin icon thingies are all about. Now you can find out:

Figure 8-5:
The Onion
Skin palette
allows you
to trace
over other
cast
members.

✔ **Toggle Onion Skinning:** Click to highlight the icon and turn on onion skinning. Figure 8-5 shows the icon turned on. Click again to turn off this feature.

✔ **Preceding Cast Members:** Click to display the cast members *preceding* the current bitmap as ghost images in the Paint window. The farther the cast members are from the current bitmap, the lighter they appear. Alter the number of preceding cast members shown by clicking the up or down arrows or by entering a value.

✔ **Following Cast Members:** Click to display the cast members *following* the current bitmap as ghost images in the Paint window. The farther the cast members are from the current bitmap, the lighter they appear. Alter the number of following cast members shown by clicking the up or down arrows or by entering a value.

✔ **Set Background:** Looking like Juan Valdez's mountain in Colombia, the Set Background icon allows you to designate any bitmap in the Cast window as the background image. Go to the chosen bitmap in the Paint window by using the Previous Cast Member or Next Cast Member button and then clicking Set Background in the Onion Skin palette.

✔ **Show Background:** Click this toggle button to display or hide the designated background bitmap.

✔ **Track Background:** If the designated background bitmap is the first frame in an uninterrupted sequence of Bitmap Cast Members in the Cast window, by clicking this button you can switch the background image to each cast member in their order every time you create a new easel.

Now that you know a little about Onion Skin's features, start putting them to use. The following steps show you how to use the Onion Skin command in the View menu.

Setting the background image

You can use Director's Onion Skin feature to designate a bitmap in the Paint window as a background image that faintly appears in the background of every Paint window easel. (If the previous sentence sounds like gobbledygook to you, try reviewing Chapter 7.)

1. **Choose Window⇨Paint or press ⌘/Ctrl+5 to display the Paint window.**

2. **Choose View⇨Onion Skin to display the Onion Skin palette.**

3. **Using the Previous and Next Cast Member buttons in the Paint window, display the bitmap you want to designate as the background image.**

   The bitmap you want for the background image can be located any-where in the Cast window. Say you created an animation sequence by using Auto Distort in the Xtras menu. Say the sequence shows a bull's-eye getting warped over ten frames, as though hit by a tremendous force. (See "Using Auto Distort" in this chapter for details on using this command.) Navigate to the beginning frame of the bull's-eye animation.

4. **Click Set Background in the Onion Skin palette.**

Previewing Previous and Next Cast Members

You can also use Onion Skin to preview one or more previous and following cast members relative to the current bitmap in the Paint window.

1. **Using the Previous and Next Cast Member buttons, navigate to the bitmap you want to use with the Onion Skin palette.**

   Say you've made a ten-frame sequence of an arrow being squeezed in half by the force of its forward motion. (You can create this sequence with the Auto Distort command in the Xtras menu.) In the Paint win-dow, navigate to the arrow bitmap that represents Frame 1 of the arrow sequence.

2. **Turn on onion skinning by clicking the Toggle Onion Skinning icon.**

3. **Enter a value or use the small arrow controls to set the number of preceding cast members that you want shown as ghost images.**

4. **Enter a value or use the small arrow controls to set the number of following cast members that you want shown as ghost images.**

   If you want to leave the background bitmap as a static image, skip to Step 6.

5. **If you want to display background animation, click Track Back-ground.**

   As you step forward and backward in the Paint window with the Next and Previous Cast Member buttons in the next step, you see that the designated background image also steps forward or backward in its animation sequence.

6. **Move forward and backward through the bitmaps in the Paint window with the Previous and Next Cast Member buttons.**

Because you have Onion Skin turned on, you can see a number of previous and following bitmaps relative to the current bitmap as ghost images, and you can now build or check the animation sequence to see if it is effective.

Special commands in the Xtras menu

Xtras extend the feature set of Director 6 the way that plug-ins enhance programs such as Adobe Photoshop and Premiere. Director Xtras come in three flavors: filters, transitions, and new cast member types. New Xtras are on the way from third-party developers, or if you're a whiz at programming in C while blindfolded, you can make your own Xtras in your spare time. Right.

Installing Xtras

To install a new Xtra filter, locate the Xtras folder/subdirectory in Director's folder/subdirectory. Add the new Xtra filter(s) to the Xtras folder/ subdirectory.

Other Macromedia products now feature Xtras, too. If you move the Xtras folder/subdirectory to the Macromedia folder/subdirectory, you make all the Xtras available to any Macromedia program you run. You Mac types can find the Macromedia folder in your System folder; you PC people can find the Macromedia subdirectory in the Windows subdirectory.

In the Xtras menu, reproduced in excruciating detail in Figure 8-6, commands include Filter Bitmap, Auto Filter, and Auto Distort.

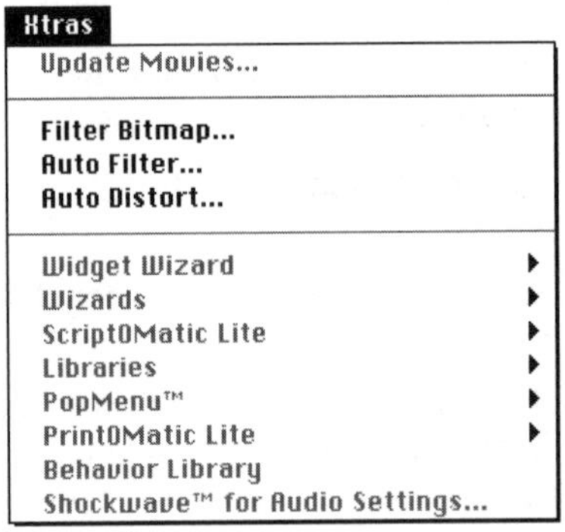

Figure 8-6:
You'll find special effect commands under the Xtras menu.

```
Xtras
    Update Movies...

    Filter Bitmap...
    Auto Filter...
    Auto Distort...

    Widget Wizard            ▶
    Wizards                  ▶
    ScriptOMatic Lite        ▶
    Libraries                ▶
    PopMenu™                 ▶
    PrintOMatic Lite         ▶
    Behavior Library
    Shockwave™ for Audio Settings...
```

Using Filter Bitmap

Filter Bitmap allows you to apply a Director Xtra filter to selected cast members in the Cast window or to a selection in the Paint window. Choosing Filter Bitmap displays the Filter Bitmap dialog box, as shown in Figure 8-7. You can even add Adobe Photoshop and Premiere filters to the Xtras folder.

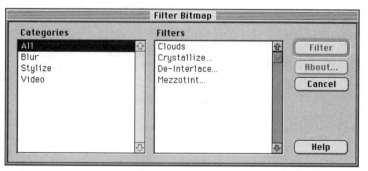

Figure 8-7:
The Filter
Bitmap
dialog box
under the
Xtras menu.

To find the Xtras folder, go to the Finder on a Mac or Program Manager in Windows and open the Director 6 folder. Inside, you'll find the Xtras folder, where all good Xtras go. (The Xtras folder is installed during Director's program installation.)

The following steps guide you through applying a filter to one or more cast members in the Cast window or to a bitmap in the Paint window, either to the entire bitmap or to a selection:

1. **Display the Cast or Paint window.**

2. **Make a selection.**

   In the Cast window, select a single cast member. Make a selection of several cast members by Shift+clicking contiguous Cast members or ⌘/Ctrl+clicking noncontiguous cast members. In the Paint window, use the Selection Rectangle tool to select all or part of a bitmap.

3. **Choose Xtras⇨Filter Bitmap to display the Filter Bitmap dialog box.**

4. **Choose a category of filter from the left Directory list in the Filter Bitmap dialog box.**

   To view all available filters, choose All from the Category list.

5. **Choose a specific filter from the right Directory list in the Filter Bitmap dialog box.**

6. **Click Filter.**

   Some filters require specific settings. To access these filter settings, click the Filter button and a dialog box or other control is displayed.

Using Auto Filter

Auto Filter is similar to Filter Bitmap, but Auto Filter automates the process and applies the effect incrementally. Figure 8-8 shows the Auto Filter dialog box, where you decide which filter to apply and the number of frames to apply the effect to.

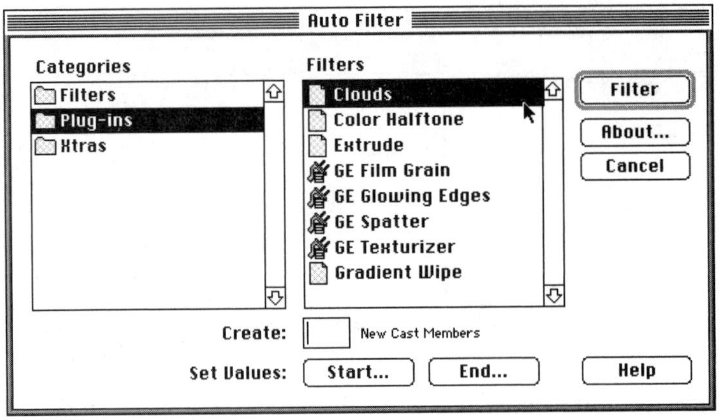

Figure 8-8:
Choose
Xtras⇨
Auto Filter
to auto-
matically
filter frames
incrementally.

The following blow-by-blow account helps you use Auto Filter:

1. **Choose Window⇨Cast or press ⌘/Ctrl+3.**

2. **Select a Bitmap Cast Member in the Cast window, or Shift+select a range of Bitmap Cast Members.**

   To filter part of one cast member, choose Window⇨Paint, click the Marquee tool, and select a portion of the current Bitmap Cast Member to alter.

3. **Choose Xtras⇨Auto Filter.**

4. **In the Auto Filter dialog box, double-click the Category of filter you want to use.**

5. **Select the Filter of choice in the Filters list.**

6. **Click Set Values: Start.**

   Filter controls appear where you can enter settings for the beginning of the sequence.

7. **Click Set Values: End.**

   Filter controls appear where you can enter settings for the ending of the sequence. Be sure that the beginning and ending values are different.

8. **Back at the Auto Filter dialog box, enter a value in the Create box for the number of New Cast Members you want to create for the sequence.**

   (If the box is grayed out or disabled, you have selected a range of cast members in the Cast window.) Auto Filter applies the filter incrementally to your selection without creating new cast members.

9. **Click the Filter button.**

Some filters may task your CPU (central processing unit) to the limit; don't be surprised if filtering takes some time to complete.

Using Auto Distort

You can use Auto Distort to create a set of new cast members for an animation sequence. Start with a bitmap you've distorted in the Paint window using the effects from the Paint toolbar. (For more on the effects, see Chapter 7.)

To use Auto Distort, follow these simple steps:

1. **Choose Window⇨Paint or press ⌘/Ctrl+5 to display the Paint window.**

2. **Using the Previous and Next Bitmap Cast Member buttons, find the bitmap you want to distort.**

3. **Double-click the Marquee tool to create a selection marquee around the entire bitmap in the Paint window easel.**

   If you want to distort a portion of the bitmap, use the Marquee tool to make a selection. Auto Distort does not work with selections made with the Lasso tool.

4. **Click one of the effects in the Paint toolbar and distort the bitmap using the handles that appear in the selection marquee.**

5. **Choose Xtra⇨Auto Distort to display the Auto Distort dialog box, as shown in Figure 8-9.**

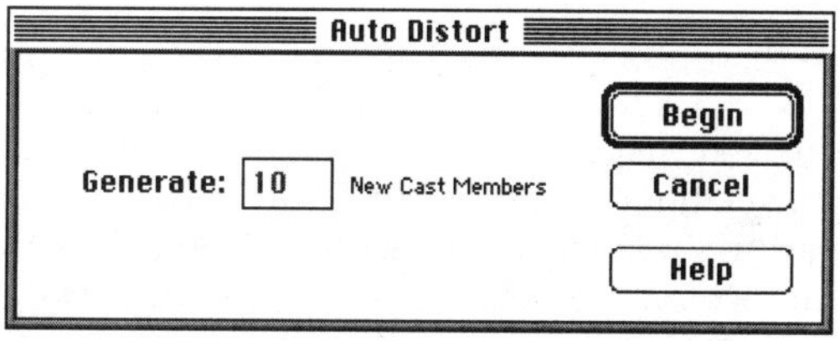

Figure 8-9:
Use Auto
Distort in
the Xtras
window to
create an
animation
sequence.

Auto Distort

Generate: [10] New Cast Members

Begin

Cancel

Help

6. **Enter a value in the Generate box for the number of New Cast Members you want Auto Distort to build.**

7. **Click Begin.**

Without knowing it, you have created keyframes, which are the beginning and ending frames for a sequence. Auto Distort fills in the difference incrementally by the value you entered in the Generate box in Step 6. You wind up with new cast members in the Cast window that make up an animation sequence that Walt would be proud of. Be sure to take time for a popcorn break after you proudly present your work to the world.

Exploring more Xtras

Under Auto Distort in the Xtras menu, you'll find another set of Xtras, including FileFlex, PrintOMatic Lite, Palettes.cst, and Animation Wizard. (Attention, Director old-timers: Animation Wizard replaces Auto Animate.)

FileFlex

FileFlex comes with Director as an Xtra in the Xtras menu. This simple database program can handle up to 1,000 records. From the submenu, you can choose Database Designer, which lets you lay out a customized database by dragging and dropping field types into the main window.

PrintOMatic Lite

PrintOMatic Lite adds basic printing features to Director 6 movies and requires light to intermediate scripting with Lingo, Director's built-in programming language. For example, you can write a simple script for a button that says

```
on mouseUp
    print "This is a test"
end
```

After you get some Lingo under your belt, you can create something Director calls an *instance*. What's that? At this point, you don't want to know. Just remember that it's more powerful, sounds more impressive, and may even get you that date you've wanted. In other words, later on down the line, it's worth learning. Look over Lingo in Chapter 14 to get your feet wet.

Palettes.cst

Choosing Xtras⇨Palettes.cst displays an external cast of assorted palettes to play with, as you can see hand-engraved in Figure 8-10. For example, you can add a Rainbow Windows palette to the Score (if you're developing for a PC) or a Cinepak palette, which is a set of colors that works especially well with Digital Video Cast Members compressed with the Cinepak codec. For more information about digital video and codecs, see Chapter 12.

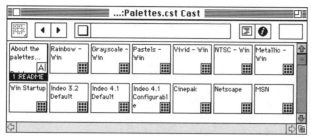

Figure 8-10:
An external
cast
bursting
with a
variety of
palettes.

Animation Wizard

The Wizard is ready to show you his tricks. He helps you put together animated presentations at the click of a button or two. He's so helpful, in fact, that I've devoted Chapter CD5 on the companion CD-ROM disc to his sly shenanigans.

SuperTechniRamaVision: All about System and Custom Palettes

Something about a known quantity is so comforting, so cozy, so . . . known. I think it's safe to say that people don't really like surprises (except for fans of Howard Stern, maybe). A surprise birthday party is about as big a surprise as most people can stomach.

Same thing goes for using a computer. Your computer works with a default color scheme, a System palette of 256 colors. The System palette's chief virtue is its lack of surprises; the colors of a System palette are relentlessly consistent. A user halfway around the world using the System palette sees the same palette of colors on the monitor as you do on this side of the globe.

Using the System palette

Director includes the System - Mac palette, the System palette for the Macintosh, and System - Win, the Windows System palette, in the Color Palettes window's pop-up list of built-in palettes. White is always the first color, black is always the last, and these two colors may not be modified. In between white and black is a range of colors — what techies call a color lookup table (CLUT), each color in its own specific, numbered slot.

You can view either set of System palettes by choosing Color Palettes from the Window menu or pressing ⌘/Ctrl+Option/Alt+7. The Color Palettes dialog box appears, looking suspiciously like Figure 8-11.

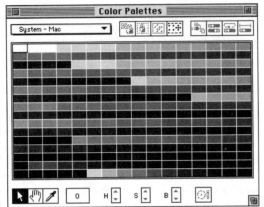

Figure 8-11:
The Color
Palettes
dialog box.

Take a look at the Palette pop-up menu shown in Figure 8-12, and you find a bouquet of palettes. When you choose System – Mac or System – Win from the selection of palettes, you know what to expect. As a multimedia producer, you constantly need to anticipate what the user, the intended audience for your epic, is going to see. Chances are that the user's going to be running off the standard, ubiquitous System palette or startup color scheme.

Figure 8-12:
The Palette
pop-up
menu in the
Image
Options
dialog box.

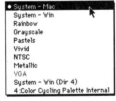

Facing problems with the System palette

You incur some problems when using the System palette, which is not to say that problems don't arise from sticking with a standard palette or color scheme. The same 256 colors that make you feel so smug also limit you in a critical way — to 256 colors. Some problems that the System palette presents you with include the following:

✔ **Poor rendering,** or display, of certain color gradients because of the limited number of colors to work with, depending on specific foreground and destination colors chosen

✔ **Posterization,** or blockiness, of some areas of scanned photographs and computer-based images, basically because of the same limited color choice problem

✔ **Artifacts,** or defects, in an image, which are little monsters in a bitmap that don't belong there, created when your computer attempts to display a range of colors that it really doesn't have the resources to create

Living with 16 million headaches

As a multimedia type, you face a classic dilemma. Use fast, 8-bit color and stay with the System palette of 256 colors. That choice ensures that the user sees what you intend to show, but the user has to put up with problems like posterization and artifacts, which degrade the aesthetics and effectiveness of your multimedia product.

Or go with 24-bit color, giving you over 16 million colors to play with, nearly photographic quality on a good monitor. But risk suffering a whole new set of performance problems, such as the fact that 24-bit color asks your computer to handle three times the amount of data and computation as 8-bit color. The result? Your multimedia slows to a grinding halt on all but the fastest machines.

Do you really want to run the risk of assuming that your user is running your beautiful multimedia on the latest, greatest computing dynamo the computer industry has to offer? Your viewer's machine may turn out to be an old clunker with 1MB (megabyte) of memory, and then your beautiful multimedia is almost all for naught.

Living with compromise

I've heard of this thing called . . . what was it? . . . oh yes, compromise. Director has heard of compromise, too, which it offers in the form of a Method pop-up menu in the Gradient Settings dialog box, shown in Figure 8-13, with several options for rendering a gradient.

Given a specific set of foreground and destination colors, one rendering method may work better than another using 256 colors. Pattern Best Colors, for example, may work better than, say, Dither Adjacent Colors. It's a visual decision rather than an intellectual one (thank goodness); if one rendering method makes a better-looking gradient, it's the best rendering method.

Another way of compromising — staying with 8-bit color when you want 24-bit, photographic-quality color — is to modify a 24-bit image in a high-level paint program such as Photoshop, Painter, or DeBabelizer by choosing

Figure 8-13:
The
Gradient
Settings
dialog box,
where you
can create
custom
gradients
for the Paint
window.

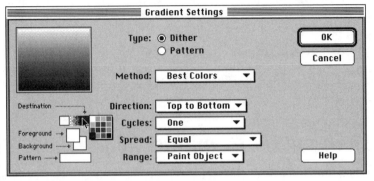

Index color. These programs offer special routines that reduce 24-bit color's 16 million hues to the System palette of 256 colors. The routine that drops the color depth from 24-bit to 8-bit uses a special trick called *dithering* in an attempt to preserve image quality. Dithering fools the eye into thinking that it sees more colors than really exist in the image. Sometimes the result of dithering is 8-bit color that can pass as 24-bit color; sometimes the result is disappointing.

Compromising, and then compromising again

A better solution when using high-end paint programs such as Photoshop or Painter to reduce colors from millions to 256 is to choose an option called an adaptive palette. The result is a graphic no longer based on the System palette or startup color scheme, but on a custom set of 256 colors analyzed by the paint program for optimum effect and combined with a special trick of the eye called dithering. The result of using an adaptive palette is often an 8-bit image that is nearly indistinguishable from its 24-bit original.

When you import a bitmap, Director displays the Image Options dialog box, shown in Figure 8-14. This is your chance to import a bitmap's adaptive palette into the Cast window as a new cast member. Otherwise, Director remaps the bitmap to the System palette, often with unhappy results.

Director gives you a gaggle of options in the Image Options dialog box. For Color Depth, choose between Image and Stage:

- **Image:** Click this radio/option button to retain the original color depth of the bitmap.

- **Stage:** Click this radio/option button to change the bitmap's color depth to the current color depth of the Stage.

Figure 8-14:
The Image
Options
dialog box
appears
when you
import a
bitmap into
Director.

For Palette, you have the honor of choosing Import or Remap to:

- ✔ **Import:** Click to import a bitmap's palette as an additional cast member, especially important for a bitmap with an adaptive palette.

- ✔ **Remap to:** Click to select a palette from the pop-up menu and have the imported bitmap remapped to the selected palette.

Last but not least, the Image Options dialog box gives you two fun check boxes to play with, Dither and Same Settings for Remaining Images:

- ✔ **Dither:** Check to apply a dithering routine to the imported bitmap. A dithering routine increases the apparent number of visible colors, similar to the idea of using four process colors in printing to create the illusion of reproducing full-color graphics and photographs.

- ✔ **Same Settings for Remaining Images:** Click to apply the same selection of options to remaining bitmaps listed in the Import Files dialog box.

Checking out those other built-in palettes

Why so many other built-in palettes? In Figure 8-12, in addition to the System – Mac and System – Win palettes discussed in the previous sections, you see several other choices.

The following list takes you through the extra built-in palettes displayed in the Color Palettes window's Palette pop-up menu and gives you an idea why they're there and what you can do with them:

- ✔ **Rainbow:** A special palette of bright colors, heavy on primary colors, as seen in a rainbow, for special effects and extra-smooth color gradients. Simply add the palette to the Score in the Palette channel.

✔ **Grayscale:** A special palette of 256 values for extra-smooth grayscale bitmaps and gradients. Add this Palette to the Score in the Palette channel when needed.

✔ **Pastels:** Another special palette of colors that is "softer" than the standard System palette, lighter and less saturated, with zero percent cholesterol.

✔ **Vivid:** A special palette similar to Rainbow but not so focused on primary colors. A more sophisticated yet bright set of colors for special effects. Take a look at this palette after drinking 10 or 12 cups of coffee for a real cheap thrill.

✔ **NTSC:** A special palette for prepping your movie for transfer to video. Novice multimedia types are often shocked at how different a Director movie looks on TV. One of the most dramatic changes in video transfer occurs with color. NTSC (National Television Standards Committee) TV, which is the kind of TV you currently watch, can handle only a very limited range of colors and saturation levels (that is, how red a particular red really is). For example, colors on NTSC TV above 70 percent of full saturation appear to spread beyond the image and bloom, meaning that the color seems to fluoresce or glow. Other colors simply translate into ugly browns, grays, and greens or make totally unexpected color shifts in the spectrum. So Director supplies you with a set of NTSC-legal colors to help reduce NTSC shock after you transfer your beautiful multimedia to videotape.

✔ **Metallic:** Another special effects palette of subtly metallic colors, designed mainly for robots that become interested in developing multimedia in their spare time. You haven't heard of robot-brewed multimedia? Well, that's 'cause robots have so little spare time. Workaholics, every one of them, bless their little tin hearts.

✔ **VGA:** A special palette for working with VGA monitors that newer Mac models can easily accommodate. VGA monitors display a color shift from standard Mac monitors; Director's VGA palette attempts to properly translate the color shift. By the way, VGA is dimmed in the Palette pop-up menu if you're not running a VGA monitor, so don't feel cheated or something.

✔ **System – Win (Dir 4):** A palette of colors for movies made with Director 4, which displays colors differently than Director 6. When choosing the standard System – Win palette over this palette, you see a definite and probably unwanted color shift in all graphics.

The best way to work on Director movies intended for video transfer is to work directly with an NTSC monitor or at least to refer frequently to an NTSC monitor during development. AV-type Mac models such as the 8500 and 8600 can switch between your computer monitor and an NTSC TV through the Monitors control panel. Second-generation Power Macs use the Monitors and Sound control panel of System 7.5.5 to send a second video signal to your TV, giving you two displays to work with. Some third-party video cards for Macs and PCs supply a separate port for outputting NTSC signals so that you can work with two monitors at one time. Check the capabilities of your own monitor, computer, and/or video card. Some settling of contents may occur. Over. Out.

Who Was That Masked Man? And How Do You Make a Mask, Man?

One of the most important ink effects available from the Score window's pop-up menu is the Mask ink effect. Matte ink makes the white, rectangular bounding box of a bitmap invisible, allowing the background to show through. But white pixels within the graphic remain opaque, which is not always the effect you want. That's when you want to turn to the more versatile Mask ink effect.

For example, the Matte ink effect on a Text Cast Member such as the letter *A* (that's a capital *A*) doesn't give you the effect you need. In the center of a capital *A* is that little bit of what typographer types call the counter, or negative space. It looks like a tiny pyramid and by all rights, the background should show through the counter, too.

When you use the Matte ink effect on the letter, what happens? Sure enough, the bounding box surrounding the *A* sprite turns transparent, and you get a silhouette effect; but the *A*'s counter remains white and defeats the effect you intended to create.

Aha, you may have discovered Bkgnd Transparent ink which turns all white pixels in a bitmap transparent. But that result may not be what you want; instead, you may want to choose which white pixels become transparent and which ones remain white. That's where Mask ink comes in.

Creating a mask

To use Mask ink, you need to use two bitmaps in the Cast window, the primary Bitmap Cast Member in any color depth you want to use and a duplicate Bitmap Cast Member immediately following the primary bitmap that has been turned into a 1-bit black-and-white Bitmap Cast Member. Follow these steps to create a mask that you can apply to a bitmap:

1. **Select a Bitmap Cast Member in the Cast window.**

   Make sure that an empty cell is to the right of the selection.

2. **Choose Edit⇨Duplicate.**

3. **Double-click the duplicate cast member, taking you to the Paint window.**

4. **Choose solid black from the Foreground Color selector (the very last color).**

5. **Select the Paint Bucket tool and click inside the area of the cast member that requires the mask, filling its shape with black paint.**

   If the bitmap were a large capital *A,* you wouldn't want to fill the *A*'s "counter," that pyramid shape in the middle of the character.

   You may need to select the Pencil tool or Brush tool and color the bitmap pixel-by-pixel. If you want some white pixels in the primary bitmap to remain white, you need to blacken their counterparts in the duplicate bitmap.

6. **Choose Modify⇨Transform Bitmap to display the Transform Bitmap dialog box.**

7. **Choose 1 bit from the Color Depth pop-up menu.**

8. **Click the OK button.**

   The Bitmap Cast Member in the Paint window is now a 1-bit graphic, which is exactly what you need to go to the next set of steps. Don't worry, there are only 534 more steps.

   Just kidding.

Applying Mask ink to a sprite

To apply the Mask ink effect to a sprite, follow these steps:

1. **Click the Score window and make sure that the original sprite is still selected.**

   The sprite also appears selected on the Stage.

2. **Choose Mask from the Ink Effect pop-up menu in the Score window.**

After Mask ink is enabled, the area of the sprite that needs the mask displays the original cast member; nonmasked areas become transparent, revealing the background. You can always return to the 1-bit cast member and edit the bitmap in the Paint window with the Pencil tool or Brush tool to fine-tune the masking effect.

While pressing the ⌘/Ctrl key, click a selected sprite on the Stage to reveal the secret Ink Effect pop-up menu. Remember, with the purchase of this book, you agreed to guard this secret with your life. Always read the small print.

Chapter 9

First, Earth versus Flying Saucers; Now, Text versus Field Windows

In This Chapter

▶ Examining different text types

▶ Revisiting the Paint window's Text tool

▶ Looking into Text and Field windows

*A*lthough people think of multimedia as a visual experience, content in the form of old-fashioned words still plays a big part in most multimedia productions. Working with Director 6 is no exception. A strong textual element exists among all the jumping, gliding, hip-hopping, generally hyperactive sprites on the Stage.

In this chapter, you can explore Director 6's text capabilities and find out more than you ever wanted to know about bitmapped text, rich text, and text in fields.

Bitmapped Text, One Step Away from Pod People

Bitmapped text is fake. It looks like text, reads like text, and even smells like text — kind of musty. Bitmapped text reminds me of those pod people from *Invasion of the Body Snatchers,* that creepy movie out of the '50s where Uncle Ira turns out to be a big cucumber.

Bitmapped text starts out like Uncle Ira, looking to all the world like the genuine article, like text created with a click of the Text tool. But this Text tool comes from the Paint window, which should be a dead giveaway. After you type some text with the Paint window's Text tool and even do some limited formatting and revising, when you're not looking the text turns into, yikes, a bitmap! And it doesn't even have to be a full moon.

Don't get me wrong — bitmapped text can claim many advantages over real text in Director. You never have to worry if the user has the right fonts installed. Bitmapped text is legally entitled to all bitmap privileges under the Constitution, such as being stretched and pulled like taffy with distortion options from the Paint toolbar or having Xtras filters applied to it ad nauseam for special effects rivaling Industrial Light and Magic stuff. But . . . .

When text becomes a bitmap, it can't be edited. And bitmapped text looks like heck warmed over when you print it out.

Rich Text, Come to Papa

Rich text is Director 6's name for text you type with the Text tool from the Tool palette or from within the Text window.

Don't confuse the Text tool in the Tool palette with the Text tool in the Paint window, which gives you bitmapped text. Two different "animules" completely.

Rich text is the closest thing to word processing-type text in Director 6. In general, it's the text of choice for most movie-making in Director with a set of features worthy of an Oscar, including:

- ✔ **Paragraph formatting:** Create paragraph-specific formatting choices just like you make in Microsoft Word and other word processing programs, including alignment, line depth (leading), and even kerning (spacing between character pairs).

- ✔ **Tabs:** Set real tabs within paragraphs of rich text.

- ✔ **Editable text:** Rich text is always editable in the authoring mode — that is, while you're making your movie with Director and before you turn the movie into a projector. Rich text in a projector becomes bitmapped text with all its benefits and disadvantages.

- ✔ **Anti-aliasing:** Rich text can be anti-aliased or smoothed out with special routines to eliminate the infamous stairstepping effect, or *jaggies,* which are common to text displayed on a computer monitor. Set text for anti-aliasing in the Text Cast Properties dialog box.

- ✔ **Imported text:** Import text from Microsoft Word and other programs that support the RTF (Rich Text Format) format. Many developers prefer to type text destined for a multimedia project in a program — such as Microsoft Word — specifically designed to handle text and then import the results into Director. Being able to import RTF text files also is important when writers become members of a creative team, working on the text on their own, and then incorporating their efforts into the final product.

Text in a Field

Create text in a field by choosing Insert⇨Media Element⇨Field or by selecting the Field tool in the Tool palette (as shown in Figure 9-1) and dragging out a field on the Stage or by typing text in the Field window.

Figure 9-1:
Selecting
the Field
tool from
the Tool
palette.

Text in a field has special uses in Director movies. Use text in a field if you need editable text during playback of the movie or projector or if text needs to be printed out at high resolution, but be aware of the following limitations:

- **System dependent:** To display properly, text in a field depends on the right fonts being installed in the user's system. Otherwise, unexpected and potentially disastrous results may occur on playback, causing you to never play the piano again.

- **Limited formatting:** Text in a field doesn't offer the full formatting features of rich text (discussed in the preceding section). You can't apply true paragraph formatting or set tabs and indents to text in a field.

- **Slow playback:** Text in a field is slower on playback than bitmapped or rich text and can significantly impede performance, especially on slower computers.

The Text Window

Go ahead, choose Text from the Window menu to display the Text window, which should look something like Figure 9-2. The beady-eyed among you who already read about Paint window stuff may notice something familiar. If you like, review the top row of the identical Paint window icons in Chapter 7.

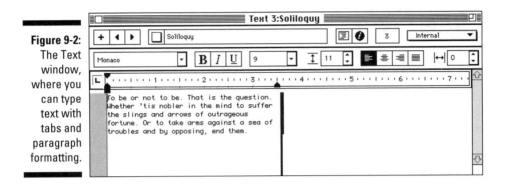

Figure 9-2:
The Text
window,
where you
can type
text with
tabs and
paragraph
formatting.

In the second row of icons, you have lots of formatting goodies to explore. From left to right, they include

- ✔ **Font pop-up menu:** Displays all fonts currently installed and available for selection.

- ✔ **Bold, Italic, and Underscore buttons:** Click to apply one or more of these formatting options to selected text.

- ✔ **Size pop-up menu:** Choose any type size from the pop-up menu or enter a value directly in the field.

- ✔ **Line Spacing:** Displays line spacing or *leading* of the Text Cast Member in points. Use the up and down arrows to alter the vertical distance from line to line. You can also directly enter a value in the entry box.

- ✔ **Left Align, Center, Right Align, and Justify buttons:** Click one of these buttons to set the alignment for selected paragraphs in a Text window. *Left Align* aligns selected paragraphs flush on the left side of the text block, leaving the right side ragged. *Center* aligns selected paragraphs along the midpoints of each line, and *Right Align* aligns selected paragraphs along the right side of the text block, leaving the left side ragged. *Justify* stretches each line of selected paragraphs so they are flush on the left and right sides of the text blocks. You often see this effect in magazine design, where two or three columns of text are on a page. Justified text is thought to be more formal and sophisticated than other alignments.

- ✔ **Tracking/Kerning control:** Adjusts two similar but distinct types of text spacing. With a block of selected text, increase the general horizontal spacing, or *tracking,* by clicking the up arrow or tighten the spacing with the down arrow. Generally, the larger the type size, the tighter the tracking can be. Normally you wouldn't even bother with adjusting spacing for body text, like the text you're reading now. You'll want to adjust tracking, though, for headlines and larger, so-called *display-size* text like banners.

Certain character pairs in a block of text are troublesome because of the very shapes of the characters. For example, the letters *W* and *A* in WATER and *o* and *w* in owl have too much space between them compared with the general spacing or fit of most characters. Without adjustment, or *kerning*, these character pairs stand out from the rest of the text, interrupting the flow of text and reducing readability. Good typesetters kern character pairs like *A* and *W*. Now you, too, can kern character pairs in Director 6. Simply click in between the characters, and then click the up arrow to increase or the down arrow to decrease character pair spacing. Like tracking, you usually apply these adjustments to text larger than body text.

Under the second row of icons is the Text ruler for setting tabs and indents in rich text. You can hide or show the ruler by choosing View⇨Ruler. To change the units displayed in the ruler, choose File⇨Preferences⇨General and select Inches, Centimeters, or Pixels from the Text Units pop-up menu.

Setting tabs

The left side of the ruler is called the *tab well,* where with each click you can cycle through four kinds of tabs: left, right, center, and decimal.

To create custom tabs, follow these steps:

1. **Select paragraphs for tabbing in the Text window.**
2. **Click the tab well until you see the kind of tab you need.**
3. **Click once in the ruler just under the displayed text units (inches, for example) to establish each custom tab.**

Change the position of a tab by dragging it to the desired location on the ruler. Remove a tab simply by dragging it off the ruler.

If you don't establish custom tabs, preset tabs align every half inch on the ruler as with most word processing programs, such as Microsoft Word.

Setting indents

Set indents for selected paragraphs by dragging left- and right-indent markers along the ruler. To set a first line indent, use the control that points down from the top of the ruler.

The Text Cast Member Properties Dialog Box

Click the Text Cast Member Properties icon, the one that looks like an italic *i* in a bowling ball, to display the Text Cast Member Properties dialog box, shown in Figure 9-3, so that you can check out its unique features.

Figure 9-3: The Text Cast Member Properties dialog box.

The Text Cast Member Name box

In this entry box, you can enter a meaningful name for the Text Cast Member instead of referring to it by its position in the Cast window or in the Score (which can change over time and cause unexpected results) — or as "Hey, you."

The Framing pop-up menu

From the Framing pop-up menu, meticulously reproduced by Alsatian artisans in Figure 9-4, you can choose one of three options for text display on the Stage, including the following:

- **Adjust to Fit:** Creates a field that automatically adjusts its depth to display the total amount of text in the field.

- **Scrolling:** Creates a field with a vertical scroll bar on the right side, allowing you to enter a large amount of text without resizing the text field. The user simply scrolls with the up and down arrows to see different parts of the field's content during playback.

- **Cropped:** Creates a text field with a fixed depth regardless of the amount of text typed in the field, although you can manually reshape the field by dragging one of its eight selection handles (the small black squares in the corners and at the center points of each side of the text field) to reveal more of the text.

Figure 9-4:
The
Framing
pop-up
menu.

Anti-alias radio/option buttons

You can apply anti-aliasing to Text Cast Members to subdue the
stairstepping effect, often referred to as the jaggies, common to text on-
screen and to increase perceived sharpness. Under the Framing pop-up
menu are three check boxes, including:

✔ **All Text:** Click this radio/option button so that all text in the Text
  window becomes anti-aliased. Keep in mind that small text with anti-
  aliasing may be difficult to read.

✔ **Larger Than:** Click this radio/option button and type a value in the
  small entry box to the right to apply anti-aliasing to text in the Text
  window that is larger than the entered value. Typing a value larger than
  so-called "body text," such as 14 point or 18 point or larger, is a good
  solution to the problem raised in the previous bulleted text.

✔ **None:** Click this radio/option button so that none of the text in the Text
  window is anti-aliased.

The Unload pop-up menu

Use the Unload pop-up menu to tell Director which cast members may be
purged (removed from memory) when they're not visible on the Stage as
sprites. Check out an extended discussion of the Unload pop-up menu in
Chapter 5.

Miscellaneous stuff

You find a few other goodies in the Text Cast Member Properties dialog box:

✔ **Text Cast Member Preview:** At the top left is a preview representing
  the contents of the Text Cast Member, with a Text Cast Member icon in
  the lower-right corner of the preview.

✔ **Size Indicator:** At the bottom-left corner, Director displays the size in
  bytes of the Text Cast Member.

- ✔ **Script button:** Under the OK button, Director provides a Script button to take you to the Text Cast Member's Script window.

- ✔ **Help button:** The ever-popular Help button displayed in all dialog boxes takes you quickly to Director's built-in Help system.

Searching for text

To search for and replace text in the Find Text dialog box, depicted in Figure 9-5, choose Edit⇨Find⇨Text, where you discover the following options:

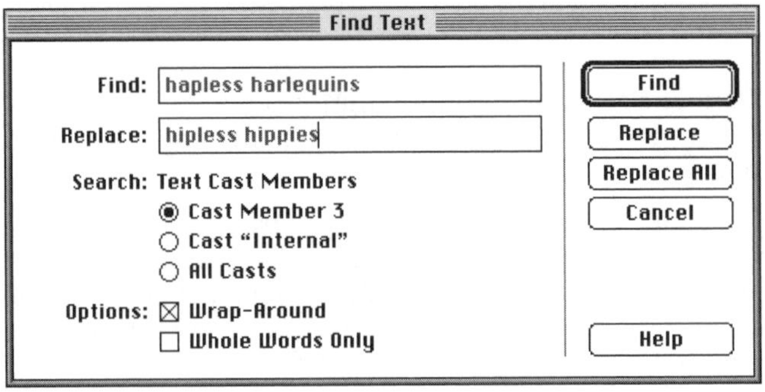

Find Text

Find:	hapless harlequins
Replace:	hipless hippies

Search: Text Cast Members
- ● Cast Member 3
- ○ Cast "Internal"
- ○ All Casts

Options: ☒ Wrap-Around
☐ Whole Words Only

[Find]
[Replace]
[Replace All]
[Cancel]

[Help]

Figure 9-5:
The Find
Text
dialog box.

Selecting Text and Field Cast Members on the Stage

A selected Text or Field Cast Member on the Stage may appear in one of two ways. This situation's kind of schizophrenic and fraught with danger, so be careful.

When you give a Text or Field Cast Member one click, a thick, hollow border with black so-called "handles" in the corners and midpoints appears, indicating that the Text or Field Cast Member is selected as an object and not as text. When you move the mouse pointer inside the cast member, the cursor remains a pointer, and you can then drag the cast member as an object to a different location on the Stage, or you can press and drag a handle to reshape the cast member.

When you double-click a Text or Field Cast Member on the Stage, the border becomes patterned with striped lines. Now, when you move the mouse inside the cast member, the pointer turns into the venerable I-beam cursor common to most word processors. You can take this cursor to mean that the Text or Field Cast Member is now in edit mode and that you can modify its text until heck freezes over.

✔ **Find:** Enter the word or phrase you're looking for, called the *search string*, here. Include only as much as you're sure that you need and watch out for typos and misspelled words. Click Replace or Replace All to continue.

✔ **Replace:** Enter replacement text when the Find Text command makes a hit.

✔ **Search: Text Cast Members:** Restrict the search to the currently selected cast member, the internal cast, or all casts by clicking the appropriate radio/option button.

✔ **Change Again:** Allows you to replace found text with the last substitute text entry made in the Find/Change dialog box.

✔ **Wrap-Around check box:** Makes Director search from the insertion point to the end of the selected field and then search from the first character in the field to the original location of the insertion point, coming full-circle in its search.

✔ **Whole Words Only check box:** Makes Director search for a match of complete words rather than partial words. For example, if you enter *part* as the search criteria with Whole Words Only checked, Director ignores words with *part* in them, like *partner* and *partisan,* and accepts only the complete word *part* as a legitimate hit.

The Field Window

The Field window, shown in Figure 9-6, is exactly like the Text window. Except the Field window is different — I mean, different in that text you enter in a Field window can be editable during playback of the Director movie and after you've turned a movie into a projector. In other words, if you have text areas in a Director movie that a viewer can fill in, like a questionnaire or a database entry, create these areas with the Field tool in the Tool palette or by choosing Window⇨Field. For Text window info, see the earlier section, cleverly titled "The Text Window."

Field windows are also different from Text windows in what they lack. Here's what's missing:

✔ No Ruler

✔ No Justify alignment option to stretch each line to its maximum width

✔ No tracking or kerning options

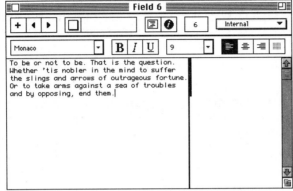

Figure 9-6:
The Field
window,
where you
can enter
text that
remains
editable
during
playback
and in a
projector.

For a quick overview of what you can and can't do with Director text, keep
Table 9-1 handy. I suggest making several copies and stapling them throughout your home.

Table 9-1	Advantages and Disadvantages of Director Text	
Type of Text	**Advantages**	**Disadvantages**
Bitmapped text	Text shapes are editable pixel by pixel	Not editable for content
	Speedy animation	Poor printing output (resolution frozen at 72 dpi)
		Not searchable with Find commands
		Not recognized as text by Lingo scripts
Rich text	Editable at any time during development	Shapes are not editable pixel by pixel during development
	Tracking and kerning options	Font mapping tables for cross-platform movies
	Searchable with Director Find commands during development	
Text in a field	Editable during playback and in a projector	Requires correct fonts to be installed in the user's system
	Prints at full resolution with smooth character shapes	Slow on playback

Chapter 10

Yet Another Set of Tools: The Tool Palette

- -

In This Chapter

▶ Fiddling around with the Tool palette

▶ Using the shape tools to create and change shapes

▶ Exploring the importance of the Tool palette

▶ Discovering the meaning of life

- -

*O*ne of the great pleasures of learning Director 6 is plowing through the kazillion windows that the program has to offer — that is, if you also happen to look forward to paper cuts during the day. As if you don't have enough windows to befriend, allow me to present the Tool palette.

A Brief Explanation of Tool Palette Tools

If you've read Chapters 7 and 8, you know that I've talked about Paint tools this and Tool palette tools that. So you just may be wondering, what the heck is the difference? Well, without getting too technical, the Tool palette tools work like ClarisDraw and CorelDRAW, two well-known computer graphics programs that make mathematical descriptions of shapes like circles, rectangles, polygons, and even freeform shapes. By contrast, when you work in the Paint window, you're putting "digital" paint on a digital easel and creating bitmaps made up of individual pixels.

When you use a program like ClarisDraw or CorelDRAW, you're drawing, not painting. And as much as I hate to admit it, when you use one of Director's tools from the Tool palette, you're really drawing, too, not painting. I feel so ashamed that I didn't bring this up earlier . . . well, not that ashamed.

Anyway, what's the difference between painting and drawing? Read on, my friend.

Painting in Director

In a painting environment, to use the big kids' lingo (no pun intended), you add digital paint to the page pixel by pixel as you push the Brush or Pencil tool around. Another way of saying this is that you turn on individual pixels on the page that look like a recognizable image from a normal viewing distance. This collection of pixels may look like a circle, an apple, or even text if you use the Paint window's Text tool. But the circle, apple, and text images are all an illusion, smoke and mirrors, nothing but individual pixels glowing on your computer screen that happen to look like a circle, apple, and text. I know, another illusion shattered forever.

Drawing in Director

Imagine that you're drawing in ClarisDraw or CorelDRAW or, better yet, using one of the Tool palette tools in Director 6. Whether you realize it or not, you're creating a description of an object rather than painting with pixels. Your computer accepts the result as an *object,* or whole entity, not just a collection of pixels that look like something due to a trick of the eye. When you draw an oval with the Circle tool from the Tool palette, you get a real oval; you can click anywhere inside the oval and drag the circle around the Stage. Try this on long, rainy weekends; time just flies by.

Watch My Lips: T-h-e-s-e A-r-e D-r-a-w-i-n-g T-o-o-l-s

What makes the Tool palette tools unique is that they draw shapes or objects, very different from the bitmap-making tools in the Paint window. If the word *object* made you utter, "Huh?" don't worry. In the section coming up, I give you a painless idea of what drawing objects, or what Director calls shapes, is all about.

Drawing on the Stage

Functionally, one of the biggest differences between Paint window tools in the Tool palette and those in the Paint window is that you can draw directly on the Stage with a Tool palette tool. Several events occur, actually, when you draw on the Stage with a Tool palette tool. To better understand what happens, set up your screen as follows:

1. From the Window menu, choose the Tools, Cast, and Score windows.

2. Drag the Resize box, located in the lower-right corner of the Cast window, to make the window about two inches square, and then click the appropriate scroll bars so that an empty cast member cell is visible in the window.

3. Drag the Score's Resize box, located in the lower-right corner of the Score window, toward the center of the window to make the Score window as small as possible.

4. Click inside the first empty cell in the Score window.

5. Click one of the filled tools in the second row of the Tool palette.

6. From the upper-right region of the Stage, drag the tool diagonally down and to the right about $1^1/_2$ inches, and then release the mouse button.

   The Stage is the one window you never have to select. It's always there, like happy, smiley-face sunbeams in California. And, oh yes, like death and taxes.

Notice what happens the nanosecond you release the mouse button: Several events occur instantaneously. In fact, if you have an atomic clock handy, it's great fun timing the following as a family project:

> ✔ A rectangular shape appears selected on the Stage, with small black squares called *handles* at the corners and midpoints of the selection.

> ✔ Director automatically adds the shape you just drew as a new Shape Cast Member to the Cast window.

> ✔ Director automatically adds the shape to the first free channel in the Score window.

And you thought Director was just another pretty face.

Modifying a Shape Cast Member

As for the type of shape, the shape you just drew directly on the Stage (see the previous section, "Drawing on the Stage") is dramatically different from any graphic you may have created in the Paint window. Well, don't act so smug about it.

For example, when you double-click a Bitmap Cast Member on the Stage, Director takes you to the Paint window, where you can edit the graphic, pixel by pixel.

The Shape Cast Member Properties dialog box

Don't expect Director to take you by the hand and lead you to the Paint window when you double-click a Tool palette shape. So, what happens when you do? Double-clicking a shape takes you to the Shape Cast Member Properties dialog box, as shown in Figure 10-1.

Figure 10-1:
The Shape Cast Member Properties dialog box for a shape drawn with a Shape tool.

You can easily recognize a Shape Cast Member in the Cast by the media type icon in the lower-right corner of its cell — like a shape on the Stage, with handles yet.

You can't edit shapes pixel by pixel, but the Shape Cast Member Properties dialog box allows you to modify the graphic in a number of significant ways, including:

- 🖊 Giving the shape a unique and meaningful identity by entering a name in the Name entry field at the top of the window
- 🖊 Changing the graphic's shape by choosing a basic shape in the Shape pop-up menu under the cast member name
- 🖊 Changing the graphic to an unfilled shape by unchecking the Filled check box

The Shape pop-up menu

Take a look at the Shape pop-up menu, shown in Figure 10-2, featuring four Shape options based on the dimensions of the currently selected shape. You can use the Shape pop-up menu to quickly transform the shape of a previously drawn shape.

Figure 10-2:
The Shape
pop-up
menu.

Shape options in the Shape pop-up menu include the following:

✔ **Rectangle:** A rectangular shape with 90-degree corners

✔ **Round Rect:** A shape with rounded corners

✔ **Oval:** An oval shape

✔ **Line:** A straight line whose angle reflects the start and stop points of the original shape that you dragged out with a Tool palette tool

Shape resizing handles

Another way of modifying a shape is to resize it by dragging one of its selection handles, as shown in Figure 10-3.

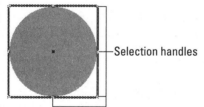

Figure 10-3:
The
selection
handles of a
shape on
the Stage.

Ah, some of you wide-awake types remember that selected bitmap sprites display selection handles, too, and that you can resize them by dragging a handle. However, an advantage of shape sprites is that you can resize them without jaggies, those infamous stairstepped edges that you get with enlarged bitmaps.

When you want to increase the size of a shape, press one of the shape's handles and drag it away from the center of the shape. You should see something like the result pictured in Figure 10-4. If you want to maintain proportions, hold down the Shift key until after you begin dragging a selection handle.

The selection marquee and handles disappear and a ghost outline of the sprite grows in size as you continue dragging the mouse. After you release the mouse button, the result is an enlarged shape (see Figure 10-5).

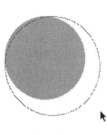

Figure 10-4:
Proportionally
scaling a
shape on
the Stage
by pressing
Shift and
dragging
one of its
handles.

Figure 10-5:
An
enlarged
shape on
the Stage.

Compare the shape in Figure 10-5 with the bitmap sprite in Figure 10-6, which has been scaled up to similar dimensions. Note the classic and, may I add, ugly stairstepping effect called the *jaggies* that results whenever you try enlarging bitmaps in Director (or any other paint program).

Another important difference between shapes and bitmaps is that shapes are objects, self-contained entities that aren't just an assemblage of pixels. Bitmaps look like self-contained shapes; they're really nothing more than a block of pixels that trick the eye into looking like something from a normal viewing distance.

Be careful not to get confused about the difference between bitmaps and shapes when adding cast members to the Stage. A bitmap on the Stage takes on some shape-like characteristics. You can click anywhere on a bitmap on the Stage and select the whole bitmap, and, after it's selected, the bitmap displays handles just like its shape-type cohorts.

Director designed things this way so that we multimedia types can work with bitmaps more easily on the Stage. But double-click that bitmap, get it into the Paint window, and its bitmap heritage comes blazing through. Zoom in and whammo. Pixels! Nasty, slimy, individual pixels that give the whole show away.

Figure 10-6:
The infamous "jaggies" raise their ugly head when you enlarge a bitmap.

Checking out the Tool palette tools

Several tools in the Tool palette, shown in Figure 10-7, look similar to tools that you find in the Paint window. Read ahead to discover more tools unique to the Tool palette.

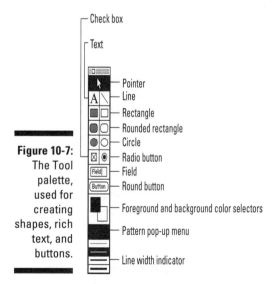

Figure 10-7:
The Tool palette, used for creating shapes, rich text, and buttons.

Misfit tools

The first tools you meet in the Tool palette are the set of tools at the top. Call them misfit tools. From top to bottom, left to right, they include the following:

- **Pointer tool:** The classic mouse pointer moves — interestingly enough — both shapes and bitmaps on the Stage.

- **Text tool:** Click anywhere on the Stage with the Text tool and type rich text, whose unique features include tabs and full-paragraph formatting. The resulting text is the same kind of text you type in a Text window and then drag to the Stage. The text adopts the current background color in the Tool palette; the text itself reflects the current foreground color. You can read all about rich text in Chapter 9.

- **Line tool:** Draws straight lines at any angle directly on the Stage; remember to Shift+drag to draw a horizontal, vertical, or 45-degree angle line. The line adopts the current foreground color and the line width displayed in the Tool palette. While the line is selected, you can change the graphic's color with the Foreground color selector and the line width with the Line width indicator. Notice that line width options in the Tool palette are very limited compared to sizes available for bitmaps in the Paint window. You win some; you lose some. *C'est la vie.*

Shape tools

The second set of tools in the Tool palette are the Shape tools with split personalities — filled on the left, hollow on the right. Come to think of it, I have a couple of friends who fit that same description. Anyway, the Shape tools include

- **Rectangle tool:** Allows you to draw a rectangle bordered in the current foreground color or a rectangle filled with the current foreground color. Remember to Shift+drag to draw a perfect square shape.

- **Rounded rectangle tool:** Allows you to draw a rounded rectangle bordered in the current foreground color or filled with the current foreground color. Remember to Shift+drag to draw a perfect rounded square shape.

- **Circle tool:** Allows you to draw an oval shape bordered in the current foreground color using an oval filled with the current foreground color. Remember to Shift+drag to draw a perfect circle shape. And to eat plenty of leafy green vegetables each and every day.

When you double-click a shape created with one of the Shape tools, Director takes you to the Shape Cast Member Properties dialog box. From there, you can change the shape with the Shape pop-up menu. For more info, see "The Shape pop-up menu," earlier in this chapter.

Button-making tools

The next set of tools comprises Director's button-making tools. From top to bottom, left to right, they include the following:

✔ **Check box button tool:** Creates a check box-style button, as shown in Figure 10-8.

During playback, the user may check one or more check boxes, initiating a script inside each checked button that you write in Lingo or add with one of Director's new behaviors. Use check boxes, for example, to enable users to change the font, size, and weight of a screen title. For more on Lingo, see Chapter 14. Read all about behaviors in Chapter 15.

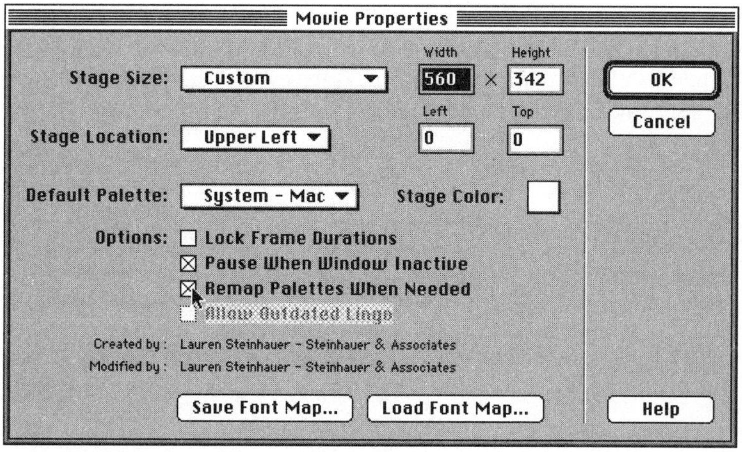

Figure 10-8: Check boxes in the Movie Properties dialog box for options that are not mutually exclusive.

✔ **Radio/Option button tool:** Creates a radio/option button. Figure 10-9 shows radio/option buttons used in the Export dialog box to give you some choices when exporting a Director movie as a QuickTime mooV. Use radio/option buttons to present a group of options that are mutually exclusive.

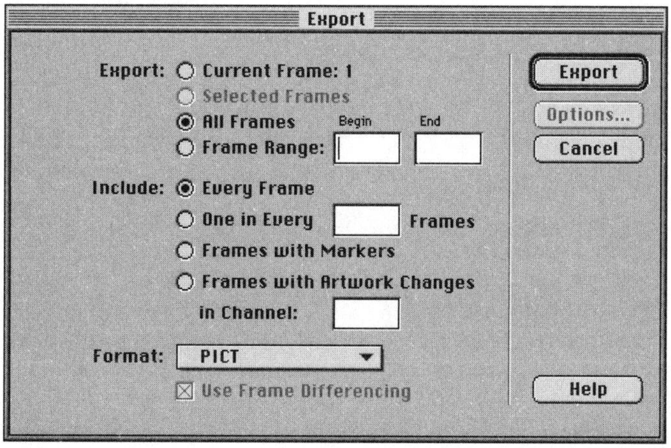

Figure 10-9: Select radio/option buttons in the Export dialog box for options that are mutually exclusive.

During playback, the user may check one of the radio/option buttons from a set, initiating an associated script. You — who else? — are responsible for writing the script that both initiates the desired action and unchecks any other radio/option buttons in the group. For more info on writing scripts in buttons, jump to Chapter 14.

✔ **Field tool:** Select to add text in a field to the Stage. For more on text in a field, jump back to Chapter 9.

✔ **Round button tool:** Your plain-vanilla Round button tool creates a rounded button, as shown in Figure 10-10, that you can name.

During playback, the user activates an associated script or behavior after clicking a round button. Guess who gets stuck writing the script or adding the behavior?

Figure 10-10:
OK, Script, Cancel, and Help buttons are like push buttons you can add with the Round button tool.

```
                 Text Cast Member Properties
  ┌──────────┐  ┌────────────────────────────┐  ┌──────────┐
  │To be or not│  │Soliloquy                  │  │    OK    │
  │to be. That │  │                           │  └──────────┘
  │is the      │   Framing:  [ Adjust to Fit ▼]  ┌──────────┐
  │question.   │                                 │ Script... │
  │Whether ' A │   Anti-Alias: ○ All Text        └──────────┘
  │            │              ◉ Larger Than [12] points  ┌──────────┐
  │3:Soliloquy │              ○ None                       │  Cancel  │
  │Internal    │                                           └──────────┘
  │            │   Unload:  [ 3 - Normal ▼]   ┌──────────┐
  │Size: 6.6 K │                              │   Help   │
  └──────────┘                                └──────────┘
```

You can easily change the button style of a Button Cast Member. Double-click the button to go to its Button Cast Member Properties dialog box, where you can select a different style of button from the Style pop-up menu.

When double-clicking a button to go to its Button Cast Member Properties dialog box, be sure to double-click within the selected button's bold, gray selection border. Otherwise, you'll place only an insertion point in the field area of the button or select part or all of the button name. Very frustrating.

If you can't wait to play with making buttons and adding secret messages in them, what we multimedia types call *Lingo scripting,* peruse Chapter 14. For more on when to use check boxes and radio/option buttons, see the sidebar, "Round versus square: the politics of selection buttons," following this commercial announcement.

Round versus square: the politics of selection buttons

In graphical user interfaces like the Mac OS (Macintosh Operating System) and Microsoft Windows, you find two distinctive styles of buttons for making choices.

Mac radio buttons and Windows option buttons look like this:

> ◉ Use Movie Settings
> ○ Match Current Movie

When you face a set of options where you may choose only one option to the exclusion of the others — whew, maybe I should have been a lawyer — a well-designed program presents you with a set of radio/option buttons. For example, the Stage Size panel in the General Preferences dialog box gives you one of two choices: Use Movie Settings or Match Current Movie. Logically, only one option can prevail. When you click your option of choice, its radio/option button adopts the "bull's-eye" style to indicate its standing in the community of selection buttons.

On Macs and PCs, check boxes look like this:

> ⊠ Center
> ⊠ Reset Monitor to Movie's Color Depth
> ⊠ Animate in Background

Check boxes offer you a set of options from which you may pick and choose willy-nilly; these options aren't mutually exclusive. Checked check boxes stand for selected options. Back to the General Preferences dialog box, you can check the Center option. And Reset Monitor to Movie's Color Depth. And Animate in Background. Or if you're anal-retentive, none of the above.

A selected check box isn't really checked. It's "Xed." I think of something checked looking like, well, a check. Anyway, I don't know of anyone who goes around saying, "I Xed the check box." Maybe it sounds too much like a naughty word. But if you want to instantly establish yourself as a free thinker and all-around character, here's your golden opportunity.

More Tool palette stuff

The bottom of the Tool palette includes the following areas:

- ✔ **Foreground color selector:** Allows you to select the current foreground color from the current palette of colors when you press the selector area

- ✔ **Background color selector:** Allows you to select the current background color from the current palette of colors when you press the selector area

- ✔ **Pattern pop-up menu:** Allows you to select the current pattern from a set of patterns when you press the pop-up menu area

- ✔ **Line Width indicator:** Allows you to set the line to invisible or to one of three different widths by clicking the desired option

The Meaning of Life

Oh, yeah, the meaning of life. Who knows?

Why You Should Care about This Palette

Why should you care about the Tool palette? Because it's there. And because its features are very useful. I've listed a number of reasons why — not necessarily ten reasons, so no drum roll please:

1. You can paint — excuse me — draw directly on the Stage.

2. You can type directly on the Stage.

3. You can search and replace text typed with the Text tool while developing your movie.

4. You can easily edit text typed with the Text tool while developing your movie.

5. You can instantly change the shape of a shape, manually or by using Lingo commands, to create magical transformations during playback.

6. You can instantly change the color of a shape, manually or by using Lingo commands, to create magical color changes during playback.

7. Field text prints at high resolution, making it the text of choice for printing out storyboards for client approval or for reports generated by a multimedia product that you've produced with Director.

8. Lingo scripts can recognize, modify, or manipulate text typed with the Text tool.

9. You can reduce or enlarge a shape right on the Stage without getting the infamous stairstepping effect known as the jaggies.

10. Shapes and text take up less memory than bitmapped equivalents.

Well, what do you know? Ten reasons! Okay, I'll take that drum roll after all. *Yes!*

Chapter 11

Getting to Those Scrumptious Palettes: The Color Palettes Window

● ●

In This Chapter

▶ Creating a custom palette

▶ Working with the Color Palettes window

▶ Using the Apple Color Picker

▶ Discovering the mysteries of 65535

● ●

*T*hroughout this book, I talk about sets of colors called palettes that you use to develop movies with Director. Surprise — palettes have their very own window. And some clever devil at Macromedia named it, of all things, the Color Palettes window.

Decisions, Decisions, Decisions

To see your very own Color Palettes window, choose Window⇨Color Palettes, and like magic, the Color Palettes window appears, bearing an uncanny resemblance to Figure 11-1. (Remember, this figure is only an artist's representation, not the real thing.)

When Director first brings up this window, it's tiny. Real tiny. Click the Zoom box in the upper-right corner of the window to fill the screen with the Color Palettes window. Simply click the Zoom box again to return the window to its original size.

Okay, so the Color Palettes window isn't quite as imposing as, say, the Score window, but it's very important in its own little way. You'll find the Color Palette pretty useful after you learn about its various features.

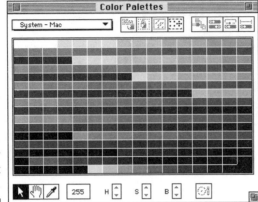

Figure 11-1:
The Color
Palettes
window,
where you
can choose
from built-in
and custom
palettes for
the current
movie.

The Palette pop-up menu

When you click the box near the upper-left corner of the Color Palettes window, a menu pops up, as in Figure 11-2, revealing ten built-in palettes and any custom palettes belonging to the current movie. Custom palettes are either imported with a bitmap or palettes you create yourself within Director.

Director's built-in palettes

Here's a look at the ten built-in palettes listed in the Palette pop-up menu shown in Figure 11-2:

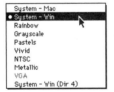

Figure 11-2:
The Palette
pop-up
menu.

✔ **System – Mac:** This is the Mac's default palette, which is the palette the Mac chooses right out of the box while it's still warm. Your desktop and most program interfaces are based on this palette of 256 standardized colors. Most of the PICTs that you import into Director display these same 256 colors.

✔ **System – Win:** A collection of 256 colors intended to translate well when porting bitmaps between a Mac and a PC.

✔ **Rainbow:** A bright collection of 256 colors meant to flower forth images of doves, angels, and big, fluffy clouds shimmering before your galvanized eyes. Great for kiddie games.

✔ **Grayscale:** Sometimes nothing's better than a beautiful set of colorless values, from pure white through incremental shades of gray to deepest velvet black. That's when you choose the good old Grayscale palette for photographic-quality black-and-white images in your movie.

✔ **Pastels:** A collection of 256 colors inspired, no doubt, by watching too many Barney adventures. A plethora of soft, snugly, coochie-coo colors for designing disposable undie packaging.

✔ **Vivid:** Whoever designed this set of colors needs to cut way down on the coffee. These are 256 very bright colors. The word vivid actually pales in comparison to the Vivid palette of colors.

✔ **NTSC:** A special collection of colors meant to translate well when copying (or printing to video, as multimedia types are apt to say) your Director movie.

✔ **Metallic:** An interesting collection of colors that definitely brings to mind thoughts of rusting tin cans, Robbie the Robot (oops, I'm dating myself), and auto derbies. Not for everyone, but that's what makes life a confusing mess. (Just kidding.)

✔ **VGA:** Grayed out in Figure 11-2, this set of VGA (Video Graphics Array) colors is available only when a VGA monitor is running off your computer.

✔ **System – Win (Dir 4):** A collection of 256 colors for movies that started out in life as Director 4 files. Director 4 handled colors differently enough under Windows that if you switched a Director 4 movie to Director 6's standard System – Win palette, you would notice a distinct and probably unpleasant color shift. By the way, you need to update a Director 4 movie to version 5 before opening it up in Director 6. It just goes to show you, never throw away anything.

Custom palettes

Look at the very bottom of the Palette pop-up menu, just below the gray rule demarcating the built-in palettes from the custom palettes. You see the line 6:Palette 6 Internal, a reference to a custom palette that tagged along with a bitmap I imported into Director when you weren't looking.

When an 8-bit (256-color) bitmap is built on a set of colors other than the System palette, the bitmap carries custom color info in a secret place within its own file. To import a bitmap that has a custom palette, follow these steps:

Free to be NTSC

Novice multimedia types are often alarmed at how dramatically colors change after video-taping their work and playing it back on a real TV. NTSC is a set of standards for TV broad-casting that was adopted, while the crust of the earth was still cooling, by a stodgy group of frustrated, old media moguls called the National Television Standards Committee. Back in the dark ages (1953), there were a number of ways to transmit and receive color television, but some people thought that there needed to be some basic specifications, lest chaos prevail.

Until contemporary debate over standards for high definition and wide-screen television, NTSC standards dictated the quality of color images broadcast to the huddled masses yearning for cable to be free. The NTSC stan-dards include a limited range of colors, bring-ing you back to the NTSC palette, a collection of 256 NTSC-legal, or safe, colors. None of these colors is so bright as to bloom, or fluo-resce, beyond an image's outline on the TV screen, and none is far enough removed from NTSC's gamut, or color range, that it could transform into an unexpected color.

1. **Choose File⇨Import.**

2. **Select the desired bitmap from the Directory dialog box, and click Import.**

   Director displays the Image Options dialog box — the showoff that Director is — boasting that it knows you're trying to sneak in a bitmap with special colors. In this dialog box, re-created in Figure 11-3, Director asks you to decide on a few options.

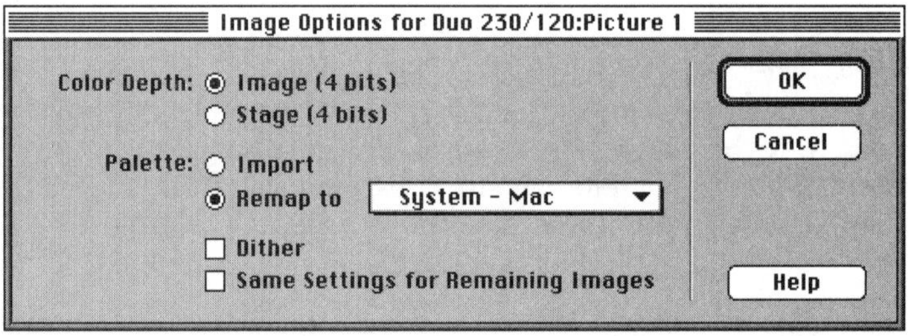

Figure 11-3:
The Image Options dialog box that appears after you import a bitmap.

Image Options for Duo 230/120:Picture 1

Color Depth: ⦿ Image (4 bits)
○ Stage (4 bits)

Palette: ○ Import
⦿ Remap to [System - Mac ▼]

☐ Dither
☐ Same Settings for Remaining Images

[OK]
[Cancel]
[Help]

3. **For Color Depth, you have a choice between Image and Stage:**

   • **Image:** Click this radio/option button to retain the original color depth of the bitmap.

- **Stage:** Click this radio/option button to change the bitmap's color depth to the current color depth on the Stage.

  Choose the Image option to import a bitmap in its original color depth.

4. **For Palette, you have the honor of choosing between Import or Remap to:**

   - **Import:** Click to import a bitmap's palette as a Palette Cast Member, especially important for a bitmap with an adaptive palette.

   - **Remap to:** Click to remap the imported bitmap to a new palette you select from the Palette pop-up menu in the dialog box.

     Choose the Import option to import a bitmap's custom palette as an additional cast member.

5. **The Image Options dialog box gives you two fun check boxes to choose from — Dither and Same Settings for Remaining Images:**

   - **Dither:** Check to apply a dithering routine to the imported bitmap. The dithering routine increases the apparent number of visible colors, similar to the idea of using four-process colors in printing to create the impression of full-color graphics and photographs.

     If you're importing a bitmap with a custom palette, leave Dither unchecked. Applying a dithering routine to the custom palette would likely change the quality of the custom colors.

   - **Same Settings for Remaining Images:** Click to apply the same selection of options to remaining bitmaps listed in the Import Files dialog box.

6. **Click OK.**

Color Palettes window tools

In the upper right of the Color Palettes window (refer to Figure 11-1) is a row of special tools, including:

 ✔ **Reserve Selected Colors:** Protects colors that you select in the Color Palettes window. Shift-select a block of colors or ⌘/Ctrl-select noncontiguous colors. (By the way, you can combine these selection techniques in one selection.) Use this command to reserve a set of colors for special effects like color cycling (an easy method of creating animation that I discuss in Chapter 20). For example, if you animate a bitmap of a roaring fireplace with color cycling, you don't want the color blend created for the fire effect to appear in other bitmaps. Choose Reserve Selected Colors to avoid using these colors in anything but the fire sequence.

✔ **Select Reserved Colors:** Selects all colors in the current palette designated as reserved colors. Use this option to take the next step to "cancel your reservation" by clicking Reserve Colors and clicking the No Colors radio/option button in the resulting dialog box.

 ✔ **Select Used Colors:** Tallies up the colors in the bitmap displayed in the Paint window and automatically selects them in the Color Palettes window. This option is grayed out in Figure 11-1 and probably on your screen because it is dependent on three conditions: The command must have a bitmap in the Paint window (whether or not the Paint window itself is visible); the Color Palettes window must be visible; and the Color Palettes window must be the active window.

 ✔ **Invert Selection:** Selects the unselected colors and deselects the selected colors in the Color Palettes window. On long, rainy weekends, I pass the time very quickly by selecting and inverting colors over and over again; in no time, it's Monday morning. Pathetic, isn't it?

 ✔ **Sort:** Displays the Sort Colors dialog box, where you decide how to sort the selection of colors by clicking one of three radio/option buttons: Hue (by red, for example, rather than blue or green), Saturation (by intensity or purity of color), or Brightness (by lightness or darkness of color).

 ✔ **Reverse Sequence:** Reverses the order of a contiguous block of selected colors. Try Reverse Color Order on the gradation of grays in the System palette at the tail end of the colors. Your computer won't allow you to move or modify black (index number 255) or white (index number 0). The moment you reverse colors in one of the default palettes, Director forces you to the Create Palette dialog box. The big bully.

 ✔ **Cycle:** Shifts a contiguous block of selected colors one color over with each issue of this command. Cycle reproduces what happens to a block of selected colors in color-cycling animation, only more slowly. If you're having trouble picturing what happens, think of a selection of colors as a rosary of color, each color a bead in the chain. Each time you choose Rotate Colors, you shift the rosary by one bead; that covers all the Catholics out there. Now, there are these worry beads. . . .

 ✔ **Blend:** Creates a blend of colors between the beginning and ending colors of a contiguous block of selected colors. If you look back at the System palette, notice that it lacks a contiguous block of smoothly graduated colors; the key to creating effective color cycling animation is to create a custom palette with a wide range of blended colors. You can select the block of colors either by dragging through colors or by clicking a beginning color and then Shift-clicking the ending color with the Arrow or Hand tool.

What do you know? You've got a bottom row of tools, too. Life is good.

✔ **Arrow tool:** Your basic mouse pointing and selection tool. Click in the Color Palettes window with the Arrow tool to make a single selection. Drag the Arrow tool through a block of colors in a palette or Shift-click a range of colors to make a contiguous selection. ⌘/Ctrl-click colors to make a noncontiguous selection.

 ✔ **Hand tool:** Use the Hand tool to move a selection in the Color Palettes window. Drag a selection with the Hand tool to another area of the palette. As it passes over colors, the Hand tool highlights the color directly beneath its pointing finger, which is where the first color in the selection lands when you release the Hand tool. After you move colors in one of Director's ten default palettes, Director presents the Create Palette dialog box. If you move a noncontiguous selection, Director deposits the selection as a contiguous block of colors when you release the Hand tool.

 ✔ **Eyedropper tool:** Common to many high-powered paint programs, including xRes and Photoshop, the Eyedropper tool allows you to sample a color anywhere on the Stage. Sampling means that you can record a color's percentage of red, green, and blue light that makes up all colors on an RGB monitor. Suppose you're working with the System – Win palette and you have an image of a bright sun on the Stage; you click the brightest area with the Eyedropper tool, and the fifth color from the top-left of the color chip selector area becomes highlighted. The number to the right of the Eyedropper tool changes to 5 to display the color's index number. For more information about indexed color, see "Color and index numbers" in this chapter.

 ✔ **Index Color number:** Gives the index number of the currently selected color that represents its position in the CLUT (Color Lookup Table) currently in use. A CLUT is another way of referring to colors when you're running your monitor in 8-bit color mode, giving you 256 colors from index number 0 to 255. Index number 0 is always white and index number 255 is always black in Mac and Windows CLUTs.

✔ **H-S-B (Hue, Saturation, Brightness) controls:** Modify the selected color in the H-S-B color model. If the current palette is the System palette, the nanosecond you begin clicking one of these controls, Director takes you to the Create Palette dialog box, where clicking OK automatically creates a new custom palette.

 ✔ **Color Picker:** Takes you to the so-called color wheel, where you can run wild, making up your own colors.

Color and index numbers

Most of the Color Palettes window is taken up by the set of colors making up a particular palette. (Yes, I'm still referring to Figure 11-1.)

Have you noticed something striking? (No, running out of beer doesn't count.) White is always the first color in the upper-left corner of the palette, and black is the last. In other words, white is always index number 0, and black is always index number 255. Always and forever. You can bet your life on it — just don't bet mine. You never know when some computer maker is going to slip up and put black in the center or something.

Anyway, this black-and-white thing applies to all Director's default and custom palettes. That's right, your computer doesn't allow you to move or modify white or black, regardless of how weird the other colors in your custom palette happen to look.

In the System – Mac, System – Win, and System – Win (Dir 4) palettes, things get even more draconian. Each color is always the same color in its respective position and always has the same index number for identification. Of course, this boring predictability is the whole point of a System palette. The only problem is that Real Life and even the world of the imagination don't always fit so neatly into this predefined handful of colors.

Custom palettes

If you ever need colors that aren't in one of Director's default palettes, you can create a custom palette by following these steps:

1. **Choose Window⊳Color Palettes.**

2. **Click the Zoom box in the upper-right corner to fill the screen with the Color Palettes window.**

3. **Choose System – Mac from the Palette pop-up menu if you're using a Mac; choose System – Win if you're on a PC.**

   One exception occurs if you're working with a Windows Director movie that was originally created with Director 4. To match its colors in Director 6, choose the System – Win (Dir 4) palette.

4. **Double-click a color you can live without.**

   On a Mac, the Apple Color Picker, shown in Figure 11-4, appears. On a PC, Windows' Custom Color Selector, shown in Figure 11-5, appears.

   In the Apple Color Picker, notice that the color you double-click shows up in the large color sample under Define a new color, is marked in the color wheel itself with a small circle, and is displayed broken down into its components in H-S-B (hue, saturation, brightness) and RGB (red, green, blue) values. In Windows' Custom Color Selector, the selected color appears in the Color|Solid panel, is marked in the large color space with a crosshair-like icon, and is shown broken down into its components in H-S-L (hue, saturation, luminance) and RGB values.

Figure 11-4:
On a Mac,
double-
clicking a
color in the
Color
Palettes
window
opens the
Apple Color
Picker.

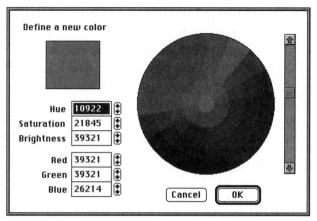

Figure 11-5:
On a PC,
double-
clicking a
color in the
Color
Palettes
window
opens
Windows'
Custom
Color
Selector.

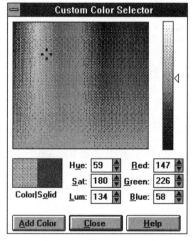

Both windows display two main color models or spaces used in the multimedia industry: H-S-B or H-S-L (essentially identical models) and RGB. (Just in case you're interested, nearly all computer monitors use RGB color to create the images on your screen.)

Few people think of colors as numbers like the ones in Figures 11-4 and 11-5, but numbers add a certain precision to the whole business of defining a color. For example, I might think of a special color, a kind of British racing green that's very difficult to describe accurately. Instead of trying to put the color into words, I can pass on the color's components in one of the color models so that it reproduces fairly accurately on your monitor.

5. Enter new RGB or H-S-B (H-S-L) values.

If that great Austin Healy green sounds appealing to you, try the following RGB values in Apple's Color Picker: 8963 for Red, 14928 for Green, and 20129 for Blue. For you PC types, try the following RGB percentages: 86 for Red, 72 for Green, and 69 for Blue.

6. Click OK.

As soon as you click OK, Director knows that you made changes to a default palette, and it displays the Create Palette dialog box, shown in Figure 11-6, where you can christen your own custom palette with a meaningful name. Or a silly name.

Figure 11-6:
After you make a change to a palette, the Create Palette dialog box appears.

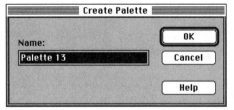

7. Enter a name for the new palette in the dialog box and click OK.

With a click of the mouse, you add a custom palette to the list under the Color Palettes window and a Palette Cast Member to the Cast window.

Hot flashes

I'll bet my mother's hot water bottle that you see an iridescent flash when switching palettes. It's not one of Director's most fetching traits. To avoid the flash, try adding a transition to the Transition channel in the same frame in which you place the custom palette. The Transition palette is just underneath the Palette channel in the Score window. The Frame Properties: Transition dialog box appears, as shown in Figure 11-7.

Switching palettes in your movie

I can think of at least three reasons why you may want to switch palettes in a movie; there are probably 5,895 other reasons, give or take.

Figure 11-7:
The Frame
Properties
Transition
dialog box,
where you
can choose
from a wide
range of
transition
effects.

Adaptive palettes

The Big Number One reason is due to the limitations of the default System –
Win and System – Mac palettes. Their 256 colors just don't do justice to
photographs, for example, displaying millions of colors, scanned into your
computer and then reduced to 256 paltry colors. Often, the result resembles
a graphic technique called *posterization,* in which light and shade variations
are reduced to a few solid blocks of color. Sometimes, you may actually want
this effect. It can be very dramatic, graphic, and artful. But not if you're
aiming for realism and photographic quality.

That's when you go into Photoshop, open the scanned photo, and choose
Indexed Color from the Mode menu. A dialog box appears, giving you a
number of choices for reducing colors to a limp 256. But one special choice,
called the *Adaptive method,* creates a custom palette that optimizes results.
Amazingly, the altered bitmap with a 256-color adaptive palette often looks
almost as good as the original photo. Director tries to do the same thing
with imported bitmaps. After you click Import in the Import Files dialog box,
the Image Options dialog box appears with Remap and Dither options that
approximate what Photoshop can accomplish, although not as well.

Wonderful as Director may be, Photoshop's the expert at remapping
bitmaps. So if you go the Photoshop route, be sure to click the Import radio/
option button in the Image Options dialog box. The imported bitmap and its
palette become new cast members in the Cast window.

Better performance through plastics, er, 8-bit graphics

Why would you want to reduce all those beautiful 16 million colors to 256
colors? Well, that's reason number two for making a custom palette. 24-bit
graphics are gigantic; they slurp up room on your hard drive and stretch
your poor machine's computing power above and beyond its limit. Unless

you can count on developing and running your movie on the latest, greatest computing dynamos Apple and IBM have to offer with umpteen gigabytes of storage and a terabyte or two of memory chips, the most common solution is to drop colors. Either go with the System palette's interpretation of your image or let Director handle it with the Remap option. Or you can try Photoshop's adaptive palette method.

Color cycling

By the way, the third reason I can think of for creating a custom palette is color cycling. If you're downright antsy to find out more, jump to Chapter 20. Just keep in mind that the color cycling palette is a limited palette, and you may want to swap back to your regular palette after color cycling is finished. Be sure to add your regular palette to the Palette channel in the Score at the appropriate frame.

When you place a bitmap with a custom palette on the Stage or in the Score, Director automatically adds its palette to the Palette channel in the Score window. Until you change palettes again, Director continues to use the custom palette, which may or may not be what you want. If not, add your regular palette, probably the Mac or Windows System palette, to the Palette channel at the appropriate frame.

Only a few transitions really overcome the flashing that occurs when switching palettes. I've used the Dissolve, Pixels Fast transition set to Changing Area with great success. How did I find the transition that works the best? Trial and error. To save you the pain, I experimented and experimented, night and day, day and night. And to what end? To end up a shell of a man with a good transition. Aargh.

Achieving that classic look

Another technique that helps when you plan to switch Palettes is to choose File➪ Preferences➪General and check Classic Look (Monochrome), as shown in Figure 11-8.

Choosing Classic Look helps Director's performance because the interface becomes black and white and doesn't need to be updated every time you switch palettes. It uses less memory, and many developers find the black-and-white interface less distracting, too.

Babbling on about DeBabelizer

There's dithering, and then there's *dithering*. Great as Director may be, Photoshop and other high-end paint programs offer dithering routines that produce superior results. A fascinating, peculiar, irritating, and necessary program called DeBabelizer from Equilibrium — Windows and Mac OS demo versions of which you'll find on the CD that came with this book (you're welcome) — does a particularly excellent job of dithering bitmaps for the Macintosh and Windows platforms.

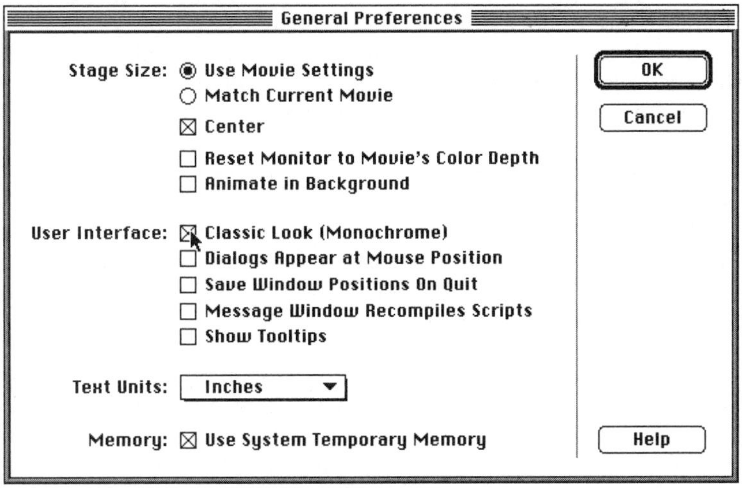

Figure 11-8:
Check
Classic
Look in the
General
Preferences
dialog box
to prevent
Director
from having
to update
the
interface
with every
Palette
change.

General Preferences

Stage Size: ⦿ Use Movie Settings
○ Match Current Movie
☒ Center
☐ Reset Monitor to Movie's Color Depth
☐ Animate in Background

User Interface: ☒ Classic Look (Monochrome)
☐ Dialogs Appear at Mouse Position
☐ Save Window Positions On Quit
☐ Message Window Recompiles Scripts
☐ Show Tooltips

Text Units: [Inches ▼]

Memory: ☒ Use System Temporary Memory

[OK]
[Cancel]
[Help]

Figure 11-8:
Check Classic Look in the General Preferences dialog box to prevent Director from having to update the interface with every Palette change.

DeBabelizer solves one of the most irksome enigmas that comes up when using two or more palettes in a Director movie. How can images common to Director sequences with different palettes appear at the same time on the Stage? DeBabelizer can analyze a wide range of color requirements in different images and create what it calls a *Super Palette* that is usually a terrific compromise palette for all the images. This is the palette you want to import as a cast member along with the special bitmaps themselves. As you're saving the bitmaps in DeBabelizer, be sure to save the files in PICT2 with CLUT file format from the pop-up menu in DeBabelizer's Save As dialog box.

The Old H-S-B Thing Again

In the "Custom Palettes" section, earlier in this chapter, I take you on a tour of the Apple Color Picker and the Windows Custom Color Selector to create a custom palette. During the tour, you discover that on-screen colors are described with two different color models, or systems: H-S-B (H-S-L) and RGB.

Hue, saturation, and brightness

H-S-B stands for hue, saturation, and brightness — not an old vaudevillian team that worked with seals — one of the major color models that multimedia types use to develop products. Take another look at the Apple Color Picker in Figure 11-4 or the Windows Custom Color Selector in Figure 11-5 and see how the H-S-B (H-S-L) model relates to colors in its color space.

In the H-S-B color system, *Hue* refers to pure color. Picture a distinctive color in your mind; that's a hue. As a color changes hue in the Apple Color Picker, it moves around the circumference of the color wheel. In the Windows Custom Color Selector, the crosshair-like icon in the rectangular color space moves horizontally through its landscape.

Saturation refers to intensity of hue. How red is a particular red? A washed-out or pastel red is less saturated than pure red, candy red, or apple red. In the Apple Color Picker, as a hue becomes less saturated, it moves closer to the white center of the color wheel. In the Windows Custom Color Selector, pure hues are at the top; as a hue becomes less saturated, it moves closer to the bottom of the color space.

Think of *Brightness* as the amount of light shining on a hue. When you turn off lights in a room at night, all hues go black, even yellow. When you set Brightness to 0 in the Apple Color Picker dialog box, you're turning off all the lights. The Apple Color Picker visualizes this scenario with the "eleva-tor" in the scroll bar sliding to the bottom. The Windows Custom Color Selector features a similar scroll bar to visualize the brightness level of a color.

Additive and subtractive primary colors

Remember school? You learned that the primary colors are red, yellow, and blue. Close, but no turkey. Actually, you need to work with two different sets of primary color schemes when playing with color. Additive primaries — red, blue, and green — are for working with pure (or incident) light, such as the light that your monitor uses. That's why monitors generally use red, green, and blue (RGB) light. Mix all three colors at the highest saturation and brightness levels and what do you get? White light. If you're a fan of the theater, those lighting technicians use the same scheme to light the stage; when the director wants a golden glow on her leading man and lady, the lighting crew had darn well splash red and green spots on them to make yellow light. That's the wacky world of additive color for you.

On the other hand, when you're dealing with light reflected off objects, you turn to subtractive primary colors: cyan, yellow, and magenta — printers' colors or *process colors.* In the desktop publishing world, printers customar-ily sneak in black as a fourth color to add bite to the printed image.

That mysterious 65535

In Figure 11-4, the Apple Color Picker, the selected hue happens to be pure red, as red as you can get on an RGB computer screen. Below the H-S-B values, RGB mode represents the same hue with red at maximum, the mysterious value 65535, while green and blue are set to 0. With saturation and brightness in the H-S-B color model turned up all the way, the additive and subtractive primaries are evenly divided in 60-degree intervals around the color wheel with pure red at number 0, pure green at 21845, and purest blue at 43690; subtractive primaries work out to pure cyan at 32768, pure yellow at 10922, and pure magenta at 54614. All based on 65535 divided by 6. And boy, wouldn't you love to know why? That makes two of us, because I haven't a clue.

I lied. Actually, I have a good idea why that mysterious 65535 keeps coming up. The Apple Color Picker is designed to handle up to 16-bit color. One way of defining 16-bit color is 2 multiplied by itself 16 times, which is "2 to the 16th power." Which is, ta da, 65536. Isn't all this math stuff bringing back fond memories of old school days, wilted peanut butter sandwiches, and the school bully grinding your new glasses into the asphalt at recess? Anyway, you may have noticed that it's not a perfect match. Since computers start counting from 0, subtract 1 and the remainder becomes . . . 65535! That's 65536 hues to click through, each color with its own identifying number in the H-S-B system.

The Windows Custom Color Selector uses a different scheme from Apple's Color Picker and specifies RGB colors in percentages. To change Apple Color Picker RGB colors with values from 1 to 65535 into Windows RGB percentages, use the following formula. Yikes!

Percent = 1.00 – (Apple Color Picker number / 65535)

If you'd studied your math instead of the redhead next to you, I wouldn't need to tell you that this means, "Divide each Apple Color Picker RGB number by 65535. Subtract the result from 1.00, and that should get you close to the number in RGB percentages." Now, where's my apple?

Complementary colors

You can also use the Apple Color Picker to find complementary colors. Four out of five rocket scientists agree that a *complementary color* is the color that creates white light when added to the original color. The technique for finding a color's complement is simplicity itself with the Apple Color Picker. After choosing a color either by clicking on the color wheel or entering values in H-S-B or RGB mode, find the complementary color directly opposite on the color wheel. You can build color schemes around opposing colors that are scientifically guaranteed to be pleasing to the eye. If you have great color sense, don't bother. But if, like many developers, you need help in putting together pleasing colors, this technique can at least point you in the right direction. Unfortunately, the Windows Custom Color Selector doesn't work with the technique.

Or try a group of three complementary colors, which is what primary colors are. To make things more interesting, start with a more subtle color and then find its complements by finding the other two colors a third of the way around the color wheel in each direction. For example, say you decide on a yellowish color by eye-clicking hither and thither on the color wheel. Better yet, click hither and yon. You note that in H-S-B color mode, the color you pick is Hue 14626, a little more interesting than pure yellow. To find a set of complementary colors, imagine dividing the color wheel into thirds like a pie, starting at your yellowish color. The other two "slices" wind up at around hues 36338 and 58316. To make things more interesting, brighten one hue by moving your choice in toward the white center of the color wheel and darken another color by scrolling down with a couple of clicks to the down arrow. The colors are no longer perfect, but that's okay; the result is visually more exciting.

Have you noticed that computers start counting with 0? For example, 8-bit color gives you 256 colors, but the first color is index number 0 and the last color index number 255. Also, on a Mac, the Apple Color Picker offers 65536 hues in H-S-B color mode, but the first hue is 0, the last 65535. You see this kind of thing very frequently when working with your computer. A little safety tip: Don't let it throw you, especially if you wind up programming for NASA.

Chapter 12

Your Very Own Digital
Video Window

In This Chapter

▶ Reviewing digital video
▶ Setting up your movie for digital video
▶ Getting close and personal with codecs
▶ Exporting your movie
▶ Touring the Video window
▶ Playing digital video in Director
▶ Using Director as a movie editor

Depending on who you speak to, digital video is either the biggest thing since sliced bread or a sham technology, doling out postage stamp-sized, cataract-inducing animations to a swelling crush of catatonic multimedia wannabes swayed by a movement more subversive than Tupperware parties. Where lieth the truth?

Can You Review That Digital Video Thing Again?

Adding video to the rest of the mix that makes up multimedia has been the dream of developer types for some time. We tried all sorts of Rube Goldberg, Scotch tape, and rubber band kinds of solutions. Some solutions actually worked, but none turned out to be as on target as digital video in the form of Apple's QuickTime, Microsoft's Video for Windows, and other flavors of digital video.

Introduction of digital video

In 1993, Apple introduced QuickTime to the world. Depending on your perspective, QuickTime was: A — a major event on the same plateau as the invention of writing, movable type, and teflon-coated frying pans; B — nice; or C — insignificant. Old-time videographers laughed at the stamp-sized images everyone suddenly showed on their monitors and the poor quality of the video images. Similar comments belittled Microsoft's entry into digital video, Video for Windows, an extension to the Windows interface.

But critics missed the point. QuickTime and Video for Windows technology was destined to improve; more importantly, digital video gave birth to desktop video, allowing anyone with a computer the opportunity to access and manipulate video-style information with the ease of using text and still graphics.

Demands of digital video

Remember contemplating your navel in the '60s and '70s? Okay, contemplate video for a moment. Video is a radically different type of information compared to traditional computer information. Most critical of all, video *changes over time.* Video presents a new image approximately every thirtieth of a thecond — excuse me, second. If you ask your computer to "read" video or record video, you suddenly make enormous demands on your software and hardware.

Now consider the size of a video-style file. A good rule of thumb is to count on about 27MB (megabytes) per second of video. 27 MEGABYTES! Sorry, I lost it for a second, but I'm all right now.

Without getting too technical, consider the demands that a second of video, about 30 frames, makes on your hardware, keeping in mind your computer's many *bottlenecks,* areas that slow down performance regardless of how fast your machine is. To make things more interesting, video-style information often includes sound effects, narration, and/or music. Not only are you asking your computer to take care of this additional burden, but you're also asking the machine to somehow synchronize sounds to images. What does your machine do if video with sound is running on a slow computer? Does the whole movie slow down so that the speaker sounds like Forrest Gump on Prozac? Or does the narration get completely out of sync so that your movie looks like a really bad Ninja film? What's a budding Steven Spielberg to do?

Digital Video to the Rescue

Maybe now you can see why Apple developed QuickTime and Microsoft gave us Video for Windows. Technically, these programs are extensions to the operating system, an INIT in the parlance of Mac lovers and a TSR (Terminate and Stay Resident) for the PC users in the crowd. Figure 12-1 shows the QuickTime icon. Apple includes QuickTime with its latest, greatest system update for Macs. Otherwise, QuickTime is available free in any number of CD-ROMs these days. Oh, and Apple actually sells QuickTime kits for Macs and Windows. Video for Windows comes with Windows 3.1 and Windows 95.

However you get digital video into your machine, you restart your computer, and ka-boom! Nada. Nothing. Not a darned thing. Your computer doesn't rev up like a Lamborghini or double in speed. Zip.

You find yourself asking, "Self, what's the big deal about digital video, anyway?" Well, the video extension e-x-t-e-n-d-s your system. In and of themselves, QuickTime and Video for Windows don't do anything you notice. Digital video works its magic after you launch a video-type program, such as Adobe Premiere. Then the extension shifts into overdrive with special video capabilities.

Figure 12-1:
The
QuickTime
icon,
Apple's
extension
for digital
video.

QuickTime Codecs

QuickTime contains a number of built-in compression schemes. Multimedia types like to call them *codecs* for *c*ompression/*dec*ompression or *c*oder/*dec*oder, depending on who you talk to. In Director, you meet codecs for QuickTime and Video for Windows when you save a movie as a digital video file to your hard drive. You can import digital video into Director, but you can also choose to turn your Director production into a QuickTime movie by choosing File⇨Export.

After you choose Export from the File menu, Director takes you to the Export dialog box, shown in Figure 12-2. Notice that Director gives you some powerful options in this dialog box, including choosing which frames to export: a single frame, all frames, or every fifth frame, if you so choose.

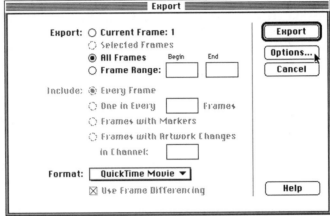

Figure 12-2:
The Export dialog box, where you may choose to turn your Director movie into QuickTime, PICTS, a Scrapbook file, or a PICS file.

Focus now on the Format pop-up menu and the Options button in the upper-right corner of the Export dialog box. If you choose QuickTime Movie from the Format pop-up menu straight away, you tell Director that you accept the default, out-of-the-box setting for your QuickTime movie, and you miss the opportunity to custom select a codec. So your first step after arriving at the Export dialog box is to click the Options button. Director takes you to the QuickTime Options dialog box, shown in Figure 12-3, to introduce you to your set of QuickTime codecs.

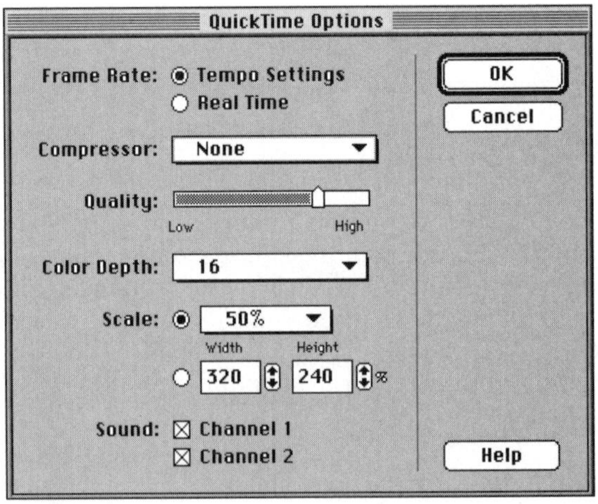

Figure 12-3:
The QuickTime Options dialog box, where Director offers you a choice of codecs for turning your movie into QuickTime.

Pressing the Compressor pop-up menu displays a list of codecs, as shown in Figure 12-4.

Figure 12-4:
The list of
QuickTime
2.5 codecs
under the
Compressor
pop-up
menu.

✓ Animation
Cinepak
Component Video
Graphics
None
Photo – JPEG
Video

Figure 12-4 shows QuickTime 2.5's current list of codecs for the Macintosh, each codec designed to compress a specific type of file. These codecs include

✓ **Animation:** This codec's main purpose is compressing computer animation, such as a sequence created in a 3-D program that takes you on a tour of a make-believe city existing only on computer. This type of file has unique characteristics that the Animation codec is designed to compress most efficiently.

✓ **Cinepak:** Cinepak is the codec of choice for many developers and is especially useful for preparing QuickTime movies destined to run off a CD-ROM. The Cinepak codec takes a long time to compress information; figure about two minutes per frame on average. But, after you compress Cinepak movies, they decompress quickly on playback and look very good. Developers often choose to compress their work overnight with the Cinepak codec in combination with utilities allowing *batch compression* (that is, compressing a log or list of selected QuickTime files).

In addition to controls for setting the degree of compression for the Cinepak codec, some QuickTime applications and utilities — not including Director, unfortunately — allow you to set the data rate (how much information is sent to the Mac or PC) in kilobytes per second. For example, using a useful shareware utility called MovieShop, you'd want to set a QuickTime movie's data rate to around 150 kilobytes per second for QuickTime destined to play on older, single-speed CD-ROM drives and around 300 kilobytes for double-speed CD-ROM drives. If you're interested, you can find MovieShop on various commercial online services, bulletin boards, and the Internet (at http://www.download.com). Movie Cleaner Pro by Terran Interactive is an excellent commercial product that does even more than MovieShop; you can order the product at http://www.Terran-Int.com.

✔ **Component Video:** For you to better understand the Component Video codec, I need to give a mini-lecture on how real TV works. What we receive on our real TVs is *composite video,* meaning that the image-making signals are essentially mixed together, as opposed to separate red, green, and blue signals. Real TV attempts a translation back to red, green, and blue data for the picture tube to work properly, but there's that old saying about stuff losing something in translation. TV is a perfect example.

Video composed of separate red, green, and blue signals is called *component video* and results in significantly higher image quality than composite video. When you want to make a QuickTime movie from a component video source, the Component Video codec is the one to go with to save all the extra info that component video offers.

✔ **Graphics:** Graphics is the codec of choice for 8-bit graphics — that is, bitmaps that display 256 colors — and a special situation for at least two reasons and possibly 3,472 more. First, QuickTime is optimized to display thousands of colors. And second, 256-color bitmaps are limited in color range. The Graphics codec is designed to achieve good compression and optimum results with 8-bit graphics, resulting in few *artifacts* (flawed pixels in the image) that typically occur during the compression process.

✔ **None:** I'll give you one guess. You got it: This selection turns off all codecs and results in a QuickTime movie with no compression. None offers the highest quality QuickTime results but is a practical choice only if you own behemoth hard drives with names like Bruiser and Powe-r-r-r-r-r-D-r-r-rive, accessorized with a Cray (as in lightning speed) computer or two.

✔ **Photo – JPEG:** This codec was developed for compressing full-screen, 24-bit (16 million+) color *still* images. Now you may be asking yourself, "Self, why offer still-image compression in a movie-making program?" Well, you need to remember that part of the beauty of QuickTime is its capability to incorporate virtually all file types into the digital video file type, including still images. For example, you can use a series of still images, such as a tour of famous paintings from the Louvre in Paris, as a QuickTime sequence, compressed with the Photo – JPEG codec and spliced together in Director with other QuickTime sequences, each compressed at its optimum value with the best codec.

✔ **Video:** The Video codec offers fast compression and decompression for files with moving images and sound. Moving images present special problems for compression schemes because all the pixels that make up the image tend to change from frame to frame. All these changes disable what any self-respecting compression scheme tries to do: namely, cut down on info by recording only what changes from frame to frame.

Of these codecs, QuickTime for Windows currently offers two Apple codecs, Video and Cinepak, plus None and Intel Indeo Video R3.2. The Intel Indeo Video codec is very similar to the previous description of Cinepak.

Notice the Quality slider under the Compressor pop-up menu back in Figure 12-3. You use the slider to set the degree of compression. (I'm working on a Quality slider for Congress.) In general, you aim for the highest possible quality by selecting the least amount of compression, however you have to balance quality against frame rate and image size. If a large video window and/or high frame rate are paramount, you need to consider compromising on quality by upping the compression rate.

 Some developers use QuickTime for purposes other than making digital movies. Because QuickTime can incorporate still-image file types such as PICT files and sounds, you may want to consider using QuickTime as a way of archiving various file types into one QuickTime standard. Use no compression or the Animation codec, which is sometimes used to organize and store high-quality PICTs. An additional benefit of this kind of QuickTime archive is being able to easily tape animations to video, one PICT per frame, the so-called single-frame technique that some high-end video recorders offer.

Preparing QuickTime for Export

Take another look at the QuickTime Export Options dialog box back in Figure 12-3. If you read the earlier sections in this chapter, you checked out the Compressor pop-up menu and found out about QuickTime 2.5's various codecs and how to adjust the amount of compression with the Quality slider, keeping in mind the inverse relationship between image quality and amount of compression. Now you can become close, personal friends with the dialog box's other features.

Tempo Settings versus Real Time

Director gives you a choice between Tempo Settings and Real Time when saving part or all of your Director movie as digital video. Choose Tempo Settings to create a digital video movie based on sprites in the Tempo channel of the Score window. Be warned that using regular transitions in the Transition channel and/or Palette transitions helps determine a digital video's file size and playability. Choose Real Time to duplicate playback of your movie from a specific computer.

Digital video has a big advantage over Director when you play the same movie on different computers. When exported as digital video, a Director sequence of 30 frames with a tempo setting of 15 frames per second plays back on any computer in precisely two seconds, with good sync between video and audio. When you play the same sequence as a Director movie, it may or may not play back in two seconds. Depending on the type of machine, color depth, and a number of other factors, the Director movie runs at different speeds on computers of varying performance.

The big difference is that Director is frame-based while digital video is time-based. Director plays all the frames of a movie no matter what, even if it limps to an agonizing crawl on an old, festering computer. Digital video keeps a sharp eye on time, dropping frames rather than letting the picture and sound get out of sync.

What color is your pop-up rainbow, er, menu?

Setting the desired color depth is another option in the QuickTime Options dialog box. Keep in mind that the color depth options depend on what codec you choose. For example, if you choose the Animation codec from the Compressor pop-up menu, you find a complete choice of color depths under the Color Depth pop-up menu, as shown in Figure 12-5; if you choose Graphics for your codec, you have only 256 colors available.

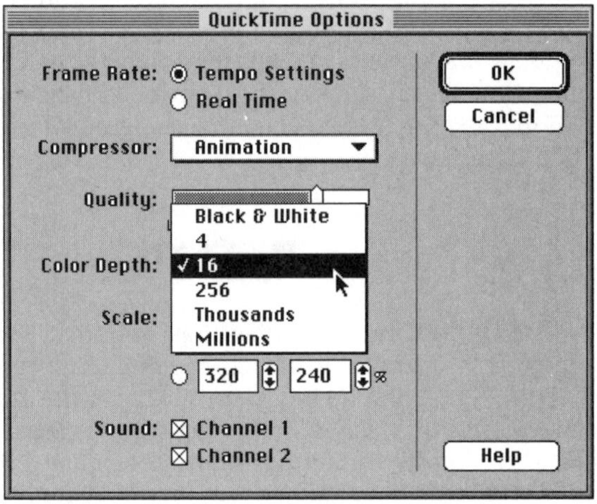

Figure 12-5:
The Animation codec allows a complete choice of color depths from the Color Depth pop-up menu.

QuickTime Options	
Frame Rate: ● Tempo Settings	OK
○ Real Time	Cancel
Compressor: Animation ▼	
Quality:	
	Black & White
	4
Color Depth:	✓ 16
	256
Scale:	Thousands
	Millions
○ 320 ⬍ 240 ⬍ ⊠	
Sound: ⊠ Channel 1	
⊠ Channel 2	Help

You can create your digital video in black and white, although I don't recommend it. The result is dithered black-and-white frames, possibly justified when considering as wide an audience as possible. There's just one problem with black-and-white video: It's ugly, although it may make an interesting special effect.

You can choose 256 colors, which multimedia types call 8-bit color. However, if you read my rantings in the previous section on codecs, you know the Graphics codec is specifically engineered to optimize 8-bit (256 colors) digital video.

Anyway, you can move up to thousands or even millions of colors. Keep in mind that QuickTime is optimized for thousands of colors, what developer types call 16-bit color. As tempting as millions of colors sounds, 24-bit digital video makes enormous demands on your computer. And experts agree that only three people in the whole world can tell 16-bit from 24-bit color. And I'm not telling.

If you want cross-platform compatibility, you better stay with 8-bit color. An army of pre-Windows 95 users out in the world are limited to 256 colors.

How do you export a color Director movie as a grayscale digital video? You don't. Within Director, you can import the color digital video, place it into the Score, and then set the palette to Grayscale in the Palette channel of the Score window. Thinking positively, the conversion is relatively easy and all done in Director. The downside? All the other sprites in the same frames turn gray along with the digital video until you change palettes again. The best way to create a grayscale digital video is to turn to a utility program like MovieShop for the Mac or a heavy-duty application like Premiere for Macs and PCs, open the color digital video, and then save the video as a grayscale movie. For more on the Score window, see Chapter 6. For more on switching palettes, see Chapter 11.

Scale options

Director gives you several ways to resize or *scale* your QuickTime movie. Choose a value from the Scale pop-up menu, shown in Figure 12-6; or choose Other and enter a specific percentage in the Scale dialog box, reproduced in Figure 12-7. You can also enter the Width and Height values manually or by clicking the little up and down arrows next to the Width and Height boxes.

In Real Life, only a handful of dimensions work well with digital video, all based on the classic 4-to-3 screen ratio inherited from the film industry since the silent screen days, passed on to television and now to digital video. The proportions of the ubiquitous 13-inch monitor, 640 x 480 pixels (or pels), reflect this 4-to-3 ratio; you can derive other dimensions by simply halving these values again and again until you arrive at the stamp-sized video window that started it all in 1993, a whopping 160 x 120 pixels.

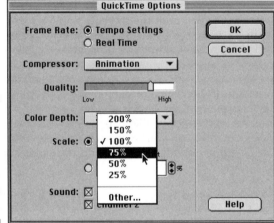

Figure 12-6:
The Scale pop-up menu in the QuickTime Options dialog box.

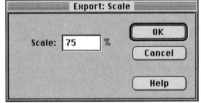

Figure 12-7:
The Scale dialog box.

Sound decisions

You can choose to include sound channels along with your animations by clicking the appropriate check boxes in the QuickTime Options dialog box. In Figure 12-3 (earlier in this chapter), I decided to include both channels of sound. If your computer doesn't support stereo sound, Director enables only one sound check box anyway.

Setting up for Real Time digital video

Use the following steps to prepare your digital video for Real Time playback:

1. **Turn off all Lingo commands by choosing Control⇔Disable Scripts.**

2. **Establish a beginning tempo for the movie by double-clicking the Tempo channel in Frame 1, clicking the Tempo radio/option button in the Set Tempo dialog box, and sliding the Tempo control to 15 fps (frames per second), a standard rate for on-screen animation barring high-end equipment, pronounced EXPENSIVE. Click OK.**

3. **Set desired tempos in other frames of the Tempo channel, by repeating Step 2.**

4. **Set desired transitions in the Transition channel by double-clicking the Transition channel in the respective frame, scrolling to the preferred transition in the Set Transition dialog box, and customizing the transition with its specific set of check boxes and other controls. Click OK.**

5. **Uncheck Loop Playback in the Control menu.**

6. **Rewind the movie by pressing ⌘/Ctrl+Option/Alt+R.**

7. **Make popcorn.**

8. **Salt and butter popcorn.**

9. **Play the movie by pressing ⌘/Ctrl+Option/Alt+P.**

10. **At the conclusion of the movie, choose File⇨Export.**

11. **Be sure to click Options in the Export dialog box and check the Real Time radio/option button in the QuickTime Export Options dialog box.**

12. **Select an appropriate codec from the Compressor pop-up menu.**

    To review codecs and their uses, jump back to "QuickTime Codecs," earlier in this chapter.

13. **Make any other desired modifications to Director's default settings in the QuickTime Options dialog box and click OK.**

14. **Make any other desired modifications to Director's default settings in the Export dialog box and click Export.**

15. **Play back your digital video to test results.**

16. **Clean fingers of salt and butter from popcorn.**

By the way, Lingo is Director's built-in programming language that's a lot easier to use than you may think. Why do you think I devote one precious chapter (Chapter 14) to Lingo in this book?

Video for Windows Codecs

Video for Windows, Microsoft's solution to digital video, offers its own set of codecs for the PC, including

✔ **MPEG-1:** An acronym for Moving Picture Experts Group; MPEG-1 is designed to display full-screen, full-motion video. The hitch to this codec is that creating and viewing MPEG-compressed video is dependent on installing a pricey MPEG decompression board. Top boards run from $4,000 to $15,000, give or take a few pennies. The QuickTime 2.5 installation includes a feature to *view* MPEG movies but not to *compress* movies with MPEG.

✔ **MPEG-2:** A new and improved version of MPEG-1 with a price tag to match. MPEG-2 boards start around $85,000, give or take a lunch.

What Good Is an Empty Digital Video Window?

It's time to dive into using digital video in Director with the infamous Video window. When you choose Window⇨Video, surprise! The Video window's blank. That outrageous price that Macromedia wants for Director, and you get a blank window, as blank as Figure 12-8.

Figure 12-8:
An empty digital Video window.

Try copying a bitmap and pasting it into the empty Video window; you can't. Sure, it's a great practical joke. It keeps you entertained for a couple of hours, but then it dawns on you. You realize that you can use a blank Video window in Director to glue together snippets of other videos.

By the way, you can open as many Video windows in Director as your memory or RAM allows — more RAM, more windows.

After you import a digital video, you can use all the standard Copy, Paste, and Clear commands under the Edit menu to move, rearrange, and delete frames within the Video window and between Video windows. Until you get Adobe Premiere, you can edit video in Director. And with Shockwave, Director's plug-in for the Web's premiere browser, Netscape Navigator, you're set for doing cutting-edge animation in Cyberspace! For more on Shockwave and the Web, turn to Chapter 18.

When you export a Digital Video Cast Member cut and pasted together in Director as a digital video file, the result is what we multimedia types call a "flattened" file, meaning that all the bits and pieces it took to put the Digital Video Cast Member together in Director are now part of the final digital video file, independent of the original sources.

Touring the Video window

Take a closer look at that blank Video window. Most of the features look familiar; some are unique to this window. Notice that the top row of buttons duplicates precisely what you find in the Paint window. To review Paint window buttons in psychoanalytical depth, take one giant step back to Chapter 7.

The only unique area of the Video window is the row of controls at the bottom. These controls are actually a standard feature called, of all things, the *controller.* Digital movies usually appear with the controller, although you can hide it in most programs, including Director. Notice how similar the controller buttons are to VCR or remote control buttons. From left to right, the controller features the following:

- ✔ **Sound Control:** Press to adjust the sound, from off to full volume, with a sliding control. You can adjust the sound during playback. If no slider appears when you press the Sound Control button, the original digital video either has no soundtrack or it wasn't imported along with the graphics for any of 5,392 reasons.

- ✔ **Play and Stop:** Click to begin video playback. On playback, the button's icon changes to a square and functions as the Stop button.

- ✔ **Scroll Bar:** Press and drag to the right to fast forward or to the left to fast rewind as with the shuttle control on some VCRs.

- ✔ **Step reverse control:** Moves the digital video back one frame for each click of the mouse.

- ✔ **Step forward control:** Moves the digital video forward one frame for each click of the mouse.

- ✔ **Resize box:** Like the Resize box on most windows. Press and drag to manually resize the Video window's dimensions.

If you don't want to assume the person viewing the digital video knows how to use a controller, you have two options. Either include a Help area somewhere on-screen, or hide the controller by unchecking the Show Controller check box in the Digital Video Properties dialog box and include a custom Play Movie button somewhere on-screen that issues the Lingo play command. See Chapter 14 for more about how Lingo commands work.

Unfortunately, Director does not have a simple play command for digital video. In this chapter's section, "Playing Digital Video Lite," is a method for playing a video from a button, which avoids a great deal of Lingo scripting. It looks like a lot of work, but the whole process goes pretty quickly. You can also try your hand at Director's new behaviors, including video playback behaviors. Check out Chapter 15 for more on behaviors.

Make the distinction clearly in your mind between a Digital Video Cast Member in the Cast window, its sprite placed on the Stage, and its Video window — three very different views of the same object, as shown side by side in Figure 12-9. By the way, Figure 12-9 shows an impossible situation in one respect: three active windows; in Real Life only one window may be active at any time. Don't let this concept throw you.

The first view, from left to right in Figure 12-9, shows an imported digital video as a cast member in the Cast window. Note the row of Cast window buttons at the top, the cast member's telltale thumbnail size, its cell number under the thumbnail followed by as much of the name as Director can show in Geneva 9-point type, and the Digital Video icon in the lower-right corner.

The second view in Figure 12-9 is the Digital Video Cast Member's sprite on the Stage. Notice the selection rectangle and handles that appear when you select the sprite. Displaying the controller at the bottom of a Digital Video sprite is optional; you can hide it by selecting the cast member, clicking the Cast Member Properties button, and unchecking the Controller check box.

Figure 12-9:
Three faces of an imported digital video movie: its Digital Video Cast Member, its sprite viewed on the Stage, and its Video window.

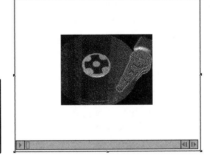
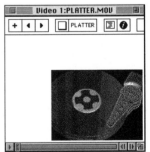

The third view in Figure 12-9 shows the Digital Video Cast Member's Video window. Display it by double-clicking a Digital Video Cast Member in the Cast window or its sprite on the Stage. Notice the telltale Add button at the top of the window and the Digital Video's permanent controller. Director doesn't allow you to hide a Video window's controller any more than its Close box, Zoom box, or Resize box.

Setting up your digital video

Click the Digital Video Cast Member Properties button, and Director takes you to the Digital Video Cast Member Properties dialog box, depicted with excruciating accuracy in Figure 12-10.

Figure 12-10:
The Digital Video Cast Member Properties dialog box offers a number of options for modifying a Digital Video Cast Member.

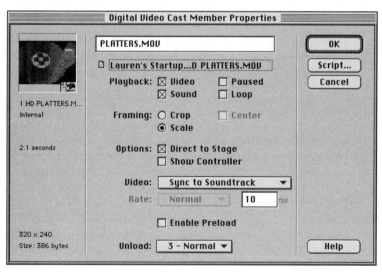

The Digital Video Cast Member Properties dialog box gives you important information about a Digital Video Cast Member. In Figure 12-10, the digital video is Digital Video Cast Member 1. At the top, Director gives you the Digital Video Cast Member's name, which may be different from the source file's name on the hard drive; remember, you can rename a cast member in its Properties dialog box at any time. Underneath the name is the video's address or path on the drive. At the left, Director informs you that the digital video runs for 2.1 seconds, its dimensions are 320 x 240, and its file size is 386 bytes. In addition to all this info, Director offers you a flock of options at no additional expense.

Playback options include

✔ **Video check box:** Check to show the video sprite on playback. An unchecked Video check box hides the video track. With only the controller showing, you can still click the Play button to play an audio track.

✔ **Sound check box:** Check to enable any sound tracks embedded in the video sprite.

✔ **Paused check box:** Check to keep the video sprite from automatically playing when it appears on the Stage; you can then click the Play button on the controller at any time. With the check box unchecked, Director plays the video sprite when it appears on the Stage.

✔ **Loop check box:** Check to make the digital video jump from the last frame to Frame 1 and replay, continuing to loop until you click the controller's Stop button.

To stop a digital video, press the spacebar. Press the spacebar again to resume playback. By the way, this keyboard shortcut works with most QuickTime-related programs.

The Framing options include

✔ **Crop radio/option button:** Click to turn the video sprite's bounding box (the outline that highlights when you select the sprite) into a frame showing more or less of the sprite as you drag the bounding box by a selection handle into various dimensions. If you set the sprite's controller to be visible, you can crop out the controller along with unwanted parts of the image.

✔ **Scale radio/option button:** Click to resize a video sprite by its selection handles. Shift+drag a selection handle to resize proportionally. Regain a sprite's original size by choosing Modify➪Sprite➪Properties and clicking Restore.

✔ **Center check box:** Check this option to center the video sprite within the dimensions of its bounding box. If the Center check box is disabled (grayed out), the Crop radio/option button is not selected, as shown in Figure 12-10. When you select Crop, Director enables the Center check box.

Additional options include

✔ **Direct to Stage check box:** Checking this box forces Director to play the video sprite at the highest layer, regardless of its real channel position in the Score.

Each frame of a Director movie contains 120 channels to work with, like transparent layers one on top of the other. Channel 1 is the farthest back, like a background layer; Channel 120 is the closest layer to you.

Playing digital video in the closest or highest channel maximizes playback speed because Director doesn't have to deal with the possibility of calculating the effect of other sprites overlapping the video sprite.

Two rules are associated with this option. First, no other sprites can play in higher channels in the Score when you call on this option, and second, the only acceptable ink type is the default ink, Copy. In other words, when you need to apply a custom ink type to a video sprite, or you want other sprites overlapping or crossing a video sprite in your animation, don't use Direct to Stage. You may cause the magnetic fields of the North and South Pole to swap places, wreaking havoc throughout the world and leading to some really bad traffic jams.

✔ **Show Controller check box:** Only enabled after you check the Direct to Stage check box, the Show Controller check box displays a digital video's controller, the subject of the next section.

✔ **Video pop-up menu:** Choose Sync to Soundtrack to play a video at its original rate even if frames are dropped. Or choose Play Every Frame, No Sound to prevent dropped frames.

✔ **Rate pop-up menu:** This menu is available if you choose Play Every Frame from the Video pop-up menu. Select a rate from the pop-up menu: Normal, Maximum, or Fixed. Enter a value in the entry box to the right.

The Fixed rate option works properly only when the entire digital video plays at the same frame rate. Some digital videos vary frame rate from sequence to sequence.

✔ **Enable Preload check box:** Checking this box automatically issues a Lingo command, preLoadCast, that initiates the copying process into memory before Director plays the video sprite.

Director has two ways to call up digital video information from the source file to play back on the Stage. The slower way is to read one frame of the source file from disk, display the frame on the Stage, read the next frame, display it, and so on. The faster method is to copy the entire source file into memory or, in a limited memory situation, copy as much of the file as possible to memory and then play the digital videos from memory. The faster method is where the Enable Preload check box comes into play.

Be sure to uncheck the Enable Preload check box when you anticipate or need to assume a low-memory situation.

When you import a digital video, Director always sets up the source document as a linked file; the Digital Video Cast Member that appears in the Cast window refers to the external digital video on your hard drive when you play back the video sprite in the Stage window.

✄ **Unload pop-up menu:** Choose one of the Purge Priority options, as shown in Figure 12-11, for the Digital Video Cast Member.

For detailed information about Purge Priority options, jump back to Chapter 5.

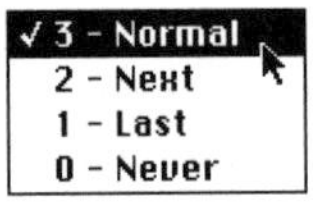

Figure 12-11:
The Unload pop-up menu for setting when Director clears a cast member from memory.

Playing Digital Video Lite

Hold onto your seats. You're about to enter the eerie, scary world of LINGO! Actually, you'll do just fine. You can try out all the basics of Lingo by reading Chapter 14. But to get your feet wet, try this section first, Digital Video Lite. Goes great with low-fat pancakes, too.

First, you need to set up a new Digital Video Cast Member in the Cast window that has only the first frame of the video you want to play.

Setting up your window

1. **Choose Window⇨Cast or press ⌘/Ctrl+3 and double-click the digital video you want to play to bring up its Digital Video Cast Member window.**

2. **Click the Cast Member Properties button or press ⌘/Ctrl+i and make sure that the Paused check box is *not* checked.**

3. **Click OK.**

4. **Choose Edit⇨Copy Video or press ⌘/Ctrl+C.**

   Basically, you copied the first frame of the video, known as the *poster* because it acts as a preview image for the file. In the rest of the steps, I refer to this one-frame video as the poster video and to the original full-framed movie as the original movie.

5. **Click the Add button in the Digital Video Cast Member window to display a blank Digital Video Cast Member window.**

6. **Choose Window⇨Cast or press ⌘/Ctrl+3 to display the Cast window.**

7. **Click the new Digital Video Cast Member and choose Edit⇨Paste Video or press ⌘/Ctrl+V.**

8. **In the Save As dialog box that appears, name the poster video something original, like Poster. Using the Directory window, select the location where you want to save the video and click Save.**

Preparing the Score

Now you need to set things up in the Score window.

1. **In the Cast window, drag the poster video to the desired frame and channel in the Score window.**

   Be sure to remember the video sprite's channel number. You use the same channel throughout the rest of these steps.

2. **Drag the original video from the Cast window two frames to the right of the poster video in the Score.**

3. **Guess the number of frames the original digital video takes to play completely in the Score.**

   This part's a little dicey. You need to guess approximately how many frames your animation runs. For example, if your movie is running at 15 fps (frames per second), and you guess that the digital video runs for 3 seconds, that's 45 frames. Adds up, doesn't it?

4. **Drag the original video sprite's sprite bar to the right to the number of frames you guessed in Step 3.**

Adding a little Lingo

Remember, I said that these steps avoid a lot of Lingo; avoiding it altogether is hard.

1. **Return to the frame where the poster video starts, noting its frame number, and double-click the Script channel in the same frame to display the Script window.**

2. **Type go to the frame in the Script window.**

3. **Click the Script window's Close box.**

   When you play the Director movie, this line of Lingo locks you in this frame until another command tells Director to do something else.

4. **Choose Window⇨Tools and select the basic Push Button tool.**

   For more on the Tool palette, page back to Chapter 10.

5. **Drag out a button at the bottom of the Stage and enter a name for the button where you see the blinking insertion point — for example, Play Movie.**

6. **Press ⌘/Ctrl+i to display the button's Properties dialog box, and then click the Script button.**

7. **Type** go to frame **in the button's Script window.**

8. **Type a space and then the number of the frame where the real full-framed digital video begins; then click the Close box.**

   The complete line should look something like go to frame 45.

Testing it out

Now you're ready to test your work.

1. **Press 0 (zero) on the keypad to rewind the movie.**

2. **Choose Control⇨Play or press ⌘/Ctrl+Option/Alt+P to play the movie and test the Lingo command you typed for the push button.**

What should happen? Your Director movie should play to the frame where your digital video (in this example, "Poster") appears. Director waits until you press the button you created (in this example, the "Play Movie" button). After you press the button, the Lingo command hidden in the button jumps you to the full video and plays to its conclusion, providing you guessed correctly about the number of frames it would take. If you didn't guess enough frames, simply stretch the video's sprite bar longer and test again.

Cutting and Pasting between Friends

If you don't have an honest-to-gosh digital video editing program like Adobe Premiere or one of the other fine products on the market, you can use Director itself as an editor. Of course, Director wasn't meant to be a dedicated video editor, so don't expect to replicate all the wondrous special effects you've heard about; but for basic editing, cutting, and pasting, Director works just fine. In a way, Director offers some features that those fancy editing programs lack.

To use Director as an editor, you need to start with some digital video. In other words, opening the Paint window, creating a masterpiece on a blank easel, copying it, and trying to paste your graphic into a blank Video window just doesn't work. Try it if you don't believe me. Gjeeeech.

Start from scratch

Remember that old saying about, "Where there's a will . . ."? Just as soon as the words leave my lips (that is, my keyboard), I find myself backtracking on them a bit. Director actually does provide a way to create a digital video from scratch — it's a roundabout way, but it works! For example, you decide to develop an animation sequence in Director, maybe the old-fashioned way, one drawing at a time, making small, incremental changes to your actors (or sprites, as we Director types call them) from frame to frame. You build your sequence over the days, the weeks, the months. You forget to make your car payment; they tow your car away. You build your sequence. Your spouse leaves you; your children run away. You build your sequence, fine-tuning each frame to perfection until you have ten frames Disney would be proud of. Sure, you sacrificed a little, but hey, that's the path of the true artiste.

Anyway, you have your ten frames. Then again, maybe you're not so dedicated. You decide to use Director's Animation Wizard features, discussed in Chapter CD 5. You build an animated bullet chart. The topics fly in; the bullets fly in. Full color, stereo sound, with just a couple of clicks of the mouse. You seriously consider CinemaScope but finally pass on that one. Either way, one drawing at a time or taking advantage of Director's built-in animation capabilities, you build your ten frames. Then you realize what makes the darned thing so powerful is the sync between graphics and sound. Now, you did swipe that musical intro from *Star Trek: The Next Generation,* didn't you? So what if you spend some big time in a maximum security federal penitentiary; you're an artiste, willing to sacrifice a little for your art. A few years in the slammer's nothing compared to building ten great frames Disney would be proud of.

What I'm trying to say is, Director is a frame-based application. With a lot of tweaking and perspiration, you can make graphics and sound sync pretty well together. Wondrous as Director is, however — kiss, kiss — the application is just not designed to do the job as well as digital video. Digital video is time-based. Digital video was developed to play at a user-set rate, to stay in sync with any accompanying soundtracks, and to drop frames if necessary in order to accomplish its mission, should it so choose to accept. Impossible, you say? No, digital video works very well indeed for synchronizing graphics with soundtracks. So why not export your ten frames as a digital video, resolve any sync problems, and, if you want to stay with Director as the software "engine," simply re-import your video back into a Director movie? Now for your editing pleasure, you have the best of both worlds: digital video's time-based technology and Director's interactive and Web publishing capabilities.

Prebuilt digital video

Another way to use Director's built-in video editing features is to start with some prebuilt video. A list of sources may include the following:

- ✔ **Your own digital videos:** What AV Macs and PC video boards are all about, complete with Video In and Video Out ports, Stereo Sound In and Out ports, and DSP (Digital Signal Processor) chips on the system board, along with other special computer stuff to digitize analog video (your videotapes) into digital info that your computer understands and Director can display in a Video window.

- ✔ **Freeware and shareware digital video:** You say you don't have a camcorder, a VCR, or talent? All the major commercial online services, such as America Online, CompuServe, and Prodigy, have tons of digital video for you to download (copy to your computer through an inexpensive modem). And don't forget the Internet, which you can access with AT&T WorldNet Service included on the companion CD. Many videos are freeware with unlimited usage rights granted to you by the originator; other files may be shareware-style files where you're obliged to send in a relatively low fee for ownership and/or usage, or perhaps a licensing fee per one-time usage of the video based on the honor system. In these legally combative times, I suggest reading all the fine print and completely understanding the contract you're agreeing to before adopting someone else's work for your own.

Freeware doesn't necessarily translate into "no strings attached." Always read the fine print. How do you think I wound up getting married twice?

- ✔ **Digital video on floppy and CD-ROM media:** Countless sources of third-party commercial digital videos and still images on floppies are on the market. Better yet, purchase a CD-ROM full of digital video. A CD-ROM can store up to 650MB (megabytes) of info, and its shelf life is longer than your own. Assuming the image and sound quality are high, prices for CD-ROM collections are usually very reasonable. Again, check and double-check usage rights before you purchase anything. My recommendation is to look for unlimited usage to get your full money's worth, unless you just can't live without that CD-ROM full of one-time usage kitties lapping up milk, ripping sofas, sinking needle-sharp, little fangs into toes, and so on.

Chapter 13

Your Pals — The Markers Window and New Window Command

● ●

In This Chapter

▶ Creating markers

▶ Using the New Window command

● ●

*N*ever let it be said that Director 6 lets you down. Out of the kindness of its heart, Macromedia Director gives you umpteen windows, and then it gives you even more. The Markers window is a note to yourself, a permanent ID for your frames, a printable outline, and a great dessert topping, too.

Introducing a close, personal friend of mine: the Markers window.

So, What Is the Markers Window?

Think of markers as bookmarks, only better. Why are markers so important, you ask? Well, for one thing, markers help organize your movie in the Score window and flag important frames, as shown in Figure 13-1. Also, you can add a name and note for each marker in the Markers window that prints out at high resolution, so you can distribute the notes as an outline to members of your design team and your clients.

Another great feature with markers is that their names and notes stay with their frames even when you shuffle frames around as you develop your movie. If you have a movie that's 100 frames long, and you add three frames to the beginning, Frame 100 becomes Frame 103. A Lingo script that refers to Frame 100 now affects or references the wrong frame, the frame that used to be Frame 97. On the other hand, if you write a Lingo script that refers to the

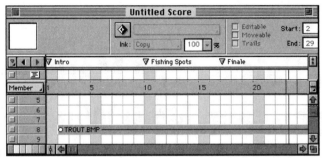

Figure 13-1:
The Score
window
with
markers for
Frames 1,
10, and 17.

contents of a frame by its marker name, the Lingo script is always correct. Markers move with the content of their frames, even after you add or delete other frames in the Score. To brush up on Lingo basics, peruse Chapter 14.

As you orchestrate your Director 6 movie in the Score window, add markers to important frames (as shown in Figure 13-1) by clicking the Markers channel in the frame you want to mark. After you have a marker in the Marker channel, you can drag the marker to a different location at any time. You can review frames in the Score in Chapter 6.

At first, markers are simply named New Marker. To give a marker a unique name, you can click the marker in the Marker channel of the Score and type a meaningful name. To name a marker in the Marker window and to add a note, display the Markers window, which is illuminated with Old World craftsmanship in Figure 13-2, by choosing Window⇨Markers or pressing ⌘/Ctrl+Shift+M. You can replace the default names of markers in the left field of the Marker window.

Figure 13-2:
The
Markers
window,
where you
can name
markers in
the Score
window and
add notes.

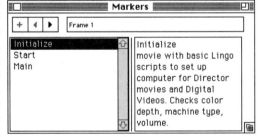

To add a note to a marker, click at the end of a marker name in the right field, press Return, and then begin your note on the *second* line. Director considers any text in the first line of the right field to be part of the marker name. Repeat this process for each marker you want to name or annotate.

To print the contents of the Markers window, display the Markers window. Then choose File⇨Print and consider the options in the Print dialog box shown in Figure 13-3. Choose Marker Comments, for example, from the Print pop-up menu and decide whether you want to print the currently selected markers, all markers, or a range of marker comments.

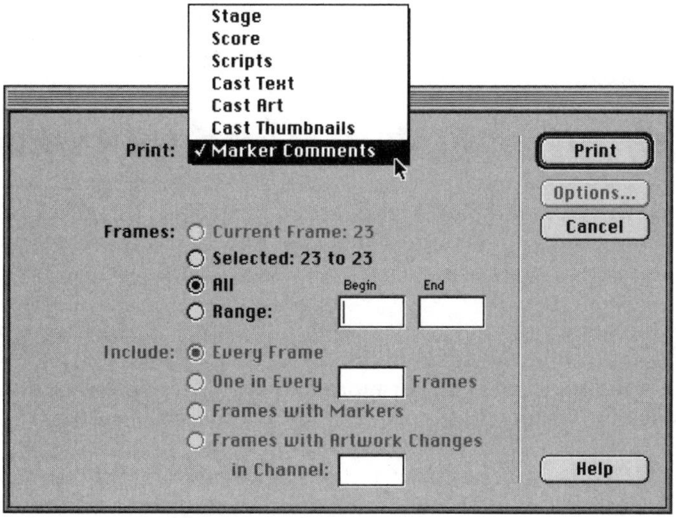

Figure 13-3:
Choose
Marker
Comments
from the
Print pop-
up menu in
the Print
dialog box
to output
comments
as high-
resolution
text.

Stage
Score
Scripts
Cast Text
Cast Art
Cast Thumbnails
✓ Marker Comments

Print: ✓ Marker Comments

Print
Options...
Cancel

Frames: ○ Current Frame: 23
○ Selected: 23 to 23
⦿ All   Begin   End
○ Range:

Include: ⦿ Every Frame
○ One in Every [   ] Frames
○ Frames with Markers
○ Frames with Artwork Changes
in Channel: [   ]

Help

You can also click Options to customize the output by deciding how many markers to include on each printed page and by adding a footer, as shown in Figure 13-4. When you're ready, click Print.

When you start writing Lingo scripts in a movie, you can use the go command with a frame's marker name in quote characters to add meaning to the line of Lingo. For example, instead of typing a line of Lingo that looks like, `go to frame 10` — which doesn't say much — you can type `go to marker "Finale"`. Director moves the playback head to the frame marked `Finale`. With luck, some dynamite special effect starting at that marker is just waiting to kick in and sweep your audience off its feet.

Use only plain quotes whenever you type Lingo commands. Director is very picky about this. In the example line of Lingo, `go to marker "Finale"`, be sure to use plain, old-fashioned quote characters (Shift+apostrophe), not those fancy beginning and ending quotes (" and ").

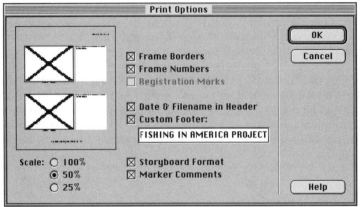

Figure 13-4:
Click
Options in
the Print
dialog
box to
customize
printer
output.

A Word about the New Window Command

The New Window command works with a Text, Cast, Digital Video, or Script window only when that window is active. New Window creates another window representing the same cast member.

New Window is great when using Director 6 to edit QuickTime movies, either to use in a Director movie as a Digital Video Cast Member or to export it as a stand-alone QuickTime file. For more info on digital video and QuickTime, jump back to Chapter 12.

In Chapter 12, I discuss cutting and pasting a new QuickTime movie together within Director. During this editing process, calling on the New Window command can be very useful, especially for a long sequence. After choosing Window⇨New Window for an active Video window, you can use the new window to move to a different part of the QuickTime movie, as shown in Figure 13-5.

Figure 13-5:
Two
different
views of the
same Digital
Video Cast
Member,
thanks to
the New
Window
command.

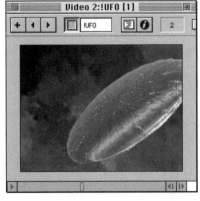

Suppose that one window shows Frame 1 of the sequence, as usual. In the second window, you can fast forward to the middle of the sequence and cut and paste between the beginning and middle sequences to a third blank Video window. Even high-powered video editing programs, such as Adobe Premiere, have a hard time duplicating the ease of this kind of editing.

Keep in mind that the original and duplicate windows refer to the same cast member, so edits in either window directly change the cast member in the Cast window. Also keep in mind that digital video in Director 6 is always linked to the original file on disk; all edits you make to the video in Director 6 actually change the original external file on disk.

Press Option/Alt when you choose New Window from the Window menu for a Text, Script, or Field window to create a new window of the same cast member. Otherwise, Director replaces the Text, Script, or Field window with a blank new window.

Part III
More Interaction, Please!

By Rich Tennant

"AND TO COMPLETE OUR MULTIMEDIA PRESENTATION..."

In this part . . .

When the Altair 8800, the world's first personal computer, hit the stands on the cover of *Popular Electronics* back in 1975, people couldn't wait to busy their hands assembling it. Funny thing was, no one could say why, or what they were going to do with all that silicon after they slapped it together.

If you've had the same kind of trouble articulating why you were just born to do interactive Director 6 stuff and whip up stunning animations for the World Wide Web with Shockwave, Part III has a haystack full of fodder for you, from why learning Lingo should be high on your To Do list (just under "Changing Underwear") to adding sound to your Director movie.

Chapter 14

A Taste of Lingo

*L*ingo's something you have to talk yourself into, like putting on a tie, washing the car, or getting married. You may have heard scary stories about Lingo. They're all true.

Just kidding. Lingo's not as bad as it used to be. It's a lot more like everyday speech in Director 6. Of course, if you're still working on everyday speech. . . .

In this chapter, I show you that learning Lingo is something a four-year-old child can handle. So if you have a four-year-old child handy, you're all set. You can even try the sample script in this chapter and live to tell about it. I also give you some essential information about using a computer language. You can use this background info for getting started with just about any programming language.

Okay, Take a Deep Breath — Lingo's Not That Hard

As programming languages go, Lingo's a breeze. Although Lingo feels conversational, the experience of learning Lingo is very close to tackling a foreign language with its special rules, distinctive syntax, and unique set of words to learn, small in number though they may be in Lingo. Syntax is the way words are arranged to form meaningful clauses or sentences. Lewis Carroll had a great time playing with syntax in *Alice in Wonderland* when he wrote, "'Not the same thing a bit!' said the Hatter. 'You might just as well say that "I see what I eat" is the same thing as "I eat what I see"!'" Or was that the Disney version?

Touring Basic Lingo Concepts

Today's Lingo is a far cry from its old VideoWorks days. By comparison, Lingo is conversational and approachable. It's still a computer language, though, and the time has come to face a few unusual characteristics most programming languages share.

Operators

You may not know it, but you're already familiar with some of Lingo's operators. In fact, in your halcyon school days, your teacher probably referred to *arithmetic operators,* such as addition (+), subtraction (–), and multiplication (*) operators. Lingo's operators are simply an extension of the same idea. For example, you'll find that Lingo's operators include a set of comparison operators including <, which means "less than," and >=, which means "greater than or equal to." You can use these operators in a line of Lingo to compare one value to another.

You can see a list of Lingo's operators in the Script window. Choose Window⇨Script or press ⌘/Ctrl+0 (zero) to display the Script window and then press the Alphabetical Lingo pop-up list (the icon that looks like a capital *L*), as shown in Figure 14-1. Table 14-1 contains basic explanations of the operators in the order they appear in the Operators submenu.

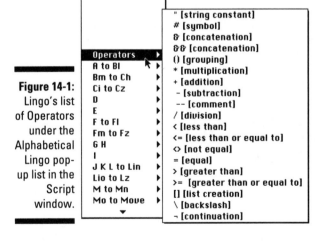

Figure 14-1:
Lingo's list
of Operators
under the
Alphabetical
Lingo pop-
up list in the
Script
window.

Operators	▶
A to Bl	▶
Bm to Ch	▶
Ci to Cz	▶
D	▶
E	▶
F to Fl	▶
Fm to Fz	▶
G H	▶
I	▶
J K L to Lin	▶
Lio to Lz	▶
M to Mn	▶
Mo to Move	▶

```
" [string constant]
# [symbol]
& [concatenation]
&& [concatenation]
() [grouping]
* [multiplication]
+ [addition]
 - [subtraction]
 -- [comment]
/ [division]
< [less than]
<= [less than or equal to]
<> [not equal]
= [equal]
> [greater than]
>= [greater than or equal to]
[] [list creation]
\ [backslash]
¬ [continuation]
```

Table 14-1	The Operators Submenu	
Operator	**Function**	**Example**
#	Used to create a symbol instead of a variable for increased speed	Put #Lauren into firstName
&	Used to "glue" text, values, and variables together in a line of Lingo	Set the text of cast "Welcome Message" = "Hello," & firstName & "."
&&	Same as & but automatically adds a space character between two elements	Set the text of cast "Welcome Message" = "Hello ," && firstName & "."
( )	Forces Director to execute enclosed operators first in a list of operators	$5 + ({}^{9}/_{3} + 1) / 4$
*	Multiplies one value by another	235 * 29
+	Adds one value to another	356 + 25
–	Subtracts one value from another	9 – 3
- -	Disables a line of Lingo in a handler to include notes in a script	-- The following line gets the machine model running Director
/	Divides one value by another	956 / 18
<	Less than	85 + 1 < 92
<=	Less than or equal to	90 + 2 <= 92
<>	Not equal	${}^{85}/_{2} <> 92$
=	Equals	85 + 15 = 100
>	Greater than	85 + 20 > 100
>=	Greater than or equal to	85 + 15 >= 100
[]	Used to specify items in a special Lingo type of variable called a list	["Sunday", "Monday", "Tuesday", "Wednesday", "Thursday", "Friday", "Saturday"]
¬ (Option+ Return on Macs, Alt+ Enter on PCs)	Use as a "continued on next line" character in a Lingo script, not read as a return character	If moneySpent > moneyEarned, then ¬ set the text of cast "Financial Condition" = "God help us."

Commands

A command is a direction telling Director to accomplish a specific task during playback. All programming languages, including Lingo, have commands. In Director, the commands appear alphabetically by initial letter in the Alphabetical Lingo pop-up menu after Operators (refer to Figure 14-1). When you scroll to the initial letter of interest, a submenu appears, and you can drag the mouse to the submenu to choose one of the listed commands.

The go command is one of the most frequently used commands. When Director encounters a go command in the Script channel of the Score window, it executes the command like the stolid genie that it is. If you type **go to frame 15** in the Script channel of Frame 10, the nanosecond Director lands on Frame 10 and the playback head jumps straight to Frame 15.

Functions

A function tries to pass itself off as an ordinary old command but makes itself conspicuously different with a telltale giveaway: A function always returns a value. For example, the date function returns the current date. Similarly, the time function returns the current time. Commands are hyper; functions are mellow — they must have been developed in California.

You can use the Message window to try out a function.

1. **Choose Window⇨Message or choose ⌘/Ctrl+M to display the Message window.**

   The Alphabetical Lingo pop-up menu is in the upper-left corner of the Message window.

   You need to use a Lingo command, often the put command, with a function to get a result in the Message window.

2. **Choose put from the Pn to Q submenu, as shown in Figure 14-2.**

   The phrase put expression appears in the Message window. *Expression* is just a placeholder and appears selected because Director expects you to replace the expression by typing something meaningful or choosing another item from the Alphabetical Lingo pop-up list.

3. **Choose a function from the Alphabetical Lingo pop-up list.**

   For example, if you choose the time from the T to Track submenu, the phrase the time replaces the selected placeholder expression. By the way, *the* is another giveaway that *the time* is a function; you find plenty of *thes* as you use functions — the time, the date, the key, and so on. Ad nauseam. *E pluribus unum.*

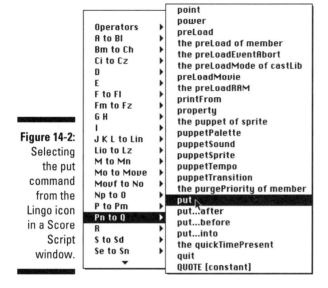

Operators ▶	point
A to Bl ▶	power
Bm to Ch ▶	preLoad
Ci to Cz ▶	the preLoad of member
D ▶	the preLoadEventAbort
E ▶	the preLoadMode of castLib
F to Fl ▶	preLoadMovie
Fm to Fz ▶	the preLoadRAM
G H ▶	printFrom
I ▶	property
J K L to Lin ▶	the puppet of sprite
Lio to Lz ▶	puppetPalette
M to Mn ▶	puppetSound
Mo to Move ▶	puppetSprite
Mouf to No ▶	puppetTempo
Np to O ▶	puppetTransition
P to Pm ▶	the purgePriority of member
Pn to Q ▶	put
R ▶	put...after
S to Sd ▶	put...before
Se to Sn ▶	put...into
▼	the quickTimePresent
	quit
	QUOTE [constant]

Figure 14-2:
Selecting
the put
command
from the
Lingo icon
in a Score
Script
window.

4. Press Return to execute the line of Lingo in the Message window.

Underneath the line of Lingo you typed, Director displays the current time prefaced with two hyphens to indicate that Director executed the command. The two hyphens actually represent one of Lingo's operators, the comment operator, which marks a line of text as a note rather than an instruction.

By the way, a function has one of two forms. For example, you can see the date function as `the /date` and `date()`. Same thing.

Handlers

A handler consists of three or more lines that follow a very strict format, as in

```
on exitFrame
    go to frame 15
end
```

The first line of a handler always consists of *on,* a space, and then the name of the handler. In this example, `exitFrame` is the name of a built-in handler that you use often in the Script channel of the Score. Director initiates an exitFrame handler as the playback head in the Score window leaves the frame that contains the exitFrame handler.

The name of the handler must always be one word. In other words, you can't use spaces in the handler's name. A well-established convention is to start the name of a handler with a lowercase letter. You can add words to the name of the handler by capitalizing the first letter of each additional word without adding spaces. For example, you can name a handler *getARandomNumber*. Notice that the name of the handler is technically still one word even though you can read it as a phrase or sentence. You can also use an underline to give the sense of separate words in a variable name. Director reads a handler name like *get_A_Random_Number* as one word, too.

The second line of a handler begins the list of Lingo commands that you use in the specific handler. In the earlier example, you find only the go command. In some complex handlers, the list of commands may be half a page or more in length.

The last line of a handler, the third line in this case, is always end. Writing Lingo is that simple, folks.

Events

Director echoes the way your computer works — probably all that empty space inside your machine. Your computer is waiting to serve you and is nervously checking whether you pressed a key on the keyboard or clicked the mouse so that it can respond appropriately. Pressing a key on the keyboard or clicking the mouse is called an event.

Director behaves the same way when playing back a movie. While a movie is playing, Director constantly checks for events that may be occurring. It checks for the following types of events:

- **activateWindow event:** When a window becomes active
- **closeWindow event:** When the active window is closed
- **deactivateWindow event:** When the active window is no longer active
- **enterFrame event:** When the playback head enters a frame in the Score
- **exitFrame event:** When the playback head leaves a frame in the Score
- **idle event:** A nonevent, when no event is occurring during playback
- **keyDown event:** When you press a key on the keyboard
- **keyUp event:** When you release a key on the keyboard
- **mouseDown event:** When you press the mouse button down
- **mouseUp event:** When you release the mouse button
- **newEvent event:** When a custom behavior or script sends a message

✔ **prepareFrame event:** When the playback head leaves a frame in the Score but before the playback head enters the next frame

✔ **rightMouseDown event:** When you press the right mouse button of a PC mouse

✔ **rightMouseUp event:** When you release the right mouse button of a PC mouse

✔ **startMovie event:** When a movie begins to play back

✔ **stopMovie event:** When a movie stops playing

✔ **timeOut event:** Another kind of nonevent, when an event does not occur at an anticipated time

✔ **zoomWindow event:** When you click a window's zoom button

Messages

Every time an event occurs, Director sends out an alarm or message. For example, with a keyDown event, Director releases a keyDown message. A mouseDown event initiates a mouseDown message.

You can actually view these messages as they occur, and you don't even have to drink a six-pack with the Coneheads. Just call up the Message window by choosing Window⇨Message or by pressing ⌘/Ctrl+M, check the Trace button (the middle button under the title bar), and play your movie. Figure 14-3 shows the Message window in action, displaying messages in a scrolling list as a movie plays.

Figure 14-3: Clicking the trace button in the Message window displays messages passed and Lingo scripts executed on playback of your Director movie.

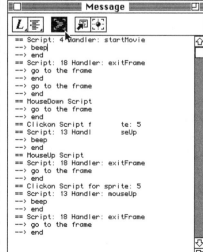

Variables

A variable is a little bit of memory you reserve and name to store a value. For example, in a handler, you may type the following line:

```
put 10 into theNum
```

That single statement accomplishes three things:

- ✔ Declares a variable. (Declare is programmerSpeak for "create.")
- ✔ Names the variable theNum.
- ✔ Stores the value 10 in the variable.

It's that simple; don't make it any more complicated.

You may decide to create another variable in the same handler with an additional line:

```
put "Lauren" into firstName
```

This line tells Director to put the name, Lauren, into firstName. Notice that when storing a value, such as 10, you don't use quote marks. To store words, such as Lauren, cat, or dog, you must use quotes to tell Director the value is a *literal,* which means that the value of the word stored is the word itself. You need to use quotes to differentiate a literal from the same group of characters (word) used as a variable.

For example, you may enter the following line in a handler:

```
put "Lauren" into cat
```

In this case, you declare, or create, a variable; name it cat; and store the word "Lauren" in the variable. Remember, a variable is just an arbitrary name you give to a little bit of memory in your computer.

Local variables

When you declare a variable in a handler by entering a line like in the "cat" example in the preceding section, you create a local variable — local because Director recognizes it only in the handler where you create the variable. If you decide to add a line in another handler that takes the value of cat and puts it in a text sprite, Text Cast Member 1, you may enter something like the following:

```
set the text of member 1 = cat
```

But Director objects, saying that you're trying to use a variable that doesn't exist. In this case, you need to use a special kind of handler called a global variable.

Global variables

Global variables are variables that you can use in any handler of your movie, ergo global. To create a global variable, simply type **global**, a space character, and the name of the variable in the second line of a handler. That's all there is to it. Staying with the example of using the variable cat, you may type a couple of lines within a handler as follows:

```
global cat
put "Lauren" into cat
```

Now, whenever you want another handler to access the value stored in the variable cat, just be sure to type **global cat** as the second line of the other handler.

Scripts

A script is the text in the Script window that consists of one or more handlers. Say you have a button in the first frame of a movie. The Script window has a mouseUp handler and a custom handler named getARandomNumber. The mouseUp handler moves the playback head to a new frame. The getARandomNumber handler generates a random number — with something called the random function — that determines the number the mouseUp handler uses to move the playback head. These two handlers form a script in the Button Cast Member Script window. It's that simple. (See Figure 14-4.)

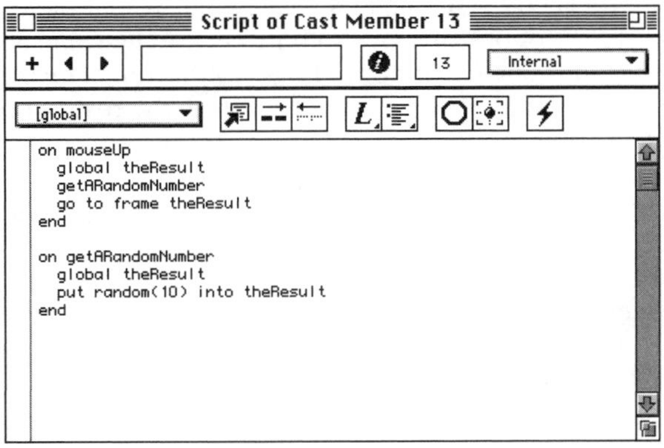

Figure 14-4:
Two handlers in the script of a Button Cast Member.

To briefly explain what this script accomplishes, the getARandomNumber handler declares a global variable (discussed in the previous section) named theResult. The handler uses the random function to pick a random number, in this case, a number from 1 to 10, and places the number into theResult. The mouseUp handler also declares the global variable so that it can use the number stored in theResult. The mouseUp handler calls on getARandomNumber, gets the random number from the global variable, and tells Director to move the playback head to the random frame number that getARandomNumber generates. You may have a different image on each frame so that viewers see a different image each time they press the button.

Script window

Choose Window⇨Script or press ⌘/Ctrl+0 (zero) to display the Script window, looking amazingly like Figure 14-5.

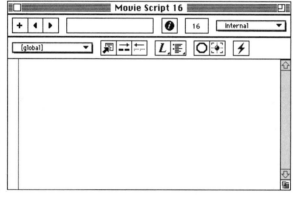

Figure 14-5:
A Movie
Script
window,
where you
can type
Lingo
scripts for
your movie.

In addition to all the accoutrements of a basic window, just beneath the title bar you find a row of buttons. These buttons are the same as Mr. Paint window's buttons, with one exception: The Script button is missing because you're already in the Script window. You can review the rest of these buttons in Chapter 8.

The stuff that's different is in the second row. Allow me to perambulate through the buttons with you from left to right:

- ✓ **Handler Name pop-up menu:** After you write a slew of Lingo handlers for a movie, Director lists them all in the Handler Name pop-up menu, a veritable Who's Who of Lingo handlers.

- ✓ **Go to Handler button:** The Script window is like a miniature word processor. Somewhere in the window is an insertion point. If the insertion point is in a line that refers to a handler, clicking Go to Handler takes you directly to that handler.

✔ **Comment button:** Click to add the comment operator (--) to the beginning of a line; it's a good idea to be generous with comments in a script.

✔ **Uncomment button:** Clicking Uncomment removes the comment symbol (--) from a line of text in the Script window.

✔ **Alphabetical Lingo pop-up menu:** Pressing this button reveals a list of operators and commands in alphabetical order (refer to Figure 14-1).

✔ **Categorized Lingo pop-up menu:** Clicking this button reveals a list of Lingo stuff organized by categories such as Navigation, Movie Control, and User Interaction.

✔ **Toggle Breakpoint button:** This button sets or clears a *breakpoint*, a special red marker like a giant bullet point to the left of a line in the Script window. As Director executes a script, it stops at each toggle breakpoint and takes you to the Debugger where you can analyze a handler that's not working properly. For more Debugger info, check out the bonus chapters on the CD.

✔ **Watch Expression button:** The Watch Expression button and the Watcher window work together to keep track of what expressions and variables stand for while you play back a movie. Add an expression and variable you want to keep track of to the Watcher window by clicking the expression or variable in the Script window and then clicking the Watch Expression button. After you add the expression or variable to the Watcher window, Director updates it as your movie plays back.

✔ **Recompile Script button:** Lingo is too conversational for your computer to understand, so you need to translate or recompile Lingo into machine language. Click to recompile and test all handlers in the current movie.

Script Cast Member Properties dialog box

In the Script Cast Member Properties dialog box, you find important info about the script you're currently exploring. Display the Script Cast Member Properties dialog box by clicking the Cast Member Properties button in the top row of Script window buttons, as shown in the margin. Take a look at the dialog box's layout, shown in Figure 14-6, which includes the following options:

✔ **Script Preview:** The square panel in the upper-left corner of the dialog box. Displays the first few lines of the script. Note the Script icon in the lower-right corner of the Script Preview panel.

✔ **Cast Member Name:** (no name) is the default name Director gives a new Script Cast Member. It's not a bad idea to give a Script Cast Member a meaningful name. In the Script window, the name appears following a colon as in "Movie Script 1:Meaningful Name Appears Here."

Figure 14-6:
Click the
Cast
Member
Properties
button in
the Script
window to
go to the
Script Cast
Member
Properties
dialog box.

- **Cast Member Number:** Each Script window sits in the Cast window as a Script Cast Member with its own location number — in this case, 16 — displayed just below the Script Preview panel.

- **Cast Type:** Tells you whether the Script window belongs to an internal or external cast. See Chapter 5 for related info.

- **Cast Member Size:** Tells you the size of the cast member in bytes, basic computer stuff nobody knows anything about.

- **Type pop-up menu:** Displays three basic types of scripts you can write for a Director movie: Movie, Score, and Parent.

Types of scripts

Where a specific script resides in your movie determines the type of script and how accessible the script is. In a sense, some scripts such as movie scripts appear in the Yellow Pages so that everyone knows about them and can call on them. Other scripts, such as button scripts, have unlisted numbers because you only use them in very restricted situations. I discuss types of scripts in the following sections.

Movie scripts

Most movie scripts are a set of initialization handlers that set primary event handlers, load values into memory, and generally set up the movie for playback. Using the startMovie message, a movie script typically looks like Figure 14-7.

Figure 14-7:
A typical
movie script
in a Movie
Script
window.

```
on startMovie
   global stateFlag
   set the mouseUpScript to "set the foreColor of cast 1 = 0"
   set the timeOutLength to 6*60
   put 0 into stateFlag
end
```

This initialization movie script in Figure 14-8 translates as follows:

- ✔ **Line 1 says:** Make a handler called startMovie.

- ✔ **Line 2 says:** When the movie starts, name a part of memory stateFlag and make it a global variable so that the value the variable holds is available to any other handler that declares stateFlag.

- ✔ **Line 3 says:** Set the color of text inside Button Cast Member 1 to white.

- ✔ **Line 4 says:** Start timing down from 360 ticks, or 6 seconds (and if nothing happens within 6 seconds, do the timeoutScript handler defined elsewhere in the movie).

- ✔ **Line 5 says:** Put the starting value, 0, into a reserved part of memory that you named stateFlag, which tells Director whether a user has pressed the button since the movie began. Another handler in the button declares the global variable, stateFlag, and sets stateFlag to 1 the first time the person running the movie presses the button.

Movie scripts want to be available to everyone, everywhere. Movie scripts and primary event handlers are the most accessible scripts in your movie.

To create a movie script, follow these steps:

1. **Choose Window⇨Script.**

2. **If the Script window is not blank, click the New Script button (the + icon) in the upper-left corner of the Script window.**

   A new Script window always starts as a movie script. If you want a different kind of script, click the Script Cast Member Properties button (the i icon) and choose a different type of script in the Type pop-up menu.

3. **Enter your movie script handlers and commands.**

   For example, you may enter one or more of the following commands in a startUp handler:

```
on startUp
  set the soundLevel to 7
  set the colorDepth to 8
  preloadCast 5
end
```

The soundLevel indicates the current volume from 0 for off to 7 for ouch, the highest sound level. Using the set command, you set the sound level to its highest setting.

The colorDepth indicates how many colors your monitor currently displays. In the second command line, you set the color depth to 8 bits, giving you 256 different colors.

PreloadCast is a Lingo command that copies designated cast members into RAM before they appear on the Stage for improved performance. The third command line copies Cast Member 5 into RAM; maybe it's a big digital video.

4. **Close the Script window by pressing ⌘/Ctrl+W.**

A dialog box appears if any problems occur with your script so that you can debug your work. Chances are the error is a typo or a syntax problem.

5. **Press ⌘/Ctrl+Option/Alt+P to play your movie and test the handler.**

By the way, you can have more than one movie script in a movie.

Primary event handlers

Actions in Director are generally considered events. Director always knows when an event occurs. Four specific actions a user can do in Director are so basic they're called *primary events.* The four primary events are

- ✔ **keyDown Event:** Whenever you press a key on the keyboard

- ✔ **mouseDown Event:** Whenever you press the mouse button

- ✔ **mouseUp Event:** Whenever you release the mouse button

- ✔ **timeOut Event:** Whenever a specific duration of time passes without an anticipated event occurring

Director 6 allows you to write a handler for each of these primary events. You can write a keyDownScript, a mouseDownScript, a mouseUpScript, and a timeOutScript for your movie. Had I designed Director, I would've stuck with the term handler. But someone in his or her infinite wisdom named them scripts; don't let that term confuse you — they're handlers. Usually, you write these special handlers as part of a movie script, which I explain in the preceding section, "Movie scripts."

Director executes primary event handlers whenever a primary event occurs during your movie's playback. To help you understand the unique consequence of including a primary event handler in your movie, consider what occurs without a primary event handler in your movie. An example of a regular mouseDown handler in a button is

```
on mouseDown
beep 2
end
```

Clicking the mouse over the button generates a mouseDown message. The mouseDown handler in the button acts like a trap, "catching" the mouseDown message. Director beeps twice because the command is activated. The mouseDown message ends there, echoing the meaning of the third line of the handler, end. That particular mouseDown event does not trigger any other handler.

On the other hand, when you add a mouseDownScript to the movie, Director executes the mouseDownScript every time the user presses the mouse, even if the mouseDown event triggers a button that would normally trap the mouseDown message.

For example, you can write a mouseDownScript to randomly change the color of a button's text label (the name of the button that the user sees on the Stage) every time the user clicks the button. If you need to create a button with the Tool palette, page back to Chapter 10.

First, add a script to a button so that it beeps when the user presses it. Follow these steps:

1. **On the Stage, click a button to which you want to add a script.**

2. **If you've already given the button a text label, skip to Step 4; otherwise, double-click the button sprite on the Stage.**

   The button sprite now displays a wide, striped selection border and a blinking insertion point in the center of the sprite.

3. **Type a text label for the button sprite.**

   This label appears to a user as the button's name (usually indicating its function).

4. **Choose Modify⇨Sprite⇨Script.**

   The Script window for the button appears with the handler on mouseUp already entered on line 1, a blank second line ready with the blinking insertion point, and end automatically entered on the third line.

5. **Type your command line(s) at the blinking insertion point, in this case** beep 2, **and then click the Mac's Close box or double-click the Windows Control menu box.**

The following set of steps shows you how to add a script to the Score so that you remain in the same frame while the movie plays back:

1. **Choose Window⇨Score.**

In Frame 1, notice the sprite representing the button on the Stage. The frame just above the sprite is the Script cell for Frame 1.

2. **Double-click the Script channel in Frame 1.**

The Script window for Frame 1 appears with the handler on exitFrame already entered on Line 1, a blank second line ready with the blinking insertion point, and end entered on the third line.

3. **Type** go to the frame.

Go to the frame is a special version of the go command that keeps the user in the frame where the command appears while the movie continues playing.

4. **Click the Mac's Close box or double-click the Windows Control menu box in the Script window.**

Now that you set up your button and Frame 1 with a couple of simple scripts, you can write a primary event handler that kicks in with a mouseDown message even if a button you click executes its handlers. Without a primary event handler, the mouseDown message would stop at the button and never reach a movie script.

Say you decide to make the primary event handler — that changes a button's color when the user presses it — a startMovie type handler.

1. **Choose Window⇨Script or press ⌘/Ctrl+0 (zero) to display the Script window.**

2. **For the first line, type** on startMovie.

3. **For the second line, type a mouseDownScript. For example, type**

```
set the mouseDownScript to "set the foreColor of cast 1
        = random(255)"
```

This line of Lingo changes the color of the button's name to different colors every time the user presses the button. Be sure to include the plain quote characters in the preceding example.

The first part of the line, set the mouseDownScript to, establishes the current handler for a mouseDown event, one of four primary events in Director.

The next part of the line, `set the foreColor of cast 1`, uses the set command to change the foreground color of cast 1, referring to the button you made, Cast Member 1 in the Cast window. The foreground color of the button is the color of the text you typed in the button.

The last part of the line, `= random(255)"`, is one of those functions I discuss earlier in this chapter. This line tells Director to return or pick a random number from 1 to 255 and to change the foreground color of the button to that random number every time the user presses the mouse. In Lingo, you set colors by number.

4. For the third and final line, type end.

Press ⌘/Ctrl+Option/Alt+P to play back your movie; you can test your scripts by clicking the button several times. The button should beep and its text label should change color each time. If you click anywhere in the background of the Stage, the button's text label should still change color but without beeping, thanks to the mouseDownScript.

Cast member scripts

A cast member script is exclusive to the cast member it belongs to. Director executes handlers in a cast member script after you click the cast member's sprite on the Stage during playback.

To make a cast member script, follow these steps:

1. Choose Window⇨Cast or press ⌘/Ctrl+3 to display the Cast window.

2. Select the cast member in the Cast window.

3. Click the Script button at the top of the Cast window.

Director takes you to the Cast Member Script window.

4. Enter Lingo commands between on mouseUp **and** end**.**

Try playing with the beep command or, if you feel up to it, check out the set foreColor of cast command in the preceding section "Primary event handlers."

5. Click the Mac's Close box or double-click the Windows Control menu box.

6. Press ⌘/Ctrl+Option/Alt+P to play your movie and test the handler.

Sprite scripts

When you drag a cast member onto the Stage from the Cast window, you create a sprite on the Stage and in the Score. A sprite script is a script for that particular sprite in that particular frame of the Score. Director can execute a sprite script when the person viewing the movie clicks the sprite during playback or when the mouse pointer touches the sprite on the Stage.

Follow these steps to make a sprite script:

1. **Choose Window⇨Score or press ⌘/Ctrl+4 to display the Score window.**

2. **Select a sprite in the Score.**

3. **Click the Script box at the top of the Score.**

4. **In the Script window that appears, add lines of Lingo between the first line,** on mouseUp, **and the last line,** end.

5. **Press ⌘/Ctrl+Option/Alt+P to play your movie and test the handler.**

Why You Want to Write Lingo Scripts but Don't Know It

As you can tell from my whirlwind tour of Lingo, adding simple Lingo scripts to a movie elevates the Director experience to a dramatic new level. With Lingo, you can check the type of machine running your movie, set the color depth of the monitor, fade in a sound, fade out a sound, adjust the volume of the sound, and at least two or three other things, actually hundreds, probably thousands.

Most importantly to you multimedia types out there in ReaderLand, you can add a level of interactivity to your movie that is accessible only through scripting with Lingo or by using behaviors. When you learn to "make your movie make decisions" with conditional statements using "if-then" lines of Lingo to branch to one of several different possible options — at random, if you so choose — and use repeat statements and a number of other advanced scripting techniques, you're well on your way to developing fully interactive products for multimedia and the Web with Director 6. Bon voyage!

Chapter 15

Behaviors, the Secret Sauce of Interactive Multimedia

*B*less you, people of Macromedia. You bequeathed to the vast multitudes programmingless programming in the form of behaviors. Because of your generous spirit, fewer nails will now be bitten, hair loss will drop significantly throughout the world, and we will have more temperate days with only moderate precipitation. Tornadoes will still favor trailer parks, however.

Drag-and-Drop Behaviors

Director 6 comes with a set of *drag-and-drop* behaviors that allow you to accomplish tasks that were previously possible only by learning Lingo programming. Now you can simply choose from a special Cast window full of behaviors and drag one or more behaviors over a sprite on the Stage or in the Score.

Each behavior is a small set of prebuilt Lingo programming. Dragging a behavior over a sprite on the Stage or in the Score window adds that Lingo programming to the sprite without needing to learn Lingo, itself.

For those of you crazy enough, er, brave enough to want to delve into Lingo, see Chapter 14.

You can access behaviors by choosing Xtras⇨Behaviors Library. The Behaviors Library Cast window appears, as shown in Figure 15-1. Scroll down the set of behaviors and note that Director organizes the behaviors into specific areas such as Navigation, Media, Control, and Bad Hair Days.

Figure 15-1:
The
Behaviors
Library is a
collection
of Behavior
Cast
Members,
prebuilt
Lingo
programming
that you
can drag
over
sprites.

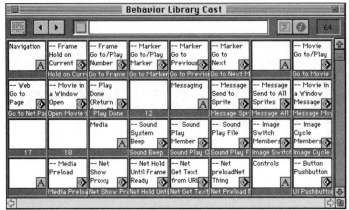

Note that Behavior Cast Members in the Cast window sport a new, diamond-shaped media type icon. For more info on media type icons and the Cast window in general, see Chapter 5.

Some of the tasks you can take care of with behaviors include:

Adding functionality to push buttons

To create a push button and add functionality to it with a drag-and-drop behavior, follow these steps:

   1. Choose Insert⇨Control⇨Push Button.

   A push button appears on the Stage, highlighted and ready for you to type a label for it.

   2. While the push button is highlighted, type a label for the button.

   The user sees the label of the button when the movie plays back. For example, you may want to label a push button that takes you to the next screen as "Next."

   Note: The label is not the same as the name of the push button. When you first create a push button, it has no name; more specifically, it's name is literally "(no name)." To name the push button, press ⌘/Ctrl+i, type a name for the button, and click OK.

   3. Choose Xtras⇨Behaviors Library.

4. Scroll to the Navigation area of the Behaviors Library and drag the behavior named Go to Frame over the push button on the Stage.

The Parameters for "Go to Frame" dialog box, shown in Figure 15-2, appears.

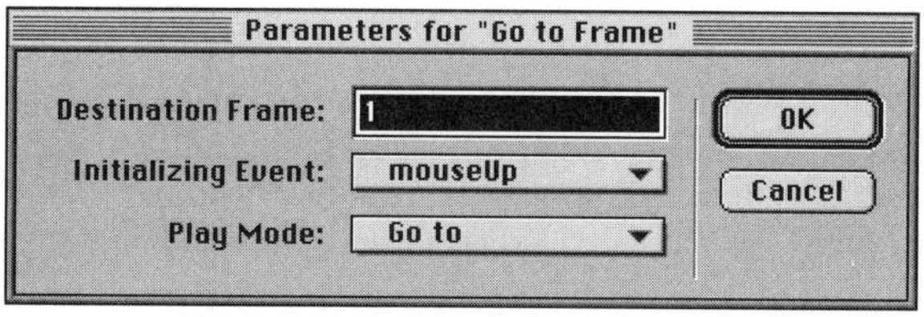

Figure 15-2:
The
Parameters
dialog box.

```
┌──────────── Parameters for "Go to Frame" ────────────┐
│  Destination Frame:  [1              ]    ┌────────┐  │
│                                           │   OK   │  │
│  Initializing Event: [ mouseUp    ▼ ]    └────────┘  │
│                                           ┌────────┐  │
│  Play Mode:          [ Go to      ▼ ]    │ Cancel │  │
│                                           └────────┘  │
└──────────────────────────────────────────────────────┘
```

The Parameters dialog box includes three areas that complete the preprogrammed behavior and make the push button functional: Destination Frame, Initializing Event, and Play Mode. For more info on these options, see the sidebar, "Customized behaviors," later in this chapter.

5. Type the number of the frame you want to go to in the Destination Frame entry box.

6. Choose mouseUp in the Initializing Event pop-up menu.

Most buttons work with a mouseUp message. Take a gander at the sidebar, "Customized behaviors," later in this chapter for the scoop on mouseUp messages.

7. Choose Go to in the Play Mode pop-up menu and close the dialog box.

To actually test the push button, you need to make the movie pause on the frame that displays the push button by adding the Hold on Current Frame behavior to your movie. Lucky devil, this behavior just happens to be the very next topic!

Making a movie pause on a frame

When you develop multimedia with Director 6, you often want to set up your movie so that it pauses at certain frames, such as a main menu screen that gives the user a set of options. By using the new Hold on Current Frame behavior, you can easily add this feature to any frame you like.

1. Go to the frame where you want the movie to pause.

2. Choose Xtras⇨Behaviors Library to display the Behaviors Library Cast window.

3. **Scroll to the Navigation area of the Behaviors Library and locate the Behaviors Cast Member named "Hold on Current Frame."**

4. **Drag the Hold on Current Frame behavior over a blank area of the Stage.**

5. **When Director frames the Stage in a bold, gray outline, release the mouse button.**

Director automatically adds some Lingo programming to the Script channel of the Score window in the current frame. The lines of Lingo cause the movie to pause on this frame upon playback. To review Score window stuff, such as the Script channel, see Chapter 6. For a taste of Lingo, see Chapter 14.

Playing a sound interactively

You may want to play a sound file that you haven't imported into a Director movie (to keep the movie's file size down). You may also want to have the sound play when the user clicks a sprite on the Stage as if the sprite is a button. To accomplish this nuttiness, use the Sound Play File behavior by following these steps:

1. **Go to the frame that contains the sprite you want to use as a button to play an external sound file.**

2. **Choose Xtras⊃Behaviors Library to display the Behaviors Library Cast window.**

3. **Add the Hold on Current Frame behavior by following Step 3 through Step 5 in the previous section, "Making a movie pause on a frame."**

You need to pause on the frame to give the user a chance to click the sprite.

4. **Drag the Sound Play File behavior over the sprite on the Stage.**

The Parameters for "Sound Play File" dialog box appears, shown in Figure 15-3, where you need to enter three items: the name of the external sound file, including its *path* or address on your hard drive (see the sidebar, "On the right path"); the sound channel you want the sound to play from Channel 1 to Channel 4 (that's right, with Lingo or behaviors you can access more than the two standard sound channels in the Score); and the Initializing Event, which you choose from a pop-up menu.

5. **In the Sound File entry box, type the exact name of the external sound file, including its path.**

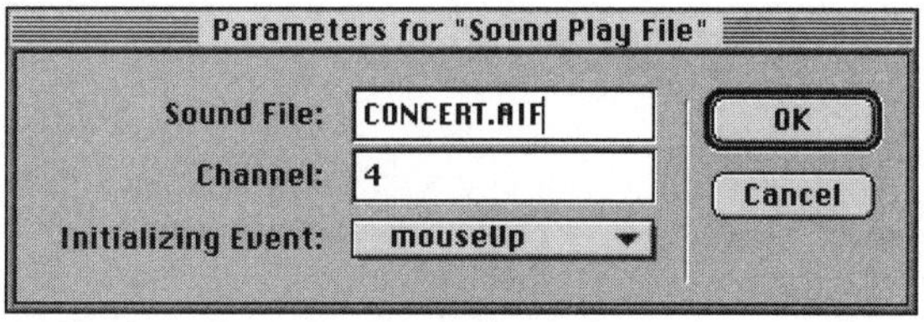

Figure 15-3:
When you drag the Sound Play File behavior over a sprite, the Parameters for "Sound Play File" dialog box appears.

Parameters for "Sound Play File"	
Sound File: `CONCERT.AIF`	OK
Channel: `4`	Cancel
Initializing Event: `mouseUp ▼`	

6. **In the Channel entry box, type a channel number from 1 to 4.**

7. **From the Initializing Event pop-up menu, choose an event, such as mouseUp, that causes the external sound to play.**

   For more on events, see the "Customized behaviors"sidebar in this chapter.

8. **Click OK.**

Creating a rollover with one hand tied behind your back

Actually, you don't need to tie up either hand to use this behavior. A *rollover* is a word from Lingo meaning that one or more programming commands kick into gear when the mouse pointer moves over a sprite. Normally, this kind of action requires some serious programming and a box or two of Tums. Lucky you, now you can just drag the UI Rollover Change Member behavior over a sprite and trade in that box of Tums for some Oreos.

Why would you want this kind of rollover to happen? Good question. You can create a great "glow" effect with this kind of rollover. By preparing a regular version of a sprite that acts like a button and a second version of the sprite with a neon-like glow (you can do this in xRes, for instance), you can set up this rollover so that when the viewer passes the mouse pointer over the sprite, the sprite suddenly glows as if jumping to life. Pretty snazzy if you ask me. Follow these steps to create a rollover:

On the right path

Sometimes when you whip up multimedia with Director, you need to deal with something called the path of a file. The path is nothing more than the address of the file on your hard drive. Take a look at the path of a Mac sound file:

```
Lauren's Hard Drive:Sound Files
    Folder:INTRO.AIF
```

The above example represents the path or address of the sound file named INTRO.AIF. Reading the code backwards, the path says that the sound file is in a folder named Sound Files Folder, which is in the hard drive named Lauren's Hard Drive.

On a Macintosh computer, you separate each part of the path with a colon (:), which is why your Mac won't let you type a colon as part of a filename (try it, you get a hyphen instead). With a PC, use the slash (/) character to separate the different parts of a file's address in the directory.

---

1. **Go to the frame that has the sprite you want to use with the UI Rollover Change Member behavior.**

2. **Choose Xtras⇨Behaviors Library to display the Behaviors Library Cast window.**

3. **Add the Hold on Current Frame behavior by following Steps 3 though 5 in the section "Making a Movie Pause on a Frame."**

   You need to pause on the frame to give the user a chance to roll the mouse pointer over the sprite.

4. **Drag the UI Rollover Change Member behavior over the sprite.**

   The Parameters for "UI Rollover Change Member" dialog box appears.

5. **In the Alternate Image pop-up menu listing other bitmaps in the Cast window, choose the cast member you want to switch to when the rollover occurs.**

   If you named your cast members in the Cast window, the Alternate Image pop-up menu shows your cast members by name. Otherwise, the pop-up menu refers to them by cast member number and Cast window number as in "member 2 of castLib 1." Director refers to Cast windows as castLibs and uses castLib 1 as your default internal Cast window. Other numbers represent additional internal or external Casts. For full disclosure on Cast window stuff, see Chapter 5.

6. **Click OK.**

Customized behaviors

When you use certain behaviors, Director displays a variation of the Parameters dialog box. The dialog box may be a simple entry box or a more complex dialog box featuring many options, such as the Parameters dialog box for the Hold on Current Frame behavior.

The Destination Frame entry box lets you type the frame number of the movie you want to move to when the behavior kicks in. For example, typing 25 in the entry box for a push button with the Go to behavior makes the movie jump to Frame 25 when the user clicks the button.

The Initializing Event pop-up menu sets up the action that initiates the behavior. Director calls this action an *event*. For example, clicking the mouse creates two events, a mouseDown event, when the user presses the mouse button, and a mouseUp event, when the user releases the mouse button. Other types of events include enterFrame, when the Score goes to the next frame in the movie, and exitFrame, when the Score leaves the frame.

The Play Mode pop-up menu lists choices for what happens after the event chosen in the Initializing Event pop-up menu occurs. You can choose *Go to* to go to another frame in the movie or even to another movie. Or you can choose *Play and Return* to set up playing an animation sequence in the current movie or another movie and then return to the original frame.

The Behaviors Library Cast Window

The Behaviors Library Cast window is the key to using Director 6's new drag-and-drop behaviors. You find the Behaviors Library under the Xtras menu. The Behaviors Library Cast window is just like the Internal Cast window that comes with each new movie you create in Director. You can read more about Cast window stuff in Chapter 5.

The Behaviors Library comes with a whole set of prebuilt Behavior Cast Members organized into specific areas within the Cast window, such as Navigation and Controls. You can scroll down the window until you find the right behavior for your movie.

To add a behavior to a sprite on the Stage or in the Score window, just drag the behavior from the Behaviors Library Cast window to the sprite. Director then adds a copy of the Behavior Cast Member to the Internal Cast window of the movie. You can also add two or more behaviors to a sprite. To choose a block of behaviors in the Behaviors Library, Shift+click a range of behaviors in the Cast window. If you need behaviors from different areas of the Behaviors Library, ⌘/Ctrl+click a set of behaviors. After you select one or more behaviors in the Behaviors Library, press any one of the selected behaviors and drag it to the sprite on the Stage or in the Score. Truth be known, sometimes you may want to drag a behavior such as the Hold on Frame behavior over a blank area of the Stage itself.

The following list describes the basic set of behaviors that comes with Director 6. You can use these behaviors without any knowledge of Lingo programming. These easy behaviors include

- ✔ **Hold on Current Frame:** This behavior is one of the few that you drag over the Stage itself instead of over a sprite, and it allows the movie to continue playing but pauses on the current frame. This way the viewer has a chance to make some kind of choice, such as clicking a button at a main menu screen to go to some other section of the Score.

- ✔ **Go to/Play Frame:** You typically drag this behavior over a sprite that functions as a button. You can choose Insert⇨Control⇨Push Button to add a classic button-type sprite to the Stage, and then you drag the behavior over the button. But in Director, any bitmap or PICT-type sprite can be a button, too. At any rate, after you drag the behavior over a sprite, the Parameters dialog box appears where you can enter the frame you want the button to take the user to. You can also choose whether to go to a frame or to play a series of frames and then return to the frame where the user clicked the button. Use this behavior along with the Play Done behavior described later in this list.

- ✔ **Go to/Play Marker:** The previous comment for the Go to/Play Frame behavior applies to this behavior as well except that instead of going to a frame, the Go to Marker behavior navigates the user to the marker you elect in the Parameters dialog box. (I fully explain markers in Chapter 13.) As with Go to/Play Frame, you can choose whether to go to a marker or to play a series of frames from a marker that you elect in the Parameters dialog box and then return to the frame where the user clicked the button. Use this behavior along with. . . .

- ✔ **Play Done:** This behavior works with the Go to/Play Frame and Go to/Play Marker behaviors by marking the end of the animation sequence you want the user to see when you set up the behaviors as a Play Frame or Play Marker behavior. To use the Play Done behavior, go to the last frame of the animation sequence and drag the behavior over the Stage itself. In the dialog box that appears, you usually want to choose exitFrame from the Initializing Event pop-up menu.

- ✔ **Go to Previous Marker:** This behavior takes the viewer to the previous marker in the Score relative to the current frame.

- ✔ **Go to Next Marker:** This behavior takes the viewer to the following marker in the Score relative to the current frame.

- ✔ **Go to/Play Movie:** This behavior takes the user to another Director movie you elect in the Parameters dialog box. When the dialog box appears, Director doesn't present you with the Directory to find the movie; you need to *type in* the exact name of the movie in the Movie entry box. And don't bother trying to copy and paste the name of the movie in the Movie entry box, that process simply doesn't work. You can also choose whether to simply go to another movie or to play the movie and then return to the movie where the user clicked the button.

✔ **Go to Net Page:** This behavior takes the user to the World Wide Web page address — referred to as the URL (Uniform Resource Locator) — that you type in the Destination URL box of the Parameters dialog box. For example, if you want a button to take the viewer to Macromedia's home page, type the address `http://www.macromedia.com` in the Destination URL box.

✔ **Sound Beep:** This behavior plays the System sound alert when the event, as in a mouseUp or mouseDown event, occurs that you designate in the Initialize Event pop-up menu of the Parameters dialog box. For more on events, see the Events pop-up menu topic in the section, "The Behavior Inspector," later in this chapter.

✔ **Sound Play Castmember:** This behavior plays the Sound Cast Member you enter in the Parameters dialog box when the designated Initialize Event occurs. Be ready to type the exact name of the Sound Cast Member in the Sound entry box of the Parameters dialog box and to type the sound channel you want the sound to play in. Because you really use Lingo when you add this behavior to a sprite, you have a choice of up to eight sound channels. You can even drag two or more of these behaviors on a sprite so that up to eight sounds play at the same time. Yikes!

✔ **Sound Play File:** The previous comments for the Sound Play Castmember apply to this behavior as well except that you type an external sound file in the Sound entry box of the Parameters dialog box. In this case, the trick is to be sure to keep the external sound file in the same folder as the Director movie because Director refers to the external file when this behavior is initiated.

✔ **Net Show Proxy:** Use this behavior to display a fast-loading cast member in a movie while a more complex image downloads from the Web. Fast-loading cast members include bitmaps with a low color depth such as 1- to 4-bit images. Be ready to type the exact name of the proxy cast member in the Parameters dialog box.

✔ **UI Pushbutton:** Use this behavior to create a push button from any Bitmap or PICT Cast Member. When you drag the behavior on a sprite, the Parameters dialog box appears and you can choose a different cast member to represent the highlighted button.

✔ **UI Toggle Button:** The previous comment for the UI Pushbutton applies to this behavior as well except that you use this behavior to create effects, such as rocker switches where the button seems to move or become locked in a depressed state after the user clicks it.

Note: The difference between the Pushbutton and Toggle Button behaviors is that the push-button effect is *temporary,* switching to another cast member for the button's highlighted state only as long as the user holds the mouse button down. The toggle effect *permanently* switches cast members until the user clicks the mouse button again. For example, if you want to create the effect of a rocker switch and the button starts out depressed on the left side, clicking the mouse kicks in the behavior, which switches the cast member to a bitmap of the rocker switch, which is depressed on the right side. In this example, every time you click the rocker switch button, it toggles from left to right.

✔ **Video Rewind:** This behavior allows you to create a push button that rewinds a Digital Video Cast Member that you name in the Parameters dialog box.

✔ **Video Play:** This behavior allows you to create a push button that plays a Digital Video Cast Member that you name in the Parameters dialog box.

✔ **Video Stop:** This behavior allows you to create a push button that stops playback of a Digital Video Cast Member that you name in the Parameters dialog box.

✔ **Video Control:** This behavior offers you Rewind, Play, Stop, or Pause functionality from one dialog box. Drag the behavior over a button. In the Parameters for "Video Control" dialog box that appears, choose the video command you want from the Command pop-up menu and type the channel number of the video sprite you want to affect with the button.

✔ **Video Slider:** This behavior seems borderline advanced, but it really just needs a bit of extra preparation. With the Video Slider behavior, you can build a custom slider control that sets the beginning frame of a video sprite during playback. You can even drag the slider to play back the video interactively.

To do so, click the video sprite on the Stage and press ⌘/Ctrl+i to display the Video Cast Member Properties dialog box where you can click the Paused check box.

In the Tool palette (see Chapter 10), choose the unfilled Rectangle tool and the No Line setting for line width and then drag a long "bar" on the Stage for the slider. Create another small sprite on the Stage for the user to slide along the invisible bar during playback.

After you drag the Video Slider behavior over the small sprite, the Parameters for "Video slider" dialog box appears. Enter the video sprite number, the number of the long sprite that serves as the bar and that Director refers to as the Extent Sprite, and the cast member that Director refers to as the Hilite Member.

If you want to build a horizontal slider, check Horizontal. If you want the user to be able to play the video interactively with the slider, check Dynamic. To make this action work, you need to add at least one button to begin playback of the video by dragging the Video Play behavior over the button on the Stage. If you need to review button-making, take a peek at Chapter 10.

That's it; whew.

✔ **UI Pointer Change:** This behavior allows you to change the mouse cursor from the default pointer or arrow to another of Director's seven built-in cursors or to a cast member while the movie plays back or while a specific sprite is on the Stage. You can hide the cursor while the movie is playing by choosing Invisible in the Parameters dialog box.

✔ **UI Pointer Animate:** This lets you designate a sequence of cast members in the Parameters dialog box as the "frames" to animate the mouse cursor during movie playback. If you're comfortable with Lingo stuff such as events, you can set up this behavior for when a specific event occurs (for example, when the user clicks the mouse button).

✔ **UI Rollover Change Pointer:** This behavior allows you to set up the mouse pointer so that it changes to one of Director's seven other built-in cursors or to a cast member designated in the Parameters dialog box when the user moves the pointer over a sprite.

Note: *Rollover* refers to a part of the Lingo programming language that discloses the sprite currently under the mouse pointer. You can then program Director to take some action, depending on what sprite is under the pointer.

✔ **UI Rollover Change Member:** This behavior works like UI Rollover Change Pointer, except that you can set up the change so that a sprite switches from one cast member to another while the user moves the pointer over the sprite on the Stage.

✔ **UI Cursor Change Mouse Down Rollover:** This behavior allows you to make the mouse pointer change to one of Director's other seven cursors or to a cast member when the user moves the pointer over a designated sprite and holds the mouse button down.

✔ **UI Drag Snap to Sprite:** This allows you to make one sprite *snap* to another sprite while being dragged during movie playback, as if you were piecing together a magnetic jigsaw puzzle. First, highlight the Moveable check box in the Score window for each sprite that snaps together. Then set up the registration point of each sprite in the Paint window by mirroring their registration points. For example, if you want a red square to snap to the left of a blue square, you want to select the Registration Point tool in the Paint window and click the center right of the red bitmap and the center left of the blue square so that the vertical registration line acts like a seam. This seam marks where the sprites snap together on the Stage. Now you can drag the behavior over the sprite you intend to drag. In the Parameters dialog box, type the number of the sprite you want to snap to in the Target Sprite entry box. Also enter a Snap Distance value in the Parameters dialog box. This number is how close the sprites need to come in pixels before they snap together. See Chapter 7 for lots more info on using the Registration Point tool.

Take note: For the UI Drag Snap to Sprite behavior, type a *sprite number* in the Target Sprite entry box, not a cast member number.

The following list describes behaviors that I would rate as advanced, meaning that you really need some basic programming and Lingo knowledge to understand and/or make full use of the behaviors. If you feel brave today, take a look at Chapter 14 for more on Lingo.

The more advanced behaviors include

- ✔ **Message Sprite:** This behavior allows you to send a message to a sprite. While you run Director 6, messages are constantly being sent from one part of Director to another. For example, when you click the mouse button, a mouseDown message is sent throughout Director. Using the Message Sprite behavior, you can set up a situation that sends a message, such as a mouseDown message, to a specific sprite — a button-type sprite, for instance — as if the user physically clicks the mouse. You can even send a custom collection of Lingo commands, referred to as a *handler,* using the Message Sprite behavior.

- ✔ **Message All Sprites:** The previous comments for the Message Sprite apply to this behavior as well except that you can set up this behavior in the Parameters dialog box to send messages to all the sprites on the Stage.

- ✔ **Image Switch Cast Members:** This behavior switches one cast member for another when an Initialize Event set up in the Parameters dialog box occurs.

- ✔ **Image Cycle Cast Members:** This behavior is similar to the previous behavior, Image Switch Cast Member, but is even more complex and needs quite a bit of setup in the Parameters dialog box. Put on your safety goggles when working on this behavior.

- ✔ **Media Preload:** This behavior offers memory management similar to the features of the Unload pop-up menu in a Cast Member Properties dialog box. You can use the Media Preload behavior to force designated cast members into memory for better movie playback. For full disclosure on the Unload pop-up menu, see Chapter 5.

✔ **Open Movie in a Window:** Definitely an advanced behavior. Use this behavior to display another Director movie in a new window of its own, referred to in Lingo parlance as a MIAW (Movie in a Window). Why make a MIAW? Developers often use a MIAW as a custom About-type box or a custom palette, such as a navigation palette. You can elect the type of window in the Parameters dialog box. See Table 15-1 later in this chapter.

✔ **Message Movie in a Window:** Sends a designated message to a MIAW. See the previous comment for basic info on MIAWs.

✔ **Net Hold Until Frame Ready:** This behavior is similar to the Hold on Current Frame behavior (discussed in the first list in this section) but stays on the current frame until Director loads into memory the media in the frame range designated in the Parameters dialog box.

✔ **Net Get Text:** This behavior imports text from a URL (Uniform Resource Locator, the address of a specific Web page or Web site) designated in the Parameters dialog box into a Field Cast Member.

✔ **UI Radio Group Item:** This behavior allows you to set up a radio button as part of a group of radio buttons to offer mutually exclusive options to the user. With radio buttons, the user can make only one choice from the available options. For instance, if you created a group of three buttons to change the color depth (the number of colors displayed in the monitor), the user would choose only one setting from radio buttons marked 8-bit, 16-bit, and 24-bit. You can't set the monitor to two or more different color depths at the same time.

When you work with multimedia, you sometimes need to create a custom window, such as a MIAW or Movie in a Window (see the Open Movie in a Window behavior comment in the previous list). You have a choice of numerous window types, although some window types are not cross-platform compatible. For the adventurous among you who want to play with creating MIAWs using advanced behaviors, Table 16-1 lists safe window types you can designate and their numbers.

Table 15-1	Window Types	
Window Number	*Comment*	*Window Type*
0	Moveable and sizeable but doesn't have a zoom box	
1	Modal *dialog* type of window that forces the user to make a decision because the user can't click outside of the window to go to the desktop or another application	

(continued)

Table 15-1 *(continued)*

Window Number	Comment	Window Type
2	Plain	
3	Shadow	
4	Moveable but doesn't have a Size or Zoom box	
5	Similar to Window 1, the *modal dialog* window, but is moveable	
8	Standard document	
12	Zoomable, nonresizeable window	
16	Rounded	
49	The infamous floating palette, a very special kind of window that floats in front of other window types; for special uses such as a navigation or custom tool palette	

Use other types of windows at your own peril. Many other window types are not cross-platform compatible.

The Behavior Inspector

Once upon a time, two inspectors lived under the Window menu, the Memory Inspector and Text Inspector. They were bored cheating each other at pinochle every evening. One night, a little sprite appeared at the stroke of midnight and gave them one wish. They wished for another inspector so they could cheat it at pinochle together. And so the Behavior Inspector came to be.

The Behavior Inspector shows the behavior(s) added to a sprite on the Stage or in the Score. It also allows you to modify a behavior if you're not squeamish about playing around with a handful of programming concepts. For those of you who feel bold, you can even create brand new behaviors from the Behavior Inspector. Like the other inspectors, the Behavior Inspector, shown in Figure 15-4, is a *floating* palette because it hovers in front of other open windows on the screen.

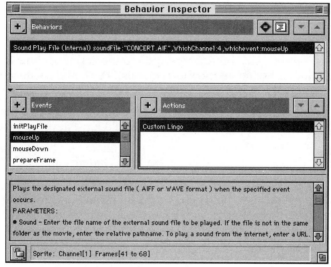

Figure 15-4:
You can modify behaviors or create new ones in the Behavior Inspector.

You can access the Behavior Inspector a number of ways. After selecting a sprite on the Stage or in the Score, Mac users press Ctrl and PC users press the right mouse button on the sprite to display a hidden menu and then choose Behaviors. You can also choose Window⇔Inspectors⇔Behavior. Either way, the Behavior Inspector makes an appearance.

At the top of the Behavior Inspector is the Behaviors panel with a row of buttons and the Behaviors list. These nifty gizmos include

▶ **Behavior Pop-up Menu:** This list, shown in Figure 15-5, displays the New Behavior command and all the behaviors currently in the Cast window. You can add another behavior to the currently selected sprite by choosing a behavior from this list, which Director adds to the sprite's Behaviors list.

▶ **Parameters Button:** This button takes you to the Parameters dialog box for the behavior you select in the Behaviors list.

Figure 15-5:
The
Behavior
pop-up
menu with a
list of
behaviors in
the Cast
window.

✔ **Script Button:** This button takes you to the Script window for the behavior you select in the Behaviors list. For Lingo cognoscenti, you can modify a behavior's Lingo programming. Definitely advanced.

✔ **Next/Previous Behavior Button:** These buttons highlight the next or previous behavior in the Behaviors list. I'd have never guessed.

✔ **Behaviors List:** This list includes all the behaviors that you added to a sprite. It also describes the behaviors, including choices you made in the Parameters dialog box.

Note: You can't edit behaviors in the Behaviors list. You need to double-click a behavior to go to the Parameters dialog box where you can change the behavior's available options. You can also select a behavior and click the diamond-shaped Parameters button in the row of buttons at the top of the Behavior Inspector.

Under the Behaviors list in the Behavior Inspector, you find the Events panel. The Events panel is where you can create a new behavior. To repeat: You really need a grasp of basic Lingo and programming concepts to work with this panel. You can get a head start in Chapter 14.

The Events panel includes the Events pop-up menu. See the sidebar "Customized behaviors" earlier in this chapter for general info on what events are. The pop-up menu lists the following events:

✔ **Mouse Up:** An event that happens when the user releases the mouse button

✔ **Mouse Down:** An event that happens when the user presses the mouse button

✔ **Mouse Enter:** An event that happens when the the mouse pointer intersects a sprite on the Stage

✔ **Mouse Within:** An event that happens as long as the mouse pointer is inside a sprite on the Stage

✔ **Mouse Leave:** An event that happens when the mouse pointer leaves a sprite on the Stage

✔ **Key Up:** An event that happens when the user releases a key on the keyboard

✔ **Key Down:** An event that happens when the user presses a key on the keyboard

✔ **Right Mouse Up:** An event that happens when a PC user releases the right mouse button or when a Macintosh user releases the single mouse button of a Macintosh mouse while holding down the Control key

✔ **Right Mouse Down:** An event that happens when a PC user presses the right mouse button or when a Macintosh user Ctrl-presses the single mouse button of a Macintosh mouse

✔ **Prepare Frame:** An event that happens after leaving one frame of a movie and before entering the following frame

✔ **Enter Frame:** An event that happens when the movie moves to a new frame

✔ **Exit Frame:** An event that happens when the movie leaves the current frame

✔ **New Event:** For creating a custom event

Underneath the Events pop-up menu, you find the Events list that shows one or more events associated with the selected behavior. You can modify the events in the Actions panel to the right of the Events list.

The Actions panel has its own pop-up menu of actions plus Next and Previous Action buttons. To change an event, you can choose a different action or add another action to the event. The Actions pop-up menu includes the following categories:

✔ **Navigation:** This category of actions is based on Lingo's Go to command. The first four actions — Go to Frame, Go to Marker, Go to Movie, and Go to Net Page — display a dialog box like the Parameters dialog box to configure the action. For example, you can elect to go to Frame 5 with the Go to Frame action. Exit refers to a Lingo command that stops a script from running the moment Director encounters the command. For more on Lingo, see Chapter 14.

✔ **Wait:** This category of actions allows you to control and measure time and act on events, such as mouseUp and mouseDown events. The actions include On Current Frame, Until Click or Key Press, and Time Duration that lets you pause the movie in ticks, Director's unit for time based on 60 ticks per second.

✔ **Sound:** This category of actions allows you to control and play sound files in the Cast window or external sound files. The Play Cast Member action plays a sound in the Cast window. The Play External File action plays a sound file that you haven't imported into Director. The Beep action plays the System alert sound, and Set volume, uh, sets the sound volume. For more info about sound in Director 6, see Chapter 16.

✔ **Frame:** This category of actions controls tempos, transitions, and palettes. Go to Chapter 6 for more info on these items and their special channels in the Score window.

✔ **Sprite:** This category of actions changes sprite stuff, such as the sprite's location on the Stage. Each type of action displays a unique Specify dialog box. For instance, when using the Change Location action, type new numbers in its Specify Location dialog box. You can also change the sprite's ink from the default Copy ink to something like Matte ink to hide any white pixels surrounding the sprite. Change Cursor and Restore Cursor let you elect a custom cursor at some point in the movie and then return the cursor to the default mouse pointer. In the Specify Cursor dialog box, be ready with the *number* of the cursor you want, which you can look up in the handy table, Table 15-2. In addition to the cursors in Table 15-2, you can also choose 0 to turn off a cursor and 200 to make a cursor invisible. You're welcome.

Don't forget to include a comma in between the first and last numbers. These numbers are the x and y coordinates for the sprite defining its location on the Stage. Take a look at Chapter 3 for info on how Director keeps a record of where sprites are on the Stage.

✔ **New Action:** This option is for creating a custom action (not for the faint of heart).

Table 15-2	Types of Cursors	
Cursor	*Cursor Number*	*Description*
▶	−1	Arrow (pointer)
I	1	I-beam
+	2	Crosshair
✛	3	Crossbar
⌚	4	Watch (Macintosh only)

At the bottom of the Behavior Inspector is a scrolling field that explains the selected behavior. If you want to protect the behavior from more edits, click the Lock button. This area of the Behavior Inspector also includes information such as the channel number and frame number of the sprite containing the behavior.

Chapter 16

You Talkin' to Me? Adding Sound to Your Movie

. . . .

In This Chapter

▶ Where you acquire sound

▶ Where you store sound files

▶ How to use smaller sound files

▶ All about sync (not including the kitchen kind)

. . . .

*Y*ou may be asking yourself, "Self, add sound to my movie? Okay, I'm all for that, but . . . ." Then all the questions come pouring into your mind. How do I add sounds to my computer? Where can I go for canned sounds? How can I get my mother-in-law to like me? And so on.

I can't help with the in-laws, but this chapter gives you a bevy of tips to help you add quality audio to your Director movies.

Where Do I Get All This Stuff, Anyhow?

Sound? What am I, a producer? As a matter of fact, that's exactly what you become when you get involved in multimedia: a multimedia producer, a wild mix of Hollywood and Silicon Valley. So knowing sources for audio becomes important. With a little thought, a number of possibilities come to mind.

Sampling your own audio

With an AV Mac, you're all set to sample sounds. On a PC, you need to buy a sound card such as Sound Blaster Pro by Creative Labs for sampling sound. Sampling uses an ADC (Analog-to-Digital Converter) to translate audio into digital information, 0s and 1s, the only thing your computer really understands. The higher the sampling rate, the better the sound: 16-bit digitized audio offers near CD-quality results.

The right connections

AV Macs, some Performas, and most PowerBooks have input for sound in the back; it's the connection with the MIC icon on top. Sound cards for the Mac and PC provide their own input and output ports. You can get your audio from a number of sources: VCRs (most hi-fi VHS decks have terrific audio specs), CDs, and even your camcorder. Hi-8 and SuperVHS camcorders offer impressive if not professional levels of audio specs. Connect either the headphone output or the RCA jack output of your audio source to your computer's sound port.

Be prepared with a slew of adapters. Radio Shack and most stereo shops have a wide selection of adapters, but remember this: Somewhere side by side with Murphy's Law, a Universal Rule of Adapters states that you never have the adapter you need. I'd relocate if I were you, cat and all, closer to Radio Shack, just for some peace of mind.

Anyway, older AV Macs such as the 660AV and 840AV feature stereo sound, but they sport a single mini-type stereo Sound-In port. So skip to your handy electronics shop and get a stereo RCA plug-to-stereo mini-plug adapter. The RCA cables go into the adapter, the adapter goes into the Mac, and you're all set for sampling fun. Luckily, Apple's latest Power Macs sport RCA plugs for sound input and output.

Be sure that you have the right to use someone else's audio professionally. You don't want to violate any copyright protection; it's not right, and it's against the law. Check whether the audio is in the public domain, that you've been granted written permission to use the material, or that purchasing the audio gives you the right to use it in a commercial product or public performance. Even then, did you pay for one-time only use (a *drop needle fee*) or unlimited usage?

Sampling sound with an AV Mac

But how do you actually sample or digitize sound after you're all connected? AV Macs come with a program called FusionRecorder, used for making QuickTime movies. You can use QuickTime technology to record only audio, and there's no law against a QuickTime mooV with only an audio track. In FusionRecorder, simply turn off the program's video capabilities. The only other decision to make is what sampling rate to use. The following list shows various sample rates and acceptable uses for them. Remember, the higher the sample rate, the better the sound.

- ✔ **48 kHz:** The AV Mac's highest sample rate in kHz, which stands for kilohertz, or 1,000 hertz, a way of describing the number of sound waves that pass a fixed point, referred to as *frequency,* and a determinant of pitch quality. Use for sampling music, especially from CDs, to obtain the highest playback quality.

- ✔ **44 kHz:** Next highest sampling rate. Use for sampling music from non-CD sources.

- ✔ **24 kHz:** This special sampling rate is available mainly for the Geoport Telecom Adapter used with AV Macs for modem and fax features.

- ✔ **22.05 kHz:** Use this sampling rate or higher for sampling narration and sound effects.

Another common sampling rate is 11 kHz, although not directly available when sampling with an AV Mac. Many utilities are available for *downsampling,* to turn sound sampled at a high sampling rate — 44 kHz or 22 kHz, for example — into 11 kHz, which is acceptable for narration (although a higher sampling rate is always preferable). You may even see 7.5 kHz listed in these downsampling utilities, but this sampling rate is for desperation time only — for example, if you need to fit tons of audio in Director movies that must fit on a double-density floppy.

Why use lower sampling rates at all? The lower the sampling rate, the smaller the sound file. With extended narration and musical scores, sound can dramatically swell a movie's size. Later in this chapter, in the section, "Great Sound for the Price of Good," I show you a way to get double the sound quality at half the file size on a Mac. Unfortunately, I'm not aware of a similar program in the PC world. Some good samaritan is welcome to send me the name of such a program for the PC and I'll include it in the next revision. You can reach me at my e-mail address: laurenrs@aol.com.

Keep in mind Director 6's ability to compress sounds with Shockwave for Audio. You can brush up on this option in Chapter 19.

Using sound editing software

You can use sound editing software to sample sound, downsample digitized sound, manipulate sound with special effects, and convert one sound file type to another.

Sonic Foundry Sound Forge XP

Macromedia bundles Sonic Foundry's Sound Forge XP, shown in Figure 16-1, with the Windows package.

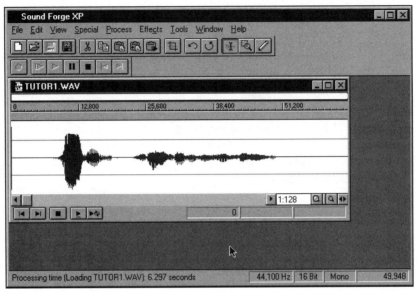

Figure 16-1:
The main
program
window of
Sonic
Foundry's
Sound
Forge XP,
bundled
with the
Director 6
Studio
package for
Windows.

Sound Forge XP is a good package with some interesting special effects. You'll find a demo version on this book's CD. But this program, and the Sound Forge 4.0 upgrade, lack a very important feature found in Macromedia SoundEdit 16: the ability to copy a track from a music CD directly to your hard drive. You can digitize or sample music as input from a CD or CD-ROM player to your sound card, but for purists, this process entails going digital to analog to digital and reduces the quality of the resulting sound.

However, Sound Forge is great at converting one sound file type to another. This capability is very important when you're developing multimedia and scrounging around (legally, of course) for music and sound effects. The audio that you find or even purchase may not be in the file type you need. Or your client may demand a sound file in a specific file type. The key to converting one sound file type to another is the Save As dialog box, as shown in Figure 16-2.

To change the file type of a sound in the Sound Forge XP program window:

1. Choose File⇨Save As.

The current file type of the sound appears in the File Save Type control in the Save As dialog box. The default file type for Sound Forge files is WAV.

2. Type t **or click File Save Type to display the list of available file types.**

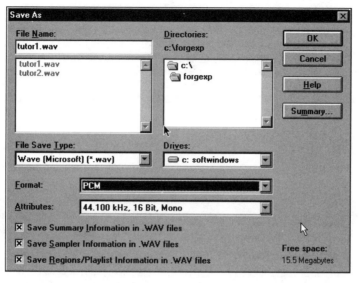

Figure 16-2:
Sound
Forge XP's
Save As
dialog box
where you
can convert
one sound
file type to
another.

3. **Select the new file type from the list of file types.**

   Another control in the Save As dialog box is the Format control. Most
   sounds are in the PCM (Pulse Code Modulation) format for standard,
   noncompressed audio. If other formats are available — usually for
   compressed sound file types — you can select another format from the
   list under the Format control.

   The Attributes control displays the current attributes of the sound. If
   you want to change the sample size, number of channels, or sample
   rate, you can choose options in the Attributes drop-down list.

4. **If you want to change the sound's attributes, type A or click Attributes; otherwise, skip to Step 6.**

5. **Select the new attributes for the sound file from the Attributes drop-
   down list.**

6. **Click OK.**

Macromedia SoundEdit 16 2.0

The Director 6 Studio package for the Macintosh includes Macromedia
SoundEdit 16 2.0, the main program window of which is shown in
Figure 16-3.

If SoundEdit's main window looks familiar, it's no accident. The folks at
Macromedia designed SoundEdit to be compatible with Director 6 right
down to the Help Pointer and toolbar at the top of the screen. Like its PC
counterpoint, Sound Forge XP, SoundEdit features a bouquet of impressive

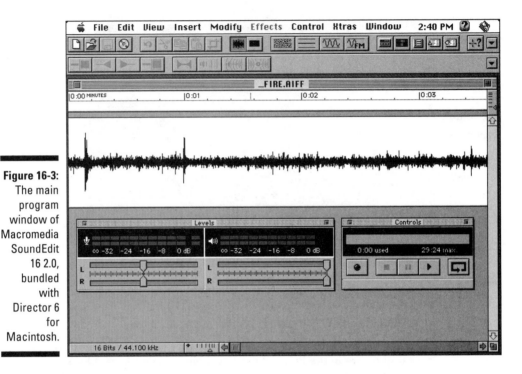

Figure 16-3:
The main program window of Macromedia SoundEdit 16 2.0, bundled with Director 6 for Macintosh.

features including great special effects. And like Sound Forge, you can use SoundEdit to convert one sound file type to another by choosing File⇨Save As, selecting a different file type from the File Format pop-up menu, shown in Figure 16-4, and then clicking Save.

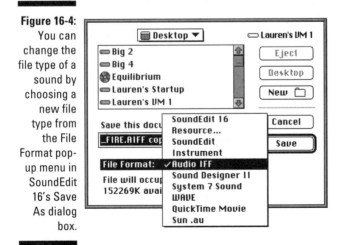

Figure 16-4:
You can change the file type of a sound by choosing a new file type from the File Format pop-up menu in SoundEdit 16's Save As dialog box.

One of SoundEdit 16's most important features is its ability to save a CD music track directly to your hard drive without losing the track's high signal quality. With a music CD in your CD-ROM drive, save a track to your hard drive with the following steps:

1. **Click Convert CD Audio, the button that looks like a little CD in SoundEdit 16's toolbar at the top of the screen, or choose Xtras⇨Convert CD Audio to display the Directory window.**

2. **Locate the audio CD in the Directory and click Open.**

3. **Select one of the tracks on the CD and click Open to display the Save Converted File As dialog box.**

4. **Click Options to display the Audio CD Import Options dialog box, as shown in Figure 16-5.**

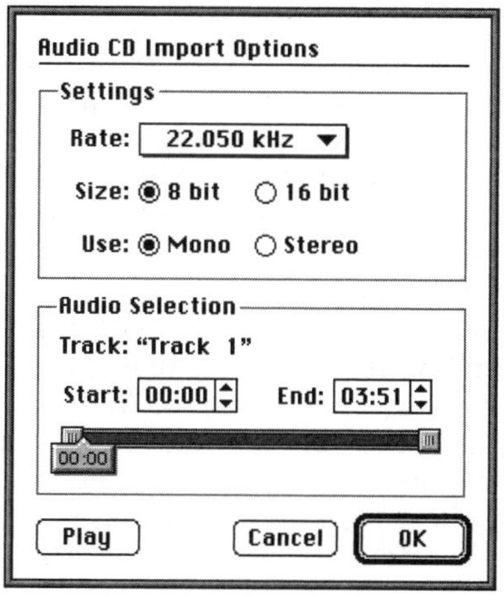

Figure 16-5: When saving a CD track to your hard drive, choose from a bouquet of options in SoundEdit 16's Audio CD Import Options dialog box.

```
Audio CD Import Options
┌─Settings──────────────────────┐
│  Rate:  [ 22.050 kHz    ▼ ]    │
│                                │
│  Size: ◉ 8 bit    ○ 16 bit     │
│                                │
│  Use: ◉ Mono    ○ Stereo       │
└────────────────────────────────┘
┌─Audio Selection───────────────┐
│  Track: "Track  1"             │
│                                │
│  Start: [00:00]⬍   End: [03:51]⬍│
│  ┌────────────────────────────┐│
│  │▥─────────────────────────▥ ││
│  │00:00                       ││
│  └────────────────────────────┘│
└────────────────────────────────┘
  ( Play )     ( Cancel )  ( OK )
```

5. **Choose a sampling rate in the Settings pop-up menu.**

   If you want to retain the highest quality, choose 44.100 kHz. To save space and memory requirements, go with 22.050 kHz for music. If you're saving a voice track, 11.025 may actually be more than satisfactory for many projects.

6. **Choose 8 or 16 bit for Size.**

   As with the previous step, for the best quality choose the higher *bandwidth,* 16 bit for 256 times the information of 8-bit sound.

7. **Choose Mono or Stereo for Use.**

8. **Set the Start and End points of the track and click Play if you want to preview the track.**

   In the Audio Selection panel, you can change the starting and ending points of the track that you want to copy into SoundEdit 16. Click the small arrow controls by the Start and End boxes, or drag the small squares in the slider control. You can drag the large rectangular control to pinpoint a starting point to preview by clicking Play.

9. **Click OK.**

10. **Back in the Save Converted File As dialog box, click Save.**

   The track appears in SoundEdit's main window where you can now apply any of the program's filters and save the sound in any of SoundEdit's supported file types.

Sampling sound without an AV Mac

By the way, if you don't have an AV Mac or use a video board-endowed PC, you can install a sound card, such as the Audiomedia card from Digidesign for the Mac or Sound Blaster for Windows, in the expansion slot of your computer. Many sound cards offer features equal to or surpassing an AV Mac's capabilities. Some cards add considerably more professional features, so results are truly CD-quality audio.

If you don't have an AV Mac or an expansion slot (where extra goodies go inside your computer) or you don't want to make an investment in a sound card, you can sample sound with an external "box." For the Mac, the MacRecorder plugs into the serial port of your Mac and allows you to sample audio from a built-in microphone, an external microphone, or a line output. You can even use two MacRecorders to sample stereo sound using both serial ports. Similar external devices are available for PCs.

Freeware and shareware

Commercial online services, such as America Online, CompuServe, and Prodigy, and Internet sites have vast libraries of sampled sound to download (copy via a modem to your computer). The Internet's the latest craze, and who knows what types of sound you can find there? You can get access to the Web with AT&T WorldNet Service, the software for which is included on this book's CD. Most freeware audio allows unlimited usage, but you'll want to double-check the privileges granted to you by the owner and read all the fine print.

Commercial floppy and CD-ROM collections

You can find vast numbers of music and sound effect collections on the market on floppies and CD-ROMs. Of course, CD-ROM collections offer a number of advantages over floppies, including storage capacity, shelf life, and sound quality. Combined with the capabilities of SoundEdit 16 2.0, which I discuss earlier in this chapter, or Disc-To-Disk software for the Mac from Optical Media International, CD audio offers the highest quality sound you can transfer to your hard drive. Again, check and double-check usage rights before you purchase anything. My recommendation is to look for unlimited usage to get your full money's worth.

Where Sounds Go in Director

Just as you can import graphics into your movie, you can import sound files. In the Import Files dialog box, you can import a sound as a *linked file,* referenced by a movie during playback but not actually incorporated into the movie itself. Your other option is to incorporate the sound into the movie. Either way, the sound appears in the Cast window as a Sound Cast Member.

One way to determine which option to choose is to consider that unlinked sounds must load completely into memory before being played and that they become the property of that one movie. A linked sound file (like an AIFF sound file) plays from a disk, reducing memory requirements and remaining available to use in several movies. A special advantage of an AIFF sound file is its portability, meaning that you can use the same AIFF sound file for Mac and Windows Director movies. You Mac users can use Easy Aiff, a shareware utility included on this book's CD, to quickly preview AIFF and AIFC (compressed) sound files.

In a Mac, sounds that you incorporate into a Director movie become part of the resource fork of the file, the place where sounds and other types of resources are stored. In MacLand, sounds are stored as resource type snd. PCs have no equivalent to the Mac resource fork.

Great Sound for the Price of Good

Wouldn't it be great to play 44 kHz sound at a 22 kHz storage and memory price? Or 22 kHz sound, great for narration, at an 11 kHz price? If you own a Mac, you can achieve the impossible with a wonderful little shareware utility called Sound Mover, created by Riccardo Ettore. You can download this utility to your Mac from most commercial online services, bulletin boards, and the Internet. For instance, America Online has Sound Mover stored in its vaults as Sound Mover Package 1.9.sit. On the Web, you can download Sound Mover from `http://www.shareware.com` as sound-mover-19.hqx. You adventurous types can even type in the whole URL:

```
http://search.shareware.com/code/engine/
        Find?cfrom=quick&orfile=True&search=sound+mover
        &category=Macintosh
```

If you remember Font/DA Mover from System 6.8, you're familiar with Sound Mover's interface, a window with a left and right scrolling field and a button underneath each field. Pressing Option and clicking the left Open button opens a pop-up menu that allows you to choose the type of sound file you want from your hard drive. Sound Mover lists sounds in the left directory, and you may copy any of these sounds to a file you find in the right directory. After selecting a sound from the left scrolling field, if you ⌘+Option+click the Copy button, Sound Mover copies the sound while cutting the size of the file in half without lowering the quality of playback.

How does Sound Mover achieve this miracle? Basically, the utility copies every other byte of sound information. Four out of five physicians claim that they can't hear the difference between the original 44 kHz file and the 22 kHz file. Try it; you'll like it.

Sync about It

Synchronizing sound to picture is every multimedia type's nightmare, although digital technology makes this task a lot easier than it used to be. When you think about it, much of the sound you hear around you and in movies and TV isn't synced sound at all. Background noise, most special effects, and musical scores aren't synced to the degree that people expect of lip-synced sound. Even then, if someone's head turns away from the camera, or if a figure is moving or in the distance, sync becomes much less critical.

Playing a sound through

Before running, maybe you'd better learn to crawl. How do you play a complete sound file in Director? Adding a Sound Cast Member to one cell in the Score's Sound channel doesn't do it. Try it; you'll hear the narration, music, or sound effect for an instant, and, as soon as the playback head moves on to the next frame, the sound dies.

To play a sound from beginning to end, you can use one of a number of techniques.

The two-frame movie

One way of playing a sound is to set up a two-frame sound sprite in the Score and to set the movie to loop by clicking the Play Loopback button in the upper-left corner of the Control Panel. Sorry, a one-frame movie simply doesn't work — go talk to the Macromedia people about that one.

When you play the movie, the complete sound plays once — the sound stops but the movie continues looping. The problem? Of necessity, the movie must loop, which limits the kind of animation that can happen on the Stage. Also, although the sound plays only once, animations continue playing over and over again as long as the movie runs.

Play "Guess My Frames"

A better way to play a sound than the two-frame movie is to add the same Sound Cast Member to as many frames as you need in the Sound channel to play back the sound from beginning to end. Not enough frames and the sound dies before the end of the piece; too many frames and you waste valuable frames in your movie. Remember: Director sees a block of frames with the same cast member as one *performance* of the sound. To play the sound again, leave at least one frame blank between the first and second performance of the sound.

You can manually stretch the sound sprite in the Score window to fill a block of frames with a Sound Cast Member. Or you can select the sprite in the Score and type a number in the End box at the top of the window to increase the sprite's sprite bar. To review these features of the Score window, jump to Chapter 6.

The number of frames needed to play a sound depends on the tempo of your movie. You can experiment with different Tempo settings for a selected block of sound cells. Changing the tempo doesn't change the sound itself but rather the number of frames needed to play the sound from beginning to end. (For more on setting tempos, see Chapter 12.) Keep in mind that you only need to set the tempo once in the Tempo channel of the Score at the beginning of the sound. After the sound finishes playing, if you want to return to a former tempo or simply change the tempo of the movie, you can add a new tempo in the last frame of the sound sprite.

Don't forget: Sync is one of those ticklish areas dependent on the speed of your computer's processor. Slower machines need different settings than Power Macs and Pentium PCs.

Wait for Cue Point tempo

In general, the best way to play a sound is with the Wait for Cue Point tempo in the Tempo dialog box, as shown in Figure 16-6.

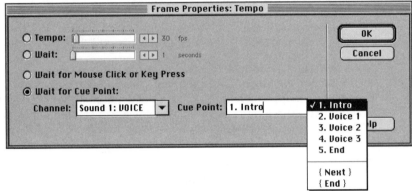

Figure 16-6:
The Wait
for Cue
Point tempo
in the
Tempo
dialog box.

To set up a sound in a Sound channel to play from beginning to end using the Wait for Cue Point tempo, try the following steps:

1. **In the first frame of the sound sprite, double-click the Tempo channel of the Score.**

   The Tempo dialog box appears, artfully depicted in Figure 16-6.

   The Tempo channel is the first channel in the Score window.

2. **Click the Wait for Cue Point radio button.**

3. **Choose {End} from the Cue Point pop-up list.**

4. **Click OK.**

These steps tell Director to pause the movie on the frame with the Wait for Cue Point tempo, play the sound from beginning to end, and then continue playing the frames in the movie. The only downside to this method is that the movie pauses while the sound plays. However, until you try using Lingo to play sounds or use some of Director 6's new drag-and-drop behaviors, this method is generally the best way to play complete sound files.

Syncing sound to your movie

Director 6 features a great new way to sync sound to your Director movie. The Wait for Cue Point tempo (see the previous section) works with special cue points you can add to sound files (and QuickTime movies) using

SoundEdit 16, which is bundled with Director 6 for Macintosh. The bad news: Unfortunately for PC users, SoundEdit 16 runs only on the Macintosh. The good news: If you can get your hands on the software and a Mac, you PC users can add cue points to AIFF sound files and QuickTime movies that Director 6 for Windows recognizes.

After you add cue points to your sound file, you can add the Wait for Cue Point tempo to various frames of your movie to sync sound to animation occurring on the Stage, such as lip-synced narration for an animated cartoon character.

Add cue points to a sound with SoundEdit 16

Macromedia Director 6 Studio for Macintosh includes SoundEdit 16 2.0. With SoundEdit 16, you can add cue points to a sound file or even to a QuickTime movie. Although SoundEdit 16 is a Macintosh-only program, when you add cue points to an AIFF sound or QuickTime movie, you can play these files and use their cue points in Director 6 for Windows as well as Director 6 for Macintosh by following the next steps.

Add cue points in SoundEdit 16

1. **Open a sound in SoundEdit 16.**

2. **If the Controls palette isn't open, choose Window⇨Controls.**

3. **Select the beginning of a music segment where you want to add a cue by dragging through the area.**

4. **Click the Play button in the Controls palette.**

5. **When you find the best spot for a cue, press the Left Arrow key to shift the insertion point at the beginning of the segment.**

6. **Choose Insert⇨Cue Point to display the Insert Cue Point dialog box, as shown in Figure 16-7.**

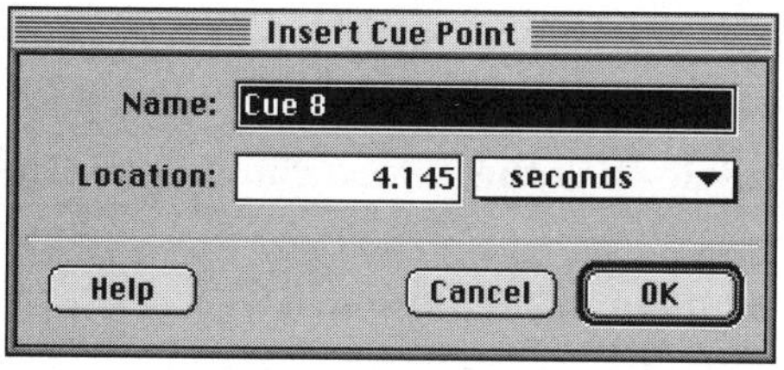

Figure 16-7:
You can name a cue point in SoundEdit 16's Insert Cue Point dialog box.

Insert Cue Point

Name: Cue 8

Location: 4.145 seconds ▼

Help   Cancel   OK

7. Type a meaningful name in the Name field or leave the cue labeled as Cue 1.

8. Click OK to return to SoundEdit 16's main window.

   SoundEdit 16 adds a marker above the insertion point, like Director 6's markers in the Score window.

9. For each additional cue, repeat Steps 2 through 7.

10. Update the file by choosing File⇨Save.

Import a sound file into Director

1. Choose File⇨Import to display the Import Files dialog box.

2. Select the sound containing cue points in the Directory area of the dialog box.

3. Choose Standard Import from the pop-up menu at the bottom of the Import Files dialog box.

   If you decide to import the sound as a linked file, choose Link to External File from the pop-up menu. Remember, a linked sound file plays from a disk instead of from memory, reducing the load on RAM.

4. Click Import.

   The sound is now a Sound Cast Member in the Cast window.

Add the sound to the Score

1. Drag the imported sound from the Cast window to a frame in one of the Sound channels of the Score window.

2. Extend the sprite's sprite bar through all the frames of the animation sequence in which you want the sound to play by dragging the last frame of the sprite to the right.

   For more info on sprites and sprite bars in Director 6, see Chapter 4.

Add Wait for Cue Point tempos

1. Locate the frame in the animation sequence that syncs with the first cue point in the sound.

2. In the same frame, double-click the Tempo channel to display the Tempo dialog box.

3. Select the Wait for Cue Point radio button.

4. Select the sound from the Channel pop-up menu.

5. Select the correct cue point from the Cue pop-up menu.

   You can select the cue by number, by name, or by simply selecting Next to go from cue to cue in sequence.

6. **Click OK.**

7. **For each additional cue point, repeat Steps 1 through 6, finding the next frame in the animation to link to the next cue point in the sound.**

During playback, the playback head pauses at each Wait for Cue Point tempo until the next cue in the sound comes up.

Getting that syncing feeling

Following are some general tips for syncing sound to sequences in your movie, be it music, narration, or creepy sound effects.

✔ Make sure that your audio is clear and well recorded. You don't want to start with source audio that has lots of noise, pops, or other distractions. When you sample audio, digital "noise" degrades the result (especially on lower-end sampling devices or settings). Also, pay close attention to audio levels; digital audio is very sensitive to high recording levels. The settings you use for your VCR or cassette player may sound very distorted when applied to digital sound.

You want to record your sound as *hot* (AudiophileSpeak for loud) as possible without going into the danger zone of your sound-level meter. Find the loudest part of your audio track, set the levels to that segment, and then record.

One exception: If you plan to play your movie on PCs running Windows 3.1, record your sound at less than maximum volume. Windows 3.1's sound drivers have trouble with high-volume sound, so keeping settings to about 85 percent maximum volume isn't a bad idea.

✔ Try changing Tempo settings for various blocks of sounds in the Sound channel of the Score window. Select a block of cells in the channel that contain the same Sound Cast Member. Double-click the Tempo channel in the first frame of the selected sound cells and set the Tempo with the slider control in the Set Tempo dialog box.

When using Tempo settings to sync sound to Director animation, use the slowest machine that you anticipate the movie will play on. Working the other way around, you lose sync as you move to slower machines and the frame rate drops while the sound plays on. Remember that Director is built to play every frame of your movie; the movie slows down on slower computers instead of dropping frames.

✔ For an animation sequence featuring synced sound, try shortening or lengthening the sprite bar(s) of the appropriate sprites in the Score window. To review sprites and sprite bars, jump to Chapter 6.

✔ If you own a digital video editing application like Premiere, export your Director movie with sound as a digital video. In Premiere, picture and sound are in separate tracks, and you can take advantage of special tricks that the program offers, like shortening or lengthening audio passages to sync sound to picture without distorting the sound. If you need to run the final video from Director, re-import the video as a Digital Video Cast Member to play back in its own Video window while maintaining the sync you established in Premiere. Remember, digital video was designed to maintain sync between audio and picture, even dropping frames if necessary.

Chapter 17

Cross-Platform Stuff No One Should Need to Know

• •

In This Chapter

▶ All the dirt on the cross-platform pack

▶ Following the rules is cool

▶ Managing your files

• •

*O*ne of the reasons people buy Director 6 is to get the four manuals that come with the package. They're great for leveling tables. Another reason is Director 6's capability to produce multimedia on different types of computers and operating systems, called *cross-platform* capabilities.

When you're ready to produce multimedia for PC-compatibles and Macintosh, you need to know lots of stuff. In this chapter, I get you started with tips on compatibility issues and how to manage your files.

Cross-Platform Which Way?

In a perfect world, you'd buy one program, whip up a multimedia extravaganza overnight, and offer it to every computer-using market you could find. Heck, you'd be happy to sell it to people who don't have a computer. That's the American way.

Now for Real Life. Director 6 is as much a cross-platform program as any out there on the market and then some. But it doesn't match the utopian picture previously described. To do serious cross-platform work with Director, you need to purchase — now sit down — Director 6 for Macintosh *and* Director 6 for Windows.

Now wait, I know I've heard of a cross-platform pack

That's right, Macromedia offers a cross-platform pack. Some people assume that the pack contains a special cross-platform edition of Director 6. Know what's inside? One copy of Director 6 for Macintosh and one copy of Director 6 for Windows, plus assorted manuals for leveling tables. You may save a few pennies with the bundle, but you're still buying two copies of Director.

In the testing phase of a cross-platform project, some developers are tempted to use emulation software like SoftWindows from Insignia Solutions, which makes your Mac think it's a PC, or MacOpener from DataViz, which tricks your PC into opening Mac files. You can also purchase hardware from companies like OrangePC that does the same kind of trick. Frankly, Macromedia doesn't encourage this practice and highly recommends testing Director 6 for Windows on a PC-compatible and Director 6 for Macintosh on a real Mac or Mac clone. I agree.

But I've heard you can use Mac Director movies in a Windows projector

Another source of confusion about Director's cross-platform features is whether you can use Mac Director movies in a Windows projector. Director movies, the files you save with the Save command, are platform-independent files. Within some limitations, you can open a Macintosh Director movie on a PC and a Windows Director movie on a Mac. As long as you stick to a few guidelines, you can also add Mac movies to a Windows projector and vice versa.

So far, so good. The catch is that projectors themselves are *not* platform-independent files. After you turn movies into a projector, they run only under the platform that built the projector, so a Macintosh projector runs only under the Mac operating system, and a Director for Windows projector runs only under Windows.

And you probably want to distribute your work as a projector. When your movies are protected as a projector, the Lingo scripting is converted to a low-level language that only your computer and Carl Sagan understand, and the user doesn't need to buy Director 6 to play your movies. See Chapter 19 for more information about projectors.

Prepping Your Director Movies

The real trick to doing cross-platform work with Director 6 is prepping your Director 6 movies. By following my guidelines, you can develop your movies on either platform, Mac or PC, and safely "port" (don't you love this stuff?) over to the other platform.

Following the rules is cool

Although Mac users have more latitude in what they can name their files, most developers strongly suggest staying with PC file-naming conventions for cross-platform work. I'm going to be even stricter with you and ask you to stick with ISO-9660 naming conventions. You may vaguely remember seeing the term ISO-9660 somewhere. If you own a CD-ROM drive, you're right. ISO-9660 is the name of one of the files that should be on your system to communicate with the CD-ROM drive.

The ISO-9660 file-naming convention calls for three parts: a filename, a period, and an extension. Following these rules pretty well guarantees compatibility across platforms and for CD-ROM publishing and doesn't hurt on the Web, either, when you prep your movies for the Internet with Shockwave. See Chapter 18 for more information about Director 6 and the Web.

These naming conventions are very strict. To work properly, you must follow them to the letter, no pun intended. (Or was it intended?)

In more detail, here's how to name your movies for cross-platform work:

- ✔ **Filename:** Begin the filename with a letter, not a numeral. The filename can be up to eight characters long including *only* capital letters A through Z, numerals 0 through 9, and the underscore (_) character (which you get by pressing Shift+hyphen).

- ✔ **Period character:** The period character is reserved for separating the filename from the following part, the extension. Do not try to substitute colons, semicolons, ampersands, or avocados for the period. These symbols do not work. Especially the avocado.

- ✔ **Extension:** Follow the period with a three-character extension, sticking with the same filename rules. And don't use just any extension. Stick with the standard extension for standard files. Director movies end in DIR, PICTs with PCT, and QuickTime movies with MOV.

Refer to Table 17-1 for common file types and their extensions.

Table 17-1	File Types and Extensions
File Type	*Extension*
Director movies	
Unprotected movies	DIR
Protected movies	DXR
Projectors	EXE
Animation files	
Autodesk Animator files	FLI
Autodesk Animator files, compressed	FLC
Bitmap images	
Bitmap	BMP
Device Independent Bitmap	DIB
Encapsulated PostScript	EPS
GIF	GIF
JPEG PICT	JPG
Kodak PhotoCD	PCD
Paintbrush	PCX
PICT	PCT
PICT	PIC
MacPaint	PNT
TIFF	TIF
Windows Metafile	WMF
Digital videos	
Video for Windows	AVI
QuickTime	MOV
QuickTime for Windows	MOV
Sound	
AIFF	AIF
WAVE	WAV

Stick with the System – Win palette

Director 6 comes with a set of palettes to start you off. For cross-platform work, add the System – Win palette to the Palette channel in Frame 1 right from the start and leave it there whether you're working with a Mac or PC. One exception is if you're working with movies that began as Director 4 movies; because Director 4 handled colors slightly differently from Director 5 or Director 6, go with the System – Win (Dir 4) palette to avoid embarrassing color shifts.

Will sticking with the good, old reliable System – Win palette stifle you? Will it limit your free-ranging creativity? Of course, but that's part of working in the cross-platform world. Actually, limitations often stir the creative force within, forcing solutions you never would have dreamed of ordinarily.

A corollary to staying with the System – Win palette is sticking with 8-bit color. Out go those beautiful 24-bit PICTs that glow with all the fire of a room-size transparency. They'd create heck on earth for you and your movies. Director 6 supports 24-bit color on the Stage for Mac and Windows 95 platforms, but again, use only 8-bit graphics. Trust me.

Believe it or not, Windows and the Mac operating system share some things in common. When displaying 256 colors (8-bit color depth), both operating systems fix white at slot 0 and black at slot 255, locking them so that you cannot modify them. But Windows goes farther. Windows reserves the first ten and last ten colors of the current palette for GUI (Graphical User Interface) elements. These colors are called *static colors*. You can modify static colors between black and white, but not black and white themselves.

This setup affects two cross-platform issues: Director's Fade to Black and Fade to White effects. Because black and white are locked, they don't work with fade effects available in the Stage Properties: Palette dialog box. If you intend to use fades in a cross-platform movie, avoid solid white (slot 0) and solid black (slot 255) pixels in the graphic. If you must use these colors, create a custom palette by making color slot 1 pure white and slot 254 pure black, duplicate black and white colors that work with fades. Then remap the graphic to your custom palette. (For more info on creating a custom palette, see Chapter 19.)

Fonts R Us

Fonts represent a problem area even without the added complexities of cross-platform development. Even when the platforms are the same, if the user doesn't have the right fonts installed in the computer — or if you and the user have the same fonts but from different type vendors — havoc reigns on your beautiful Director movie wherever you display rich text. To review rich text, skip to Chapter 9. Basically rich text is word-processing text that relies on the fonts currently installed in the system. Very tricky.

Director gives you a way of mapping fonts from one platform to another by modifying the FONTMAP.TXT file in the Director folder or directory. But it's a little technical and a little tricky, too.

The safest, easiest way to work around the problem is to stick with *bitmapped* text, text you enter with the Text tool in the Paint window. See Chapter 7 for more on using the Text tool.

You can also convert Director's other types of text into bitmaps when you've completed development by selecting a Text Cast Member in the Cast window and choosing Modify⇨Convert to Bitmap. If you must use editable text, the safest strategy is to stick with boring old Helvetica and Times.

Prep your digital videos

QuickTime movies may be used in Director movies for cross-platform projects. However, you need to coax movies with a little preening by using one of several programs and converter utilities. You need a program that *flattens* or converts the QuickTime movie to a cross-platform format and makes the movie self-contained, independent of any linked files.

MoviePlayer 2.1, whose icon is portrayed at left, is a ubiquitous little program for the Mac that can handle both assignments. To convert a QuickTime movie to a cross-platform format and make it self-contained, do the following:

1. **Open MoviePlayer 2.1.**

2. **Choose File⇨Open and open the QuickTime movie from the Directory.**

3. **After test playing the movie, choose File⇨Save As to display the Save As dialog box, as shown in Figure 17-1.**

4. **Click the Make movie self-contained radio/option button.**

5. **Check the Playable on non-Apple computers check box, which is MoviePlayer's term for "flatten."**

6. **Click Save.**

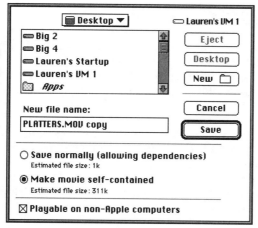

Figure 17-1:
MoviePlayer
selections
to make
your
QuickTime
movie self-
contained
and
flattened.

PC owners do not have the option of using MoviePlayer to make a movie self-contained and flattened. PC users can, however, use a QuickTime for Windows package that Apple sells, which includes a conversion utility, or Adobe Premiere. Open Premiere and find your QuickTime movie in the Open dialog box. Choose File⇨Export⇨Flattened Movie and click Save. Premiere flattens the movie and makes it platform-independent. That's it.

You don't have to pay a lot to get a program designed for prepping QuickTime. FlattenMooV is a shareware program that carries a paltry $10 price tag and does a great job. You'll find it in the Shareware folder on the accompanying CD-ROM. You can contact its author, Robert Hennessy, at 39495 Albany Common, Unit B, Fremont, CA 94538.

Managing Your Files

One of Director 6's best features, linking external files to a movie, is also problematic. The feature is great because you can share information and graphics among several Director movies when the files aren't imbedded in one movie alone. But the catch is that you better keep track of those linked files. If Director can't find the files, you're in deeper than you know.

Note: QuickTime movies are always imported as linked files. The external files must tag along with your Director movies.

The project folder

When you include linked files in a Director movie, the original external files must be available and locatable for a presentation to play back properly. The best solution to this file management dilemma for cross-platform work is to put everything in one folder or directory, which you can call a project folder.

Everything goes into the project folder: the Director application and its assorted folders or the projector; any digital video like QuickTime and AVI movies; external sound files; external casts; and other movies called by the main Director movie. Everything. To pretty things up a little, you can arrange the icons you want the user to see in one area of the folder's window and resize the window so that all other files are hidden.

The stub projector

A more technical way of handling file management for cross-platform work is to create what's known as a *stub projector,* a little movie that automates initialization and maintenance stuff that should be taken care of before, during, and after a movie's playback. In this case, you'd make a stub projector to keep Director on top of its ancillary files by working with two of Lingo's functions, the searchPath and the pathName, and a Lingo command, append.

Because a Director movie looks for external cast members before reading Lingo scripts, design your production so that the stub projector plays first and does its magic with the searchPath function.

Suppose Mr. Big hires you to create a CD-ROM entitled "How I Made a Killing in the Cement Business," and you produce a gorgeous cross-platform production for him. Using the backslash (\), the PC convention for directory (folder for Mac-ites), you create two folders/directories. In one, \MOVIES, you store all the QuickTime demos; in another, \AIFFS, you archive important speeches that Mr. Big has given about cement. The beginning Director movie is entitled INTRO.DIR and uses the play command to navigate to additional movies during playback.

Follow these steps to make a stub projector:

Create the Movie script

1. **In Director, start a new movie by choosing File⇨New⇨Movie or pressing ⌘/Ctrl+N.**

2. **Choose Window⇨Script or press ⌘/Ctrl+0 (zero) to display a Movie Script window.**

3. **Type** on startMovie.

4. **Press Return and type** append the searchPath, the pathName &.

5. **Type a space, a plain quote character (Shift+apostrophe), the name of a project folder, and another plain quote character.**

6. **Repeat Steps 4 through 5 for each additional project folder your movie uses.**

7. **Press Return and type** end.

In my example, my handler for Mr. Big would now read

```
on startMovie
    append the searchPath, the pathName & "MOVIES"
    append the searchPath, the pathName & "AIFFS"
end
```

Notice how the second and third lines of my handler are indented. Director indents lines to tell you that the Lingo script seems to be okay. When you don't see this kind of indentation, check for typos in your handler.

8. **Click the Script window's Close button.**

Create the Score script

1. **Choose Window⇨Score or press ⌘/Ctrl+4 to display the Score window.**

2. **Double-click Frame 1 in the Script channel to display the Score Script window.**

Director types the first line, on exitFrame, for you. Director also adds the last line, end. This wonderful program even places the blinking insertion point at the beginning of line 2 and makes your next mortgage payment. Now all you need to do is begin typing.

3. **Type** go to movie.

4. **Type a space, a plain quote character (Shift+apostrophe), the name of the movie that begins your multimedia production, and another plain quote character.**

5. **Press Return and type** end.

In my example, this new handler for Mr. Big would look like

```
on exitFrame
    go to movie "INTRO.DIR"
end
```

6. Click the Script window's Close box.

7. Choose File⇨Save As and save the movie, giving it a clever title like CLICK_ME.DIR.

Create the stub projector

1. Choose File⇨Create Projector to display the Create Projector dialog box.

2. Find the movie in the left directory and double-click it to enter it in the right directory.

3. Click Create and name the projector CLICK_ME.EXE. (EXE is the extension for a projector).

4. Put your opening Director movie (INTRO.DIR in my example), all other project movies, and the stub projector, CLICK_ME.EXE, in the root directory of the CD-ROM.

Director shouldn't have any trouble accessing the linked files of your presentation during playback.

Chapter 18
WWW S.O.S.

● ●

In This Chapter
▶ Director in Cyberspace
▶ The shocking truth about what's new in Shockwave
▶ Testing your shocked movie in Netscape Navigator
▶ Streaming your video and audio

● ●

The World Wide Web. The World Wide Web? Where have I heard that before? Only everywhere. It's the latest and greatest thing and just about no one saw it coming. Corporate types are scrambling trying to find someone like you to help them get on the Web with attitude. And everyone, and I mean e-v-e-r-y-o-n-e, wants to have his or her very own Web page in Cyberspace. Most of the time, they're not even sure why.

The big news is all the new Web stuff those kooky folks at Macromedia have added to Director 6. Read on, oh faithful one.

Why All the Fuss?

Well, compare the World Wide Web to the Internet. Using the Internet is like stepping back in time to the days of DOS (Disk Operating System) with its reams and reams of text. In other words, the Internet is for nerds (affectionately said), not Real Human Beings.

In contrast to the Internet, the Web is a graphical environment with all the advantages of operating systems such as the Macintosh OS (Operating System) and Windows. People like working with pictures rather than typing in arcane code.

By any standard, Web technology is slow. It's slower than a CD-ROM drive, a floppy drive, or the simplest of networks. In terms of speed, the Web is directly opposed to what animation and multimedia demand, high speed. One minute of uncompressed video takes up 27MB (megabytes) of information. Said another way so you really hear the numbers I'm talking about, to view one minute of video on the Web coming through your phone line, you need to squeeze 27MB of information through the whole mess of a system in under a minute. Have you tried copying, or downloading, a simple file to your computer from a Web site lately? I started my last download around the time of the Great Depression.

So How Do I Get Started on the Web?

Aside from a basic computer setup, you need some hardware and software to enter the wacky world of Cyberspace:

- ✔ **Modem:** You need to purchase a modem. Demand your right as an American citizen to buy at the very least a 28.8 baud modem with V.34 plus protocol. The U.S. Robotics Courier modem is an example of this standard. Even better, get your hands on one of the new 56 Kbps (kilobits per second) modems, the fastest in regular modem technology, and you won't be happy with anything less. One cavent, though: Check that your web service provider supports 56 Kbps modems (most larger providers probably feature such support by now).

- ✔ **Web service provider:** This company becomes your liaison with the Web. Ordinary human beings don't connect directly to the Web but to the service provider's servers that connect you to the Web. Look for an organization that offers unlimited usage and 1 to 2MB (megabytes) of their storage space for your very own Web page for a monthly rate around $20, give or take.

Software for AT&T WorldNet Service, an Internet service provider, is included on this book's CD.

- ✔ **Web browser:** You need Netscape Navigator 3.0 or Microsoft's Internet Explorer 3.0 or newer, especially to work with Shockwave. You can find them both on the companion CD-ROM. Navigator is part of the AT&T WorldNet Service package. A customized version of Explorer is also on the CD. You can also download (copy) a browser from either company's Web site or get it from one of a number of other CD-ROM collections of Web-related material. If a friend has a copy, whining works pretty well, too. When you sign up with a service provider, the company should supply you with a good Web browser along with other Web goodies. If not, I'd report them to the UnAmerican Activities Committee.

Shocking News about Shockwave

This section is where Director and Shockwave step into the Web picture. Shockwave started out as a dynamic duo of special programs, something called AfterBurner and Shockwave. AfterBurner began as a separate application that compressed Director movies, and Shockwave was a plug-in for a select group of Web browsers to play regular Director movies and Director movies compressed with AfterBurner in a Web page. With Director 5, AfterBurner became an Xtra (Director's name for plug-in) in the Xtras menu.

Now, AfterBurner is fully integrated into Director 6. The File menu command that's misleadingly named Save as Shockwave Movie is the new home for AfterBurner. To create a Director movie compressed with AfterBurner, choose File➪Save as Shockwave Movie. It's that easy.

The latest version of Shockwave is still a plug-in for browsers such as Netscape Navigator and Internet Explorer. The section that follows is a nice, informal introduction to using Shockwave in its current iteration.

When you're ready for more details about Shockwave, consider the new title, *Shockwave For Director For Dummies,* 2nd edition, by Greg Harvey (IDG Books Worldwide, Inc).

Web browsers

Where does the Shockwave plug-in, well, plug in? That's where Web browsers such as Netscape Navigator 3.0, shown in Figure 18-1, and Microsoft's Internet Explorer enter center stage.

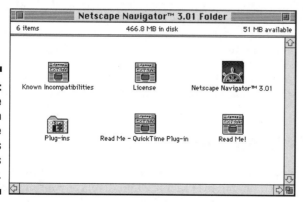

Figure 18-1: Shockwave goes in Netscape Navigator's Plug-ins folder.

The Web browser is the program that allows you to see all those beautiful Web pages everyone's been surfing lately. The browser's a kind of interpreter that translates a list of funny looking lines of nonsensical text called HTML (HyperText Markup Language) tags into the readable text and graphics you happily view on a Web page.

With Shockwave installed and a few extra lines of HTML, you can use browsers to include your Director movies in Web pages along with the other graphics. Shockwave is designed to prime your Director 6 movies for broadcast over the Web, along with several network-related additions to Director's Lingo language, which are beyond the scope of this book to explore. Again, for in-depth coverage of this topic and lots more, see *Shockwave For Director For Dummies* at your friendly bookstore now. Okay, IDG, hand over that fiver.

AfterBurner

AfterBurner's sole task in Life is to dramatically compress your Director 6 movies by about 50 percent, a very effective solution to the problem I pose earlier on in this chapter: How do you pass massive quantities of information through ordinary phone lines?

Compression is the key to everything you see on the Web. The two main types of graphics you encounter on the Web, GIF (Graphics Interchange Format) and JPEG (Joint Photographic Experts Group) files, represent more compression schemes. Compression is the key to everything you see on the Web. The two main types of graphics you encounter on the Web, GIF (Graphics Interchange Format) and JPEG (Joint Photographic Experts Group) files, represent more compression schemes. You Mac users can take advantage of GIFConverter and GraphicConverter, two shareware utilities included on the companion CD, to create GIFs and convert files into GIF, JPEG, and many other file types. You PC types can play with the Save-disabled version of Equilibrium's powerful DeBabelizer Pro that does the same kind of file conversion but on a commercial level.

Director also contributes to higher sound quality on the Web with Shockwave for Audio compression, which I cover later in this chapter.

Shockwave plug-in

The Shockwave plug-in recognizes movies you prepare with the Save as Shockwave Movie command in Director 6 and displays your movie as part of the Web page. Macromedia made it that simple to add high quality animations to Cyberspace.

Exciting as other Web solutions may sound — like Java, JavaScript, and VRML (Virtual Reality Markup Language) — they ask a lot in return. With Java, for example, you need to learn a full-blown programming language at least as difficult as C++, a very popular high-level computer language.

High-level means that the language seems conversational and designed for us human beans to read and understand. Low-level languages like Assembly language are meant for computers to understand.

JavaScript is a subset of the Java language, easier to learn than Java but still not exactly intuitive. And VRML is a markup language like the Web standard itself, HTML (HyperText Markup Language), no Sunday picnic either. The brave among you PC users can check out a triplet of HTML shareware helper utilities on the companion CD — Webforms, Webmania, and Macromedia's own Backstage. Sorry, Macaholics, nothing for you, but Adobe PageMill 2.0 makes those first few HTML pages a whole lot easier.

OK, So How Do I Install Shockwave?

When you're happy with your Director movie and you save the latest changes to disk, choose File⇨Save and Compact, forcing Director to do some important housecleaning. The file size should drop dramatically, especially if you've worked a long time on the movie.

You Macaholics can install the Shockwave plug-in by running the Shockwave installer program. You can also drag the Shockwave plug-in into Netscape Navigator or Internet Explorer's Plug-ins folder.

For you Windows people with 486 PCs or better running Windows 95, Shockwave is called Active Shockwave in the form of an ActiveX control. You need Internet Explorer 3.0 or newer to use Active Shockwave.

ActiveX is Microsoft's multimedia solution for cross-platform publishing on the Web, featuring modular snippets of code — similar to Director's behaviors — called ActiveX controls that can be glued together, Lego-like, to create new components and functionality.

First, you need to do a little housekeeping. Uninstall any earlier version of Shockwave installed in your browser by double-clicking the uninstall file named delsw2.bat. Then, in Internet Explorer choose View⇨Options⇨Navigation. Click Clear History to clear the *cache,* a small file created by browsers to record your travels through the Web.

Now, you're ready to install Active Shockwave. Oddly enough, Macromedia doesn't have a stand-alone installer for Active Shockwave unlike its Mac brother, so you need to go to Macromedia's Shockwave home page and let a remote server install Active Shockwave to your browser. In the Internet Explorer's Address box, type:

http://www.macromedia.com/shockwave/download/alternates/index.html

This Web address takes you to the index page shown in Figure 18-2. Click Go! for Shockwave under the Win95/NT column and follow Macromedia's directions from there.

Shockwave limitations

Before Director 6 and the latest version of Shockwave, I would have included a *long* list of do's and don'ts (mainly don'ts) in this section. Instead, I'm happy to say the list has dwindled down to a couple of cautionary notes.

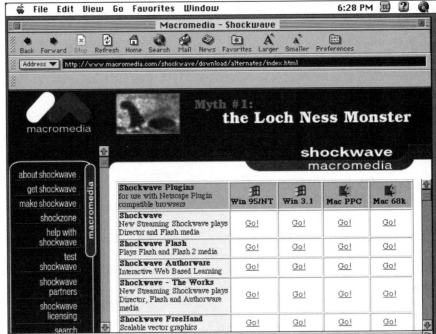

Figure 18-2: Navigate to Macromedia's Shockwave index page to begin loading Active Shockwave for Internet Explorer.

One area that Shockwave still doesn't support is MIAWs (Movies in a Window), a feature for advanced Director users allowing a second movie to appear in its own window. You can use this feature to build custom palettes and alert boxes. If you decide to play with MIAWs, leave that exploration for non-Web movies. Another item to avoid with Web-bound movies is the Loop Playback setting in the Control Panel. If you need to create a looping movie, add one line of very simple Lingo by following these steps:

1. **Double-click the last frame of your movie in the Script channel of the Score.**

2. **In the Script window that appears, type** go to frame 1.

3. **Click the Close box or press ⌘/Ctrl+W to close the Script window.**

   That's it. The snippet of Lingo jumps the playback head back to Frame 1 every time the movie comes to the last frame. And Shockwave has no problem with this line of Lingo.

The only other major problem area Shockwave still has is with custom menus, another advanced feature of Director. Unfortunately, I can't give you a workaround for adding custom menus to a Web-bound Director movie at this time.

Looking over any Read Me files that come with your installation of Director 6 is always a good idea to get the latest info on Shockwave that may not have even made it to the manuals.

Prepping Director movies for Shockwave

Because the Web is so slow, you need to do everything possible to make the original movie as small as possible. Aim for a final file size of 60K (kilobytes) for a 30-second movie. That's a basic rate of 2 kilobytes per second. Try the following hints to shrink your movie down to microscopic size.

Keep the Stage size small

The file size of a movie is directly related to the Stage size. Choose Modify⇨ Movie⇨Properties and choose the smallest Stage size you and your conscience can live with.

Don't be alarmed if you type in a value for the Stage width that's not divisible by 16 and Director changes the value for you. Keep in mind that because of Director's internal architecture, the Stage width must be in 16-pixel increments. Curiously enough, the Stage height can be any size you like.

Use 1-bit color

Director features the ability to colorize 1-bit sprites on the Stage, which opens a world of creative opportunities to populate your movie with nearly any number of animated, colorful sprites at a very low cost, file size-wise. Begin by creating 1-bit, black-and-white bitmaps in the Paint window. After dragging each bitmap on the Stage, choose Window⇨Tools palette. Now you can colorize each 1-bit sprite by selecting it and choosing a color from the Foreground Color pop-up palette in the Tools palette. Even with 1-bit Bitmap Cast Members, keep the number of cast members down. Keep in mind that you can drag any number of sprites on the Stage from just one 1-bit Bitmap Cast Member and you can give each sprite a different color.

Use Shape Cast Members

For sprites that don't move on the Stage, create Shape Cast Members with tools from the Tool palette. Shapes are much more efficient than bitmaps, but they're slow to animate. You can read all about the Tool palette and its shape tools in Chapter 10.

Use film loops

For animations, add repetitive kinds of animation sequences, such as a running figure or a bird with flapping wings, that you can use to build long animations efficiently by creating a film loop. You can review the ins and outs of film loops in Chapter 20. Keep the number of frames down in the film loop. Drop the color depth of the participating cast members as low as possible. And keep the size of each cast member in the film loop as small as you can.

Downsample sound at 11.025 kHz

When you digitize or sample sound for your movie, see if a sampling rate of 11.025 kHz (kilohertz) or lower is acceptable. Four out of five doctors consider 11.025 kHz fine for voice applications such as narration and for many sound effects.

However, you can achieve better sound quality if you sample sound originally at CD-quality 44 kHz, then resample or downsample the sound in Macromedia's SoundEdit 16 for the Mac or Sound Forge XP for the PC, both bundled with the Director Studio package. Demo versions of both also are on this book's CD.

You can also use these programs to create small snippets of sound that you can loop in Director instead of playing big sound files. The key to creating a successful sound loop is to edit the sound so that the beginning and tail end of the sound match visually in SoundEdit or Sound Forge's main window.

Use Shockwave for Audio

The Director 6 package includes Xtras (Director's name for plug-ins) for compressing and streaming audio. The Shockwave Compression Xtra is capable of compressing sound files with a ratio of 176 to 1. Of course, all compression schemes are best when used conservatively, and Shockwave for Audio is no exception. In general, use the lowest compression ratio you and your Web page can live with.

A musical interlude needs the highest quality possible because of its dynamic range, the highest and lowest pitches in the piece, and its loudness factor. Experiment and find the lowest compression ratio you and your ear drums can live with.

Voice doesn't require the same quality as music because the vocal range is pretty limited compared to a symphonic or rock piece. Try a fairly high compression ratio with recorded voice sequences. Remember, we're talking about a Director movie destined for the Web, which — next to blackstrap molasses — is the slowest entity known to man.

Sound effects are another story. With some effects, you need the highest possible quality. With others, you may actually want to experiment by intentionally lowering the quality way down to enhance the effect, such as the scratchy record effect (remember records?) or some other unusual sound effect.

The adventurous among you might consider playing with some of the sound-related shareware included in the companion CD. You Mac users might want to check out SoundHack, an unusual program that allows you to manipulate sounds in extraordinary ways. The PC users among you might want to look into Music Sculptor and MOZART the Music Processor.

Shockwave for Audio compresses sounds that have been imported into Director 6 for Macintosh and Windows but *does not* offer streaming audio at the same time. The first task is to choose settings for Shockwave for Audio by following these steps:

1. **Choose Xtras⇨Shockwave for Audio Settings to display the Shockwave for Audio Settings dialog box, as shown in Figure 18-3.**

2. **Check the Enabled check box.**

   Selecting Enabled turns on Shockwave for Audio compression for imported sounds.

3. **From the Bit Rate pop-up menu, choose 32.**

   You can try this rate first for a good compression ratio for Web-bound movies or for movies to play from a CD-ROM.

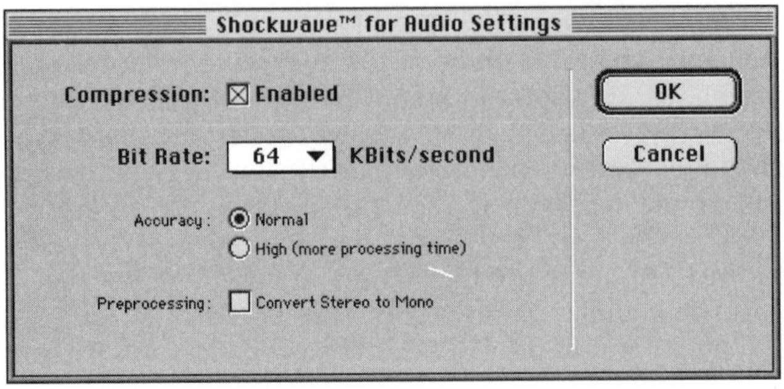

Figure 18-3:
Call up the
Shockwave
for Audio
Settings
dialog box
to set
options for
compressing
Sound Cast
Members.

Shockwave™ for Audio Settings

Compression: ☒ Enabled

Bit Rate: ▢ 64 ▼ KBits/second

Accuracy: ⦿ Normal
○ High (more processing time)

Preprocessing: ☐ Convert Stereo to Mono

OK

Cancel

4. **Click the Normal radio button.**

This setting keeps the processing time as low as possible.

5. **To have Director convert stereo sound to mono sound for higher compression, check the Preprocessing checkbox and click OK.**

Director automatically converts stereo to mono for a Bit Rate setting lower than 48.

Although you can test many Web-related features directly in Director 6, you need to first turn a movie with Shockwave for Audio compression into a Shockwave movie or projector to test compressed sound. Audio set for Shockwave for Audio compression is actually compressed during the process of turning a Director movie into a Shockwave movie or a projector. Remember, Director 6 offers you three ways to compress a movie:

✔ File⇨Create Projector

✔ File⇨Save as Shockwave Movie

✔ Xtras⇨Update Movies

One other point to keep in mind, Director movies use another Xtra to decompress the sound during playback. To ensure that the decompression Xtra and other required Xtras are incorporated into a projector, follow these steps:

1. **Choose Modify⇨Movie⇨Xtras to display the Movie Xtras dialog box, as shown in Figure 18-4.**

In the Movie Xtras dialog box, you see a list exclusively of Xtras used in the Score of your movie. To add Xtras used in Lingo scripts to the list, go to Step 2; otherwise, go to Step 5.

2. **Click Add to display a list of the Xtras stored in the Xtras folder inside the Macromedia folder/directory.**

Figure 18-4:
You can
set up
incorporating
Xtras into a
projector
from the
Movie Xtras
dialog box.

3. **Click OK.**

4. **Repeat Steps 2 and 3 for each Xtra you want to add to the list.**

5. **Make sure that the SWA Decompression Xtra is included in the list and click OK to go back to Director's main interface.**

Use Streaming Audio

Streaming Audio is a bit of smoke and mirrors that makes audio seem to begin playing as soon as a user opens a Director movie within a Web browser. What happens is that the beginning of the sound loads very quickly and begins playing while the remainder of the sound is downloaded from the remote server. You can also use this feature to "stream" audio from a CD-ROM.

Sorry, you Macaholics. You can't set up streaming audio directly in Director 6, but you can in Macromedia's sound editing program, SoundEdit 16 2.0, that comes bundled with the Director 6 Studio package. However, after you create the streaming audio file, you can use the file as a linked cast member for both the Macintosh *and* Windows platforms.

To create a streaming audio file from SoundEdit 16, follow these steps:

1. **Open the sound file in SoundEdit 16.**

2. **Choose File⊅Export.**

3. **In the Save As dialog box that appears, choose SWA File from the Export Type pop-up menu.**

4. **Type a name for the streaming audio file.**

5. **Maneuver in the Directory box to where you want to store the file and click Save.**

6. **In Director, choose File⊅Import.**

7. **Select the sound file in the Directory box and choose Link to External File from the pop-up list at the bottom of the Import Files dialog box.**

8. Click Import to import the file as a linked Sound Cast Member.

With Director 6 for Windows, all you need to do to create a streaming audio file is to choose Create Shockwave Audio File Xtra from the Xtras menu within Director.

Testing a Shockwave Movie in Netscape Navigator

After you create a Shockwave movie, you can test the movie from your hard drive rather than from a remote server on the Web. The following steps are for testing a movie with Netscape Navigator, but the steps are pretty much the same for most browsers.

1. Double-click Netscape Navigator.

Netscape Navigator tries to connect to its home page on the Web when you open the program. If you don't have a modem or it's not on (or if there's a problem), you see an alert letting you know it tried to do its job. Just click OK and continue.

When you arrive at Netscape Navigator, you see a Web page, as shown in Figure 18-5. In the top left corner, find the line, Go To. To the right is a long horizontal box, an entry field with the words, http:// home.netscape.com/. This is Netscape Navigator's address on the Web, which is called a URL (Uniform Resource Locator). You're going to replace Netscape's address with the address of your Shockwave movie on your hard drive.

Figure 18-5: Netscape Navigator's graphic interface, where you can test your Shockwave movie.

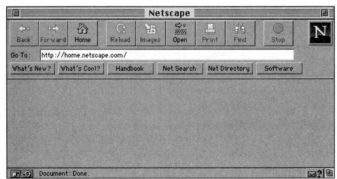

2. Click in the Go To field and press ⌘/Ctrl+A to select the contents of the field.

3. **Type the following:** file:///.

4. **Type the name of your hard drive followed by a slash (/).**

   You PC types have it easy. Just type **C** (for your main hard drive) and a slash (/) and jump to Step 6. However, it gets a little dicey for you Mac people. Netscape doesn't recognize a common, ordinary old space character (the one you type with the spacebar) in the entry field.

5. **Replace any space characters in your Mac hard drive's name with %20.**

   %20 is the ASCII (plain text) equivalent of the space character, which makes Netscape happy as a lamb. By the way, does anyone out there have any personal experience about how happy lambs are?

6. **Finally, type the name of your Shockwave movie.**

   What you see in the box now is the address or path of your file on your hard drive, Web style. If I had a Shockwave movie just inside the hard drive of my 8500, the address in the box would look like the following:

   ```
   file:///Lauren's%20HD/HOHOHO.DCR
   ```

7. **Press Enter.**

   If all's well, Netscape goes to the address of your hard drive and opens the Shockwave movie in the blank Web page — thanks to the Shockwave plug-in. If nothing happens, you may get some kind of error message from Netscape. Message or not, the problem is probably just a typo. Check your work and try again.

Streaming Video

 Santa Claus came early in 1997. He brought the Shockwave world what it wanted for so long, *streaming video,* which means that the first frames of a movie are quickly downloaded to a user's computer and displayed while the rest of the movie continues being downloaded from the remote server on the Web. You can also use this feature to stream video from a CD-ROM.

Set up streaming video

Check out the section earlier in this chapter, "Prepping Director movies for Shockwave," for numerous tips on getting your movie ready for the Web. Afterward, try the following steps to set up streaming video for your Web-bound Director movie:

1. **Choose Modify⇨Movie⇨Playback to display the Movie Playback Properties dialog box, as shown in Figure 18-6.**

2. **Select Use Media As Available for the Streaming option.**

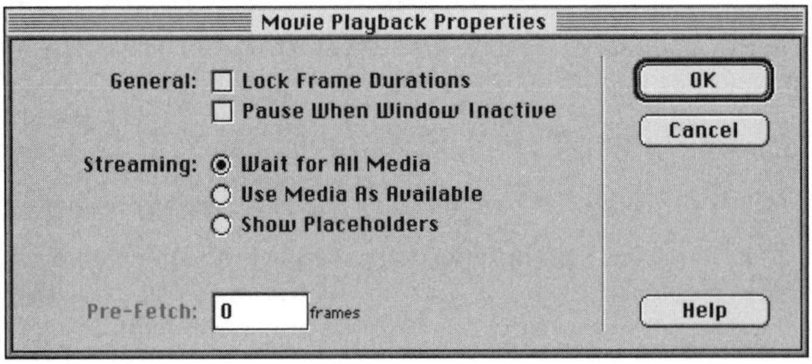

Figure 18-6:
Making
choices in
the Movie
Playback
Properties
dialog box
is the first
step in
setting up
streaming
video.

> **Movie Playback Properties**
>
> **General:** ☐ Lock Frame Durations
> ☐ Pause When Window Inactive
>
> **Streaming:** ⦿ Wait for All Media
> ○ Use Media As Available
> ○ Show Placeholders
>
> **Pre-Fetch:** [0] frames
>
> [OK]
> [Cancel]
> [Help]

Wait for All Media is Director's sly term for turning off video streaming, so you don't want to choose that option in this case. Show Placeholders displays a low-resolution image while the movie completely downloads, another option you want to avoid at this time.

3. **Type a number in the Pre-Fetch entry box.**

The value in this box represents the number of frames Director streams when the user opens the movie. The recommended value is 5 or thereabouts. While these first frames begin playback, the remote server continues downloading the remainder of the movie.

4. **Click OK.**

Prep your movie for streaming video

When a Director movie is streamed from a server on the Web, cast members are downloaded in the order in which they appear in the Score. The movie begins to play only after all cast members appearing in the designated number of frames set in the Pre-Fetch entry box are loaded into memory. So prepping your movie and cast members with the following tips in mind isn't a bad idea.

Pre-Fetch cast members

Try to minimize the number and file size of cast members appearing in the first few frames of your movie, keeping in mind the number you typed in the Pre-Fetch entry box of the Movie Playback Properties dialog box.

Avoid references to other cast members

In the first frames of your movie, avoid using Lingo or behaviors that refer to other cast members.

Use small background images

Use small background images in the first few frames of your movie that will be streamed. If you can live without any background, you'll help the streaming process even more. Remember that you can color the Stage without using a background sprite by choosing Modify⇨Movie⇨Properties and choosing a colorful background color for the Stage from the Stage Color pop-up palette. For you brave souls, you can add a snippet of Lingo to the frame in the Script channel to color the Stage at different times throughout the movie. Try the following line of Lingo:

```
set the stageColor = insertTheColorNumberHere
```

How do you know the number of the color you want? Call up the Color Palettes window and click the color you want for the Stage color. At the bottom of the window, to the right of the Eyedropper, Director displays the number of the currently selected color. That's the number you type in the line of Lingo.

Linked Media

Unlike its former version, Director 6 allows you to used linked cast members, such as QuickTime movies, streaming audio files, and even URLs (Uniform Resource Locators), with Shockwave movies. You can add any of these elements to a Web-bound Director movie using the standard Import Files dialog box.

For linking a URL to a Director movie, click the Internet button, rather than the Import button, to display the File URL dialog box, as shown in Figure 18-7.

Figure 18-7:
Type a URL in the File URL dialog box to link a Web page to a Director movie.

File URL: `http://www.macromedia.com`

OK

Cancel

You need to prep Director for linked URLs by going to the Network Preferences dialog box and following the next steps:

1. Choose File⇨Preferences⇨Network to display the Network Preferences dialog box, as shown in Figure 18-8.

2. Click Browse to display the Select Browser dialog box.

There's not much to this dialog box, just the standard Directory box.

3. Locate your browser of choice in the Directory, select the browser, and click Open.

Director records the browser's location under the Browse button.

4. Click Launch When Needed.

This command automates the opening of the browser when linking to a URL.

5. Leave the Cache Size 100K, the default setting.

If you need to clear the cache, click Clear to the right of Cache Size.

6. Select Once Per Session.

Once Per Session is the default setting and is usually the safest choice. For example, if you choose Every Time instead, you force Director to continually compare a cached document to the source document on a Web site's remote server. This added effort could dramatically slow down the performance of the Director movie.

7. If you're not going through a *firewall,* select No Proxies.

If you don't know if you have a firewall, ask your Web guru or systems administrator.

8. Click OK.

Part IV
The Part of Tens

The 5th Wave   By Rich Tennant

Principal

"I found these two in the multimedia lab morphing faculty members into farm animals."

In this part . . .

If you know anything about the *...For Dummies* tradition, you know that these books like to leave you with a part full of chapters to peruse in sets of tens — really ten glorified bullet points. If these points were written on stone tables, Charlton Heston would feel right at home.

Anyway, relax and enjoy my collection of Director 6 tips and tricks. Hey, it's Miller time.

Chapter 19

Ten Common Director Questions and Answers

· ·

· ·

*P*erfect strangers pop out of nowhere pleading with me to answer questions about Macromedia Director. The following are the ten most common questions they ask and my answers for your "edutainment" and "amusecation."

How Can I Cut Down the Size of My Movie?

You can use a couple of techniques to cut down the size of a Director movie, which is never a bad idea, by the way. Movies that have been cut down run faster on slower hard drives, older computers, the Web, and CD-ROM drives, should they be destined to star on a CD-ROM.

Rather than choosing File⇨Save, choose File⇨Save and Compact, especially after you complete a large Director movie. The Save and Compact command offers special features, including the following:

- ✔ **Trashing unneeded info from the Director movie:** As you develop a movie, Director tends to hang on to outdated info that it recorded along the way, causing bloated files. Running Save and Compact makes Director dump this digital flotsam and jetsam, effectively compacting the file.

- ✔ **Internally rearranging cast members:** Choose File⇨Save and Compact helps to help further optimize the Director movie for playback. You won't necessarily see a change in the Cast window, but whatever Director does contributes to building the smallest and fastest-running Director file possible.

Another way of trimming the fat from a Director movie is to move the Score to a new movie. Here's the scoop, step by step:

1. **Choose Window⇨Score.**

2. **Choose Edit⇨Select All.**

   Selecting frames in the original Score by choosing Select All is very important. If you try selecting frames by dragging the mouse pointer or Shift+clicking a range of frames, the markers set in the Score won't be included in the selection and won't transfer to a new file with the Paste Cells command. You would need to reestablish the markers, a chore worse than laundering underwear.

3. **Choose Edit⇨Copy Cells.**

4. **Choose File⇨New⇨Movie.**

   A new movie appears with the Score window open and active.

5. **Choose Edit⇨Paste Cells.**

6. **Choose File⇨Save As.**

7. **Type a unique name and click OK.**

   If you want to replace the original movie, enter the original movie name in the Save As dialog box, click OK, and then click OK again when your computer asks whether you really want to replace the file.

This second method of reducing the size of your movie actually has an advantage or two over the Save and Compact command. Copying selected cells from the Score of one movie and pasting the selection into the Score window of a new Director file fills the new Cast window only with cast members that appear in the Score window. Just be sure that you don't mind losing all those deadbeat cast members too lazy to make an appearance.

Deleting unused cast members in this way makes your file even smaller than if you used the Save and Compact command. In addition, Director eliminates any empty pockets of cells that may have been present in the original movie's Cast window, because Director fills consecutive cells of the new Cast window with cast members for the new movie.

If you're tight on memory, you can achieve the same benefits from the second method I just described without leaving the original movie by choosing Edit➪Find➪Cast Member and clicking the Usage radio/option button in the Find Cast Member dialog box. Director highlights all the unused cast members. Delete them by choosing Edit➪Clear Cast Members. Then choose File➪Save and Compact for a Director pick-me-up.

What Can I Do to Make Movies Play Faster?

Use a bouquet of strategies to make your movies play faster:

- ✔ Compact your movie with one of the methods discussed in the previous section "How Can I Cut Down the Size of My Movie?"

- ✔ Change single-color cast members to 1-bit cast members by choosing Modify➪Transform Bitmap. Then apply a color to the bitmap selected on the Stage with the Foreground Color selector in the Tool palette.

- ✔ Change 16-bit and 24-bit cast members to dithered 8-bit cast members by choosing Modify➪Transform Bitmap. A 16-bit cast member asks your Mac to process roughly 32,000 colors at one time. A 24-bit cast member tasks your processor even further, with over 16 million colors. Dithering to 8-bit cuts down the number of colors to a mere 256, along with a special trick reminiscent of what the Impressionists accomplished with dabs of oil paint. Up close, all you see in the Impressionists' paintings is flecks of color, but from a normal viewing distance, the spots of color blend into new color combinations. That's the idea behind dithering, creating the illusion of seeing more than 256 colors by placing the right colored pixels, or pels, next to one another in an unobtrusive pattern. To convert 16- or 24-bit images to 8-bit PICTs using Macromedia xRes 3.0, which is bundled with Director 6, see the sidebar "Converting graphics to 8-bit PICTs with Macromedia xRes 3.0" in this chapter.

✔ Take advantage of Director's memory management features. If you have tons of RAM, select all cast members from the Cast window and choose Purge Priority 0 from the Cast Member Properties dialog box so that all the cast members stay in memory. Director can access anything in memory about 1,000 times faster than having to find a cast member on disk and load the cast member into RAM. In limited RAM situations, choose Purge Priority 3 for your most important cast members and Purge Priority 2 for secondary cast members whenever possible so that Director quickly dumps from RAM cast members not frequently used. Director releases cast members with Purge Priority 2 from memory before cast members assigned Purge Priority 3. See Chapter 5 for more on prioritizing your cast.

✔ Apply Copy ink to all sprites whenever possible. When you have a white background, assign Background Transparent ink to nonrectangular sprites that must pass in front of other sprites on the Stage; otherwise, choose Matte ink for these sprites. Choose Mask ink if you must have a doughnut hole effect, but avoid all other ink effects unless they're absolutely vital to your production. Review ink types in Chapter 6. For more on Mask ink, see Chapter 8.

Converting graphics to 8-bit PICTs with Macromedia xRes 3.0

Reducing the number of colors in a bitmap is important for most multimedia projects to allow Director movies to run their fastest. You can change the color depth of a bitmap and create a custom palette for it using Macromedia xRes 3.0 and following these steps:

1. **Choose File⇨Open to open a bitmap in xRes.**

2. **From the Modify menu choose Color Mode⇨Indexed 256.**

3. **Choose Adaptive.**

The Adaptive option changes the bitmap's color depth to 8-bit color and builds a custom palette based on the colors in the original graphic. The other options, Custom, Uniform 8-8-4, and Uniform 6-6-6 are based on prebuilt sets of colors.

4. **Click OK to return to xRes's main window.**

5. **Choose File⇨Save As.**

6. **In the Save Image dialog box, choose a file type from the Save as Type drop-down list and click Save.**

What's the Best Way to Speed Up Digital Video in Director?

To speed up digital video in Director, use Director's Direct To Stage feature, which optimizes the playback of digital video in a movie. Just follow these steps:

1. **Choose Window⇨Cast.**

2. **Select the desired Digital Video Cast Member in the Cast window.**

3. **Click the Cast Member Properties button at the top of the Cast window, as shown in Figure 19-1.**

   The Digital Video Cast Member Properties dialog box appears.

Figure19-1:
The Cast Member Properties button.

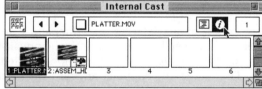

4. **Check the Direct To Stage check box, as shown in Figure 19-2.**

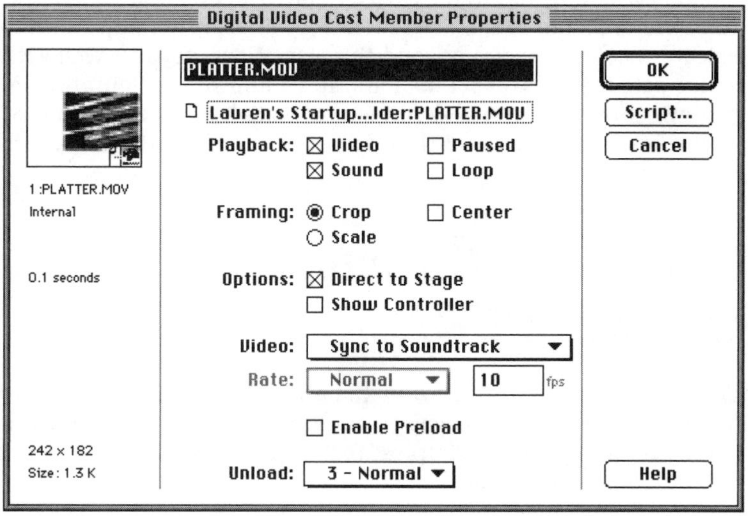

Figure19-2:
The Direct to Stage check box in the Digital Video Cast Member Properties dialog box.

When you apply Direct To Stage to a digital video, remember The Rules. The Rules state: No other object will animate across the digital video and no special inks may be applied to the digital video. For more information about the Direct To Stage option, peruse Chapter 12.

Why Do I Keep Losing Part of My Screen When I Tape My Movies?

The differing makeup between computer video and NTSC TV (the stuff you and I watch at home, blech) reveals itself again when you tape a Director movie or print-to-video. You find that the beautiful image you carefully composed on your computer monitor partially disappears. Some of the title may be missing, resting in nether regions beyond the border of the TV screen, along with other lost details you worked so hard to perfect. If you can't get enough about NTSC TV, check out Chapter 8.

NTSC TV is designed to create an image larger than the picture area of the TV so that the image fills the screen, bordered only by the physical, plastic frame of the Ray-O-Vision TV set itself. This phenomenon is called *overscan* by broadcasting types. The same thing happens to your Director movie when its video signals are converted to NTSC-compatible signals as you print to video. The image is blown up, and you lose a good inch or more of the picture all the way around.

The solution is to anticipate overscan when you're preparing a Director project for taping and to designate a safe title area that is 512 x 384 pixels, or pels, and centered in the Stage. Don't let titles, other copy, or important objects touch or extend beyond this area. Keep borders well within an inch of this safe area. If you set up a multiple monitor configuration as described in the section "A better way to be NTSC safe," you can visually adjust areas on the RGB display so that they don't get cut off on the TV screen.

How Can I Tape Director Movies to My VCR?

Unless you own an AV Mac or install a video edit board in your computer, there's really no effective way to put your Director movies on videotape. If you insist on trying, the simplest technique involves your computer's monitor and a camcorder.

Simple, cheap, but not terribly impressive

The simplest, most inexpensive but least effective way of videotaping a Director movie is to videotape the monitor itself with your camcorder. You lose a lot of definition, color, and quality along the way. You may also get weird, shimmering patterns and vertically rolling bars in the image because of the difference in synchronization signals between the camcorder and the computer monitor.

But you can minimize many of these pitfalls with a few tricks:

- ✔ If your camcorder features a variable shutter, visually adjust the shutter until the vertical roll disappears from the image on the monitor or is minimized. Many high-end consumer camcorders, especially Hi-8 and Super-VHS models, feature a variable shutter these days. Check your manual. For Mac owners, Apple includes a control panel called VideoSync that alters the way the on-screen image is formed to minimize vertical roll.

- ✔ To reduce distortion, shoot from a distance using the longest telephoto setting your camcorder has to offer.

- ✔ Soften the screen's pixels by shooting slightly out of focus. Better yet, shoot through a Hasselblad diffusion filter to minimize screen pixels on the tape. Nikon diffusion filters are the next best choice.

- ✔ Adjust your monitor's settings to reduce contrast, and shoot in a darkened room to avoid glare.

- ✔ If at all possible, use a color laptop computer that features an active matrix LCD (liquid crystal display) screen. How do you know whether your laptop has an active matrix screen? Break down and read the manual. Because LCD screens work differently than conventional computer monitors, they don't display rolling bars or annoying distortions when you videotape them. LCD panels are flat, too, which helps minimize distortion.

AV Macs

If you're the proud owner of an AV-type Centris, Quadra, or Power Mac, you're all set to copy your Director movies to videotape. For highest quality, use the S-Video Video Out port from your AV Mac to the S-Video Video In port available on Hi-8 or Super-VHS camcorder and VCR models. Otherwise, use premium quality, shielded RCA-type video cables for the connection.

For first-generation AV Power Macs, you need to purchase an adapter at your friendly electronics shop to convert the stereo miniplug Audio Out port to left and right audio cables, most likely RCA-type cables. Either way, use the best-shielded cables you can afford.

The videotape is no place to skimp on cash, either. Buy the highest quality brand-name videotape you can find. And break down and buy a brand-name head-cleaning kit to clean the recording heads of your VCR before taping.

If you record in real time, the way your movie plays back on your monitor, be sure to take some precautions before taping. Choose Window⇨ Inspectors⇨Memory and click Purge, which eliminates or *purges* all cast members not currently visible on the Stage from RAM. And remember to follow my suggestions for optimizing your playback speed in "What Can I Do to Make Movies Play Faster?" earlier in this chapter.

Video boards

If you don't have an AV Mac, you need to install a video board in your Macintosh or PC, such as Radius's VideoVision for Telecast, the Mac's NuBus or PCI slot, or one of miro's selection of video boards for Macs and PCs, such as the miroVIDEO DC-30. These boards do the job of converting computer video into real TV signals compatible with your camcorder or VCR.

Why Am I Getting Weird Colors When I Tape My Director Movies?

One of the biggest differences between real TV, the stuff we watch at home with our shoes off, and computer video is the gamut, or range, of colors available on each system. (By the way, it is technically possible to watch TV with your shoes on.) If you're fortunate enough to be working with 24-bit color, you're playing with 16 million-plus colors on your monitor. With your monitor properly adjusted, any one of these colors appears relatively pure on-screen, although your monitor does have limitations of its own that I won't get into (to thunderous applause).

In comparison to 24-bit color, real TV color is atrocious. It's atrocious compared to just about anything, especially compared to the beautiful images beaming off your pristine, perfectly adjusted computer monitor. Real TV's gamut of colors is extremely limited; only a small portion of the spectrum of colors appears at all. And of these colors, only a percentage are acceptable for viewing purposes. These colors are called NTSC, or *legal,* colors. *Illegal* colors that display beautifully on your computer monitor may *bloom* on TV, meaning that the colors spill over the borders of their object and in motion, smear across the rest of the television image. The colors may look Day-Gloish and psychedelic, similar to the way colors look on your TV when you crank up the color control. Generally, these colors are above 70 percent of their saturation (the intensity of a hue, how blue a blue sky is, for example) point.

So the answer to the question is, you're getting weird colors because so few of the colors that look fine and dandy on your computer monitor translate into NTSC colors on your Ray-O-Vision TV set at home. If you're interested in how to overcome this seemingly impossible technological hurdle, read on.

How Can I Improve the Color of My Movies on Tape?

Okay, you just installed your high-definition, surround-sound, wide-screen, 80-foot, monster Ray-O-Vision television set and anti-aircraft radar detector, you've settled back to enjoy watching your Director 6 *pièce de résistance* you transferred to tape, and . . . bad color! All that work for bad color. What's a videophile to do?

NTSC palette

The easiest, least technologically challenging, and least costly method to improve colors when you print to video (as multimedia types say) is to use Director's NTSC palette, one of the special collections of colors included with Director out of the box. No extra charge.

To set an entire Director movie to NTSC-legal colors, do the following:

1. **Choose Window⇨Cast.**

   Next, you need to change the color depth of all cast members to 8-bit color.

2. **Choose Edit⇨Select All.**

3. **Choose Modify⇨Transform Bitmap to display the Transform Bitmap dialog box.**

4. **Choose 8 Bits from the Color Depth pop-up menu and click Transform.**

An alert box appears, telling you the transformation cannot be undone and giving you a chance to change your mind.

5. **Click OK.**

Next you need to make certain that the display is set to 8-bit color, too.

6. **Choose File⇨Preferences⇨General.**

7. **Check the Reset Monitor to Movie's Color Depth check box and click OK.**

8. **Choose Window⇨Score.**

9. **In Frame 1, double-click the cell in the Palette channel, as shown in Figure 19-3.**

Director displays the Palette dialog box.

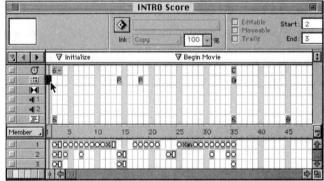

Figure 19-3:
The Palette channel in Frame 1 of the Score window.

10. **Choose NTSC from the Palette pop-up menu, as shown in Figure 19-4.**

11. **Be sure that the Palette Transition radio/option button is on.**

12. **Click OK.**

Until you change palettes again, all screen images are built on the NTSC collection of legal colors.

The best strategy is to anticipate printing to video at the beginning of a project and to use an NTSC palette at all times. You can remap bitmaps to NTSC colors in Macromedia xRes (bundled with Director 6) to create bitmaps exclusively with legal colors before importing them into Director. Use the same steps in the sidebar, "Converting graphics to 8-bit PICTs with Macromedia xRes 3.0," but choose Custom instead of Adaptive in Step 3.

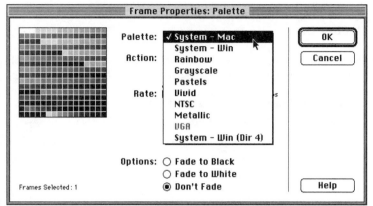

Figure 19-4:
NTSC is one
option in
the Palette
pop-up
menu in the
Palette
dialog box.

When you import a bitmap into Director 6 that was created with the default
System palette, be sure to choose Remap Colors and Dither from the Image
Options dialog box that appears after you click the Import button. To review,
Remap Colors and Dither translate the colors in the bitmap into the colors
belonging to the chosen palette, often the default System palette, and apply
a so-called "dithering routine" that arranges color pixels side by side in such
a way that the eye perceives more colors in the image than actually exist
(256). The basic scenario plays something like the following:

1. **Choose File⇨Import.**

   The Import Files dialog box appears.

2. **Locate and select the bitmap to import in the directory, and then
   click Import.**

   The Image Options dialog box appears, as shown in Figure 19-5.

Figure 19-5:
Director
lets you
remap a
bitmap's
colors
before
importing it
into the
Cast
window.

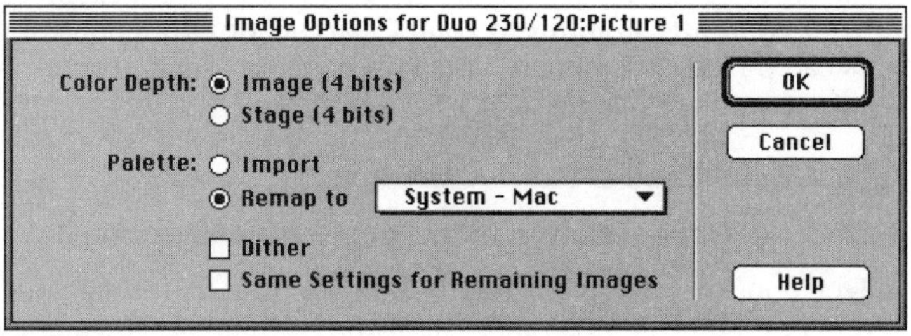

Image Options for Duo 230/120:Picture 1

Color Depth: ● Image (4 bits)
　　　　　　　○ Stage (4 bits)

Palette: ○ Import
　　　　　● Remap to 　[System - Mac ▼]

☐ Dither
☐ Same Settings for Remaining Images

[OK]
[Cancel]
[Help]

3. **Choose the Remap To and Dither options.**

4. **Click OK.**

With a Bitmap cast member built on the System palette already in the Cast, try the following to remap the cast member to the NTSC palette:

1. **Select the cast member in the Cast window and choose Modify⇨Transform Bitmap.**

   The Transform Bitmap dialog box appears, as shown in Figure 19-6.

Figure 19-6:
The
Transform
Bitmap
dialog box,
where you
can remap
a Bitmap
Cast
Member's
palette.

2. **Choose NTSC from the Palette pop-up menu.**

3. **Click the Remap Colors radio/option button; then click Transform.**

A better way to be NTSC safe

Working with an NTSC monitor is the best way to prepare a Director movie for printing to video. If you have a first-generation AV Mac, you can switch from your computer monitor to your TV in the Monitors control panel. (You PC-ites can purchase a video board with an extra video port for NTSC TV. Break down and read its manual.)

1. **Choose ⬛⇨Control Panels⇨Monitors.**

2. **Click the Options button in the Monitors control panel.**

   The Monitors dialog box appears. In addition to setting your monitor to different color depths (256, Thousands, Millions), you can control video output from here.

3. Click the Display Video on Television radio button.

If your monitor is set to 256 colors or less, your Mac allows you the option of checking the Use flicker-free format check box so that all your images are free of annoying flicker. When you set your monitor to thousands or millions of colors, Director automatically checks this check box to disable the flickering.

4. Click OK.

An alert box appears asking whether you really want to switch monitors.

5. Click Switch in the alert box.

Your monitor goes black as your Mac begins sending an NTSC signal to your real TV set. When you want to return to your RGB monitor, select the Display Video on RGB Monitor radio/option button from the Options window of the Monitors control panel.

Now you can work using your TV as your computer screen. You have instant feedback for colors in use and can instantly note the effect on your NTSC "monitor." The only problem with this setup is that the resolution is so poor on a real TV compared to the crisp pixels of a good RGB monitor that you may begin suffering eye strain and headaches in a very short time.

With Power Macs such as the 8500 and 8600, you'll find the Monitors and Sound control panel of System 7.6 (see Figure 19-7) in place of the dusty old Monitors control panel. Several other windows are associated with the new control panel. Here's how you use the new windows:

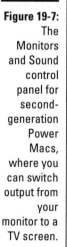

Figure 19-7: The Monitors and Sound control panel for second-generation Power Macs, where you can switch output from your monitor to a TV screen.

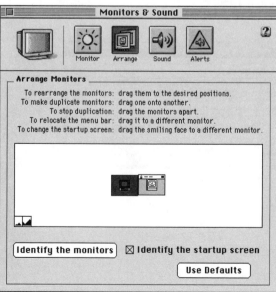

1. **Set your TV to Channel 3 (the channel you watch videos on; in some areas, it's Channel 4).**

   Be sure to run video and audio cables from the Video Out and Audio Out ports on your Mac to the Video In and Audio In ports on your VCR or TV monitor.

2. **Choose ⌘⇨Control Panels⇨Monitors and Sound.**

   In addition to choosing your monitor's color depth from this set of control panels, you can set up different options for running two displays at one time.

3. **Choose Window⇨Arrange Displays.**

4. **In the Arrange Displays window, drag the title bar of the computer monitor thumbnail over the TV thumbnail.**

   Your Mac instantly moves the display on your computer monitor to your TV while keeping your computer monitor active. To your Mac, your TV and computer monitor have merged into one "virtual screen." You may want to use the other display options available in the Arrange Displays window. For example, you may decide to "mirror" the setup so that your TV and monitor show the same display.

You PC types can access similar video drivers by following these steps:

1. **Double-click Windows Setup in the Main program group.**

2. **In the Windows Setup dialog box, choose Options⇨Change System Settings to display the Change System Settings dialog box.**

3. **Click the top line in the Display list to reveal the Display options, as shown in Figure 19-8.**

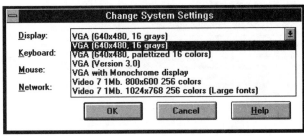

Figure 19-8:
Display
options in
the Change
System
Settings
dialog box.

4. **Click the desired video setting.**

5. **Click OK.**

The best of all worlds is running both an NTSC TV and a computer monitor at the same time, using the NTSC screen to check regularly on the progress of your work, especially the colors and patterns. For PCs, some high-end video edit boards support running your computer monitor and an NTSC TV concurrently.

I suggest taking a look at FAST Electronic's Fast video edit board featuring video input and output for VHS, S-Video, and Hi-8 tape formats. FAST Electronic U.S. Inc. claims the board performs at 30 frames/60 fields/second at 640 x 480 resolution playing AVI digital video files. The board's price is around $550.

Miro Computer offers several video boards, including the miroVIDEO DC-30. Miro claims performance of full-screen video (640 x 480) at 30 frames/60 fields/second with Motion-JPEG compression up to 5:1. The card outputs to VHS, S-VHS, Video8, or Hi8 with a choice of NTSC or PAL video formats. The price is just under $1,000.

The upscale candidate for video edit boards is Truevision's TARGA 2000 PCI featuring built-in hardware acceleration for Adobe Premiere, 16MB of on-board memory, 30 frames/60 fields/second NTSC video capture, and 24 frames/50 fields/second video capture for PAL (a European video standard). The TARGA 2000 board provides a port for previewing NTSC video on a separate monitor. The price tops the $3,000 mark.

Using a setup like the preceding examples along with Director's NTSC palette is the ultimate print-to-video configuration. If you feel adventurous, you can always create a custom color within the NTSC palette and save the new palette as a custom palette. Just be sure to avoid raising the saturation level of any new color above 70 to 75 percent, and you'll probably be okay.

Can I Set Up My Movie to Play Right on Any Computer?

The trick to producing your Director movie so that it plays at the right speed on any computer is twofold. First, you need to decide on the minimally acceptable configuration for playing back your movie and then reproduce the configuration in your studio. If you decide you want anyone with a Mac LCIII, 4MB of RAM, and a stick of bubble gum to run your movie off a high-density floppy, you must design the movie on that platform. For the sake of speed, work in other programs and do some of the tinkering in Director on a high-powered Mac, but do the serious tempo settings and playback on the dusty, old LCIII when you start timing and syncing stuff for the final production. The same strategy applies to working on the PC platform with a 386MHz computer.

After you've got everything timed down to the nanosecond on the sluggish LCIII or PC, the second ploy comes into play: locking the tempo. To prepare for locking the tempo, do the following steps with Director running on the target platform (in this example, the LCIII):

1. **Choose Control⇨Disable Scripts.**

2. **Choose Control⇨Loop Playback so that Loop Playback is *not* checked.**

3. **Press ⌘/Ctrl+Option/Alt+R to rewind the movie.**

4. **Press ⌘/Ctrl+Option/Alt+P to play back the movie after it's on the target computer.**

Now you're ready to lock your movie's tempo. Choose Modify⇨Movie⇨ Playback and check the Lock Frame Durations check box in the Movie Playback Properties dialog box, as shown in Figure 19-9.

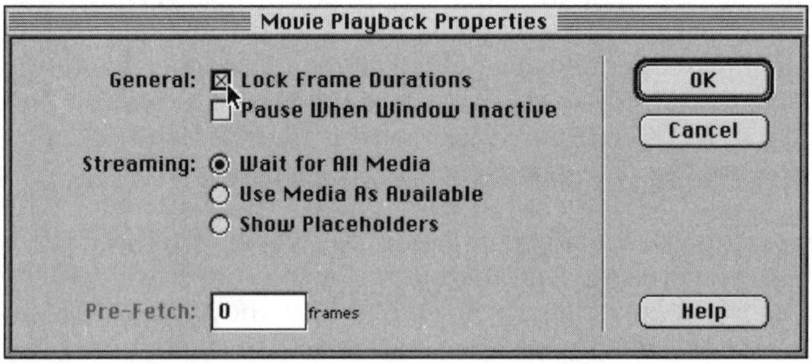

Figure 19-9:
Checking
the Lock
Frame
Durations
check box
in the
Movie
Playback
Properties
dialog box.

```
╔══════════════ Movie Playback Properties ══════════════╗
║                                                        ║
║   General: ☒ Lock Frame Durations        ┌────────┐   ║
║            ☐ Pause When Window Inactive   │   OK   │   ║
║                                           └────────┘   ║
║   Streaming: ⦿ Wait for All Media         ┌────────┐   ║
║              ○ Use Media As Available     │ Cancel │   ║
║              ○ Show Placeholders          └────────┘   ║
║                                                        ║
║   Pre-Fetch: [0        ] frames           ┌────────┐   ║
║                                           │  Help  │   ║
║                                           └────────┘   ║
╚════════════════════════════════════════════════════════╝
```

Remember, this technique doesn't ensure optimal playback. Locking the movie's tempo ensures *consistent* playback from computer to computer by designing for the lowest common denominator. Sigh — this is the stuff that makes multimedia great.

I've Never Done Programming Before. How Do I Know My Lingo Scripts Are Okay?

First, go slowly with scripting; it's like learning a foreign language. Then, the best way to check your first Lingo scripts is to test them line by line in the Message window as you include them in your Director movie. For each line of Lingo you want to test, enter it in the Message window and then press Return. You don't want to wait until you amass hundreds of lines of scripts and then discover errors you need to trace back to who knows where. As you add scripts to your movie, include plenty of comments in the scripts, explaining why the line of Lingo is needed and what it's intended to do. Contrary to stories you may have heard, comments don't slow down scripts. Director simply ignores them. Remember, choose Text⇨Comment or use the keyboard shortcut, ⌘/Ctrl+>, for each line in a script you want to mark as a comment.

When you think you're finished with your movie, choose Window⇨Message or press ⌘/Ctrl+M to display the Message window, click the Trace button, and play back your movie. Don't be surprised if Director stops your movie and slaps a script error on-screen. Go to the script and look for the problem in the line with the blinking insertion point. Remember, odds are that the problem's either a simple typo or a syntax problem. Sometimes a script doesn't work because of a memory problem; check that you're allocating the best Purge Priorities to your cast members. Review the Lingo material in this book again (see Chapter 14), and don't forget Director's wonderful online help.

Can I Play My Director Movies on a Macintosh and a PC?

One of Director's strengths is its cross-platform compatibility. Director movies are platform-independent, meaning that you can open a movie created with a Macintosh on a PC and vice versa. You can even create a stand-alone projector incorporating both Macintosh and Windows movies. The hitch is that whereas movies are cross-platform compatible, projectors are not. In other words, you need both the Mac and Windows program or Studio package to truly work in the cross-platform compatible world. If you have a tight budget, stick with Director movies rather than projectors to reach both Mac and PC users with your work.

The real trick is to use a PC monitor (VGA or Super VGA) to prep Mac movies intended for playback in a Windows projector and vice versa. Take the following precautions to avoid nasty surprises:

✔ **Use the strictest file-naming rules for Windows:** Begin the name with a capital letter. The name can be up to eight capital letters long, not including the period and extension that Windows needs to see at the end of a filename. Don't use spaces or punctuation characters, including the period, which is reserved to precede the filename's extension.

✔ **Use the Windows – System palette included with Director:** Jump back to the "How Can I Improve the Color of My Movies on Tape?" section in this chapter to review how to set up a custom palette for your movie.

✔ **Prepare for font wars:** PC fonts are dramatically different from Mac fonts. The easiest way to avoid font problems is to turn text into bitmaps while in Director. If you must use editable text, meaning word-processing like text in a text box, stick with boring, old Helvetica and Times.

✔ **Prep your digital videos:** QuickTime movies can be included in a Director file destined for a Windows projector, but each movie must be prepped in a utility program such as MoviePlayer 2.0 or FlattenMooV (included on the companion CD-ROM). Open each QuickTime movie in MoviePlayer 2.0 and then choose File⇨Save As. Click the Make movie self-contained radio/option button and check the Playable on non-Apple computers check box, as shown in Figure 19-10, and then click Save. Repeat with each QuickTime movie featured in your Director movie. This process is called *flattening* a movie.

Figure 19-10:
The Save As dialog box in the QuickTime utility and player, MoviePlayer 2.0.

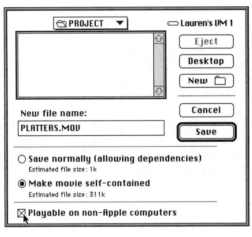

Chapter 20

Ten Ways to Animate Your Movies

Director 6 offers a number of techniques for adding animation to your movies, some with near push-button ease, many others only slightly more complex. Use the following list o' techniques as a useful reference for yourself. When you're stumped, just say, "Self, take a look at that useful list Lauren put together just for me."

Use Animation Wizard's Built-In Special Effects

Consider using Director's Animation Wizard Xtra, which is especially helpful for creating presentations on a super-tight deadline. You can create impressive animation sequences with little more than a couple clicks of the mouse and a few keystrokes to enter a title and a little bit of copy.

The following is a summary of Animation Wizard's features for your perusal:

- ✔ **Banners:** Text scrolls across the screen horizontally, bringing to mind Times Square and crackly old Movietone newsreels of winning World War II and the like.

- ✔ **Bullets:** An animated bullet chart with flying type and bullets.

- ✔ **Credits:** Classic Hollywood-style film credits scrolling vertically on-screen.

- ✔ **Zooms:** Choose one of three options for creating the effect of a zoom lens, placing you closer and closer to the subject with Zoom in, Zoom out, or Zoom in then out effects.

For more on the Animation Wizard, see the bonus chapter on the CD.

Remember In-Betweening

In Chapter 4 and Chapter 6, I discuss the dark art of *tweening*. In prehistoric days, human beans were actually hired by people with funny names like Walt Disney to tween twixt sunup and sundown. And what is tweening, you may well ask? It's the art of breaking up an animation sequence into milestone frames referred to as keyframes and then developing intermediate frames from keyframe to keyframe. In other words, tweening develops all the in-be*tween* frames, which is where the term tweening comes from.

Lucky you, Director 6 automatically tweens keyframes for you. But you need to set up the animation correctly.

Using Director 6's automatic tweening

For example, say you want to start your movie with a car driving across the Stage from left to right in half a second. In the following steps, I describe how to create this animation sequence in very general terms, and you can apply the formula to whatever you like.

1. **Create a bitmap in the Paint window.**

   For my car example, whip up a bitmap of a car in Director's Paint window with your eyes closed, automatically adding the Bitmap Cast Member to the Cast window. Actually, this happens even with your eyes open.

2. **Click and drag the bitmap from the Paint window onto the Stage using the Drag Cast Member button at the top of the Paint window.**

   Director 6 automatically adds the bitmap to the first available frame in the Score. It's usually Frame 1, unless you couldn't resist and clicked some other frame in the Score window before attending to Step 2. By default, Director 6 stretches the sprite in the Score across 28 frames, called the *sprite bar,* with one keyframe at the beginning of the bar.

3. **Move the bitmap to some beginning location on the Stage.**

   In my example, drag the car on the Stage to the far left of the screen so that half the car is actually hidden.

4. **Select the sprite's last frame in the Score.**

5. **Choose Insert⇨Keyframe.**

   At this point in my example, the car appears on the Stage in exactly the same location as the bitmap in Frame 1. In fact, all the frames show the sprite in the same location.

6. **With the playback head still in the last frame of the sprite, click and drag the sprite to some other location on the Stage.**

   In the example, drag the car to the far right of the screen. You can hold down the Shift key to constrain the car's movement horizontally. Because the last frame of the sprite is a keyframe, Director 6 automatically tweens the frames for you between Frame 1 and Frame 28.

7. **Press 0 (zero) on the keypad to rewind your movie.**

8. **Press Enter on the keypad to play the tweened frames.**

The sprite now appears to move across the Stage. In my example, the toy car scoots across the screen. You determine the car's speed by how many frames you choose to tween, the current tempo settings, and, of course, whether you fill up with high-octane gas.

Using the Sprite Tweening command

The Sprite Tweening command adds additional animation opportunities by setting up a curved path for a sprite to follow after tweening is complete. In previous Director versions, the Sprite Tweening command was called the In Between Special command.

To create a curved path, follow these steps:

1. **Follow Steps 1 through 6 in the preceding section, "Using Director 6's automatic tweening."**

   Returning to my car example, you have a sprite in Frame 1 of the Score, and on the Stage the sprite is positioned at the far left side of the screen. You also have a sprite in Frame 28, which you positioned to the far right of the screen.

2. In the Score, Option/Alt+click a frame between the first and last frames of the sprite's sprite bar.

For my example, Option/Alt+click Frame 14. Ordinarily, clicking a sprite selects its entire sprite bar; Option/Alt+clicking selects the sprite only in the current frame.

3. Choose Insert⇨Keyframe.

4. On the Stage, click and drag the sprite to a new location different from the first or last locations.

For the car example, drag the sprite on the Stage to a point near the top center of the screen.

5. Back in the Score, click the sprite on any nonkeyframe.

6. Choose Modify⇨Sprite⇨Tweening.

The Sprite Tweening dialog box appears, as shown in Figure 20-1.

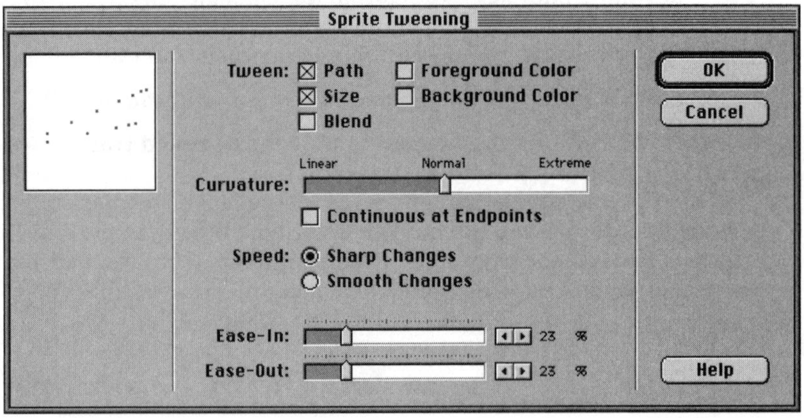

Figure 20-1:
The Sprite
Tweening
dialog box,
where you
can set up a
curved path
for a bitmap
to follow.

7. Click one or more Tween options at the top of the dialog box.

In the car example, check the Path and Background check boxes in the Tween options area. Drag the Curvature slider control to the right toward the Extreme label to make the sprite's path more curvaceous. And with the Ease-In and Ease-Out slider controls, choose 8 percent so that the little car appears to accelerate as it begins its journey and decelerate as it comes to a stop.

8. Click OK.

When you play back the movie in the example, the little car appears to drive in a curved path up to the top of the screen by Frame 14 and then back down as it completes its trip across the Stage. Try experimenting with other Ease-In/Ease-Out options in the Sprite Tweening dialog box.

Try Color Cycling

Ever notice the animation happening behind your favorite weather reporter's back? You know, the little icon-like animations indicating snowfall over a particular region of the country, rain pouring here, or the sun beaming down there, with radiant energy streaming from its little happy face?

All these animations were probably created with the same kind of color cycling that you can use in Director 6 to add animation to your movie. Color cycling — a fast but often very effective technique for animating bitmaps by rotating the order of a special set of colors in the palette — is especially well suited to repetitive movement, like the weather map examples, and is very efficient because you set up the whole sequence with one custom palette placed in the Color Palettes channel of the Score.

Say you want to create an animation that features repetitive action, such as a fire crackling and popping in a beautiful brick fireplace. First, you need to set your display to 256 colors. Color cycling works with only 8-bit color, so check your Monitors control panel or Monitors and Sound control panel for Macs and your System Setup in the Windows Setup control panel for PCs. See Chapter 19 for info on making these settings.

Next, create a custom palette and then import or paint your special Bitmap Cast Members.

Creating a custom palette

1. **Choose Window⇨Color Palettes.**

   In my example of creating a fireplace scene, check that System – Mac is the current palette for the Mac or System – Win for the PC.

2. **Choose Edit⇨Duplicate.**

3. **Enter a meaningful name for the new palette and click OK.**

   Your new palette becomes the current palette in the Color Palettes window. Next, create a special blend of colors (for the fire, in my example).

4. **If you want to create a special blend of colors, select the color chip that starts the color blend or *gradient*.**

   In my example, choose a lemony yellow from the palette.

5. **Shift+click the ending color for your custom gradient.**

   Make sure that the second color is at least 10 or more colors away from the first color. The more colors you have between the first and last selected colors, the smoother the gradient. For my example, a bright red is in order to make the fiery gradient.

6. **Click the Blend button, the last button at the top of the Color Palettes window.**

Using the first and last colors in the selected range of color chips, Director creates a smooth color gradient in the custom palette.

Painting color-cycling artwork

Now you can call up the Paint window and create special bitmaps for color cycling animation.

1. **Press ⌘/Ctrl+5 to display the Paint window.**

2. **In the Gradient Colors panel, choose the first color of the custom blend as the Foreground color.**

3. **In the Gradient Colors panel, choose the last color of the custom blend as the Destination color.**

4. **Choose Cycle from the Ink pop-up menu and paint the bitmap that you want to animate with color cycling.**

For example, if you're creating a fireplace scene, paint tongues of fire for a fireplace with various brush shapes set to Cycle ink. Also try Gradient ink for a different effect. Try inks such as Smudge, as well, to make interesting blurred and blended effects with the colors that are set to cycle during color cycling animation. Feel free to experiment.

See Chapter 8 for the scoop on using Director's Paint tools to whip up glorious digital graphics for the amusement of family and friends alike.

Painting support graphics

After you complete all your artwork that features color cycling, you can alter your custom palette for painting support graphics. First, you want to temporarily eliminate color cycling colors from the palette so that you're free to paint with any of the remaining colors.

1. **Choose Window⇨Color Palettes or press ⌘/Ctrl+Option/Alt+7 to display the Color Palettes window.**

2. **Drag through the custom blend of colors in the custom palette to select them in the Color Palettes window.**

3. **Click the Reserve Selected Colors button.**

4. **Click the Selected Colors radio/option button in the Reserved Colors dialog box and click Reserve.**

The color cycling blend in your custom palette is now *reserved* or disabled.

5. **Choose Window⊃Paint or press ⌘/Ctrl+5 to display the Paint window and create the noncolor-cycling artwork to complete your scene.**

6. **Choose Window⊃Color Palettes or press ⌘/Ctrl+Option/Alt+7 to display the Color Palettes window.**

7. **Select the custom color-cycling palette from the Palette pop-up menu.**

8. **Click the Reserve Selected Colors button.**

9. **Click the No Colors radio/option button and click Reserve to restore the custom palette to its full set of colors.**

Beware of the following caveats. After you create a palette with reserved colors, you can import a bitmap and remap its palette to the limited custom palette currently in use. For non-people pictures, the colors are probably acceptable. If people appear in your imported graphic, you may need to do some serious retouching in the Paint window to make skin tones look hunky-dory. No, I have no idea where that expression came from.

If you decide to create a bitmap from scratch for a color-cycling sequence, remember to add your custom palette to the Palette channel in the Score window at the beginning of the sequence.

You'll be working with a limited palette, depending on how many colors you choose to include in the color-cycling effect. This limitation may strain your creativity to the max, leading to surprise migraines and unexpected urges to impersonate Lola Montez. (Who's that? Look it up, Jack.)

Setting up for color cycling

To set up your custom palette for color cycling, follow these steps:

1. **Choose Window⊃Score and double-click the Palette channel in the frame where you want color cycling to begin.**

   The Palette dialog box appears, as shown in Figure 20-2.

2. **From the Palette pop-up menu, choose the custom palette you created for color cycling.**

3. **Drag the Rate slider control to set the frame speed.**

   Try 15 fps for starters.

4. **Click the Color Cycling radio/option button.**

5. **Click and drag to select the blend of colors in the palette of the Palette dialog box and click OK.**

   Clicking the Color Cycling radio/option button and the OK button in the Palette dialog box tells Director to cycle through the selected colors. The color-cycling effect continues until you change the palette in the

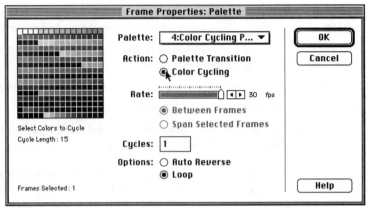

Figure 20-2:
The Palette
dialog box,
where you
can set up
color-
cycling
animation.

Palette channel of the Score or turn off color cycling manually or with advanced Lingo scripting.

For color cycling to work: The monitor must be set to 256 (8-bit) colors; the color-cycling palette must be the current palette in the Palette channel of the Score; and color-cycling colors must appear in one or more bitmaps on the Stage.

6. **Drag support bitmaps from the Cast window to the Stage and position them as needed.**

7. **Click and drag color-cycling bitmaps from the Cast window to the Stage and position them correctly.**

8. **⌘/Ctrl+click each color-cycling sprite on the Stage to display the hidden Ink pop-up menu and choose Bkgnd Transparent.**

Any white background surrounding the color-cycling sprite becomes transparent with Bkgnd Transparent ink.

Adding a line of Lingo

Back in the Score, add a line of Lingo to pause the playback head where your color-cycling sequence begins.

1. **Double-click the Script channel in the same frame in which you added the color cycling Palette.**

2. **Type** go to the frame **in the Script window.**

3. **Click the Close box of the Script window.**

4. **Test your movie by pressing ⌘/Ctrl+1 to hide all windows and ⌘/ Ctrl+Option/Alt+P to play back your movie.**

As you admire your color-cycling animation, you may find that you need to speed up or slow down the frame rate in the Control Panel for optimal effect, or return to the Palette dialog box and try a different value in the Cycles entry field or the Rate control.

Buy Good Clip Animation

Using good clip animation is not cheating. The operative word is good. Many clip animation packages are now available on floppies and CD-ROMs, and they can save you a lot of development time or help you complete a project with an extremely tight deadline that you otherwise couldn't meet.

The rule of reading all the fine print applies to using clip animation to ensure that you're using royalty-free material or, if not, that you understand the conditions you agree to on opening the package. Recent court cases suggest that even if you modify the artwork substantially, you may be violating the agreement with the use of clip animation that's not completely royalty-free or in the public domain.

Turn Cast Members into Moveable Sprites

You can easily add real-time animation to your Director movie by turning cast members into moveable sprites so that the person viewing the movie can drag the sprite to different locations on the Stage while the movie is playing. For example, in some of my courses, I demonstrate what I call *simulations,* real-time animations that illustrate how to disassemble various computer models. During playback, I interact with the movie, moving various components of the computer aside as if I were actually disassembling the machine before my students' eyes.

This bit of digital wizardry is accomplished by making each component a separate Bitmap Cast Member and then "assembling" the computer component by component from back to front in one frame's channels. The final step is to select all the sprites in the frame and check the Moveable check box under the title bar of the Score window. By the way, to keep the playback head in the same frame, double-click the Script channel for the frame and type **go to the frame**, a variation of the go command that basically means "Stay in this frame." Don't ask me why there isn't a Stay in this frame command, please.

Import Digital Videos

In Chapter 12, I discuss what digital video is and how you can add digital video as Digital Video Cast Members to your Director movies. If you've played with QuickTime movies or AVI movies, you may be able to salvage some of your work as self-made clip animation.

As I suggest in an earlier part of this chapter, tons of commercial clip animation, including QuickTime and AVI movies, exist in the marketplace as well as on commercial online services, private bulletin boards, and numerous Internet sites. As long as you thoroughly understand your rights for using the material, you should be able to find a digital video to satisfy any basic need of yours.

Director automatically imports digital video as a linked file, meaning that the movie is not incorporated directly into the Director file; only a reference to the movie is recorded in the Cast window, linking the external movie to the Director file, thus the term *link*. The digital video remains an independent, external file that needs to be present in the same folder as the Director movie itself.

Import Bitmaps or PICS Files

Some animation programs don't offer a digital video file format when saving the document, which may be the case if you have an older version of a program and haven't upgraded. If you work exclusively in the Mac platform and digital video is not a save option, save your work as a PICS file. PICS is a special Macintosh format that contains a series of PICTs glued together into one file; Director for Macintosh understands the PICS file format and can successfully import such a graphic, creating one cast member for each PICT within the PICS file. The new cast members are automatically *cast to time* in the Score window, too. Cast to Time places cast members in the Cast window into separate frames of the Score starting with the first free frame in the Score that Director can find.

In the Import Files dialog box, be sure to choose PICS or All Files from the Show pop-up menu; otherwise PICS files won't appear in the directory.

After selecting a PICS file in the directory, click Options to bring up the Import Options dialog box, as shown in Figure 20-3. Check the Contract White Space check box if you want Director to crop each PICT in the PICS file down to its smallest *bounding box*. An image's bounding box is the rectangular frame enclosing the graphic, defined by the image's maximum width and height. Contract White Space creates a smaller Director file that runs faster than a file containing PICTs with large borders of white space surrounding them.

Figure 20-3:
The Import
Options
dialog box,
where you
can direct
Director to
crop each
PICT in the
selected
PICS file.

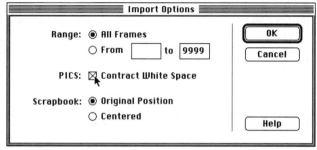

On the downside, because the PICTs are now probably different sizes, they're no longer aligned as an animation sequence and tend to jump around on playback. The best solution is to anticipate the problem and to settle on a minimal file height and width in the original application that creates the PICS file without cutting off any of the images.

As for the Range radio/option buttons in the Import Options dialog box, after selecting a PICS file in the directory, you can click From and enter a set of range values. For example, entering 5 to 9 tells Director to import only PICTs 5 through 9 in the PICS file. Of course, you need to know in advance that these particular images are of interest to you.

When importing a PICS file, Director places the row of PICTs in the Score, beginning with the current channel of the current frame, eliminating any unsuspecting sprites in its path. If you don't want this sad melodrama to happen to you, listen up. Before importing a PICS file, check that the currently selected channel in the Score contains enough free cells to hold each image within the imported PICS file. And remember: By default, Director spreads a sprite across 28 frames in the Score.

Both the Mac OS and Windows can work with PICTs, an odd file format that can hold just about any other kind of graphic document including bitmaps, drawings, and a low-resolution preview for display during production.

PCs don't take kindly to PICS, so if you're working cross-platform, follow these steps:

1. **Create a new folder/directory.**

   I usually save the folder to the desktop so that I can find it easily.

2. **Save your animation file as a set of bitmaps or PICTs in your shiny new folder/directory.**

3. **Choose File⇨Import or press ⌘/Ctrl+R.**

4. **In Director's Import Files dialog box, double-click the folder full of graphics and click Add All.**

   The graphics files fill the list at the bottom of the dialog box, ready to be imported.

5. **Click Import.**

Record Real-Time Animations

One of the most enjoyable things you can do without taking off your clothes is to record real-time animations in Director. With a Bitmap Cast Member in the Cast window, follow these directions to make those long winter nights just melt away:

1. **Choose Control⇨Loop Playback or press ⌘/Ctrl+Option/Alt+L so that the Loop Playback command is checked.**

2. **Choose Window⇨Cast or press ⌘/Ctrl+3 and move the Cast window to the upper-left corner of the screen to gain a clear view of the Stage.**

3. **Choose Window⇨Score or press ⌘/Ctrl+4 and move the Score window to the lower-right corner of the screen to gain a clear view of the Stage.**

4. **Click and drag a cast member from the Cast window to its beginning location on the Stage.**

   Notice that Director adds the cast member's bitmap to the Score in the selected cell. Now for the special keyboard command . . . .

5. **Press and hold down Ctrl and the spacebar.**

   Notice in the Score that Director places a special bull's-eye icon to the right of a channel number, designating real-time recording is now in progress.

6. **With the Ctrl key and spacebar still held down, click the sprite on the Stage and begin dragging the sprite around.**

   Director 6 records your movements into the Score window as successive frames until you release the mouse button.

7. **After you're finished mousing around, release the mouse button.**

   If your movie is set to loop (as in Step 1), Director automatically replays all the movements of the sprite. Instant déja-vu!

Use Film Loops

Making film loops is the second-most enjoyable thing you can do with your clothes on. Actually, it's a toss-up between real-time recording, making film loops, and drinking a steaming mug of Ovaltine. For sequences of repetitive movement, film loops are invaluable and very economical because you can extend an animation sequence simply by running the film loop longer in the Score window.

A classic example of applying a film loop to animation is The Flying Dove. Imagine you're videotaping a dove in flight, following its movement in the sky. If you follow it perfectly, the dove's body doesn't seem to move at all; the only movement you see and record is its wings flapping up and down. This kind of movement is perfect for making a film loop. Another classic example of repetitive movement is The Walking Man. After you capture the stride in several frames, you're ready to make your film loop.

Say you've drawn or scanned in ten frames of the dove, ranging from its wings positioned above to below its body, and the frames are represented as Cast Members 1 to 10. To make your film loop, with or without doves, start by setting up sprites in the Score window.

1. **Press Shift and select cast members in the Cast window belonging to the animation sequence.**

   If the cast members aren't contiguous, ⌘/Ctrl+select them instead. In my dove example, select Cast Members 1 to 10.

2. **Choose Modify⇨Cast to Time.**

   Director places the cast members as a sprite in Frames 1 to 10 of the Score window.

   In my example, if you play the movie, you see the dove flapping its wings from above to below its body. In general, you want to complete the cycle of movement by adding the frames that make the dove move its wings from below to above its body, which is simply a copy of the ten frames in reverse sequence.

3. **If you need to complete a cyclical sequence, select the new sprite in the Score window.**

4. **Option/Alt+drag the selection to the right, making a copy of the sprite, and place the first frame of the duplicate sprite just to the right of the original sprite.**

5. **Choose Modify⇨Reverse Sequence.**

   Notice the 20 frames you now have in the Score. You have a couple of extra frames to delete. Currently Frames 10 and 11 and Frames 1 and 20 are identical and unnecessary twin frames.

6. **Option/Alt+double-click each sprite.**

   This tells Director to let each frame of a sprite appear individually in its sprite bar in the Score and lets you select a sprite individually.

7. **Click the last frame of the duplicate sprite.**

8. **Choose Edit➪Clear Sprites.**

9. **Click the last frame of the original sprite.**

10. **Choose Edit➪Clear Sprites.**

11. **Click and drag the duplicate sprite to the left to close up the gap between sprites.**

Now you have a complete sequence of the dove flapping its wings up and down. You're all set to create the film loop.

1. **Shift+click the two sprites in the Score.**

2. **Click and drag the selection to an empty cell in the Cast window.**

   Director 6 displays the Create Film Loop dialog box, as shown in Figure 20-4.

Figure 20-4: Name your new cast member in the Create Film Loop dialog box.

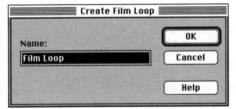

3. **Enter a name for the film loop and click OK.**

4. **Delete the sprites in the Score and click and drag the film loop from the Cast window to the Stage.**

5. **Press ⌘/Ctrl+Option/Alt+P to play back your film loop.**

A really great thing to do is combine your film loop with real-time recording. For example, you can make the flying dove sail across the Stage, flapping its wings along the way, by placing the film loop on the Stage, pressing Ctrl+spacebar, and dragging the loop across the Stage.

Switch Color Palettes

In the "Try Color Cycling" section earlier in this chapter, I walk you through setting up a custom palette in the Palette dialog box to cycle through a selected range of colors for relatively easy animation effects. Another option in the Palette dialog box allows you to create a different kind of animation by setting up a *palette transition*. This kind of animation is especially effective for situations where color changes globally on the Stage. As with color cycling, you need to set your monitor to 8-bit or 256 colors to play a palette transition in Director 6.

The classic example crying out for a palette transition is The Sunset. Say you have a beautiful desert day scene as a Bitmap Cast Member, featuring the ever-popular System palette. The image presents you with the bleached, white sand of the desert, bright green cacti hither and yon, and a brilliant azure sky specked with creamy fluffs of clouds. But you want this gorgeous image to change to a cool nighttime scene filled with blues and grays using the same bitmap. Follow these steps to accomplish this miracle, beginning with creating a custom palette:

1. **Choose Window⇨Color Palettes and choose Edit⇨Duplicate.**

2. **In the Create Palette dialog box that appears, name the palette something meaningful, such as Sunset Palette, and click OK.**

3. **Back in the Color Palettes window, click the Zoom box in the upper-right corner so that the window zooms to full-screen size, making the colors easier to see and work with.**

4. **Double-click the second color chip from the upper-left corner of the palette to display the Apple color wheel or the Windows Custom Color Selector.**

5. **Click an interesting contrasting color and alter its brightness if you like, by dragging the scroll bar elevator; then click OK in the Apple color wheel or click Add Color to the Windows Custom Color Selector; and then click Close.**

   In my example, select a deep blue and deepen the color more by dragging the scroll bar's elevator down toward the bottom.

6. **Repeat Step 5 to alter other colors at your discretion.**

   In the Apple color wheel, notice the grayscale — from light gray to black — at the bottom-right corner of the System palette. In my example, double-click the deep color just to the left of the light gray chip. In the Apple color wheel, slide the scroll bar elevator about halfway to the top. Following along, click a medium blue chip in the color wheel and click OK. In the Windows Custom Color Selector, select a medium blue color and deepen its value by sliding the scroll bar elevator toward the bottom. Click Close to return to the Color Palettes window.

Now you can make a custom blend in the Color Palettes window:

1. **Shift+select two colors of differing value and/or color in the Color Palettes window.**

   In my example, highlight the medium blue chip, then Shift+click the deep blue chip that you created.

2. **Click the Blend button (the last button in the row) to create a custom color gradient in the palette.**

   In my example, create a blend from deep blue to medium blue in your custom palette.

3. **Click the Zoom box to reduce the Color Palettes window's size.**

Now set up the Score for the palette transition:

1. **Choose Window⇨Cast or press ⌘/Ctrl+3.**

2. **Choose Window⇨Score or press ⌘/Ctrl+4.**

3. **Click and drag the Bitmap Cast Member for the palette transition from the Cast window to a frame in the Score.**

   In my example, after you drag the desert scene to Frame 1 in the Score, Director centers it on the Stage.

4. **Type 2 in the End entry box and press Return to change the sprite's sprite bar from 28 frames to two frames.**

5. **Double-click the Palette channel in the second frame of the sprite to display the Palette dialog box.**

   In my example, double-click the Palette channel in Frame 2.

6. **Choose the custom palette from the Palette pop-up menu.**

7. **Click the Palette Transition radio/option button in the Action area of the Palette dialog box.**

8. **Set a frame rate with the Rate sliding control and click OK.**

   Try 6 fps to begin with.

9. **Choose Control⇨Loop Playback so that the command is *not* checked.**

   Generally, you don't want this kind of effect to loop, so make sure that Loop Playback is turned off.

10. **Press ⌘/Ctrl+1 to hide all open windows.**

All that's left to do is to rewind the movie and play back your Director animation to thunderous applause.

Part V
Appendix

"NOT ONLY DID WE GET YOU AN APPLE WITH A MOUSE, LIKE YOU ASKED, WE ALSO GOT YOU A BANANA WITH A LIZARD."

In this part . . .

The observant among you have no doubt concluded that this book came with a CD inside the back cover. Maybe you were enlightened by the little advertisement for the CD on the cover. Maybe it was one of my many references throughout the text to the contents of the CD. Or maybe you wondered, "Hey, why can't I bend this back cover?" No matter. The appendix tells you what's on the CD and how to install the CD's contents.

After you've followed the installation instructions, don't forget to check out the bonus chapters I included on the CD. You'll find my list of Director 6 resources to make your life easier; my list of the most important Director 6 behaviors; my list of the most important Lingo words; a chapter on debugging, for those of you who really want to delve deeply into Lingo; and a chapter on Director's Animation Wizard. That, and all that great software. You're welcome.

Appendix

About the CD

● ●

*H*ere's some of what you can find on the *Macromedia Director 6 For Dummies* CD-ROM:

✔ A demo version of the Macromedia Director 6 software

✔ AT&T WorldNet Service, a popular Internet service

✔ Software programs to help both Mac and Windows users

✔ Bonus chapters containing additional great information about Director 6

System Requirements

Make sure your computer meets the minimum system requirements listed below. If your computer doesn't match up to most of these requirements, you may have problems in using the contents of the CD.

✔ A PC with a 486 or faster processor, or a Mac OS computer with a 68030 or faster processor.

✔ Microsoft Windows 95 or later, or Mac OS system software 7.5 or later.

✔ At least 16MB of total RAM installed on your computer. For best performance, we recommend that you have at least 32MB of RAM installed, because computers with only 16MB of RAM will struggle to run Director 6 and another program.

✔ At least 190MB of hard drive space available to install all the software from this CD. (You'll need less space if you don't install every program.)

✔ A CD-ROM drive — double-speed (2x) or faster.

✔ A sound card for PCs. (Mac OS computers have built-in sound support.)

✔ A monitor capable of displaying at least 256 colors or grayscale.

✔ A modem with a speed of at least 14,400 bps.

If you need more information on the basics, check out *PCs For Dummies,* 4th Edition, by Dan Gookin; *Macs For Dummies,* 4th Edition, by David Pogue, or *Windows 95 For Dummies* by Andy Rathbone (all published by IDG Books Worldwide, Inc.).

How to Use the CD Using Microsoft Windows

To install the items from the CD to your hard drive, follow these steps:

1. Insert the CD into your computer's CD-ROM drive.

2. Click the Start button and click Run.

3. In the dialog box that appears, type D:\SETUP.EXE.

Most of you probably have your CD-ROM drive listed as drive D under My Computer in Windows 95. Type in the proper drive letter if your CD-ROM drive uses a different letter.

4. Click OK.

The first time you use the CD, a license agreement window appears.

5. Because I'm sure you'll want to use the CD, read through the license agreement, nod your head, and then click the Accept button. After you click Accept, you'll never be bothered by the License Agreement window again.

From here, the opening screen of the interface appears. The CD interface lets you install the programs on the CD without typing in cryptic commands or using yet another finger-twisting hot key in Windows.

6. Click anywhere on the opening screen.

The next screen that appears is the category screen, which lists the categories the software is organized into.

You can get help any time by clicking the Help button, which opens a text screen with additional information about the interface.

7. Click a category button to see a list of products in that category.

8. Click once on a product name.

The interface opens a text page that gives a brief description of what the program does and any special information you may need to know about installing it.

9. To install the product, just click the Install button and follow the on-screen setup instructions.

When installation is complete, the interface usually reappears in front of other opened windows. Sometimes the installation will confuse Windows and leave the interface in the background. To bring the interface forward, just click once anywhere in the interface's window.

10. **To install other items, repeat steps 7 and 8.**

    You can click the Go Back button at any time to back up through the previous screens.

11. **After you've finished installing the software you chose, click the Quit button to close the interface.**

    You can eject the CD now. Carefully place it back in the plastic jacket of the book for safekeeping.

How to Use the CD Using a Mac OS computer

To install the items from the CD to your hard drive, follow these steps:

1. **Insert the CD into your computer's CD-ROM drive.**

   In a moment, an icon representing the CD you just inserted appears on your Mac desktop. Chances are, the icon looks like a CD-ROM. Some computers may open the CD directory automatically; if your computer does, skip to Step 3.

2. **Double-click the CD icon to show the CD's contents.**

   The directory contains folders that categorize the programs. Click a category folder to see the programs in that folder. But first . . . .

3. **Double-click the End User License agreement and read it.**

4. **Double-click the Read Me First icon.**

   This text file contains information about the CD's programs and any last-minute instructions you need to know about installing the programs on the CD that I don't cover in this appendix.

5. **To install most programs, just drag the program's folder from the CD window and drop it on your hard drive icon.**

6. **To install AT&T WorldNet Service and other larger programs, open the program's folder on the CD, and double-click the icon with the words "Install" or "Installer."**

   After you have installed the programs that you want, you can eject the CD. Carefully place it back in the plastic jacket of the book for safekeeping.

What You'll Find

Here's a summary of the software on this CD. If you use Windows, the CD interface helps you install software easily. (If you have no idea what I'm talking about when I say "CD interface," flip back a page or two to find the section, "How to use the CD using Microsoft Windows.") If you use a Mac OS computer, you can enjoy the ease of the Mac interface to quickly install the programs.

- **Director 6.** *For Mac OS and Windows.* On the CD, I've included a demo version of Director 6, the multimedia authoring and animation software from Macromedia, which I discuss in this book. This demo is fully-featured but cannot save files. *In the Macromedia Tools category.*

- **xRes 3.0.** *For Mac OS and Windows.* xRes is the painting and compositing program from Macromedia bundled with the Director 6 Studio package. The demo version included on the companion CD is fully-featured but cannot save files. *In the Macromedia Tools category.*

- **Extreme 3D.** *For Mac OS and Windows.* Extreme 3D 2.0 is the 3D modeling and animation program from Macromedia bundled with the Director 6 Studio package. The demo 1.0 version included on the companion CD is fully-featured but cannot save files. *In the Macromedia Tools category.*

- **Freehand 7.0.** *For Mac OS and Windows.* Freehand 7.0 is the latest version of Macromedia's powerful vector-based or drawing program. The demo version included on the companion CD is fully-featured but cannot save files. *In the Macromedia Tools category.*

- **Fontographer 4.1.** *For Mac OS and Windows.* Fontographer 4.1 is font-making software from Macromedia allowing you to create new PostScript, TrueType, and even Multiple Master typefaces. The demo version included on the companion CD is fully-featured but cannot save files to disk. *In the Macromedia Tools category.*

- **Flash 2.0.** *For Mac OS and Windows.* Flash 2.0 from Macromedia is a Web page and animation creation tool featuring vector-based or drawing tools (rather than painting tools) and works with a special Shockwave Flash plug-in for Netscape Navigator. Flash 2.0 on the companion CD is a special fully-functioning trial version that expires 30 days after your installation date. You can contact Macromedia for more information at http://www.macromedia.com. *In the Macromedia Tools category.*

- **Authorware.** *For Mac OS and Windows.* Authorware is Macromedia's icon-based interactive multimedia authoring program for developing high-end cross-platform compatible applications. The version included on the companion CD is a fully-functioning copy of Authorware but cannot save files to disk. You can contact Macromedia for more information on Authorware at http://www.macromedia.com. *In the Macromedia Tools category.*

✔ **SoundEdit 16 2.0.** *For Mac OS.* SoundEdit 16 2.0 is the sound editing software from Macromedia bundled with the Director 6 Studio package for Macintosh users. Like the other demo commercial software included on the companion CD, this special version is fully-featured but cannot save files. *In the Macromedia Tools category.*

✔ **Backstage Internet Studio.** *For Windows.* Backstage Internet Studio is Macromedia's answer to Adobe PageMill for developing professional-level Web sites with database connectivity. The demo version included on the companion CD allows you to explore Backstage Internet Studio's visual, WYSIWYG approach to authoring for building intranets, commerce sites, and much more. *In the Macromedia Tools category.*

✔ **Sound Forge XP.** *For Windows.* Sound Forge XP from Sonic Foundry is the sound-editing software bundled with the Director 6 Studio package for Windows users. Like the other demo commercial software included on the companion CD, this special version is fully-featured but cannot save files. You can get more information from the Sonic Foundry Web site at `http://www.sonicfoundry.com`. *In the Multimedia Tools category.*

✔ **DeBabelizer Pro.** *For Windows.* DeBabelizer Pro is the Windows version of Equilibrium's popular and powerful file conversion and batch processing program. The demo version included on the companion CD is fully-featured but cannot save files. Learn more about DeBabelizer at the Equilibrium Web site at `http://www.equilibrium.com`. *In the Multimedia Tools category.*

✔ **DeBabelizer Toolbox.** *For Mac OS.* DeBabelizer Toolbox is the Mac OS version of Equilibrium's popular and powerful file conversion and batch processing program for bitmap graphics. The demo version included on the companion CD is fully-featured but cannot save files. *In the Multimedia Tools category.*

✔ **DeBabelizer Toolbox Lite LE.** *For Mac OS.* DeBabelizer Toolbox Lite LE is a functional version of Equilibrium's popular and powerful file conversion and batch processing program for bitmap graphics but with fewer features than the commercial versions of DeBabelizer Lite or DeBabelizer Toolbox. DeBabelizer Toolbox Lite LE can read, batch convert, and save BMP, GIF, PICT, and TIFF (Mac & IBM) bitmap graphics from one file type to another. *In the Multimedia Tools category.*

✔ **Adobe Acrobat 3.0 Reader.** *For Mac OS and Windows.* The Adobe Acrobat 3.0 Reader opens up the world of PDF (Portable Document Files) files to you. PDFs are Adobe Systems's answer to the search for a single, platform-independent file type for desktop publishing, Internet, Intranet, e-mail, and CD-ROM publishing. In addition to the free viewing companion included on the companion CD, Adobe Systems offers a full publishing system in its commercial version of Adobe Acrobat 3.0. *In the Utilities, Etc. category.*

✔ **AT&T WorldNet℠ Service w/Netscape Navigator 3.0.** *For Mac OS and Windows.* The AT&T WorldNet℠ Service ISP (Internet Service Provider) invitational package includes a full version of one of the most popular and powerful Web browsers of all, Netscape Navigator, with support for audio, VRML, QuickTime animations, and Shockwave movies developed with Macromedia Director 6.

AT&T WorldNet Service is an Internet service provider. To sign on, you need a modem connected to your computer, a phone line, and a credit card to register. For more information and updates of AT&T WorldNet Service, visit the AT&T WorldNet web site: `http://www.att.com/worldnet`. *In the Utilities, Etc. category.*

Note: If you currently use another Internet service provider, be aware that installing AT&T WorldNet Service software may change your computer's current Internet software configuration. You may not be able to access the internet through your original provider anymore, after you install AT&T WorldNet Service.

✔ **Internet Explorer 3.0.** *For Mac OS and Windows.* Internet Explorer 3.0 is the powerful and free World Wide Web browser from Microsoft that displays HTML (HyperText Markup Language) documents rich with graphics and animations, including support for QuickTime movies and Shockwave movies made with Macromedia Director 6. *In the Utilities, Etc. category.*

✔ **DropStuff w/ Expander Enhancer 4.0.** *For Mac OS.* DropStuff with Expander Enhancer 4.0 is copyrighted shareware from Aladdin Systems, Inc. After you install it, DropStuff works with Stuffit Expander to expand a file compressed with virtually any compression format. You can also use DropStuff to join files segmented with other Aladdin Systems products. Like all shareware, you're invited to sample on a trial basis the features of DropStuff with Expander Enhancer 4.0 included on the companion CD. For a full description and to register, contact Aladdin Systems at `http://www.aladdinsys.com`. *In the Utilities, Etc. category.*

✔ **StuffIt Expander.** *For Mac OS.* StuffIt Expander is freeware from Aladdin Systems, Inc., and is included on the companion CD. StuffIt Expander expands files compressed with four compression formats (commonly used on the World Wide Web, e-mail and bulletin board services, and by individual computers users) including Stuffit, Compact Pro, BinHex, and MacBinary formats. Although you do not need to register StuffIt Expander, you may contact Aladdin Systems, Inc. at `http://www.aladdinsys.com`. *In the Utilities, Etc. category.*

✔ **ShrinkWrap 2.0.** *For Mac OS.* ShrinkWrap 2.0 from Aladdin Systems is a drag-and-drop freeware utility included on the companion CD for creating "disk images" for archival purposes and for "mounting" disk images to quickly run installation programs and to make backup copies of disks. You may contact Aladdin Systems, Inc. at `http://www.aladdinsys.com`. *In the Utilities, Etc. category.*

✔ **FileTyper 5.3.1.** *For Mac OS.* FileTyper is a small drag-and-drop shareware utility (included on the companion CD) from developer Daniel Azuma. This utility allows you to change a Macintosh file's Type and Creator codes in order to view and modify the file without having access to the original application. *In the Utilities, Etc. category.*

✔ **GIFConverter 2.3.7.** *For Mac OS.* GIFConverter is shareware included on the companion CD from developer Kevin A. Mitchell. GIFConverter can open, read, and write several graphic file formats including GIF, TIFF, RIFF, PICT, JPEG, MacPaint, and black-and-white EPS (Encapsulated PostScript). Use GIFConverter to view, convert, and print files you find online. *In the Multimedia Tools category.*

✔ **Disk Wizard.** *For Mac OS.* Disk Wizard is an advanced disk cataloging shareware program from developer François Pottier. After installation, Disk Wizard automatically creates a searchable table of contents for your hard disks, floppies, CDs, SyQuests, and any other media, even if files are compressed with StuffIt or Compact Pro formats. You'll find Disk Wizard on the companion disc, and you can contact François Pottier on the Web for more information or to register at pottier@kagi.com. *In the Utilities, Etc. category.*

✔ **EasyAIFF.** *For Mac OS.* EasyAIFF is a simple but elegant freeware program from developer Matthias Wuttke that allows you to preview AIFF (Audio Interchange File Format) cross-platform compatible sound files and AIFC (Audio Interchange File Compressed) sound files. You can e-mail Matthias at wuttke@stein.teuto.de. *In the Multimedia Tools category.*

✔ **FlattenMooV.** *For Mac OS.* FlattenMooV is a freeware utility from developer Robert Hennessy that performs one important task, removing the so-called "resource fork" of a Macintosh QuickTime movie to make the movie playable on IBM-compatible computers running Windows. You can reach Robert Hennessy over the Internet at theFunCompany@compuserve.com. *In the Multimedia Tools category.*

✔ **SoundHack.** *For Mac OS.* SoundHack is a shareware sound file processing program from developer Tom Erbe. It performs many utility and esoteric sound processing functions available nowhere else, making SoundHack invaluable to computer musicians, sound effects designers, multimedia artists, and webmasters. You can find more info on SoundHack and upgrades on the World Wide Web at http://shoko.calarts.edu/~tre/SndHckDoc/. *In the Multimedia Tools category.*

✔ **Paint Shop Pro, from JASC Inc.** *For Windows.* Paint Shop Pro is a shareware graphics viewing and editing tool. A version is available on the companion CD for Windows 95. Check out http://www.jasc.com on the World Wide Web for a full description. *In the Multimedia Tools category.*

- **WinZip.** *For Windows.* WinZip is a shareware utility from Nico Mak Computing, Inc., allowing Windows users to use the zip compression format so popular among DOS and Windows users to compress Windows files. You'll find WinZip on the companion CD. *In the Utilities, Etc. category.*

- **GraphicConverter.** *For Mac OS.* GraphicConverter is a shareware utility from developer Thorsten Lemke that performs file conversion on individual bitmap graphics and batch conversion on a folder full of bitmaps. You'll find GraphicConverter on the companion CD. *In the Multimedia Tools category.*

- **MIDI Made Music for Windows.** *For Windows.* MIDI Made Music for Windows is a shareware utility from LLERRAH Inc. that plays MIDI, Wave, Microsoft Video, Apple QuickTime Video, and audio CD selections in the background and includes ten MIDI songs. A commercial version of MIDI Made Music is also available. Contact LLERRAH Inc. at LLERRAH@aol.com or on the Web at http://www.dfw.net/~llerrah. *In the Multimedia Tools category.*

- **Music Sculptor 1.7 for Windows.** *For Windows.* Music Sculptor 1.7 is a shareware MIDI sequencer from Aleph Omega Software that works with any Windows-compatible sound card or MIDI interface. For users without a MIDI keyboard, you can use the featured music keyboard window. You'll find Music Sculptor 1.7 on the companion CD. You can contact Aleph Omega Software on the Internet at 72613.3574@compuserve.com. *In the Multimedia Tools category.*

- **Wave After Wave Player.** *For Windows.* Wave After Wave is a shareware utility from developer Ben Saladino for playing MIDI, Wave, and music tracks from audio CDs with the correct sound drivers installed on the PC. You can contact Ben on CompuServe at 71052,2416 or on the Web at http://www.interplaza.com/bensware. *In the Multimedia Tools category.*

- **MOZART the Music Processor v2.0.** *For Windows.* MOZART is a shareware music processor from developer Dave Webber. MOZART allows you to create and edit sheet music using only your computer keyboard, print out compositions featuring standard notation, and even export compositions as MIDI files. The shareware version of MOZART is included on the companion CD but a "virtuoso" nonshareware version is also available. For more information, contact Dave Webber at dave@mozart.co.uk. *In the Multimedia Tools category.*

- **Mod4Win v2.30.** *For Windows.* Mod4Win is a shareware utility written and designed by Kay Bruns and Uwe Zonker for playing Commodore AMIGA SoundTracker and NoiseTracker files on IBM-PC compatible machines running Windows. The commercial version of Mod4Win is also available through secure online ordering at the Web site, http://www.mod4win.com. *In the Multimedia Tools category.*

✔ **WebForms.** *For Windows.* WebForms is a shareware forms generator for HTML (HyperText Markup Language) documents from Q&D Software Development. WebForms automatically creates forms, reads user responses, and sends the responses to your e-mail address. You'll find WebForms on the companion CD. Contact Q&D Software Development on the Web at `http://www.q-d.com`. *In the Utilities, Etc. category.*

✔ **WebMania!** *For Windows.* WebMania! is a shareware HTML (HyperText Markup Language) editor and forms generator from Q&D Software Development that requires little or no scripting. WebMania! supports tables, lists, graphics, and many other features with a set of over 60 programmable buttons. *In the Utilities, Etc. category.*

Bonus Stuff

In addition to all that great software, the CD contains four bonus chapters that wouldn't fit in the book. These don't contain any information that you must know to run Director 6, but include some interesting material that you may want to know after you have the rest of this book down pat.

To access these chapters, you need to install Adobe Acrobat Reader (also included on the CD). After you have Reader installed, follow these steps to open the bonus chapters:

1. **Open Adobe Acrobat Reader.**

   For the Mac OS, simply find the Reader icon and double-click. For Windows 95 users, click the Start button in the Toolbar, and then choose Programs⇨Adobe Acrobat⇨Acrobat Reader 3.0.

2. **After the Reader software is running, choose File⇨Open.**

3. **In the Open dialog box that appears, locate the bonus chapter file you want to open.**

   If you installed the files to your computer, you should find them at C:\My Documents\Bonus. If you haven't installed the files to your computer, switch to your CD-ROM drive. The files are on the CD at D:\Bonus.

   The bonus chapters have a PDF extension, so CD1 is listed as CD1.PDF, and so on. CD1, "The Mother of All Resource Lists," contains neat contacts to help advance your Director skills. CD2, "Important Behaviors," emphasizes some of the more important behaviors (object-oriented programming methods, which you can also read more about in Chapter 15) new in Director 6. CD3, "Important Lingo Words," emphasizes some of the most powerful commands in Lingo, Director's scripting language (discussed in more detail in Chapter 14). If you prefer to script with the Lingo route, then CD4, "Messages from Beyond — the Message, Debugger, and Watcher Windows," shows you some of the finer points to Lingo programming. And CD5 gives you insights on using Director's Animation Wizard.

4. Click Open to call up the file you want.

If You've Got Problems (Of the CD Kind)

I tried my best to compile programs that work on most computers with the minimum system requirements. Alas, your computer may differ, and some programs may not work properly for some reason.

The two likeliest problems are that you don't have enough memory (RAM) for the programs you want to use, or you have other programs running that are affecting installation or running of a program. If you get error messages like `Not enough memory` or `Setup cannot continue`, try one or more of these methods and then try using the software again:

- ✔ Turn off any antivirus software that you have on your computer. Installers sometimes mimic virus activity and may make your computer incorrectly believe that it is being infected by a virus.

- ✔ Close all running programs. The more programs you're running, the less memory is available to other programs. Installers also typically update files and programs. So if you keep other programs running, installation may not work properly.

  Close the interface and install the program through the CD directory. Do this by opening the CD directory, opening the folder for the program you want, and then double-clicking the setup or install program.

- ✔ Have your local computer store add more RAM to your computer. This is, admittedly, a drastic and somewhat expensive step. However, if you have a Windows 95 PC or a Mac OS computer with a PowerPC chip, adding more memory can really help the speed of your computer and allow more programs to run at the same time.

If you still have trouble with installing the items from the CD, please call the IDG Books Worldwide Customer Service phone number: 800-762-2974 (outside the U.S.: 317-596-5261).

Index

(continued)

(continued)

AT&T WorldNet℠ Service

A World of Possibilities...

Thank you for selecting AT&T WorldNet Service — it's the Internet as only AT&T can bring it to you. With AT&T WorldNet Service, a world of infinite possibilities is now within your reach. Research virtually any subject. Stay abreast of current events. Participate in online newsgroups. Purchase merchandise from leading retailers. Send and receive electronic mail.

AT&T WorldNet Service is rapidly becoming the preferred way of accessing the Internet. It was recently awarded one of the most highly coveted awards in the computer industry, *PC Computing*'s 1996 MVP Award for Best Internet Service Provider. Now, more than ever, it's the best way to stay in touch with the people, ideas, and information that are important to you.

You need a computer with a mouse, a modem, a phone line, and the enclosed software. That's all. We've taken care of the rest.

If You Can Point and Click, You're There

With AT&T WorldNet Service, finding the information you want on the Internet is easier than you ever imagined it could be. You can surf the Net within minutes. And find almost anything you want to know — from the weather in Paris, Texas — to the cost of a ticket to Paris, France. You're just a point and click away. It's that easy.

AT&T WorldNet Service features specially customized industry-leading browsers integrated with advanced Internet directories and search engines. The result is an Internet service that sets a new standard for ease of use — virtually everywhere you want to go is a point and click away, making it a snap to navigate the Internet.

When you go online with AT&T WorldNet Service, you'll benefit from being connected to the Internet by the world leader in networking. We offer you fast access of up to 28.8 Kbps in more than 215 cities throughout the U.S. that will make going online as easy as picking up your phone.

Online Help and Advice
24 Hours a Day, 7 Days a Week

Before you begin exploring the Internet, you may want to take a moment to check two useful sources of information.

If you're new to the Internet, from the AT&T WorldNet Service home page at www.worldnet.att.net, click on the Net Tutorial hyperlink for a quick explanation of unfamiliar terms and useful advice about exploring the Internet.

Another useful source of information is the HELP icon. The area contains pertinent, time saving information-intensive reference tips, and topics such as Accounts & Billing, Trouble Reporting, Downloads & Upgrades, Security Tips, Network Hot Spots, Newsgroups, Special Announcements, etc.

Whether online or off-line, 24 hours a day, seven days a week, we will provide World Class technical expertise and fast, reliable responses to your questions. To reach AT&T WorldNet Customer Care, call **1-800-400-1447**.

Nothing is more important to us than making sure that your Internet experience is a truly enriching and satisfying one.

Safeguard Your Online Purchases

AT&T WorldNet Service is committed to making the Internet a safe and convenient way to transact business. By registering and continuing to charge your AT&T WorldNet Service to your AT&T Universal Card, you'll enjoy peace of mind whenever you shop the Internet. Should your account number be compromised on the Net, you won't be liable for any online transactions charged to your AT&T Universal Card by a person who is not an authorized user.*

*Today, cardmembers may be liable for the first $50 of charges made by a person who is not an authorized user, which will not be imposed under this program as long as the cardmember notifies AT&T Universal Card of the loss within 24 hours and otherwise complies with the Cardmember Agreement. Refer to Cardmember Agreement for definition of authorized user.

Minimum System Requirements

IBM-Compatible Personal Computer Users:
- IBM-compatible personal computer with 486SX or higher processor
- 8MB of RAM (or more for better performance)
- 15–36MB of available hard disk space to install software, depending on platform (14–21MB to use service after installation, depending on platform)
- Graphics system capable of displaying 256 colors
- 14,400 bps modem connected to an outside phone line and not a LAN or ISDN line
- Microsoft Windows 3.1x or Windows 95

Macintosh Users:
- Macintosh 68030 or higher (including 68LC0X0 models and all Power Macintosh models)
- System 7.5.3 Revision 2 or higher for PCI Power Macintosh models: System 7.1 or higher for all 680X0 and non-PCI Power Macintosh models
- Mac TCP 2.0.6 or Open Transport 1.1 or higher

- 8MB of RAM (minimum) with Virtual Memory turned on or RAM Doubler; 16MB recommended for Power Macintosh users
- 12MB of available hard disk space (15MB recommended)
- 14,400 bps modem connected to an outside phone line and not a LAN or ISDN line
- Color or 256 gray-scale monitor
- Apple Guide 1.2 or higher (if you want to view online help)
  If you are uncertain of the configuration of your Macintosh computer, consult your Macintosh User's guide or call Apple at 1-800-767-2775.

Installation Tips and Instructions

- If you have other Web browsers or online software, please consider uninstalling them according to the vendor's instructions.
- If you are installing AT&T WorldNet Service on a computer with Local Area Networking, please contact your LAN administrator for setup instructions.
- At the end of installation, you may be asked to restart your computer. Don't attempt the registration process until you have done so.

IBM-compatible PC users:
- Insert the CD-ROM into the CD-ROM drive on your computer.
- Select *File/Run* (for Windows 3.1x) or *Start/Run* (for Windows 95 if setup did not start automatically).
- Type *D:\setup.exe* (or change the "D" if your CD-ROM is another drive).
- Click *OK*.
- Follow the onscreen instructions to install and register.

Macintosh users:
- Disable all extensions except Apple CD-ROM and Foreign Files Access extensions.
- Restart Computer.
- Insert the CD-ROM into the CD-ROM drive on your computer.
- Double-click the *Install AT&T WorldNet Service* icon.
- Follow the onscreen instructions to install. (Upon restarting your Macintosh, AT&T WorldNet Service Account Setup automatically starts.)
- Follow the onscreen instructions to register.

Registering with AT&T WorldNet Service

After you have connected with AT&T WorldNet online registration service, you will be presented with a series of screens that confirm billing information and prompt you for additional account set-up data.

The following is a list of registration tips and comments that will help you during the registration process.

I.   Use one of the following registration codes, which can also be found in the Appendix of *Macromedia Director 6 For Dummies*. Use L5SQIM631 if you are an AT&T long-distance residential customer or L5SQIM632 if you use another long-distance phone company.
II. During registration, you will need to supply your name, address, and valid credit card number, and choose an account information security word, e-mail name, and e-mail password. You will also be requested to select your preferred price plan at this time. (We advise that you use all lowercase letters when assigning an e-mail ID and security code, since they are easier to remember.)
III. If you make a mistake and exit or get disconnected during the registration process prematurely, simply click on "Create New Account." Do not click on "Edit Existing Account."
IV. When choosing your local access telephone number, you will be given several options. Please choose the one nearest to you. Please note that calling a number within your area does not guarantee that the call is free.

Connecting to AT&T WorldNet Service

When you have finished installing and registering with AT&T WorldNet Service, you are ready to access the Internet. Make sure your modem and phone line are available before attempting to connect to the service.

For Windows 95 users:
- Double-click on the ***Connect to AT&T WorldNet Service*** icon on your desktop.
  OR
- Select ***Start, Programs, AT&T WorldNet Software, Connect to AT&T WorldNet Service.***

For Windows 3.x users:
- Double-click on the ***Connect to AT&T WorldNet Service*** icon located in the AT&T WorldNet Service group.

For Macintosh users:
- Double-click on the ***AT&T WorldNet Service*** icon in the AT&T WorldNet Service folder.

Choose the Plan That's Right for You

The Internet is for everyone, whether at home or at work. In addition to making the time you spend online productive and fun, we're also committed to making it affordable. Choose one of two price plans: unlimited usage access or hourly usage access. The latest pricing information can be obtained during online registration. No matter which plan you use, we're confident that after you take advantage of everything AT&T WorldNet Service has to offer, you'll wonder how you got along without it.

Explore our AT&T WorldNet Service site at http://www.att.com/worldnet.

IDG Books Worldwide, Inc., End-User License Agreement

READ THIS. You should carefully read these terms and conditions before opening the software packet(s) included with this book ("Book"). This is a license agreement ("Agreement") between you and IDG Books Worldwide, Inc. ("IDGB"). By opening the accompanying software packet(s), you acknowledge that you have read and accept the following terms and conditions. If you do not agree and do not want to be bound by such terms and conditions, promptly return the Book and the unopened software packet(s) to the place you obtained them for a full refund.

1. **License Grant.** IDGB grants to you (either an individual or entity) a nonexclusive license to use one copy of the enclosed software program(s) (collectively, the "Software") solely for your own personal or business purposes on a single computer (whether a standard computer or a workstation component of a multiuser network). The Software is in use on a computer when it is loaded into temporary memory (RAM) or installed into permanent memory (hard disk, CD-ROM, or other storage device). IDGB reserves all rights not expressly granted herein.

2. **Ownership.** IDGB is the owner of all right, title, and interest, including copyright, in and to the compilation of the Software recorded on the disk(s) or CD-ROM ("Software Media"). Copyright to the individual programs recorded on the Software Media is owned by the author or other authorized copyright owner of each program. Ownership of the Software and all proprietary rights relating thereto remain with IDGB and its licensers.

3. **Restrictions on Use and Transfer.**

    (a) You may only (i) make one copy of the Software for backup or archival purposes, or (ii) transfer the Software to a single hard disk, provided that you keep the original for backup or archival purposes. You may not (i) rent or lease the Software, (ii) copy or reproduce the Software through a LAN or other network system or through any computer subscriber system or bulletin-board system, or (iii) modify, adapt, or create derivative works based on the Software.

    (b) You may not reverse engineer, decompile, or disassemble the Software. You may transfer the Software and user documentation on a permanent basis, provided that the transferee agrees to accept the terms and conditions of this Agreement and you retain no copies. If the Software is an update or has been updated, any transfer must include the most recent update and all prior versions.

4. **Restrictions on Use of Individual Programs.** You must follow the individual requirements and restrictions detailed for each individual program in Appendix A, the "About the CD" section of this Book. These limitations are also contained in the individual license agreements recorded on the Software Media. These limitations may include a requirement that after using the program for a specified period of time, the user must pay a registration fee or discontinue use. By opening the Software packet(s), you will be agreeing to abide by the licenses and restrictions for these individual programs that are detailed in Appendix A and on the Software Media. None of the material on this Software Media or listed in this Book may ever be redistributed, in original or modified form, for commercial purposes.

5. **Limited Warranty.**

   (a) IDGB warrants that the Software and Software Media are free from defects in materials and workmanship under normal use for a period of sixty (60) days from the date of purchase of this Book. If IDGB receives notification within the warranty period of defects in materials or workmanship, IDGB will replace the defective Software Media.

   (b) **IDGB AND THE AUTHOR OF THE BOOK DISCLAIM ALL OTHER WARRANTIES, EXPRESS OR IMPLIED, INCLUDING WITHOUT LIMITATION IMPLIED WARRANTIES OF MER-CHANTABILITY AND FITNESS FOR A PARTICULAR PURPOSE, WITH RESPECT TO THE SOFTWARE, THE PROGRAMS, THE SOURCE CODE CONTAINED THEREIN, AND/OR THE TECHNIQUES DESCRIBED IN THIS BOOK. IDGB DOES NOT WARRANT THAT THE FUNCTIONS CONTAINED IN THE SOFTWARE WILL MEET YOUR REQUIREMENTS OR THAT THE OPERATION OF THE SOFTWARE WILL BE ERROR FREE.**

   (c) This limited warranty gives you specific legal rights, and you may have other rights that vary from jurisdiction to jurisdiction.

6. **Remedies.**

   (a) IDGB's entire liability and your exclusive remedy for defects in materials and workmanship shall be limited to replacement of the Software Media, which may be returned to IDGB with a copy of your receipt at the following address: Software Media Fulfillment Department, Attn.: *Macromedia Director 6 For Dummies*, IDG Books Worldwide, Inc., 7260 Shadeland Station, Ste. 100, Indianapolis, IN 46256, or call 800-762-2974. Please allow three to four weeks for delivery. This Limited Warranty is void if failure of the Software Media has resulted from accident, abuse, or misapplication. Any replacement Software Media will be warranted for the remainder of the original warranty period or thirty (30) days, whichever is longer.

   (b) In no event shall IDGB or the author be liable for any damages whatsoever (including without limitation damages for loss of business profits, business interruption, loss of business information, or any other pecuniary loss) arising from the use of or inability to use the Book or the Software, even if IDGB has been advised of the possibility of such damages.

   (c) Because some jurisdictions do not allow the exclusion or limitation of liability for conse-quential or incidental damages, the above limitation or exclusion may not apply to you.

7. **U.S. Government Restricted Rights.** Use, duplication, or disclosure of the Software by the U.S. Government is subject to restrictions stated in paragraph (c)(1)(ii) of the Rights in Technical Data and Computer Software clause of DFARS 252.227-7013, and in subparagraphs (a) through (d) of the Commercial Computer–Restricted Rights clause at FAR 52.227-19, and in similar clauses in the NASA FAR supplement, when applicable.

8. **General.** This Agreement constitutes the entire understanding of the parties and revokes and supersedes all prior agreements, oral or written, between them and may not be modified or amended except in a writing signed by both parties hereto that specifically refers to this Agreement. This Agreement shall take precedence over any other documents that may be in conflict herewith. If any one or more provisions contained in this Agreement are held by any court or tribunal to be invalid, illegal, or otherwise unenforceable, each and every other provision shall remain in full force and effect.

Installation Instructions

The CD-ROM in the back of this book contains software for both Macintosh and Windows users. Not all the software works on both platforms, so be sure to read the appendix for complete information.

Note: You do not need to install all the items on the CD-ROM. Just install the programs that appeal to you.

To start the CD-ROM using Windows 95, follow these steps:

1. **Insert the CD-ROM (label side up) into your computer's CD-ROM drive.**
2. **Choose Start⇨Run.**
3. **In the Run dialog box that appears, type** D:\Setup.exe.

   This assumes that your CD-ROM drive is the D drive in your computer. If not, replace D with the appropriate letter.
4. **Click OK, and the CD software starts up.**

To start the CD-ROM using a Mac, just pop the CD-ROM in the CD-ROM drive and double-click the CD icon when it appears on your computer desktop. The CD-ROM starts up without another word.

For more information about installing the programs from the CD or using the Windows CD interface, please see the appendix.

IDG BOOKS WORLDWIDE REGISTRATION CARD

Visit our Web site at http://www.idgbooks.com

ISBN Number: 0-7645-0224-7

Title of this book: Macromedia® Director® 6 For Dummies®

My overall rating of this book: ❑ Very good [1] ❑ Good [2] ❑ Satisfactory [3] ❑ Fair [4] ❑ Poor [5]

How I first heard about this book:

❑ Found in bookstore; name: [6]

❑ Advertisement: [8]

❑ Word of mouth; heard about book from friend, co-worker, etc.: [10]

❑ Book review: [7]

❑ Catalog: [9]

❑ Other: [11]

What I liked most about this book:

What I would change, add, delete, etc., in future editions of this book:

Other comments:

Number of computer books I purchase in a year: ❑ 1 [12] ❑ 2-5 [13] ❑ 6-10 [14] ❑ More than 10 [15]

I would characterize my computer skills as: ❑ Beginner [16] ❑ Intermediate [17] ❑ Advanced [18] ❑ Professional [19]

I use ❑ DOS [20] ❑ Windows [21] ❑ OS/2 [22] ❑ Unix [23] ❑ Macintosh [24] ❑ Other: [25]

(please specify)

I would be interested in new books on the following subjects:

(please check all that apply, and use the spaces provided to identify specific software)

❑ Word processing: [26]

❑ Data bases: [28]

❑ File Utilities: [30]

❑ Networking: [32]

❑ Other: [34]

❑ Spreadsheets: [27]

❑ Desktop publishing: [29]

❑ Money management: [31]

❑ Programming languages: [33]

I use a PC at (please check all that apply): ❑ home [35] ❑ work [36] ❑ school [37] ❑ other: [38]

The disks I prefer to use are ❑ 5.25 [39] ❑ 3.5 [40] ❑ other: [41]

I have a CD ROM: ❑ yes [42] ❑ no [43]

I plan to buy or upgrade computer hardware this year: ❑ yes [44] ❑ no [45]

I plan to buy or upgrade computer software this year: ❑ yes [46] ❑ no [47]

Name: Business title: [48] Type of Business: [49]

Address (❑ home [50] ❑ work [51]/Company name:)

Street/Suite#

City [52]/State [53]/Zip code [54]: Country [55]

❑ **I liked this book!** You may quote me by name in future IDG Books Worldwide promotional materials.

My daytime phone number is _____

IDG BOOKS WORLDWIDE

THE WORLD OF COMPUTER KNOWLEDGE®

☐ YES!

Please keep me informed about IDG Books Worldwide's
World of Computer Knowledge. Send me your latest catalog.